Planet Earth

Planet Earth

Jonathan Weiner

BANTAM BOOKS
TORONTO • NEW YORK • LONDON • SYDNEY • AUCKLAND

PLANET EARTH
A Bantam Book / February 1986

CREDITS

Grateful acknowledgment is made to the following as sources of previously published material reprinted in *Planet Earth:*

The Bodley Head: Lines taken from *The Prose Edda: Tales From Norse Mythology*, by Snorre Sturluson, translated by Jean I. Young. Reprinted by permission of The Bodley Head.

Cambridge University Press: Excerpt from *Weather Prediction by Numerical Process*, by Lewis F. Richardson. Copyright 1922. Reprinted by permission of Cambridge University Press.

Clark R. Chapman, excerpted from *Planets of Rock and Ice*. Copyright © 1977, 1983 by Clark R. Chapman. Reprinted with the permission of Charles Scribner's Sons.

Enslow Publishers: Quote taken from *Ice Ages: Solving the Mystery*, by John Imbrie and Katherine Palmer Imbrie, Enslow Publishers, Box 777, Hillside, NJ 07205.

Harcourt Brace Jovanovich, Inc.: Line reprinted from *Four Quartets* by T. S. Eliot. Copyright 1943 by T. S. Eliot; renewed in 1971 by Esme Valerie Eliot. Reprinted by permission of Harcourt Brace Jovanovich, Inc. in the United States and Faber & Faber Ltd. in England.

Howell-North Books: Excerpts from *Copper*, by Ira B. Joralemon. Copyright © 1973.

John Wiley & Sons, Inc.: Excerpt from *Economic Mineral Deposits* (Third Edition), by Alan M. Bateman & Mead L. Jensen. Copyright © 1979. Reprinted by permission of John Wiley & Sons, Inc.

Little, Brown & Co.: Lines by Hesiod, reprinted from *Mythology*, by Edith Hamilton. Copyright 1940, 1942 by Edith Hamilton.

McGraw-Hill Book Company: Excerpt from *Climate Through the Ages*, Revised Edition, by C. E. P. Brooks. Copyright 1949 by McGraw-Hill Book Company. Reprinted by permission of the publisher.

The National Aeronautics and Space Administration: Quote by Astronaut Edward G. Gibson, taken from *A New Sun: The Solar Results From Skylab*, by John A. Eddy. Copyright © 1979. Reprinted by permission of the National Aeronautics and Space Administration.

Simon & Schuster, Inc.: Excerpts from *The Lean Years: Politics in the Age of Scarcity*, by Richard Barnet. Copyright © 1980 by Richard J. Barnet. Originally published in *The New Yorker*, March 31, 1980. Reprinted by permission of Simon & Schuster, Inc.

W. W. Norton & Company, Inc.: Quote by Paul Ehrlich taken from *The Cold and the Dark*, by Paul R. Ehrlich, Carl Sagan, Donald Kennedy, and Walter Orr Roberts. Copyright © 1984. Reprinted by permission of W. W. Norton & Company, Inc.

Library of Congress Cataloging-in-Publication Data

Weiner, Jonathan.
  Planet earth.

  Bibliography: p. 355
  Includes index.
  1. Earth sciences—Popular works. I. Title.
QE31.W45 1986   550   85-47795
        ISBN 0-553-05096-6

Published simultaneously in the United States and Canada

PRINTED IN THE UNITED STATES OF AMERICA

WAK 0 9 8 7 6 5 4 3 2 1

To my parents,
and to the memory of
Hugh Odishaw

Contents

Acknowledgments

This book is the companion volume to a seven-part public television series produced by WQED/Pittsburgh, in association with the National Academy of Sciences. I am grateful to Lloyd Kaiser, President of WQED, and to Tom Skinner, the station's Executive Vice President and Executive Producer of the "Planet Earth" series, for inviting me to join such an exciting project.

The project's offices are divided between Los Angeles and Pittsburgh, and staff members in both cities worked hard to help me write this book. In Los Angeles, Gregory Andorfer, Series Producer, and Georgann Kane, Coordinating Producer, spent hours with me discussing each film in the series. They arranged for me to receive thousands of pages of on-camera and off-camera interviews, magazine clippings, reading lists, and shooting scripts. In these and other ways, they made it possible to coordinate the shaping of the series and the book.

Robin Bates, Georgann Kane, and Ted Thomas produced individual hours of the television series; William Walter, Debbie Glovin, and Deane Rink were Associate Producers. I drew upon their scripts, and upon transcripts of interviews they conducted, in writing each chapter. Deane, in particular, helped research and read over several chapters, between his trips to the glaciers of Switzerland and Antarctica, and the sands of Rajasthan.

Patricia Colvig, Photo Editor, found most of the pictures for this book. She did the job with high enthusiasm, and delighted the author by caring as much about the book as he did. Patricia was ably assisted by Kay Fanslow.

Michelle Rodriguez, Production Assistant, served as chief liaison, with help from Bonnie Waltch, Sue Frankenberger and Amy Barraclough, cheerfully shepherding manuscripts and memos on their way to and from Los Angeles and New York.

In Pittsburgh, WQED's Design Director, Mark Friedman, designed the book. He saw the project through from the first long, tentative meetings to the last long, hectic ones, and helped from beginning to end. I am grateful not only for his sense of style but also his sense of humor and his sage counsel. Russ Martz helped to administer the project; Meg Cheever assisted at several key stages. Allen Blaschak and many other members of the station contributed their time and their talents.

The "Planet Earth" series received major funding from The Annenberg/CPB Project, and corporate funding from IBM.

Many distinguished members of the National Academy of Sciences served on panels and review committees, and advised the producers at each stage of production. Barbara Valentino served as the academy's Project Administrator, and several times she helped me find the right scientist at the right time. Stanley Ruttenberg of the University Corporation for Atmospheric Research was the academy's Consultant to Production. I owe him thanks for his help, his conversation, and his hospitality.

I am grateful to Richard Birnie of Dartmouth College, who read the entire manuscript in its penultimate revision. His comments and warm encouragement were invaluable. Peter Bower of Rutgers University tackled many research problems early in the project. He was very generous with his time, and lent me books from his personal library.

Many Earth scientists were kind enough to read portions of the manuscript pertaining to their own specialties, and some of them read and commented upon entire chapters. They understood the needs of a book for the general reader, and helped me try to be accurate while avoiding the technical and obscure. For "The Living Machine," I thank Don L. Anderson, Brent Dalrymple, Charles L. Drake, Gordon Eaton, David Jones, Donald B. McIntyre, C. Dan Miller, Otto Nuttli, Pete Palmer, Stanley Ruttenberg, Christopher Scotese, Irwin Shapiro, Kerry Sieh, and Robert B. Smith. For "The Blue Planet": John Baross, Jenifer Wartha Clark, John Edmond, William Haxby, Henry Stommel, and Marie Tharp. For "The Climate Puzzle": Eric Barron, Charles Bentley, Reid Bryson, Robert Bunting, Harold Fritts, James Hays, Edwin Kessler, Edward Lorenz, Verner Suomi, Warren Washington, Ian Whillans, James Wilson, and Pat Zimmerman; special thanks to Raymond Pierrehumbert and Stanley Ruttenberg. For "Tales from other Worlds": Bruce Bohor, James Head, Torrence Johnson, Harold Masursky, Richard Muller, Tobias Owen, David Raup, David Roddy, Peter Schultz, Bradford Smith, and Steven Soter. For "The Solar Sea": Syun-Ichi Akasofu, Philip Bliss Duffy, Stamatios Krimigis, Ralph Markson, Martin Pomerantz, Walter Orr Roberts, Robin Stebbins, Charles Stockton, George E. Williams, and Richard C. Willson. For "Gifts from the Earth": G. Arthur Barber, Derek M. Freeston, R. W. Hutchinson, Alvin Lewis, Paul Lowman, Floyd Sabins, and Steve Scott. For "Fate of the Earth": Stanley Awramik, Thomas Lovejoy, Stephen Schneider, Daniel Simberloff, Starley Thompson, and David Usher. If, in spite of all this expert review, I have let any errors slip into the book, the responsibility is mine.

I was lucky in my sympathetic editor, Peter Guzzardi. He helped to guide the project, to shape the manuscript, and to make hard work fun. Many thanks to his able assistant Alison Acker; to Tom and Shirley Hamilton, who set the type; and to Donna Ruvituso and Barbara Cohen, who handled the book's production.

I could not have written the book without the warm support and sound advice of my agent, Victoria Pryor. Nor could I have met my deadlines without my research assistant, Lewis Zipin, whose dedication to the project often drove him to read until dawn, and who became almost a native guide. He wrote long preliminary reports on many topics; we worked closely together in outlining each chapter, and afterward in checking it for accuracy. It is a pleasure to be able to thank him here for his substantial and intelligent help.

I am also lucky to live with a gifted writer and editor. My wife, Deborah, read each rough draft, and helped keep the book on target. I am grateful for her wit, insight, love, and patience. Like Atlas' wife, she lived with a man who could not put down Planet Earth.

JONATHAN WEINER

Foreword

It was in the winter of 1983 that Jonathan Weiner enthusiastically accepted public television station WQED's invitation to author a popular book as a companion to the public television series *Planet Earth*. The result is this stunning volume full of the excitement of scientific revelation.

I was originally introduced to that excitement by Hugh Odishaw, Dean of the College of Earth Sciences at the University of Arizona. It was Hugh Odishaw's vision that sparked what was to become the *Planet Earth* television series. Nearly twenty-five years before, under the auspices of the National Academy of Sciences, he had headed the American endeavors in the 1957–58 International Geophysical Year—an unprecedented effort by scientists of sixty nations to understand how the Earth works. As he later described the effort, "It was the single most significant peaceful activity of mankind since the Renaissance and the Copernican revolution." Hugh Odishaw did not think small.

Until his early death in 1984, Hugh's excitement about the extraordinary scientific discoveries made since the International Geophysical Year and his desire to reach a broad international audience fueled our efforts to create the unique television series upon which this volume is based. As we refined the concept we knew that we were creating something new and special, but it was only after an additional two years of work in association with scientists worldwide and with many committee members of the National Academy that we came to understand how great Hugh's vision really was.

I remember one early meeting in particular when he enumerated the accomplishments in the Earth sciences since the International Geophysical Year. "Do you realize," he said, beaming, "what we didn't know in 1957? We only suspected that the Earth's land masses might be in motion, and our search for the origins of earthquakes was in its infancy; we still thought that interplanetary space in our solar system was a void, and we were unaware of the threat to our atmosphere posed by the greenhouse effect and acid rain." We went on to spend a long and fascinating afternoon discussing the recent discoveries that the Earth has a tail, like a comet, millions of miles long; that the sea floor is constantly being renewed by volcanoes; that sunspots may affect the Earth's climate; that there are bizarre ecosystems in the ocean's depths.

These ideas now propel this new television series and this book—revolutionary ideas based on discoveries that could not have been made thirty years ago. For at the beginning of the International Geophysical Year, there were no space probes or manned space systems. There were no high-speed computers, miniature high-precision electronic instruments, modern radio telescopes, or communication satellites. There were no submersibles with which to explore the ocean depths, and no one had drilled the ocean floor to confirm the theories of magnetic reversal and sea-floor spreading.

Now the earth sciences are both global and interdisciplinary in their scope. We have learned more in the past thirty years than in the previous three hundred. Most significantly, we have acquired the ability to radically change the face of Planet Earth—for good or ill. And we have come to realize that science can no longer be separated from its implications.

I am deeply grateful to my friend Hugh Odishaw, who opened the door on the great adventure that has become *Planet Earth*. I am indebted to our imaginative and energetic series producer, Gregory Andorfer, and his talented staff, as well as the many scientists who shared our enthusiasm and provided the expertise that is the "stuff" of this project.

In these pages, we embark on the most fantastic of voyages—to a place unique in all the solar system. And the end of our voyaging will bring with it a new and better understanding of the place on which we all live—Planet Earth.

THOMAS SKINNER, EXECUTIVE PRODUCER, *Planet Earth*
EXECUTIVE VICE PRESIDENT, WQED/PITTSBURGH

Planet Earth

The Living Machine

We shall not cease from exploration.
And the end of all our exploring
Will be to arrive where we started
And know the place for the first time.

T. S. ELIOT   *Four Quartets*

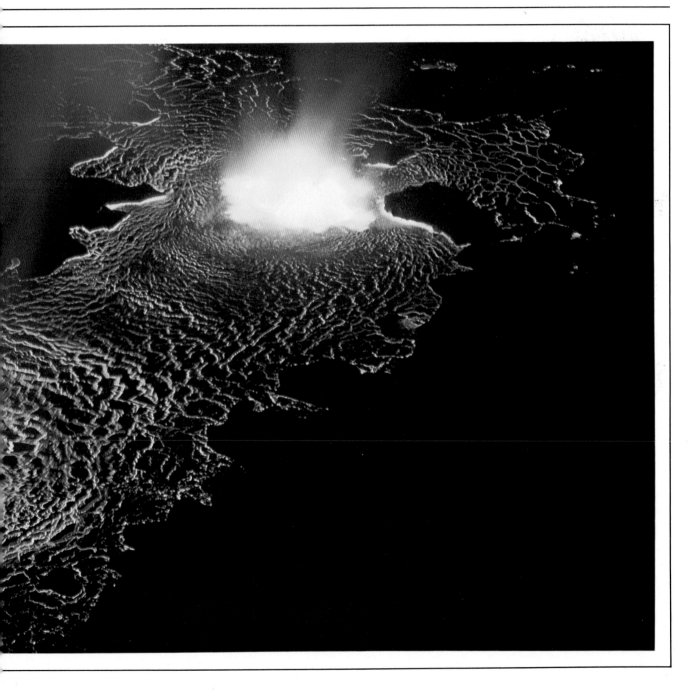

Overleaf: A bubbling lake of lava within the crater of Nyiragongo volcano in Zaire.

1 / The Living Machine

This planet has regions of sound and fury, where the earth from below destroys the earth above. In Iceland, in Hawaii, in Zaire, in New Zealand, lava bursts from rock like the spoutings of whales, or the exhalations of demons. The ground shakes as if giants wrestled in it, or fitfully slept. Those of our ancestors who lived in such places had to endure an uncertain landscape, and their dreams of Earth were brooding and dark.

It was a fearful thing when molten fire crept down from a mountain and buried a farmer's fields, or an earthquake one sunny spring morning flattened the next village. Disasters like that cried out for explanation and propitiation. In the Valley of Mexico, the Aztecs slaughtered captives on the peak of an extinct volcano; they burned the hearts of human sacrifices to keep the Sun alive, and keep earthquakes away.

In Western Africa, to one tribe of aborigines, the jungle was the hair of a giant, and all that crept and crawled and raced and flew in the jungle was lice in the giant's hair. When he shook his head the earth trembled. In New Zealand, the ragged mountains, it was said, had been cast up by the thrashings of a huge fish, hooked by greedy brothers who should have known better. In Polynesia, the islanders spoke of the goddess Pele and her older sister Namakaokahai, who battled across a good part of the Pacific. Their war left its mark upon the sea—the chain of the Hawaiian islands. Pele settled, more or less, in the cone of the volcano Kilauea, and during fits of temper—when she was spurned, as she often was, by some handsome Hawaiian chief—she threw explosive tantrums.

The old Norsemen of Iceland blamed earthquakes on a quarrel among their gods. Long ago, Loki the Trickster, out of pure spite, arranged the death of Balder, Odin's saintly son. For punishment, Loki was bound upon three flagstones in an underground cave. A snake hovered above his face, its venom dripping in his eyes. Loki's wife stood by him, holding out a goblet to catch the poison drop by drop. Now and then, however, when she turned aside to empty the cup, a drop struck her husband, and his thrashing shook the earth. "Thus Loki shall writhe," the Norsemen told each other, sitting by the fire, "until the Twilight of the Gods." And when the fire crackled, they said, "That is Loki whipping his children."

Later, the Norsemen renounced these stories, and converted to Christianity. They decided then that earthquakes and volcanoes proceed from Hell. In the Middle Ages, all Europe came to believe that Iceland's most dangerous volcano, Hekla, was Hell's gate. The hissing bombs of lava that flew out of its crater were souls of the damned.

As recently as 20 years ago, when the earth shook, and burned, there were no answers that satisfied the modern longing for explanation. Late on the afternoon of Good Friday, 1964, in Anchorage, Alaska, without warning, the land fluttered and snapped like a flag in a sudden wind. It shook for four to seven minutes. Some 200,000 megatons of energy were released, 400 times more than the combined force of all the nuclear bombs ever exploded in peace and war; it was the worst quake ever measured in North America, 8.5 on the Richter scale.

In the business district, shops and sidewalks sank twenty feet into the earth; parts of Fourth Avenue and L Street slid downhill and mingled at the corner; 130 acres of a suburb, Turnagain Heights, slid into the sea. The Alaskan town of Valdez was utterly destroyed, first by landslides, then by floods, and then by giant waves called tsunami. Tsunami sheared trees off cliffs and bluffs eighty feet above sea level. The quake was felt 800 miles north, at Point Hope and Point Barrow.

Amid such widespread destruction, the number of deaths was miraculously low. There were no tall buildings in Anchorage, and there was only one person per square mile in all Alaska. A hundred people died. If shocks of such power ever strike California, where there are several hundred people per square mile, the loss of life will be disastrous. The towering skyscrapers of San Francisco are engineering experiments that have never been tested.

At the time of the Good Friday Earthquake, geologists knew that quakes occurred along faults—cracks in the crust of the Earth. But why the cracks were there, and what moved the Earth along them, the geologists could not say.

Indeed, until that date geology had a bad press. The British physicist Lord Kelvin, in the heat of a dispute over the Earth's age, said geology was about as intellectually respectable as collecting postage stamps. The physicist was eventually proved wrong on both counts—wrong about the planet's age, and wrong about the earth sciences. But it was true that many geologists spent careers simply gathering rocks, and comparing the sandstone of Madagascar with the sandstone of India. They

During the Great Alaskan Earthquake of 1964, giant waves battered the southern coast of Alaska. In Seward, the fishing boat Taku Maid *was hurled out of the harbor and into a railroad yard.*

had no way to explain the endless comparisons and contrasts they catalogued. They could not say why those sandstones, separated by the Indian Ocean, were so similar. No single hypothesis explained mild tremors in western Africa and sudden and deadly ones in Alaska; or explained Hekla in Iceland and Kilauea in Hawaii. There was a globe, but no global theory. As one early student of the Earth, Alexander von Humboldt, lamented, "We examine the stones, but not the mountains, we have the materials but ignore how they fit together."

What are the forces that make and shape the Earth? What accounts for the torments of Mexico, Iceland, Hawaii, Zaire, New Zealand? Why is the pinnacle of Mount Everest made of rock and fossils that once lay in the bottom of the ocean—and, with some irony, now called "the roof of the world"? What accounts for the vestiges in the Sahara of massive glaciers; and in Alaska of tropical jungles? Have parcels of land wandered from one address to another?

Twenty years ago, geologists began a breathtaking succession of intellectual leaps that transformed their science. The years since the Great Alaskan Earthquake have brought a revolution in the study of the globe. Like other revolutions in the history of science, this one was a long time stirring. Indeed, certain keen minds anticipated parts of it decades, or even centuries, ago, long before they had tools with which to test their hunches. At last, in our time, the right tools, the sophisticated tests, and the decisive evidence arrived all in a rush.

Earth seen from space. The continents—the foundations of human life—are now thought to be drifting and slowly spinning, like rafts in the eddies of a river, or masses of clouds.

To approach fiery fissures, scientists wear protective suits. Lava is some 1,000 degrees centigrade—which still is only a quarter as hot as the core of the Earth. Norsemen thought volcanoes were the gateways of Hell.

The revolution brings together hundreds of thousands of observations, many of which were gained at some hazard in the field. They were won by scientists rappeling down ice cliffs in Antarctica, diving deep into sea floor rifts in tiny submarines, drilling the basement of the continent, helicoptering over the wasteland of Mount St. Helens's effluvia, lowering themselves into the Nyiragongo crater. The results have changed forever the way we see our world.

This new view is not easy to take in. It is hard to imagine that the continents are adrift, ferried about on great fragments of the Earth's shell, which incessantly grind against each other all around the Earth. The plates shudder and quake more than a million times a year. What we have been pleased to call "solid Earth" is not as solid as we thought. It is energetic, dynamic, and fundamentally restless. Its poles wander, and its magnetic field flickers and wavers like a fire in a grate. It is continually creating its own surface, destroying it, repairing it, renewing it like a skin. We have dreamed for years of life on other planets, but we have hardly noticed the life of our own. This Earth is Terra Nova—a land new to us.

Consider Earth as it looks from orbit, suspended in the black of empty space. Except for the swirls of cloud and the glitter of seashine, this is the schoolroom globe we all grew up with. How odd it would have been if the first astronauts had looked down and seen not the patchwork scraps of land they expected, but a whole other array of continents; if they had radioed back to Cape Canaveral that centuries of maps and Mercator projections were wrong. It seems improbable; yet that, in effect, is what geologists now believe. The charts are right for the moment. But they are wrong if we take them to describe the face of the Earth as it always was and always shall be. Instead, they depict only the most temporary of arrangements in the life of the planet, a casual scattering of lands and seas, changing at this moment.

In this new view of the planet there is, if anything, even more action than one might imagine looking down into the lavas of the Nyiragongo volcano. The drama unfolds with such deliberation that it is all but invisible to us, because our lives are too brief to see it. It is nonetheless dramatic. And there is in this view some tint of the wisdom of the ages: for we now understand that the volcano is as much creator as destroyer. Its fires at last build lands. And the earthquake is part of the grand movement that has given us Earth to walk upon.

The new theory of the planet has the ring of truth, and the elegance of myth.

The modern way of looking at the Earth began in a rather surprising spot: in and around Edinburgh, Scotland, at the end of the eighteenth century. Edinburgh was known then as the "Athens of the North." Beyond the walls of the medieval Old Town—which clung like swallows' nests to the steep sides of an extinct volcano, Castle Rock—the city fathers were planning a New Town, a grid of long, straight streets and grand squares. The design was bold for the day; so was the very notion of city planning.

This was a time of revolution in America and France. Yet it was the Industrial Revolution, more than these political bonfires, that was changing the ways of the world. The mechanical loom was invented, and the steam engine, and the factory system itself. Inventors and philosophers across Europe were part of the great Enlightenment—they hoped strong minds, and wide publication of the truth, could dispel the world's ignorance, to them the root of all evil. Intellect alone could "put light into" the world. Rationality became all but a new religion.

In this heady atmosphere Edinburgh flourished. It was the center of the Scottish Enlightenment, which included such brilliant men as James Watt, inventor of the steam engine; Adam Smith, whose *Wealth of Nations* set out a new economics based on free enterprise; John Clerk, who dreamed up novel and ingenious approaches to naval warfare (yet never went to sea); Joseph Black, the pioneering chemist who discovered carbon dioxide; and James Hutton, who founded the modern view of the Earth. Many of these men met, one evening a week, to unbend at the Oyster Club, which Hutton had helped to found. Benjamin Franklin, who once visited Edinburgh, called them "a set of as truly great men, Professors of Knowledge, as have appeared in any age or country." To an astonishing degree, they brought into the world not only the engines of the Industrial Revolution but also the ideas and attitudes that made the revolution possible.

Hutton was trained as a doctor, but he made his fortune as a chemist and a farmer. While farming, he became fascinated by soil, rock, and the rolling surface of the Earth; he looked—a historian of geology later wrote—"with anxious curiosity into every pit or ditch or bed of a river that fell his way." And by his forties he had a new vision of the Earth. He saw in the layering of rock in Scotland's provinces, the limestones, sandstones, and shales, evidence that they had been laid down in distant times as soft sediments that settled to the bottom of the sea. These sediments had been compacted and slowly turned to stone by the pressure of further layers of sediment settling above them. At last the sea had withdrawn, or the

Portrait of a Scottish genius. James Hutton was the father of modern geology. He saw the Earth as a living machine, immensely old and powerful.

seabed had risen, exposing some of the rock to the open air. The wearing of wind and weather had broken up the topmost layer of rock into fine bits, helping to make the rich mix we call soil.

Rains, said Hutton, are continually washing soil into streams and rivers and thence to the sea, where the sediment is compacted once again into solid rock. Heat within the Earth heaves this bedrock up above the sea to form new mountains. Molten liquid—lava—forces its way up and hardens into rock; and this rock, too, the elements wear away, until the bits and pieces find their way to the bottom of the sea. This cycle from rock to soil to rock, from sea to air and again to sea, has endured for an extraordinary length of time, and will go on, Hutton presumed, into eternity. In 1788, in a report to the Royal Society of Edinburgh, he concluded, "The result, therefore, of this physical inquiry is, that we find no vestige of a beginning—no prospect of an end."

This was a turning point in our understanding of the Earth: Hutton had perceived the gulf between human and geological time, between the clock in the church tower and the clock in the mountain. Scientists today take for granted that the Earth is vastly older than the written history of our own species. But until Hutton's day, most saw the Earth very differently. Archbishop James Ussher, Primate of Ireland, had calculated the age of the Earth by totting up all the generations of men and women mentioned in the Bible, beginning with Adam and Eve; and Ussher claimed the Earth had been created just 6,000 years before (on the evening of October 22, in 4004 B.C., to be precise). Most people believed, with Ussher, that the planet had been put together back then all at once—rather as one might lay out a landscape garden—and that it had changed little since, except perhaps during the Great Flood.

Hutton himself was not irreligious. But in studying nature, he preferred to rely on the evidence of his senses, and reason from facts he had gathered himself, than speculate upon the world's cloud-wrapped beginnings and endings, which were in the hands of God. If Earth were only 6,000 years old, Hutton said, there was simply no time for the country he saw around him to have formed. He knew that rock and soil, sediments and seas require vast stretches of time to pass through their cycles. He could not measure these cycles' duration (he would not even venture an estimate), but he could tell that the wheels grind exceedingly slow.

After all, 16 centuries had passed since the Roman Emperor Hadrian had built his great wall across the top of Britain, to keep out the wild Scots. The wall drapes across the countryside, over hillocks and down glens. If one believed Ussher, almost a third of the Earth's history had passed since Hadrian's armies built that wall; yet in all that time the lay of the land must have changed little, for any reshuffling of hills and valleys would long since have toppled the wall. Sixteen hundred winters had done small harm to its paving stones.

Since erosion had done such trifling work in a third of the Earth's history, it could not possibly have carved great mountains and valleys in the other two thirds. The roots of time had to be far deeper than anyone had supposed.

Hutton found graphic evidence of this fact at Siccar Point, by the North Sea. There the waves had exposed a cliff of two colors. The upper half was old red sandstone, and the lower half was a dark rock he called *schistus*. The sandstone was in horizontal layers, but the schistus layers were nearly vertical.

Hutton's friend John Playfair was along that day at Siccar Point. Playfair was a brilliant geologist himself, and his book *Illustrations of the Huttonian Theory* did more to popularize Hutton's ideas than the master's own writings, most of which were, in the phrase Hutton used to describe the Scottish soils, "loose and incoherent materials." Playfair and Hutton knew that no rock could be laid down in vertical layers: one might as well drop a sheaf of papers and expect them to land

James Hutton deduced that the lowest layer of rock shown here was horizontal when it first formed; then stupendous forces within the Earth tilted the layer nearly vertical; then it was worn flat by erosion; and finally it was buried beneath horizontal rock layers: one brief episode in the life of the Earth. The engraving, "Unconformity at Jedburgh, Borders," was made by a friend of Hutton's, James Clerk of Eldin.

poised on edge. The bed of schistus must first have been deposited horizontally, hardened into rock, and only afterward was disturbed, and tilted. The top of the jagged mass, exposed to the elements, had been worn flat by erosion; then the sandstone had been laid down on top of it.

The two friends were powerfully impressed as they contemplated the time all this must have taken. Playfair wrote:

> We often said to ourselves, What clearer evidence could we have had of the different formation of these rocks, and of the long interval which separated their formation, had we actually seen them emerging from the bosom of the deep? . . . Revolutions still more remote appeared in the distance of this extraordinary perspective. The mind seemed to grow giddy by looking so far into the abyss of time.

The history of the world, Hutton and Playfair saw, was not, as most assumed in his day, a Creation, followed by a Deluge, followed by millennia of tranquility. No, Earth's story was written in the same style in the past as it is written today. The past, present, and future are only a long series of ordinary

At Siccar Point by the North Sea in Scotland, there is a layer of rock tilted nearly vertical, like that at Jedburgh (far left). When Hutton found this cliff, he was awed by the long series of revolutions that went into its creation. He and his friend John Playfair felt giddy "looking so far into the abyss of time."

cycles, of wearing down and building up, of erosion and creation. To explain Siccar Point, or the hills of Scotland, or the soil of his farm in Berwickshire, there was no need to invoke miracles. As Hutton put it, "No powers are to be employed that are not natural to the globe, no action to be admitted of except those of which we know the principle."

This tenet, that the history of the Earth is even, steady, and consistent, became known as *uniformitarianism.* In the most general sense, it is a doctrine taken for granted in the sciences. If nature were not uniform, then one could not use the results of one experiment to predict the outcome of the next; neither could one assume that laws founded on a thousand varied observations would remain true. Without uniformity in nature, doing physics, chemistry, and biology would be like traveling in Alice's Wonderland. Logic, science, and life itself would fall to pieces. Still, in geology, uniformitarianism was for years controversial, in part because Hutton's work posed problems for those who wished to interpret the words of the Bible literally, and in part because the features of the Earth—mountains, gorges, cataracts, volcanoes—cry out to the imagination: Disaster! Miracle! Catastrophe!

Drawing on his knowledge of chemistry and medicine, kept lively and current by his sessions at the Oyster Club, Hutton described the Earth sometimes as a sort of chemical machine, and sometimes as a living body. Like his friend Watt's steam engine, it churns and labors, driven by the heat within it; and like a body it heals the harm done by its own erosion and continually renews itself. He saw the Earth as a great, living machine.

Once, five centuries ago, human beings thought the Sun, Moon, and stars revolved around human beings, that Earth was the hub and center of the universe. Then the Polish astronomer Mikolaj Kopernik—Copernicus—argued that the Sun is at the center, and it is we who whirl around it. Since the Copernican revolution, people have, over the centuries, slowly grown used to the fact that vast space surrounds us; that our world is merely a spinning point in the universe.

What Copernicus did for space, it has been said, Hutton did for time. Since Hutton, we know that we are pinpoints on an extraordinarily long time line. The span of years that we human beings have watched the sunrise is nothing, virtually nothing, in the history of the planet.

In a way, Hutton's point was simple: Given enough time, the slow cycles of the Earth can work wonders. The revolution that has taken place in the study of the Earth over the last two decades is only an elaboration of this idea of Hutton's. He described one grand cycle of creation and destruction, and in our time, a century and a half later, geologists have added another. This new cycle, too, leads to wonders. It explains more fully the heavings and settlings of the Earth's surface—the dynamics of the living machine.

The hero of the modern revolution is the German scientist Alfred Wegener. Like Hutton, he was a visionary, and like Hutton, his vision was widely accepted only after his death.

Wegener was one of a breed of explorer-scientists who mixed research and adventure, and he did nothing by halves. He was fascinated by meteorology and studied the upper atmosphere's weather from the gondola of a balloon. In 1906 he and his brother Kurt made a balloon flight that lasted 52 hours, a world record. He spent several strenuous winters in Greenland making weather observations ("We feel," he wrote, "like shock troops of humanity in the battle with the deadly powers of nature.") and in 1913 he crossed its ice cap with only one companion, using sledges hauled by ponies. He taught not only meteorology but also astronomy and geophysics, and he studied biology, paleontology, and much else. Yet he was obsessed with a single great idea, which he had developed as a young man while recuperating from a neck wound he had received in the First World War.

As Wegener tells it, the idea first occurred to him when he noticed that the coastlines of South America and Africa, were they to slide together, would fit as neatly as two pieces of a puzzle. To explain the coincidence, he proposed that the two continents might once have been one, and split apart. Eventually he saw them as parts of a single supercontinent, Pangaea— *pan* meaning "all," and *gaia*, "Earth." Pangaea had begun breaking up in the age of the dinosaurs, some 200 million years ago, "like pieces of a cracked ice floe." The pieces, he said, are still drifting apart to this day.

Wegener was not the first to speculate along these lines. There were many speculators, illustrious and obscure, before him. Three hundred years earlier, the courtier and philosopher Sir Francis Bacon had wondered about the coincidence of coastlines, and mentioned it in his *Novum Organum*. In 1666, a French monk, François Placet, whose name is otherwise forgotten, suggested that the continents had been broken apart by the Deluge (his title: *The Breaking Up of the Greater and Lesser Worlds: Or, It Is Shown That Before the Deluge, America Was Not Separated from the Other Parts of the World*). At the turn of this century, an American, Fránk Taylor, suggested that the tidal pull of the moon might have tugged the continents about on the surface of the planet. Another American, H. Baker,

A SUPERCONTINENT SHATTERS

Experts called his theory "a scientific fairy tale," but Alfred Wegener clung to his belief that continents drift.

thought the continents might have been set in motion by the planet Venus. Venus, he said, had swooped close enough to tear out a chunk of the Pacific floor, which became the Moon (an idea first espoused by George Darwin, Astronomer Royal of Great Britain, and grandson of Charles).

But Wegener was the first to investigate in exhaustive detail the idea of drift, and make others take it seriously. To do so, he collected evidence in many widely scattered fields. (Today, his admirers call him a Renaissance man; then, many colleagues thought he should stick to meteorology, and called him a crank.) He pointed to a mountain range that runs from east to west in South Africa, and another that matches it on the other side of the Atlantic, in Argentina. A plateau in Brazil corresponds neatly to another in Africa's Ivory Coast. Fossils of a primitive fern, *Glossopteris*, are common in certain parts of both Africa and Brazil, and these spots line up as neatly as their coastlines. Indeed *Glossopteris* is found on so many scattered landmasses, including India, Australia, and even Antarctica, that the evidence of the fern alone might have suggested the idea of Pangaea. As for the northern continents, the Appalachians of America's east coast could be traced up into Nova Scotia and thence across the ocean to Scotland and Scandinavia. Taken together, the mass of such evidence, Wegener felt, was utterly convincing: "It is just as if we were to refit the torn pieces of a newspaper by matching their edges and then check whether the lines of print run smoothly across. If they do, there is nothing left but to conclude that the pieces were in fact joined in this way."

The idea was too radical for the time, however. Wegener's book, *The Origin of the Continents and Oceans*, first published in 1915, brought him more notoriety than praise. The continents, after all, are not really like ice floes, afloat on seas. They are rooted in the bedrock of the ocean basins. Wegener was ridiculed for failing to explain what sort of force would permit "continents of granite to plow through oceans of rock." "Whatever Wegener's own attitude may have been originally," said one critic, "in his book he is not seeking truth; he is advocating a cause. . . . He has suggested much, he has proved nothing." Another critic was more to the point: "If we are to believe Wegener's hypothesis," he said, "we must forget everything which has been learned in the last seventy years and start over again."

Wegener lost his life on the Greenland ice in 1930, at the age of 50, during a mission to establish a mid-ice observatory. At the time of his death, most geologists considered his drift idea to have been thoroughly debunked. As the years passed, a few mavericks in Europe and Australia spoke up for

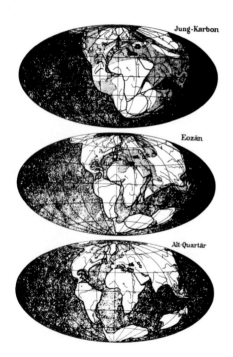

Jung-Karbon

Eozän

Alt-Quartär

In Wegener's vision of the history of the Earth, the continents were once united in a supercontinent, Pangaea; they were torn apart, and have been drifting ever since.

Wegener's ideas. In the United States, however, it became scientific suicide to attempt to revive the outlandish notions of the German meteorologist.

UNDISCOVERED COUNTRY

The proofs Wegener needed were found years later, quite by chance and on another frontier—at the bottom of the sea.

By then—the 1940s—while few believed in wandering continents, there was no doubt that the world could drift apart. World War II proved that thoroughly, as nation turned upon nation, and Axis submarines stalked Allied fleets across the Atlantic. These World War II sea chases actually made a rare contribution to the sciences. Ships watched for subs using the new sonar (*so*und *na*vigation *r*anging), reading the darkness beneath them by sending out high-pitched sounds and analyzing the echoes (a method pioneered by brown bats and bottlenosed dolphins). With another device, the Fathometer, which works on the same principle, the Navy mapped the ocean floor around Iwo Jima before the famous amphibious assault.

Harry Hess, a geologist from Princeton University who was aboard the U.S.S. *Cape Johnson* at Iwo Jima, was fascinated by these glimpses of the sea floor. It was still uncharted territory then, blank as the New World in the maps of Amerigo Vespucci. Most people assumed the sea floor was merely a vast, empty, and lifeless plain, dotted with random plateaus and seamounts (underwater mountains, whose summits the sun never sees). Hess realized that the sea hides livelier terrain. And with the new echo sounders this territory—three quarters of the world's surface—could be mapped at last.

In 1947, when the war was over, Hess went back to Princeton. But a group of scientists from the Lamont Geological Observatory, in Palisades, New York, put to sea, using the new instruments to explore the ocean floor, and dredging up rocks as they went. They were led by Maurice Ewing of Columbia University, a friend of Hess's who shared his fascination with the sea floor. Early on, their goal was fairly simple: to map a string of seamounts known as the Mid-Atlantic Ridge. They sounded it out with echoes, using sonar and Fathometers, and with data from undersea earthquakes, which, it was noticed, occur with curious frequency along the ridge.

As their undersea maps grew detailed, they found that the Mid-Atlantic Ridge is a peculiar structure of a kind never before encountered. It is a mountain range some six to ten thousand feet high, with a steep and narrow valley at the center. The Mid-Atlantic Ridge is part of a system of ridges 46,000 miles long; they have been compared to the seams of a giant baseball, winding virtually all the way around the world. The

Harry Hess,
Princeton geologist
and World War II troop
transport commander.

long valley of the Mid-Atlantic Ridge runs the length of it like the groove in a spine. No one could imagine what the ridge was doing there, but it was incontestably the longest mountain range, with the longest valley, on the planet.

In India it was once believed that the Earth's mountains and valleys formed when Sky asked his bride Earth to make herself smaller, so that he could surround her "and go to her in love." And for a long time that was more or less how geologists explained the Earth's great mountains and valleys—they formed when the Earth shrank, like wrinkles in the shriveled skin of a dried apple. This theory seemed to fit the Himalayas, the Rockies, the Andes, and the Alps, all of which represent great stretches of territory that have been massively compressed. (As Mark Twain once quipped, Switzerland would make an impressive country if it were rolled out flat.)

Yet the Mid-Atlantic Ridge, the greatest mountain range of all, did not fit the theory. The terrain around it bears marks of having been stretched, not compressed. If mountains on land suggest a shrinking Earth, these seamounts suggest an expanding Earth. Surely the planet could not be shrinking *and* expanding.

As they dredged up rocks from the bottom, the expeditions' crews noticed something equally unsettling. Most researchers had assumed the sea floor was quiet, and undisturbed. Some hoped they could find, beneath the freshest, soft layers of silt and clay, the oldest rock on Earth, the original crust that formed when Earth cooled from a molten ball. The basement of the oceans, they thought, must be billions of years old. Yet the researchers found only young rock, nothing older than about 150 million years. This was an important and puzzling discovery, which they made simply by virtue of being there first. As Chuck Drake of Dartmouth, who joined some of these early cruises, remembers, it was a delightful time to be a geologist "because you didn't have to be very smart. All you had to do was be willing to go to sea, and if you measured anything, what you measured would be new."

Harry Hess, now back at Princeton, began to wonder what it all meant. The result of his musings was a work of speculation, which he modestly called "an essay in geopoetry." Could it be, Hess asked, that the long valley was a rift in the crust of the Earth, from which hot rock was continually rising upward from deep in the interior? That idea seemed likely enough, because it would account for the occurrence of undersea earthquakes all along the ridge, around the world. Could it be, he continued, that this upwelling rock made its way through the rift as the sea floor spread apart to either side?

If so, he thought, the entire Atlantic sea floor might

be moving half toward the west, half toward the east. Hess saw the result as a sort of conveyor belt—actually twin conveyor belts, one traveling west, the other east. The upwelling rock is forever creating fresh ridge, and new ocean crust, which then moves away from the ridge. It travels across the bottom of the sea at centimeters per year, which is rapid motion by geological standards. When it reaches a barrier—the edge of a continent or the wall of an island arc—it is forced down beneath the barrier and dives deep beneath the crust, there to be melted down again. This cycle was dubbed *sea floor spreading* by the geologist Robert Dietz, and the name stuck. Something of the kind had been proposed earlier in the century by a Scottish geologist, Arthur Holmes; but now, with the new maps of the sea floor, the idea was more compelling. Sea floor spreading, said Hess and Dietz, might just be the clue that Wegener died without glimpsing—it might prove that continents really are driven across the surface of the planet. For if a sea expands, can the continents stand still?

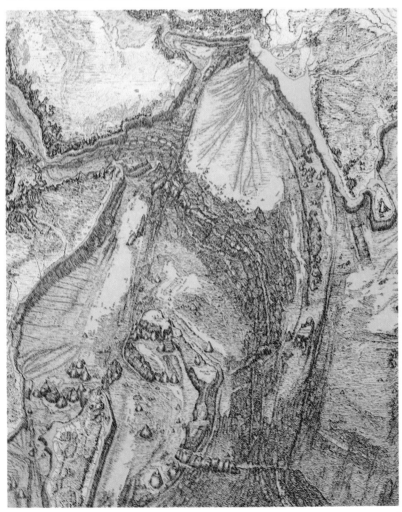

The Carlsberg Ridge, in the north-western Indian Ocean. It is one small part of an undersea ridge that winds all the way around the Earth, like the seams of a giant baseball. The Carlsberg Ridge gave Fred Vine and Drum Matthews their great inspiration.

"Harry called this geopoetry," says Chuck Drake of Dartmouth, "because he recognized that a great deal of data was needed either to substantiate or disprove this idea." The tool that proved Hess's hypothesis came, as often happens in science, from out in left field. It arose from an obscure question in an odd and specialized discipline, paleomagnetics, the study of the magnetic properties of rocks.

The whole Earth can be seen as a single giant magnet, with north and south magnetic poles. Put a bar magnet beneath a piece of paper, sprinkle the paper with iron filings, and the filings align themselves with the bar's magnetic field: if they are nearer the north pole, they point north; nearer the south pole, south. Just so, a compass needle swivels on its pivot and points to the planet's nearest pole. Cover the planet with compass needles, and they would trace much the same pattern as iron filings on a piece of paper.

Scientists have long known that certain minerals in molten rock, as they cool, become magnetized by the Earth's magnetic field, and are aligned with the planet's north and south magnetic poles. When the lava hardens, its magnetic field becomes permanent, and points north like a compass needle. A good compass needle can be locked in place with the turn of a screw. Likewise the hardened rock: unless the rock is moved, or melted down, its magnetic field should point north forever.

One common kind of hardened lava is the black rock called basalt. Oddly enough, since the turn of the century, outcrops of basalt had been discovered here and there with their magnetic fields pointing in the wrong directions. Two Britishers, Patrick Blackett and S. Keith Runcorn, systematically testing basalt compass needles across North America and Europe, found that rocks of different ages pointed off toward different spots on the horizon, like witnesses who disagree. To explain this, Blackett and Runcorn suggested at first that the poles had wandered; then, that the rocks, and the continents they rest on, had wandered too.

The two men became outspoken champions of continental drift, but they made few converts among the scientific establishment. Most thought the testimony of the compass needles too equivocal and indirect to be convincing. And the needles *were* confusing. Some of the basalt Blackett and Runcorn had found in Iceland pointed in precisely the wrong direction: dead south. Other scientists had found basalt pointing south in Japan, and in the mountain range that runs through France, the Massif Central. This basalt contradicted all the rest. Had these rocks reversed themselves in some strange chemical reaction? Or were these natural compasses accurate—when they hardened, was the Earth's north magnetic pole actually in the south? Either the rock's compasses had reversed, or the poles of the Earth had flipped. Both notions seemed slightly mad.

This intrigued a young geology student at Berkeley, Allan Cox. He and Richard Doell, who were friends at Berkeley, attacked the problem. The best way to decide about the eccentric basalt, they saw, was to date it—date samples of it from widely scattered places on Earth. If all basalt that hardened, say, 5 million years ago pointed north, and all basalt 6 million years old pointed south, that would prove that the rocks' compasses were consistent, and that between 5 and 6 million years ago the poles themselves had flipped.

The experiment would work only if the rocks could be dated precisely. Brent Dalrymple, who had also been a graduate student at Berkeley, was expert in a dating technique then quite new. Most rocks contain potassium, and some of this potassium is radioactive, decaying atom by atom into another element, argon. The argon, a gas, is trapped within the rock "like a bird in a cage," as Dalrymple says. In the laboratory, one can measure the relative amounts of potassium and argon in each sample. In very young rock, the potassium has had little time to decay, so there is barely a trace of argon. In very old rock, much more potassium has decayed, and there is more argon in it. Knowing the precise rate at which potassium decays, one can calculate the age of the rock.

Cox and company began this experiment around 1960, in California, collecting samples from some of the volcanic cones and ash flows in the foothills of the Sierra Nevada. About half the lava flows they tested were magnetized to the north, and half to the south. They found nothing peculiar about the minerals themselves; those magnetized to the south had the same composition as those magnetized to the north. "So we quickly became convinced," says Cox, "that the magnetic field of the Earth had indeed flipped from north to south—that this wild idea was in fact true."

At first, the researchers assumed that these reversals would prove to have occurred regularly, every million years or so, regular as the ticks of a clock. And indeed, Cox recalls wryly, their first data seemed to fit this pattern. ("I think that it's always true that if you don't have very much data, it will fit your theory.") But then they began to find reversals that had lasted a mere 100,000 years. For a while thereafter they said the ticking is slightly irregular, but at last they had to acknowledge that it is totally irregular, random. "For me, this was a very frustrating experience," Cox says. "Scientists always like to find some very simple, regular pattern in nature. You're always looking for order. And the odd kind of order we found was almost perfect disorder."

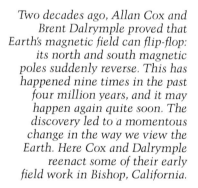

Two decades ago, Allan Cox and Brent Dalrymple proved that Earth's magnetic field can flip-flop: its north and south magnetic poles suddenly reverse. This has happened nine times in the past four million years, and it may happen again quite soon. The discovery led to a momentous change in the way we view the Earth. Here Cox and Dalrymple reenact some of their early field work in Bishop, California.

By 1966, Cox and his colleagues, and others in Australia, had confirmed that the Earth's magnetic field had reversed itself no less than nine times, at odd intervals, and for varying periods, over the past 4 million years alone (the long periods they called *epochs*, the short ones *events*).

Why the magnetic field of the Earth should flip like this is not well understood. The Earth is not really as simple as a bar magnet: its magnetic field is thought to be generated by molten metal churning within the core. Precisely how this natural dynamo might work is a subject of hot research today; perhaps changing patterns of churning abruptly alter the field. But the discovery of pole flips, and the fact that they can be measured precisely, led, indirectly, to a proof of continental drift. Pole flips became the key to deciphering certain cryptic patterns that had been detected on the sea floor.

In the early 1960s, while Cox, Doell, and Dalrymple struggled to make sense of pole flips, Fred Vine and Drummond Matthews in Cambridge, England, were staring at "zebra stripes" at the bottom of the Indian Ocean.

From the H.M.S. *Owen*, Matthews had spent half a year in 1961 surveying the Carlsberg Ridge, in the northwest Indian Ocean. Such research ships often towed a small school of "fish," torpedo-shaped casks that trailed behind the ship, filled with instruments, scanning the bottom. In a "fish" behind the *Owen* was a magnetometer, which recorded the magnetization of the rocks deep below. Magnetometer studies of this kind off the coast of California, and others made by aircraft south of Iceland over the Mid-Atlantic Ridge, had found a curious pattern. Long ribbons of sea floor seemed to be magnetized more strongly than normal, and other ribbons more weakly. On sea floor maps, when these ribbons were drawn in—the strongly magnetized ones in black, the others in white—they alternated like a rumpled zebra hide. The stripes averaged miles wide, and many miles long, and, it was noticed, they tended to run parallel to the midocean ridges. Nothing like this had ever been found on land, and no one knew what to make of it.

Matthews had recorded some of these zebra stripes in his surveys of the Carlsberg Ridge. In Cambridge, looking at these stripes, it occurred to Vine that the proof of Harry Hess's idea could be staring them in the face. He and Matthews decided that the stripes might be the signature of magnetic reversals, the same reversals that Cox, Doell, and Dalrymple had found on dry land.

It was fairly certain by the mid-sixties that lava is exuded along the midocean ridges, though this had not yet been observed directly. The lava, Vine and Matthews reasoned, must be magnetized the instant it oozes up from the interior of the Earth and freezes in the dark, icy water at the sea bottom. All along the ridge, the entire length of the ocean, this newformed rock, basalt, should be magnetized in the same direction. Then, after it hardens, fresh, molten rock oozes up; the cold, hardened rock moves away to either side. If the poles flipped, the new lava would be magnetized in the reverse direction. Then, in turn, it would be forced away from the ridge.

The result would be just the sort of steady motion of the sea floor that Harry Hess had envisioned in his essay of geopoetry.

If the sea floor is really spreading, Vine and Matthews reasoned, then the basalt that forms in the trenches is carried at last clear across the floor of the Atlantic—the process called sea floor spreading. And *if* Cox, Doell, and Dalrymple's theory was correct, this sea floor spreading should result in zebra

"Zebra stripes" on the sea floor. The alternating black and white stripes reveal epochs during which Earth's magnetic field reversed itself. This pattern was recorded at the Reykjanes Ridge, southwest of Iceland.

stripes running parallel with the ridge all across the bottom of the ocean. Each stripe should mark a flip of the Earth's poles.

Thus, the sea floor, suggested Vine and Matthews, might be like the tape in a tape recorder, marked in closely spaced strips by magnetic reversals. Played back, the tape could tell a large part of the story of the Earth. If, for example, these flips could be matched up with the reversals that Cox, Doell, and Dalrymple had dated on land, then the sea floor could be dated precisely from one end to the other. What is more (though they did not think of this at first), it would be easy to use the stripes to calculate how fast the sea floor is spreading.

Vine, who was still a graduate student, described the idea to the head of the geophysics department in Cambridge. "I think he thought I was totally mad," Vine later confided to historian of science William Glen. "He was polite enough not to say anything; he just looked at me and went on to talk about something else." When Vine and Matthews published their hypothesis in 1963, "it went over like a lead balloon in a vacuum." At the time, almost nobody was taking either magnetic reversals or sea floor spreading seriously, so it was hard to use one to prove the other. Vine and Matthews's theory was the roof of a house of cards—a speculation resting on speculations.

A few scientists, however, were interested enough to follow up the idea. It occurred to geologist J. Tuzo Wilson, who visited Vine and Matthews in Cambridge, that the zebra-stripe pattern should be symmetrical on either side of the midocean ridge. Since fresh lava welling up in the ridge spreads simultaneously east and west, one should see the same alternation of stripes, some thick, some thin, on each side. Soon this prediction was proved right—in places, the zebra stripes are strikingly symmetrical east and west of the ridges—and the pattern attracted more attention, though mostly skeptical.

Then, in November 1965, Vine met Brent Dalrymple for the first time, at the meeting of the Geological Society of America held in Kansas City, Missouri. What happened is described in lively detail in William Glen's definitive history, *The Road to Jaramillo.*

Between sessions, Dalrymple told Vine privately that he and his colleagues had found yet another pole flip, the most recent yet discovered, only .9 million years ago. This reversal, because it was found in rocks near Jamarillo Creek in New Mexico, they called the Jamarillo event.

Not long after, Vine stopped by a lab at the Lamont Observatory, and he saw pinned on the wall magnetic profiles of the floor of the South Pacific, data fresh from a voyage of the research vessel *Eltanin*. "We've discovered a new event and we're just about to publish it," Vine's friend Neil Opdyke told him, ". . . we've got an event at about .9 million years." They planned to call it the Emperor event, after the Emperor Seamounts, which the *Eltanin* was mapping when it recorded the magnetic reversal.

This was a wonderful moment of serendipity. By chance, without knowing of each others' work, two teams had discovered the same pole flip: one on dry land, the other at the bottom of the sea. The magnetic profile taken from aboard the *Eltanin* on leg 19 of its trip was found to match line for line the magnetic reversals so meticulously studied by Cox, Doell, and Dalrymple; they matched right down to the new and as-yet unannounced event of .9 million years.

Vine knew that one of the great scientific controversies of all time was finished—"it was all over but the shouting." The match between the two teams' work was too neat to be ignored by even the most skeptical. (According to Glen's history, one geologist at Lamont stared at the *Eltanin* patterns on the wall and said at last, "Well, that knocks the sea-floor-spreading nonsense into a cocked hat." "What do you mean, Joe?" someone asked. "It's too perfect," Joe said, and walked out of the room.) The evidence strongly suggested that Vine and Matthews were right; and if they were right, so were Cox, Doell, Dalrymple, Wilson, and Hess. All three theories in the house of cards became at once solid and substantial: first, that the poles do flip; second, that the sea floor does spread; third, that one can trace the pole flips in the spreading sea floor. It was as if the geologists from California had discovered the Rosetta Stone and the oceanographers at Cambridge had learned how to read it.

What is more, if the sea floor has spread, the oceans must have grown. If the oceans have grown, the continents must have moved. Wegener, it seemed, was right too. Virtually overnight, confirmed "fixists" became "mobilists" and "drifters." Wegener's theory had been hooted off the stage because he could not explain what forces move the continents. By the late 1960s, it was *still* unclear what propelled all this motion; but evidence for the motion itself was inescapable. New converts cited what is sometimes called Ayer's law: "What *has* happened, *can* happen." Earth scientists old and young had to adapt themselves to Wegener's vision of a restless and driven globe.

THE PLATED PLANET

In the late 1960s, the deep-sea research vessel *Glomar Challenger*, taking core samples across the Atlantic, found strong evidence of sea floor spreading. Analysis of the cores proved that the ocean floor is one of the youngest places on the planet, as one would expect if it is being rapidly and steadily recycled.

What is more, the ocean basement is older the farther it is from the ridge, just as theory predicted. The very oldest rock the *Glomar Challenger* found in the Atlantic was quite young by geological standards, 150 million years, and it was found buried beneath the base of North America's continental slope—again, as theory predicted.

Then, in the early 1970s, several years after the first men landed on the moon, a few men managed to get down into the inky-black ravine in the center of the Mid-Atlantic Ridge, deeper below the surface of the sea than any human being had ever ventured. The aquanaut-scientists arrived there in the submersibles *Cyana, Archimede,* and *Alvin,* in what came to be

In some ways, building a vessel that can survive the enormous pressures at the bottom of the sea is harder than building a space-ship. Indeed, men reached the Moon years before they visited the great ridge on the floor of the Atlantic. In this photograph, the tiny submarine Alvin *slips beneath the surface, to explore what has been called "inner space."*

called Project FAMOUS (French-American Mid-Ocean Undersea Study). In the beams of these tiny submarines, the scientists saw a bizarre landscape worthy of Hieronymous Bosch: fields covered with black pillows and dark boulders grotesquely budded with basalt; huge, broken stone bubbles and long, twisted tubes they called "toothpaste lava." These were the fossils of a recent volcanic eruption, frozen—just as Vine and others had imagined—as the lava emerged from beneath the sea floor.

In later dives, scientists aboard *Alvin* explored the counterpart of the Mid-Atlantic Ridge on the other side of the globe: the East Pacific Rise. There, two and a half miles down, they discovered a landscape equally bizarre, full of strange new species of life. The sea at that depth is for the most part cold, dark, and lifeless. But in the rift, water that sinks into cracks in the floor touches magma and spouts back up from pillars, chimneys, and vents. These undersea geysers are superheated, and they are full of minerals. Because warmth and minerals are precious at such depths, colonies of giant clams, tubeworms, and crabs have clustered by the vents the way European tourists gather at health spas: they are there "for the waters."

Further evidence of sea floor spreading was found aboveground. Iceland, for instance, lies smack in the middle of the Mid-Atlantic Ridge, and it is believed to be part of the ridge itself—one of the only stretches that is not submerged at the bottom of the Atlantic. In fact, the cliffs beneath which, a thousand years ago, the Icelanders debated whether to convert to Christianity, are thought to be part of the V-shaped valley in the center of the Mid-Atlantic Ridge. These cliffs run up and down the island, from north to south. Measurements indicate that their banks may be moving slowly apart from each other, as one would expect if they are part of the ridge. So the island's earthquakes and volcanoes, once attributed to the mischief of the gods, then to the gates of Hell, can now be seen as part of the global drama of sea floor spreading. The molten rock that wells up on the island is only a fraction of the lava that oozes out daily along the rest of the ridge, out of sight. The fires of creation flare beneath the sea.

Wherever these fires burn—wherever new rock is created—the earth shakes and trembles. Scientists have recorded many shallow quakes along the midocean ridges, and deeper ones at edges of continents and ocean basins. These quakes suggested an answer to the problem Wegener never resolved: how continents can wander despite their roots in the bedrock of the seas.

The earthquakes show that the Earth's outer shell, some sixty miles thick, is cracked like a giant eggshell. It is fractured into many huge slabs (somewhere between a dozen and twenty), which because of their rigidity are called *plates*. The plates are not anchored to the planet, but drift about, rubbing and chafing and sometimes crashing against one another, all in slow motion, and it is this that makes earthquakes.

When the plates move, the continents move. And since the outlines of the plates do not always follow the coastlines of continents, but run now beneath sea, now beneath land, it very often happens that an ocean floor and a continent move *together*, carried by the single plate below them.

Thus, with the discovery of plates, the greatest objection of Wegener's critics has been finessed. To move, continents do not have to plow through oceans. They have only to ride about on plates. Were it not so well entrenched, the theory of continental drift perhaps would be rechristened "plate drift," for it is plates that do the drifting—our lands are only passengers. Plate drift is usually called *plate tectonics,* from the Greek *tekton,* "to build."

It is odd to think that the features of Earth we set most store by, oceans and continents, are not the fundamental ones. They are like puddles and thin soil atop the shifting plates. If you were to take a map of the Pacific, for instance, and draw a dot for each of its hundreds of active volcanoes, and add more dots for its thousands of earthquakes, you would outline the Pacific Plate. Your dotted line would curve up along the coast of California, touch Alaska at Yakatat, sweep across the Pacific to Kamchatka, and make its way down, looping way below Australia before curving back up north to Southern California. This has long been known as the Ring of Fire: and it is fiery because the plate is in constant motion.

Others of the planet's plates, too, can be traced by looking at records of earthquakes and volcanoes and playing "connect the dots." Just as the borders of human townships, counties, states, and nations often run along rivers, mountains, and coasts, the plate's great borders run along the midocean ridges, deep-sea trenches, and sometimes along the edges of continents. Their boundaries are more volatile than any of the contested national borders in the human geography.

The story of plate tectonics accounts for most of the planet's volcanoes and earthquakes. It accounts for the midocean ridges; the compression on land that has heaved up mountains; the birth and death of oceans and the wanderings of continents. And it brings together in one global theory many of the scattered troubles commemorated in the myths and legends of the world.

The Japanese, for example, live at one edge of the Ring of Fire, which outlines the Pacific Plate. They have to cope with alien forces that invade their homeland at will. The islands that make up Japan shake perceptibly more than a thousand times each year. Tokyo alone has been devastated an average of once a century for the past 2,000 years. Each time, the city rebuilds.

In the terrible shock of 1923, 143,000 people were killed in Tokyo and Yokohama. In Yokohama, a survivor said, "We felt as though we were about to be torn to pieces, and the great Earth was trying to shake off everything on it. We seemed to be grains shaken in a sieve." Some died in falling buildings during the five or six minutes the quake lasted, others in the great waves, the tsunami, that swept through later, and more in the fire storms that raged across the cities for two days.

Such disasters have helped shape in the Japanese what one prominent psychiatrist, Takeo Doi, has called "a consciousness of helplessness." The feeling, for which the word "vulnerability" is not strong enough, "approaches a national obsession," writes Robert C. Christopher in *The Japanese Mind*.

The late Arthur Koestler remarks on this state of mind in his book *The Lotus and the Robot*. One popular proverb, he says, lists as the five main terrors of Japan: earthquakes, fires, thunder, floods, and fathers. The first four, of course, are what Koestler calls "terrors of crustal instability." These fears, he suggests, affect Japanese art's approach to Nature. "Nature is too hostile and frightening to be approached 'in the raw.' To be aesthetically acceptable, it must be stylized, formalized, miniaturized." He notes the Lilliputian art form *bonseki*, "the miniature representation of a mountainous landscape by stones, pebbles and sand on a tray." The Japanese also love hill gardens that "feature on a miniature scale artificial hills, ponds, winding streams, islands and waterfalls, curving bridges and warped trees." Perhaps, Koestler writes, one purpose of this trompe l'oeil scenery is "to represent Nature at a safe distance, seen through the reversed lenses."

Plate tectonic theory explains the pain of the island in terms of forces at work beneath it. Out in the Pacific, at the bottom of the sea, is the East Pacific Rise, this ocean's counterpart of the Mid-Atlantic Ridge. From the Rise, the sea floor is spreading outward to either side at the rapid rate of ten centimeters per year—eighteen in some places—making it the fastest-spreading ridge in the world. It is blocked in its advance toward China by the Asian Plate. Because the sea floor is made mostly of basalt, which is much denser than the continental rock, the Asian Plate rides over the Pacific Plate, and the Pacific sea floor sinks back into the interior of the Earth. Japan is on the edge of a precipice more than 6,000 meters deep, known as the Japan Trench. At this trench, the Pacific Plate begins its long slide into the bowels of the Earth. There are several such trenches, where plates sink under; they are called *subduction zones*, and they are invariably violent. The rude burial of so much rock releases a great deal of energy, and as the edge of the plate slides downward, friction causes frequent earthquakes. In addition, though just how it happens is still debated, friction and pressure apparently melt some of the rock, which rises back to the surface in long, hot plumes, and causes volcanic eruptions. Thus, for its burial, the sea floor takes a double revenge—first in earthquakes, then in volcanoes.

In Japanese mythology, the world rides on the back of

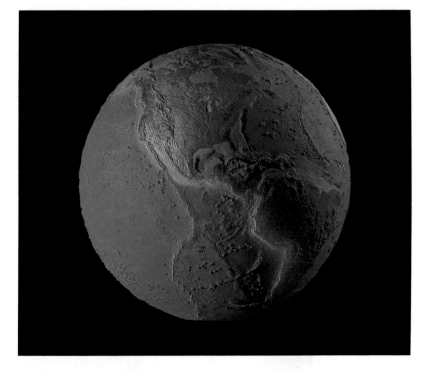

a giant catfish, whose movements cause the Earth to tremble. In the theory of plate tectonics, the islands are seen as no less precarious. Yet the forces that shake the islands also helped to create them: Japan owes its existence partly to the upwelling of lava from the sinking, melting, Pacific floor. Indeed, these forces are still building Japan today. In April 1973, there was a series of volcanic eruptions from three separate vents off the coast of Japan, south of Tokyo. By September, lava had risen above sea level and the three streams flowed together to form a new island, Nishimo. In this way, geophysicists say, much of the Japanese archipelago rose in the sea during the past thirty million years.

Because the sea floor is spreading in both directions from the East Pacific Rise, it causes trouble for North America as well as for Asia. The northwest coast of North America also lies on the Ring of Fire. Beneath this coastline, as beneath Japan's, the Pacific ocean crust is being subducted; it is sinking beneath the North American Plate at a rate of five centimeters per year. The subduction zone is marked by a string of volcanoes, the Cascade Range, of which Mount St. Helens is the best known. And the stresses of subduction caused the Great Alaskan Earthquake of 1964 in Anchorage.

Subduction is only one of several ways that plates can interact when they jostle each other. Another is outright collision. The landmass we call India, for instance, was not originally part of

The Earth's surface is cracked like a giant eggshell—broken into drifting fragments, called plates. Highlighted in this model is the African Plate. Above, the Nazca Plate.

Asia. It is not even part of the same plate. It is in fact the northern tip of the Australian Plate, and has been rammed up against Asia by the collision of the Australian Plate with the Eurasian. The Himalayas, once thought to be evidence of a shrinking Earth, are now believed to result from this crash of plates. The long arc of mountains marks the welt where the two plates have been sutured together. India is still crashing into Asia, at a speed of two inches a year. Over the course of 40 million years, the crash has thrust Mount Everest—once the rock bottom of a shallow sea—to the top of the world.

So intense is the collision that for thousands of miles northward and to the sides, the East Asian mainland is contorted like a giant bow wave as it is squeezed aside by the push of the Indian Plate. In 1976, a series of earthquakes struck Russia and China. Some geologists think the disasters were caused by a sharp surge of the Australian Plate, which led to shifting along the faults that radiate out from the plate borders. Worst hit was the city of Tangshan, China; the city was leveled, and several hundred thousand people died. Such violent earthquakes have tormented the Asian mainland all through its long recorded history, and most of them testify to the collision of the two plates. No wonder seismology, the study and analysis of earthquakes, was born, more than 2,000 years ago, in China.

Sometimes plates do not collide head-on, but instead slide against each other. This can be violent too. The plates do not glide by each other smoothly, and there is not grease enough in the world to slick their sides. Their motion is jerky, stop-and-go. The process generates violent earthquakes.

This, in essence, is what is happening along the west coast of the United States. The Pacific Plate is sliding along it, headed northwest. Between the plates is a giant shear zone, in some places miles wide. It begins in the Gulf of California, in Mexico, extends up through Southern California, and ends near a giant, three-mile-high underwater wall called the Mendocino Escarpment, off the coast of Northern California. This shear zone is the notorious San Andreas fault.

As the Pacific Plate slides by, a piece of the west coast rides with it and is being carried off to the north. The southern part of this piece, the Baja Peninsula, was split from the Mexican mainland nearly 4 million years ago, and the Gulf of California is slowly opening between it and this continent. More of the coast will follow. Thus, despite popular misconception, California will not sink into the Pacific. It will instead slide ever northward. In 15 million years, Los Angeles, if it still exists, will be a suburb of San Francisco. The Giants and the Dodgers will again be crosstown rivals.

Under this strain, the region's faults slip more easily

in some places than others. In the town of Hollister, sidewalks, curbs, fences, irrigation ditches, and tilled fields are being slowly offset, just a fraction of an inch at a time. Because the strain is relieved gently and gradually, in what is called *creep*, there is little danger here of a destructive earthquake.

In other places, the two sides of the fault hold together more tightly. As the Pacific Plate slides north, at a rate of five or six centimeters per year, these areas withstand the pressure for decades at a time, and do not give an inch. The result is disastrous. When the pressure is finally too much, the fault slips, all at once, as much as five or ten meters. That is what happened along the San Andreas fault near San Francisco in 1906, and scientists think it is due to happen again—perhaps overdue. There is a redwood tree on the San Francisco Peninsula that stands as a monument to the disaster of 1906. Because it straddles the fault, it was neatly split apart. The tree is still alive, but a piece of the trunk stands some eight feet away from the rest. In the next great earthquake the two pieces of the redwood tree will probably be jolted apart another eight feet.

The geometry of the San Andreas fault system is complex, making accurate prediction of earthquakes difficult, despite one of the most sophisticated networks of seismic monitors in the world. Geologists are still debating the details of the plate motions responsible. The obvious source of tension, of course, is the East Pacific Rise. Lava oozes from it, becomes fresh Pacific floor, and moves away from the rise. The floor has to go somewhere. Half of it goes south, and half north, where it shears the west coast of the North Pacific Plate. But this sliding boundary is so complicated, with so many different pieces and stresses, that it is still not fully understood.

The cities along the fault will continue to wait—asking not whether but when and where.

Subduction—literally, the "carrying under" of a plate. This model shows two plates. The plate at left, A, is moving from left to right. The plate at right, B, blocks its path. So A slides beneath B, into the hot depths of the Earth. There, A will be melted down. The subduction of such a great mass of the Earth causes earthquakes. Long molten plumes rise from the buried plate to the surface, erupting in volcanoes.

A GLOBAL GAME OF SKEET

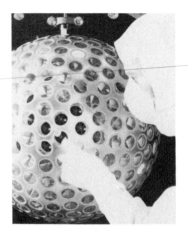

The satellite Lageos *before its launch.*

Every day, a small, very heavy, and very odd-looking satellite orbits the planet. It is only two feet in diameter, but weighs 900 pounds. It is studded with 426 specially designed reflectors called *corner-cubes*, which reflect any beam of light straight back on the path along which it came. It looks rather like those mirrored balls that are hung from the ceiling at rock concerts, and pinned by spotlights, to dazzle an audience.

And every day, around the world, lasers mounted on pads fire upon this satellite, Lageos (Laser Geophysical Satellite). The mirrored ball is the focus of a global game of skeet. There are laser pads on Otay Mountain, California, and in Plattville, Colorado; Fort Davis, Texas; Green Bank, West Virginia; Arequipa, Peru; Matera, Italy; and Wettzell, Germany. The Egyptians have a pad, and the Israelis are interested in building one. The Australians have several. The Greeks, the Dutch, and the Chinese are also in the game.

Each time the pulsed beam of one of these lasers strikes Lageos, from any country in the world, the light rebounds from a corner-cube mirror and returns to the laser pad that sent it. There, the length of time the pulse took to reach the satellite, and return, is recorded electronically. The path of the satellite's orbit, and the location of each laser pad, are ascertained with enormous care. The laser measurements should tell us the speed at which the laser pad, and the continent beneath it, and the plate beneath that, are drifting.

In a related experiment, radio telescopes around the world are timing the radio signals of quasars, which are mysterious objects far across the universe. Observatories in the United States and Sweden receive these messages from outer space at slightly different moments, depending which one happens to be closer to the quasar as the world turns. This tiny interval can be used to measure the distance between the two continents. It should eventually provide a precise measure of drift (according to present theory, the United States and Sweden are moving apart about two centimeters per year).

These two high-tech programs have been running only a few years—not quite long enough to record clear-cut results. No one has yet found a simpler way to measure continental drift, partly because the motions are so vanishingly small and slow, and partly because everything on Earth is adrift. We are like surveyors on rafts, spinning on a lake. The only way to find a fixed point of reference is to look at the distant shore. To measure the movements of Earth's plates, surveyors have to find a point of reference that is out of this world.

Having explained why continents drift—they are attached to plates—geologists still have to explain why plates drift. What force propels them? Is the action on the surface a sign of motion in the depths?

We know much less about the Earth's interior, unfortunately, than we do about its crust. Earth has several layers. In the center is a heavy inner core, probably of pure iron. Around it is a molten outer core, composed of iron alloyed with some metal lighter than nickel. The outer core is some 3,500 kilometers in radius.

Wrapped around the outer core is the mantle, 3,000 kilometers thick, whose composition is still debated. It may be mostly a dense rock called peridotite, which consists mainly of the mineral olivine. The mantle is extremely hot, but it is under such enormous pressure that much of it stays solid.

On the mantle is the Earth's thin skin, the crust. This is the only layer we know in detail. It consists of the ocean basins, which are basalt slabs at most ten kilometers thick, and the continents, which are amalgamations of much lighter rocks, but are many kilometers thicker than the ocean basins.

In 1906, a Yugoslavian geologist, Andrija Mohorovičić, looked closely at the records of seismographs, which record the waves that radiate outward from earthquakes. (In those days the record was written on a drum of paper by a trembling needle; modern seismographs are electronic, the information encoded in digital computer code.) Mohorovičić noticed that the seismograph records each earthquake *twice*; the waves from a quake, as they travel, get separated, and one set of waves arrives at the machine slightly ahead of the other. He deduced that waves travel at different speeds at varying depths within the Earth. At a certain depth, they are able to race ahead of the waves traveling above them. Below the sea floor, the boundary between these two layers is about five kilometers down, on average, and below the continents, about forty kilometers.

This transition marks the boundary between crust and mantle. The upper layer is crust, and the lower layer is mantle, which transmits waves more quickly because it is denser and more rigid. The boundary came to be called the Mohorovičić discontinuity, or "Moho."

In 1926, a German scientist, Beno Gutenberg (who later emigrated to the United States), detected a still deeper layer, about 150 kilometers down. At this level waves travel slightly more slowly than they do in the upper mantle. Perhaps, he suggested, waves are slowed there because the lower mantle is softer.

Such studies have advanced rapidly since World War II, in part because underground nuclear testing provides crisp

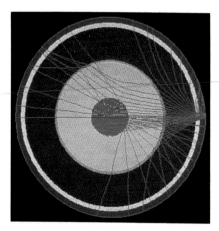

Waves from earthquakes can be analyzed by computers to illuminate the hidden world beneath our feet. This image shows the paths of waves that began from an earthquake epicenter on the equator, and travelled down through the planet's deep interior. The seismic waves were reflected and refracted by the boundaries of the main shells inside the Earth, like light rays passing through a series of lenses. The blue and white zones represent the Earth's lithosphere and asthenosphere, the orange zone is the solid mantle, the yellow zone is the fluid outer core, and the blue central zone is the solid inner core.

wave patterns that are easy to analyze, and in part because a global seismic network has been developed to watch for nuclear explosions. (Thus we may learn to understand our planet before we wipe ourselves off it.) It now seems that the discontinuity Gutenberg found is more significant than Mohorovičić's. It marks the lowest reaches of the plates.

Judging by the Gutenberg discontinuity, each plate is, on average, about 70 kilometers thick. A plate consists of a thin veneer of crust on a thick chunk of dense, solid mantle. Taken together, the dozen and a half plates make up a tough layer called the lithosphere (from the Greek *lithos*, "stone"), and they float about on the soft lower mantle, called the asthenosphere (from the Greek *asthenes*, "weak"). On this weak asthenosphere, the plates can slide and glide like toy boats in a bathtub.

This does not mean the asthenosphere is actually molten. In Europe one sometimes sees stone benches so old that the horizontal piece has had time to sag, and dip, of its own weight. This is the sort of motion that is thought to take place in the lower mantle. Under enormous heat and pressure, the solid rock does not liquify but becomes somehow *pliant*, like tar or candlewax on a hot day. If we could ever tunnel down to it (which we probably can't) we would find not lava, but something very different, which geologists often liken to Silly Putty.

How heat moves through the mantle is not well understood. The mantle rock is heated partly by the decay of radioactive elements within it, such as the potassium isotope that proved so useful to Cox, Doell, and Dalrymple. And some of the mantle's heat is left over from the first days of the planet—remnants of the original heat when the raw materials came together. It is conceivable that because of this heat, hot rock rises in long, slow updrafts from deep in the Earth, cools off near the surface, and then sinks again into the depths.

Such a circular pattern of movement, with hot updrafts and cold downdrafts, is called *convection*, and it is familiar to anyone who has ever watched soup boiling in a pot on the stove. The soup at the bottom of the pot is heated by the range and rises to the top, where it is cooled somewhat, and then sinks back down, the movement keeping the surface in a state of constant agitation.

This movement, if it does occur somehow within the solid rock of the planet, must be extraordinarily slow: the rise and fall of a single particle from the bottom of the mantle to the top might take hundreds of millions of years. Still, the currents set up by this pattern of rising and falling rock would be powerful. If convection is indeed stirring the mantle of the Earth, it could account for the constant agitation of the planet's surface—the drifting of plates.

Remarkably, Ben Franklin had an inkling of this possibility. He speculated in a letter to a friend, Abbé Soulavie, that Earth's interior "might be a fluid more dense . . . than any of the solids we are acquainted with; which therefore might swim in or upon that fluid. Thus the surface of the globe would be a shell, capable of being broken and disordered by the violent movements of the fluids on which it rested."

Franklin knew he could not test this, and apologized to the Abbé for his flight of fancy. "If [these thoughts] occasion any new inquiries and produce a better hypothesis, they will not be quite useless. You see I have given a loose to imagination; but I approve much more your method of philosophizing, which proceeds upon actual observation, makes a collection of facts, and concludes no farther than those facts will warrant."

That is the modern view, plates and all. But convection is a complicated phenomenon. Even the motion of boiling water in a pot is so chaotic that predicting its course accurately is impossible. If convection does indeed occur within the Earth, it must be even more complicated than it is in a pot on a stove, because its course varies at different temperatures and pressures, and in different kinds of rock.

Don Anderson, director of the Seismological Laboratory at the California Institute of Technology in Pasadena, is now using seismic waves to study convection within the Earth. His work carries on the analysis begun by Mohorovičić and Gutenberg, but with far more sophistication.

Anderson's team has borrowed a technique from high-tech medicine. Many large hospitals now have a CAT (computerized axial tomography) scanner. The scanner takes X rays of a patient from many angles; then a computer rapidly assembles a composite image, showing the brain, or lungs, in three dimensions. In the same way, Anderson uses a computer to analyze the records of seismometers around the world, as they provide pictures of the Earth's interior from many angles. When assembled by computer in what is known as *seismic tomography*, the waves illuminate the globe the way a lightbulb lights a room, or a CAT scan a skull. "What we'd really like," Anderson says, "is to have a three-dimensional picture of the whole inside of the Earth."

Though the technique is young and its results are controversial, Anderson says that pictures from the Cal Tech computer suggest patterns of convection. His team can make out large cycles of flow, and smaller-scale eddies, all in slow motion. But the data are so complex that at present the computer is able to work only with a simplified model, in two dimensions, and it takes three weeks to solve each problem. To model the seismic data in three dimensions would take the computer three years. So Anderson's team is eager for the next generation of computers, which are expected to be 100 to 1,000 times more powerful. Then, Anderson hopes, computer-driven graphic plotters will use the data from the global seismic network to draw a portrait of the interior of the Earth. With detailed pictures, we may be able to *see* what drives the plates— and watch the churning that has agitated the continents for billions of years.

HOT SPOTS

We do not have to plumb the depths to seek evidence of this churning. We can look for it at the planet's surface. But here, too, the patterns are ambiguous.

Two decades ago, when J. Tuzo Wilson first read Hess's essay in geopoetry, he realized that sea floor spreading might explain an old puzzle: the Hawaiian chain. These volcanic islands stretch some 3,000 kilometers along a straight line from the northwest to the southeast (and farther to the northwest, they link up with the Emperor Seamounts, which makes them longer yet). Oddly enough, the long string of atolls and islands runs in order of age from oldest to youngest, northwest to southeast. One of the oldest, Kure, at the northern end, is a coral atoll; the ancient volcano that uplifted it has long since died and subsided beneath the sea. One of the youngest, at the southern end, is Hawaii itself, the island that gave its name to the chain. Hawaii has two lively volcanoes, Mauna Loa and Kilauea, which have been making headlines for the past few

Though scientists are now beginning to chart it, the Earth's interior is still as dimly known to us as the New World was in Shakespeare's day. This image, based on computer analysis of seismic waves, suggests that the mantle may be churning, very slowly, with convective currents.

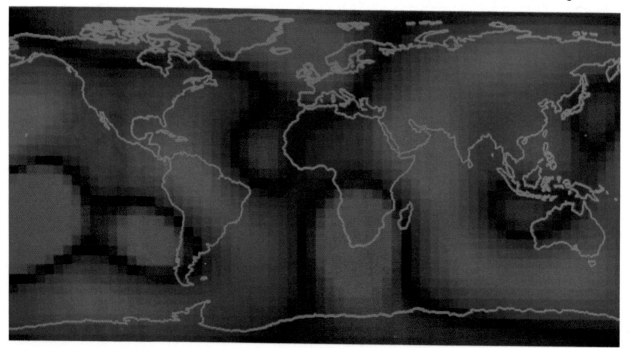

years. From one end of the Hawaiian chain to the other is a span of 30 million years.

The old geological explanation for this chain was simple: It formed when a sheet of magma leaked up through a long crack in the Earth's crust. The Hawaiian chain, however, is not at the edge of a plate, but in the middle, where one would expect peace and quiet. And why should the islands be lined up by age, like the children in the Trapp family? (The Polynesian tale handled that rather well. As the divine sisters Pele and Namakaokahai wrestled across the Pacific, they left behind, as traces of their combat, one island after another.)

Perhaps, Wilson suggested in 1963, what formed the chain was *not* a sheet of magma. If magma rose from some point deep within the Earth, and continued to well up in the same place long enough, it would burn a hole through the ocean basin, like a candle held beneath a piece of paper. Then, if the ocean basin moved, the fountain of magma would burn through in a new place. If the basin kept moving steadily in the same direction, the magma would cut a long slice through it, in a straight line dotted with numerous volcanoes, just as we see in the Pacific.

This sort of upwelling has been called a *hot spot*. As an explanation of the Hawaiian chain, it jibes neatly with the predictions of continental drift theory. The trail of the Pacific hot spot is in precisely the direction one expects if the Pacific Plate is moving northwest as the sea floor spreads from the East Pacific Rise. The path of the hot spot changes course sharply, like a bent elbow, where it meets the Emperor Seamounts; and this deflection occurred at just the time when the Pacific Plate and the North American Plate collided.

One can see signs of the hot spot trail even on the island of Hawaii itself. Volcanic action seems to have begun in the northwest corner of the island, and traveled southeast. There are five volcanoes on the island, from Kohala in the north to Mauna Loa and Kilauea in the south. Kohala is now dormant; Mauna Loa and Kilauea are still lively. Eruptions still farther to the southeast, off the coast, suggest that the island is moving off the hot spot at last. Nineteen miles south of Hawaii, a submerged volcano, Loihi, is now 8,000 feet above the sea floor, but still 3,000 feet below the sea surface. Loihi will be the next island in the long chain. It is one more piece of evidence for the drift of the Pacific Plate, and for convection below.

Still, this hot spot is one of the puzzles of plate tectonics. It seems to be all but stationary relative to the restless Pacific Plate. Why should a rising plume of magma stay put, while plates move above it and currents of mantle slowly roil around it? One might as well expect the plume from a smokestack to

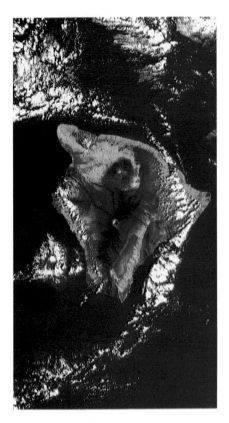

The island of Hawaii, seen from space by Landsat. *The old, dormant volcano to the north is Mauna Kea; the young, active volcano to the south is Mauna Loa. The long string of volcanic islands we call the Hawaiian Chain are lined up in order of age, with the oldest in the northwest and the youngest in the southeast—a clue to the life of the Earth's interior.*

AN ISLAND OF FIRE

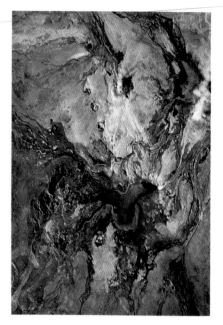

Clepsydra Geyser

Hawaii is not the only "hot spot" on the planet. Parts of Yellowstone National Park, in Wyoming, are 60 times hotter than the rest of the continent, perhaps because of another plume.

In winter, Yellowstone is a steam-blurred landscape. Clouds billow from the ground as if the park concealed secret factories, buried up to the chimneys. At the Firehole Basin, near the famous geyser Old Faithful, huge patches of ground stay bare year-round, and large herds of elk and bison winter there (steam jetting from their nostrils). It is an island of fire in a sea of ice. The first explorers who got lost and wandered through Yellowstone, among its geysers and boiling mud pools, thought they had stumbled into Hell.

This corner of Wyoming has been the site of the greatest volcanic eruptions in North American history, far more violent than Kilauea's and much larger in volume than the recent eruption at Mount St. Helens. Six hundred thousand years ago, in the last of a series of three catastrophic eruptions, some 1,000 cubic kilometers of volcanic debris poured out, and spread over millions of square miles, reaching as far as Kansas and Texas. The blast, together with the numerous smaller eruptions that followed over the next several hundred thousand years, melted right through the Rocky Mountains, leaving a plateau 7,000 feet high among mountains that are 10,000 to 12,000 feet high. The heat also cooked the rock, turning it a distinctive yellow, for which the region takes its name.

After the Yellowstone eruption, the surface sank several hundred meters. It left a crater so vast—75 kilometers by 45 kilometers—that only in the last decade or so have geologists perceived the crater's rim and traced its outline. Such a crater is called a *caldera*, from the Late Latin *caldaria*, "caldron."

Today, there are two swellings, called resurgent domes, in the caldera, and they are rising fast. In one place, between the two domes, the crust is rising more than fourteen millimeters per year—heaving like the crust of a meat pie. The region has suffered many swarms of small earthquakes and a few large shocks (the largest was at Hegben Lake in 1959, which registered 7.1 on the Richter scale). This action is being monitored by a network of seismographs, by highly accurate laser measurements of the domes' uplift, and by less expensive procedures, such as simply taking the ground's temperature.

Robert Smith of the University of Utah is the leading expert on the geophysics of Yellowstone. The geysers and boiling pools are only the surface of his subject; he is interested in

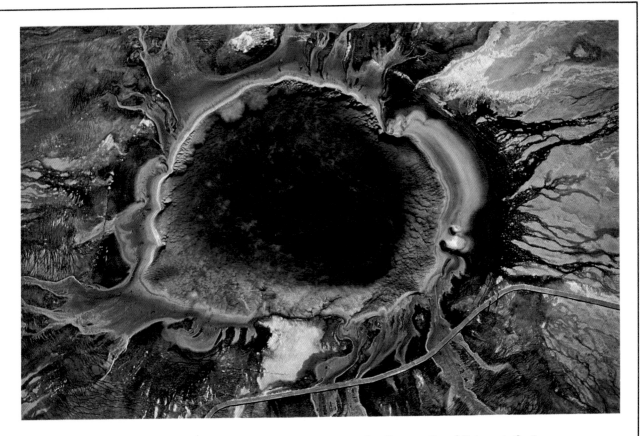

Grand Prismatic Spring

what the region implies about the driving mechanism, the flow of heat within the Earth. For this, Yellowstone is a spectacular outdoor laboratory. Using the data they have gathered, Smith and others are drawing computer profiles of a great mass of magma and hot rock they believe lies beneath the surface of the park, and extends 100 kilometers down.

Smith believes that Yellowstone, like Hawaii, is just one stepping-stone on a hot spot trail. As the North American Plate has traveled southwest in the last 18 million years, at about 4.5 centimeters a year, the hot spot has melted through the continent time after time. The scars from these eruptions cross the state of Idaho, forming the Snake River Plain.

In a sense, then, Smith says, there have been many Yellowstones. Eighteen million years ago a tourist in search of geysers and boiling mud pots would have gone to look near Boise, Idaho, 15 million years ago around Twin Falls, and 10 million years ago around Pocatello.

Since the North American Plate is expected to continue to move in the same direction, and at the same velocity, for a long time, the next Yellowstone will be to the northeast—perhaps in Cook City, Montana, many tens of millions of years from now.

Minerva Hot Spring

rise smoothly in gusty winds. And from how deep in the mantle does the hot spot rise? Chemical analysis of lava in Hawaii suggests that it comes from a source that has not mixed well with the rest of the mantle. Apparently, some of the mantle has remained apart from the rest for about a billion years.

SUSPECT TERRANE

The word "continent" comes from the Latin verb *continere*, "to hold together." But we now know that the continents do *not* hold together. Besides being blowtorched from below by hot spots, they are continually torn apart, and reassembled, by the shuffling of plates. Bits and pieces are tacked on to their coasts rather as a sculptor adds and subtracts from a rough bust. What we see as a finished sculpture is really a work in progress.

This process has endowed the famous Golden Gate Bridge in San Francisco with a touch of schizophrenia. To sightseers, it is one of the loveliest—and at 9,266 feet, one of the longest—suspension bridges in the world. To geologists, however, the span it covers is really remarkable. It connects territories that properly belong at least 1,000 miles apart, and perhaps much farther.

Such territories, which, though close together today, have separate geological histories, are called *terranes.*

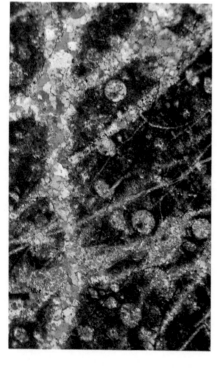

The Golden Gate Bridge links the city to the Marin Headlands, great hills that are brown most of the year, and worn almost as round as beach dunes. The rocks that form this terrane hold the fossil skeletons of microscopic oceanic organisms, closely packed together. The terrane is thought to have formed far away, at the bottom of the Pacific, probably along an ancient and long-vanished spreading center. It spent 100 million years as an ocean basin before drifting to San Francisco.

A second terrane in the bay is the island of Alcatraz, home of the old maximum security prison known as "The Rock." Like the Marin Headlands, Alcatraz formed in deep water, but unlike Marin, it was born close to a shore. Mingled with its fossil skeletons, debris of the sea, are quartz, sandstone, and shale, debris of a continent.

Angel Island, just north of Alcatraz, is a third terrane, known as Yollabolly. It is built of much the same materials as the Marin Headlands, but it has undergone a different history. The rock is remarkably folded and metamorphosed, and must at some time in the past have been suddenly and powerfully compressed. Some geologists say this happened in a subduction zone, where the rock was carried under and then found its way back up. Others say it was crushed in a collision of plates. Either event must have taken place far from Alcatraz and Marin, for they show no signs of it.

All told, geologists have now found ten different terranes in the bay area. Virtually no territory can be said positively to have originated where it is today. There are relics of coral atolls in the hills of Palo Alto, and there are islands off the coast that were once part of a continent—but not *this* continent. There is a large sandstone mountain, San Bruno, near the San Francisco Airport, that probably formed close to a continental margin, and farther down the peninsula is a terrane called Permanette, whose limestone contains fossils that can only have come from out in the ocean, near the equator.

It was J. Tuzo Wilson, in 1968, who first suggested that the North American continent is a kind of collage. He named several regions in this continent that might not be native ground, including parts of Nevada, which may have come originally from Asia, and the whole of Florida, which may have come from Africa. "I have never been very good at details," he has said, "but it struck me that, once you proposed continental drift, the logical conclusion seemed to be that pieces of North America had come from elsewhere."

This was another of Wilson's inspired guesses. In the last six years, geologists have found that almost every part of the Pacific coast, from Baja California to Alaska, is built of alien blocks. Two hundred separate terranes, large and small, have been discovered to date, as far inland as Utah and Colorado. The blocks arrived between 100 and 200 million years ago, and extended the continent west by 500 kilometers, or 25 percent.

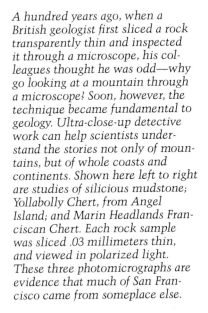

A hundred years ago, when a British geologist first sliced a rock transparently thin and inspected it through a microscope, his colleagues thought he was odd—why go looking at a mountain through a microscope? Soon, however, the technique became fundamental to geology. Ultra-close-up detective work can help scientists understand the stories not only of mountains, but of whole coasts and continents. Shown here left to right are studies of silicious mudstone; Yollabolly Chert, from Angel Island; and Marin Headlands Franciscan Chert. Each rock sample was sliced .03 millimeters thin, and viewed in polarized light. These three photomicrographs are evidence that much of San Francisco came from someplace else.

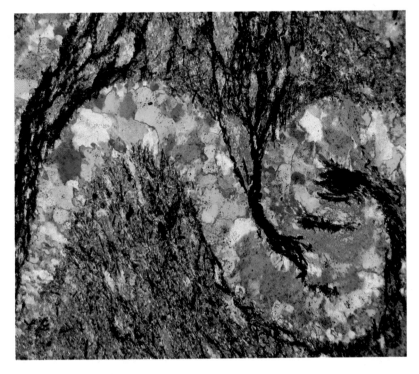

Some are fragments of ocean basins, some of continents, though of which ocean or continent it is usually impossible to say.

In fact, the whole of this continent, and every other, from Asia to Australia to Antarctica, seems to be made of accreted terranes. These are not just odd patches, but the whole cloth: the continent as crazy quilt. Asia is a notable jumble of bits and pieces. The latest piece to arrive is India, whose crash some 50 million years ago makes it the world's most spectacular example of a wandering block.

Such juxtapositions have been found even among the most ancient rocks in the Earth's crust, which are more than three and a half billion years old, so the process of accretion must have begun very early. These ancient terranes may help us study Earth's remote epochs, for which most of the record has been obliterated. The Pacific, for instance, is destroying its own floor at a great rate; its old floors have long since spread to the edges of the Pacific basin, sunk into trenches, and disappeared. The accreted terranes scattered around the Pacific's margins are the only antique pieces that survive.

Tracing such exotic terranes is done in part through paleomagnetic measurements of the kind that Allan Cox, Richard Doell, and Brent Dalrymple used so successfully in proving that the Earth's poles flip. Researchers also look at microscopic fossils embedded in the rock. In the sunlit upper sea, myriad one-celled organisms, called radiolaria, secrete beautiful shells of opal, which settle to the bottom when they die, and are preserved in the marls and clays of the sea floor. Species of radiolaria, and other tiny shelled animals and plants, have come and gone throughout the last 500 million years. Having studied the animals' long and complicated evolutionary history, specialists can now use the shells to date a sample of rock. If the species in question is known to have flourished on the equator, for instance, then its presence tells an expert not only the date, but the latitude where the rock was formed.

Working together, paleontologists, paleomagneticists, and geologists are revising the life history of the continents. Indeed, according to Davey Jones of the U.S. Geological Survey in Menlo Park, California, there would be no continents without accretion. The first bits of crust probably formed on the surface of the planet nearly 4 billion years ago—just how, no one agrees—and since then these bits, or nuclei, have grown mostly by collecting others. "We see this," Jones says, "as the way all continents originated."

THE TIME MACHINE   Thanks in part to such studies, the broad motions of plates now seem clear. When they meet, sometimes one plate is forced beneath another, as in Japan or the Pacific Northwest; sometimes the two plates lock horns, as in the subcontinent of India; sometimes they slide past each other, as along the west coast of the United States. The meetings and partings of plates cause earthquakes, and volcanoes, which line their borders, and make the edges of plates precarious places to live. And in the end, they make and break the continents themselves.

Knowing something of the ways plates move, geologists can infer in some detail what the continents looked like in the remote past, and what they may look like in the future. The Earth as we know it today is rather like a frame in a magnificent time-lapse film, most of which has been lost. With plate tectonic theory, together with data gathered by generations of geologists, we can now reconstruct many frames, enough to watch the dance of the continents for the last 200 million years. We can sketch, with much more detail than Wegener could, the unification and dissolution of Pangaea. (The accomplishment is impressive, but 200 million years is only a brief episode in the life of the Earth, only 4 percent of its 4.6-billion-year history. If *Planet Earth* were a feature-length film, the Pangaea episode would last only five minutes.)

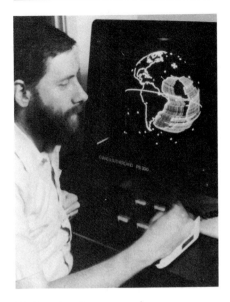

Christopher Scotese pushes continents around using a computer, to figure out how they once fit together.

Geologists interested in such work use a new tool. The field worker has the rock hammer, the paleomagnetician has the magnetometer, and the student of drifting plates has the computer console. Using interactive computer graphics, the plates, each curved like a contact lens, each with its own irregular margins, can be made to slide about on a screen with more precision than was ever possible before. One specialist in this work is Chris Scotese, a geologist at the University of Texas, Austin, and a member of the Paleogeographic Atlas Project of the University of Chicago. Members of this project have developed computer programs to test the theories of plate tectonics, and model the theories' implications. "Trying to unravel the history of plate motions," Scotese says, "is like trying to solve a jigsaw puzzle whose pieces continually change shape and size." With the aid of a computer, Scotese has generated animated movies of the last 500 million years of the Earth.

This reconstruction is quite speculative in its first half; but according to current opinion, the world 500 million years ago looked very different than it does today. Many land masses, including North America and what is now Siberia, lay along the equator. Below the equator, South America, India, Australia, Antarctica, and Africa were all melded into a single supercontinent, Gondwana. (It was named by a contemporary of Wegener's, the Austrian geologist Edward Suess, for an ancient tribe in India, the Gonds.) This great southern conglomerate, over the next 100 million years or so, swung down across the

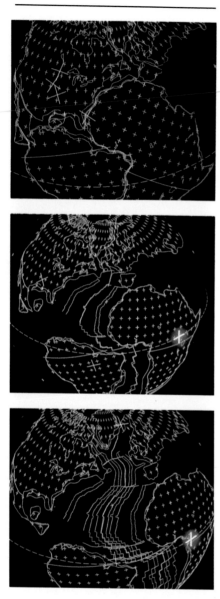

Putting Pangaea together again. This is what Planet Earth may have looked like some 220 million years ago, when the dinosaurs had just begun their reign.

Eighty million years ago, the South Atlantic had begun to open. The line that runs through its center is the midocean ridge. There new sea floor is being forged.

The North Atlantic opens, thirty-eight million years ago.

south pole. While there, Africa was covered with glaciers, its ice cap as thick as Antarctica's is today (traces of this epoch of ice have been dug up in the Sahara, which is now one of the hottest places on Earth).

In the next 250 million years, much of what is now North America, Europe, Africa, and South America drifted together, whole oceans closing between them. The Appalachians were heaved up, first north, then south, by the collisions. The supercontinent Pangaea placed North America and Western Europe (cheek by jowl) along the equator, where grew lush tropical forests that we are now harvesting as coal in Pennsylvania and Wales. It was the Age of Reptiles. Dinosaurs were conquering the world, and Pangaea paved the way for them. Scotese says, "Pangaea was sort of a superhighway for the dinosaurs. They could get almost anywhere from Siberia to Antarctica without having to cross a major body of water."

But the union was short-lived. While the last bits of land were colliding in what is now Asia, North America and Africa were already rifting, the Atlantic Ocean opening between them. So Pangaea probably existed for only a brief moment in geological history, tens of millions of years. It no sooner came together than it began breaking apart.

Fifty million years ago, the Earth looked almost as it does now. But India was still an island, and was still headed on its collision course with Asia. (In Scotese's film, it is clear how rapid and aberrant this course was. India suddenly lurches away from Africa and charges Asia.) Fifty million years ago the island of India was just within hailing distance of the southeast coast of Asia. Australia, meanwhile, was parting from Antarctica, and the ocean between them was still a narrow strait. Along the west coast of North America, Baja California was snug against Mexico, and the Gulf of California had not yet opened. So there was still no San Andreas fault.

Indeed, the breakup of the supercontinent Pangaea, which so intrigued Wegener, probably happened more than once. J. Tuzo Wilson proposed in 1966 that the Atlantic may have opened and closed and reopened again. There is evidence for this in the worn nubs of ancient mountains we call the Appalachian Range. Unlike the Himalayas or the Alps, the Appalachians probably did not form during a single collision of plates. The Appalachians seem to have formed in several separate mountain-building cycles. Parts of it formed 260 million years ago, some 370, others 500. The oldest parts of the range, then, are older than Pangaea. They may have formed during the collisions of continents whose shapes and stories we do not yet know. From the massive amounts of sediment in the area, it is clear that these mountains were once of alpine stature; they were craggy peaks jutting into the sky like the Grand Tetons.

Some day, Scotese and others believe, Australia will smack against Mainland China, completing the long sweep of the plate that began when India pulled loose from Africa. But we don't yet understand plate motion well enough to sketch the future as we can the past. There is even some question whether our moment of geological history is typical in the life of the Earth. Has this series of collisions and partings gone on at the same rate throughout the Earth's history? Has the action sometimes sped up or slowed down?

"My research interests really all go back to a childhood fantasy, to invent a time machine," Scotese says. "And I think what I'm doing comes close." Those involved in such projects sometimes feel as stirred as the explorers of the 15th and 16th centuries. They are looking at oceans and continents no human being has ever visited, or ever will. Like Columbus, they cross uncharted seas—not on a voyage in space but a voyage in time.

THE LONGEST JOURNEY

The modern revolution of plate tectonics parallels others in history: Copernicus and astronomy, Darwin and evolution, Einstein and relativity, Bohr and the atom. Hutton started us down the road by his discovery of a dynamic Earth. Plate tectonics reveals cycles of creation and destruction that prove the planet more dynamic yet. We now understand with sophistication, but still with awe, the living machine.

Plate tectonics may help resolve many planetary mysteries; how many, it is too early to say, but it is a powerful new tool. Already, in its first 20 years, it has altered our views of past and present climates, and of likely places to look for oil, coal, diamonds. The theory has changed biologists' views of the evolution and distribution of life. Like all important theories, it has prompted hundreds of subsidiary ideas and hypotheses, which are today being followed up in some of the Earth's remotest places.

The craggy, dark island of Ascension, lost in the very middle of the Atlantic, near the equator, is the scene of one of the more remarkable mysteries in the history of the planet. Here, every year, come great numbers of green turtles, who have swum 2,000 kilometers, all the way from South America. The journey takes them about two months, and they have no food to sustain them on it (unless one of them lucks on the stray turnip top some ship's captain threw overboard). The turtles plow through strong equatorial currents, dodge the rocky promontories and escarpments that guard the coast of the tiny island, and crawl ashore to nest on its seven small sandy beaches. They lay their eggs, and a new generation of green turtles is born.

To the naturalist the sight of these great turtles, which when full grown weigh up to 400 pounds, pulling themselves ashore at Ascension has seemed puzzling and ironic. Back in Brazil there are hundreds and hundreds of miles of beautiful beaches. Here there are only a few small, cold crescents of sand, ringed by rocks. The island is so small that it is hard even for sailors and pilots with sophisticated navigational equipment to find it. Why make such a strenuous journey to nest on this speck of rock? What could have prompted the first turtles to make the trip, millions of years ago? How could they even know the island was out there, half an ocean away?

To Archie Carr, a zoologist at the University of Florida who has been studying green turtle migration for 30 years, the theory of plate tectonics suggests an answer.

About 200 million years ago, when the supercontinent Pangaea was just splitting apart, the Atlantic was just a narrow sea between South America and Africa. Beneath this sea was the Mid-Atlantic Ridge, where lava welled up vigorously, dotting the sea (then little more than a broad river) with volcanic islands.

Distant ancestors of the green turtles could see and smell such an island from their beaches in South America. And if their lives then were anything like their lives now, they had good reason to nest on an island rather than on the coast. Today, jaguars in the South American jungle prey upon full-grown green turtle adults, dragging them off into the bushes. Almost everything living, from dogs to birds, preys on the turtles' eggs. So it would have been natural for ancient turtles to nest on offshore islands: with fewer predators, more of their eggs would hatch, and more young would survive.

As the sea floor spread, South America was pushed slowly farther from the Mid-Atlantic Ridge. So was the turtles' nesting island, which, as it traveled down the slope of the Ridge, sank slowly beneath the sea. But by the time it sank, the rift had sent up another volcanic island. This new island was farther from shore than the first, because the Atlantic was widening. It was no longer a broad river, but a small sea. The second volcanic island was still within easy reach, however, and it became the turtles' nesting ground.

Over millions of years, Carr suggests, the turtles have continued to swim in the same direction to nest, but they have gone to a series of islands. As the Atlantic has widened, each journey has been a little longer than the last. The distance has lengthened so gradually, and the turtles are guided by so strong an instinct, that they have remained unswervingly committed to the journey, even though it is no longer easy for them, but an epic that rules their lives.

Indeed, the trip has changed the turtles. In each generation, the fittest swimmers survived longest, bringing into the world the most offspring. Slowly, by natural selection, they became a race of marathon swimmers. The modern turtle has enormous and powerful shoulder muscles, and heavy fat deposits, which allow it to fast for weeks. The skeleton, too, has evolved and is strong enough to meet the demands of the lengthening voyage. Yet despite all these changes in physique, the instinct remained intact.

If Archie Carr is right, the drifting of continents has shaped the DNA, the genetic endowment, of these green turtles. Life itself has been programmed by the hidden powers that drive the plates.

Green turtles swim from their home in South America, and lay their eggs on a lonely speck of rock, Ascension Island, in the middle of the Atlantic. Then they swim laboriously home. Perhaps the turtles got in the habit of this long journey before the continents drifted so far apart. Here, a solitary green turtle leaves Ascension as dawn breaks.

The Blue Planet

That which is far off and exceeding deep,
who can find it out?

ECCLESIASTES

Overleaf: The sea is far more restless than scientists ever supposed—from the surface to the deepest abyss.

2 / The Blue Planet

Viewed from a spot above the center of the Pacific—looking down upon the Marquesas, or Samoa, or the Phoenix Islands—the globe is almost all blue, like a sky with a few clouds on the far horizon. The surface of our world is nearly three quarters water, and there are those who think it should be called Planet Ocean. The northern hemisphere is 50 percent water; the southern hemisphere, 90 percent. We call these waters the Indian, the Arctic, the Antarctic, the North and South Atlantic, the North and South Pacific. But they are all linked; water circulates between them. The continents are merely islands in one vast ocean. The Pacific Ocean alone is larger in area than all the land on Earth.

No other world in our solar system has an ocean of water. In ancient Greece, Aristotle taught that the world was made of just four elements: water, earth, air, and fire. Today, scientists have identified many times that number of chemical elements—more than 100 of them. Yet when modern scientists look at Planet Earth, they still like to speak of four fundamental elements, or four *spheres:* first, solid Earth, the *lithosphere;* then water, the *hydrosphere;* third, air, the *atmosphere;* and fourth, life, the *biosphere.*

The hydrosphere works intimately with the other three elements in the living machine, and 97 percent of the water on the planet is in the ocean. The ocean holds enough food to make a difference to the future of our exploding human population. It is a key to the vagaries of our weather and our climate. For all these reasons, the ocean will help decide whether our planet remains inhabitable.

J. Tuzo Wilson, one of the revolutionaries in the past quarter century of earth science, once remarked that he liked the old view of the planet. Everything seemed fixed, static, solid, clearly lit, and substantial, like the landscape in a classical painting. But, Wilson said, he enjoyed the new view even better. The solid Earth is full of motion from the surface to the depths. It is as if an old, familiar canvas has been taken off the wall and a new one put up in its place, a landscape by an Impressionist—Planet Earth in the swirling brushstrokes of Vincent van Gogh.

The ocean, like the solid Earth, was once thought to be static. Though its surface was stirred by currents and rippled by winds, the deeps were supposed to be still, dark, and silent as the grave. They were stagnant wastes, Davy Jones's locker. But the world ocean is proving to be like the solid Earth: The closer we get, the more restless it looks, alive with currents and gyres from top to bottom. Oceanographers using futuristic ships, submarines, robot buoys, and even satellites are discovering more and more profound and exotic turbulence, and swirling brushstrokes, including great storms at the bottom as violent as any at the surface.

Today's scientists sometimes feel they are sailing on a totally new sea.

DRAGON SHIPS   The earliest sailors sensed that the world's lands were surrounded by water before they even knew there were seven seas and seven continents. One of the first attempts to portray the whole Earth, a Babylonian clay tablet 3,000 years old, shows the world as a disk with a band of water around it, with Babylon, of course, at the center. The Greeks spoke of "a great Stream of Ocean that encircles the Earth"—with Greece at the center. In Christian Europe in the Middle Ages, the most common scheme for a world map was the *orbis terrarum*. This religious conception of Planet Earth showed the Don River, in Russia; the Nile River, in Africa; and the Mediterranean Sea, all in the form of a great T, a crucifix of water. This T divided the known world into three pieces: Asia, Europe, and Africa. The T was surrounded by an immense O, the "Circumfluent Ocean," and the center of the world was Jerusalem.

We are only just beginning to understand the immense and powerful influences of this world ocean upon our planet. Until recently, plain survival at sea was hard enough. In the years from 800 to 1050, for instance, the Vikings were the world's greatest sailors. They conquered much of Europe with their dragon boats, called *drakkars*, whose wooden prows were shaped like the arching necks of sea serpents. To the east, the Vikings got as far as Kiev, on the Dnieper River, mother city of medieval Russia. To the west, Eric the Red, exiled from Iceland for murder, sailed in a smaller, plainer style of ship called a *knorr* and reached Greenland. His son Leif, sailing on westward in hopes of finding another Iceland, was blown off course and discovered America 500 years before Christopher Columbus.

Thus Vikings won footholds in the territories of both today's superpowers. But according to sea historian Susan Schlee, these master sailors crossed oceans the way drivers today handle long highways on sleety nights, by gritting their teeth and keeping their eyes straight ahead. The *drakkars* and *knorrs* were wet ships, with no cabins. The only protection from the elements was a hooded smock of *wadmal*, coarsely woven wool, and a sheep's-wool sleeping bag. Schlee says, "Viking chronicles of life at sea are marvelously matter-of-fact: 'And then we bailed.'"

Those who contemplated the sea two centuries ago— natural philosophers, as scientists were called then—foresaw the need for crews of investigators. An Italian count, Luigi Ferdinando Marsigli, conducted some of the first systematic studies of currents in the Mediterranean (his scientific career was briefly interrupted when he was captured by Turks and enslaved by a pasha). Major John Rennell, wounded in Bengal in 1776, retired to London and devoted himself to studies of currents in the Atlantic and Indian oceans. Marsigli and Rennell, two of the world's first oceanographers, realized that their subject was too big for them. Each man called for large and coordinated sea projects and, because these would be expensive, for government support. Rennell was particularly frustrated in trying to chart ocean currents alone. He wrote, "The want of simultaneous observations is an incurable defect. By this we are kept in ignorance of the state of things in every other quarter, save the one in which our *own* observation was made."

Governments, however, while pleased to finance explorers, were reluctant to fund the study of the sea itself. The sea was assumed to be lifeless in the nether depths—below the reach of the longer fishing lines—which diminished the charm of deep-sea research. For a while, this latter notion was widely assumed to have been "proven." Working from the British surveying ship *Beacon* in 1841, the young Manx naturalist Edward Forbes dredged 230 fathoms deep in the eastern Mediterranean (a fathom is six feet). Forbes hauled up very few animals or plants. Anything more than 300 fathoms below the surface of the oceans, he concluded, was an "azoic zone," with "a probable zero of life."

By bad luck, Forbes had lowered his dredge into some of the most sterile and lifeless water on the planet. In the decades that followed, however, naturalists discovered worms, starfish, snails, eels, and sharks in ever deeper water. The sea's perpetual night gradually became, in the popular mind, what outer space is today—a place to explore, a region romantic, alien, cold, dark, and dangerous. Sea studies made headlines; each new find became a matter of national pride. In 1871, when the United States announced plans to send its most famous biologist, Louis Agassiz, on a cruise aboard the survey ship *Hassler*, the British responded in much the way Americans did in the next century to the ascent of the first Soviet satellite,

This T-O map was drawn by Saint Isidore of Seville in the early seventh century. Saint Isidore saw the world ocean as one great, circumfluent O, and a T formed by three mighty rivers.

Sputnik. One British doctor and amateur naturalist, William B. Carpenter, wrote an open letter to the editors of the journal *Nature.* Carpenter inquired whether,

> having shown other nations the way to the treasures of knowledge which lie hid in the recesses of the ocean, we are falling from the van into the rear, and leaving our rivals to gather everything up. Is this creditable to the Power which claims to be Mistress of the seas?

THE VOYAGE OF THE *CHALLENGER*

Within a year, the British arranged for what became the first great oceanographic expedition to circle the globe. The ship, HMS *Challenger,* was a corvette, a fast warship that had been stripped of all but two of its guns to help make room for laboratories, supplies, and hundreds of miles of coiled rope for soundings and dredgings. Noted naturalist Sir Charles Wyville Thomson (who had succeeded Edward Forbes as professor of natural philosophy at the University of Edinburgh) was talked into running the expedition, though, at age 42, he felt he was too old for it and was reluctant to leave his family. Thomson had three fellow naturalists working with him, in addition to a chemist, an artist, and a large crew furnished by the British navy. They set out just before Christmas in 1872.

The HMS Challenger *under sail.*

The Natural History Workroom aboard the Challenger.

The expedition had an ambition far ahead of its time. Thomson and his interdisciplinary team hoped to study every aspect of the sea, from the life in the deeps to the shape of the bottom, to currents and chemistry. The *Challenger* was fitted not only with sails but also with a steam engine. At each midsea stop, the crew pointed the ship into the wind and turned on the steam engine to hold position. Then they lowered buckets with cleverly designed valves and stops and hoisted up water samples from various depths. They also lowered thermometers whose bulbs were reinforced with brass to withstand the enormous pressure of the deeps—more than a ton per square inch.

Just lowering and raising the dredge took the crew hours, using a steam-driven winch (a "donkey engine") to help with the backbreaking hand over hand. The sailors hated this work, but the gentleman-naturalists were as excited as if they were drawing up Botticelli's Venus on the half shell. Near the West Indies, they found new species of annelid worms, which live in tubes, buried in the red clay and ooze of the bottom more than three miles down. In shallower waters, one mile down, the team found sea urchins, sea anemones, sea cucumbers, filmy jellyfish, squid, snails, and barnacles. Many of these species had never been seen before. "Strange and beautiful things were brought to us from time to time," wrote Thomson, "which seemed to give us a glimpse of the edge of some unfamiliar world." (And cold mud from the bottom, after being passed through a sieve, chilled bottles of champagne.)

In three and a half years, Thomson and his crew charted about 140 square miles of ocean bottom, collected 4,717 new species, 1,441 water samples, and sounded every ocean but the Arctic. Among their adventures, they rescued two shipwrecked brothers on an island called Inaccessible, cannonaded one iceberg, rammed another (accidentally), and made incredibly deep soundings. Their record was 26,850 feet, off the Marianas Islands, in a Pacific trench. This remains the deepest spot ever found in the ocean. It is often called the Challenger Deep.

The voyage established the tradition of large-scale team effort that earlier researchers such as Marsigli and Rennell had longed for, the hallmark of modern oceanographic research. The *Challenger* data eventually filled 50 large volumes written by 76 authors over 23 years. This, too, is typical of modern oceanography. Each sea foray is followed by years of analysis.

Sadly, Thomson did not live to see the voluminous records of his voyage. He died, exhausted, a few years after the *Challenger*'s return.

The *Challenger* expedition might have launched the modern epoch of exploration, an Age of Aquarius. But for decades, nothing of its size and scope was attempted again, and the science of oceanography languished. Perhaps a presentiment of the subject's difficulties prevented people from trying sooner. It took disaster, war, and revolutionary new technology before world attention focused once more upon ocean studies.

At the time the *Titanic* went down, in 1912, a former assistant of Thomas Alva Edison named Reginald Fessenden had been tinkering for some time with a way of detecting icebergs with echoes. Fessenden hustled his invention into shape within two years. He used an electric gadget like an underwater doorbell to send sound waves out through the sea in all directions, and he listened to the echoes on shipboard using an underwater microphone and a pair of earphones. In much this way, a blind man tapping his cane on the pavement can sense when he is approaching a wall by a subtle change in the quality of the echoes. Fessenden's invention worked, and sonar devices (as they came to be called) were soon in demand for detecting not only icebergs but also submarines and shoals, and the distance to the bottom. In the war-filled first half of the 20th century, the technique was strenuously refined, and by World War II, the seaborne geologist Harry Hess, using sonar to watch out for submarines, could begin to distinguish the shapes of individual peaks and mesas on the sea floor.

A wild Texas geophysicist named Maurice "Doc" Ewing was easily the most energetic field scientist to use soundings to advance the cause of science; sometimes he dumped dynamite charges overboard from a lifeboat while the mother ship, far off on the horizon, recorded the echoes. (The biggest trick, he said, was to keep passing ships from trying to rescue him.) Ewing was interested in the geology of the ocean floor,

Living dangerously, Maurice 'Doc' Ewing, on the deck of the Atlantis, in 1951, attaches a fuse to a rucksack full of dynamite. 'Doc' used the echoes of explosions to sound out the floors of the oceans.

not the ocean itself, which was nothing to him but "a murky mess that keeps you from seeing the bottom."

After the war, two scientists in particular gathered together the new sounding data and drew up new and historic maps of the sea floor. They were Bruce C. Heezen and Marie Tharp, both of Columbia University's Lamont-Doherty Geological Observatory. Before the days of echo sounding, the general picture of the oceans had been, in Tharp's words, "saucers of great thicknesses of mud in a motionless abyss." Yet each successive pass of the echo sounder over the center of the Atlantic revealed more rugged terrain, a hobgoblin landscape of crags, spires, and rifts. Heezen and Tharp soon saw that they were collecting "profiles" of a giant mountain range.

The maps these two scientists put together changed our vision of the planet. They showed that a single, long ridge runs through the basins of the world ocean. This ridge is the most prominent thing on the planet, after the continents and the ocean basins themselves. It is a deep sea monster larger than all the fancies that embroidered medieval maps; in the extraordinary new maps of Heezen and Tharp (first published in the late 1950s) the ridge looks like the sinuous and wriggling back of a giant crocodile 46,000 miles long. Its back pokes right up above the surface in many places—in the Atlantic at Iceland, Tristan da Cunha, St. Helena, and Ascension Island, for example, and also in the Pacific, at the Galapagos. Its spine shudders with earthquakes. Studies of the ridge and of the Heezen-Tharp maps led to the revolution of plate tectonics (as described in the first chapter). The biggest secret of the solid Earth had been found beneath the sea.

Spurred by these discoveries, scientists from all over the world joined forces to observe the Earth for a single, intense year. The program (which actually lasted for 18 months, from July 1, 1957 to December 31, 1958) was called the International Geophysical Year (IGY). It was the largest concerted effort in the history of science (bigger even than the Manhattan Project), and for the first time the Earth was studied from all sides at once, by scientists cooperating on the same experiments with the same kinds of instruments. For ocean studies, this was the fulfillment of Major James Rennell's dream. And in the midst of the IGY came an event that not only changed the study of the Earth and the seas but also transformed the modern age.

It was announced in the United States on the evening of October 4, 1957, at the Soviet Embassy in Washington, D.C. The Soviet ambassador held a dinner party there for Soviet and American scientists working together on the IGY. At the embassy, Walter Sullivan, veteran science reporter for *The New York Times*, got an emergency call. Someone at the *Times* had just heard, on Radio Moscow, that the Soviets had successfully launched a satellite. Sullivan dashed over with the news to Lloyd V. Berkner, the American geophysicist who had first proposed the IGY, and Berkner promptly stood up on a chair. Though the United States had been beaten in the race to space, Berkner felt at least he could beat the Soviet ambassador to the announcement in Washington. Thus the Western world first heard of *Sputnik* from an American scientist in a Soviet embassy.

In Washington, following the McCarthy era, this news caused an unpleasant sensation. American newspapers made matters worse when they translated *Sputnik* as "fellow traveler," which meant, in those days, "closet Communist." In fact, *sputnik* is only the Russian word for "satellite"—which is a fellow traveler, too, but innocent of politics. Even though the first U.S. satellite, *Explorer I*, went up only four months later, Americans never forgot the humiliation of being beaten into space. Rivalry between the superpowers fueled the Space Age.

For earth scientists, satellites meant a quantum jump in resolving power. One of the very first American satellites, *Vanguard II*, carried two *photocells* (devices that translate light into electric current). *Vanguard II* sent back to Earth, in radio signals, a crude, wobbly picture of the planet's cloud cover. Satellite imaging of clouds, lands, and seas (*remote sensing*) was refined rapidly into a high art. It is astonishing how much can be seen from far off now that is hard to see from nearby. And it is amazing the tales that can be told from even the simplest satellite measurements.

In 1978, for instance, an experimental satellite called *Seasat* orbited most of the globe's oceans from 500 miles up. One of the instruments it carried was a radar altimeter designed to determine the satellite's altitude above the sea with the utmost precision. This instrument was a simple extension of Reginald Fessenden's echo sounder. It sent a fine beam of radio waves, in a thousand pulses a second, straight down to the surface of the sea. The beam traveled there at the speed of light, hit the tops of the waves, and was reflected back up to the satellite. Tracking stations on Earth knew the position of the satellite at all times; and since the speed of light was also a known quantity that never varied, the time each pulse took to make the trip was a kind of yardstick. It allowed scientists to map the height of the surface of the sea in much the way that Ewing, Heezen, and Tharp, from ships at the surface, mapped the sea floor. The radar altimeter's measurements were precise enough to determine the average height of the ocean at each point to within two or three inches.

Nearly three quarters of the Earth's surface was terra incognita *until Bruce Heezen and Marie Tharp, working with 'Doc' Ewing, made maps of the world ocean floor. Their charts unveiled the most prominent mountain range on Planet Earth: the great, spiny ridge that winds its way through all the ocean basins.*

In 1978, the satellite Seasat *lifted the study of the sea into the Space Age.*

Oddly enough, Seasat *gave us this view of the bottom of the sea—by measuring sea level from outer space.*

This effort may seem the height of folly: Why measure the altitude of the sea? When you average out the waves and tides and wakes of ships—all the little disturbances of God and man—isn't the sea level? It is not.

The solid Earth holds the sea in its bed by virtue of gravity, that mysterious and still unexplained force by which matter attracts matter over vast distances. Though few people realize it, the force of gravity is uneven over the face of the Earth. Wherever matter is concentrated at the surface—say in a dense black mountain of basalt—the pull of gravity is slightly but measurably greater than average. Wherever matter thins out at the surface—say in a yawning chasm, filled with nothing but air—the pull of gravity is slightly less than average.

This has a curious effect upon the sea. A big seamount (a peak submerged at the bottom of the sea), because of its extra gravitational attraction, pulls a little extra water toward itself. As a result, there is generally a small pile of water above it on the surface—a gentle hill of water above each mountain! Above a valley or fissure in the ocean floor, there is often a faint dip in the sea surface. "Sea level" is a myth. Some seamounts in the Hawaiian chain raise watery hills as much as 30 feet high. Deep trenches in the Pacific cause dips of 30 feet. These watery hills and dales cannot be seen from a ship at the surface; their slopes are too broad, too gentle, obscured by waves, tides, and currents. But the hills and hollows can be seen from a satellite.

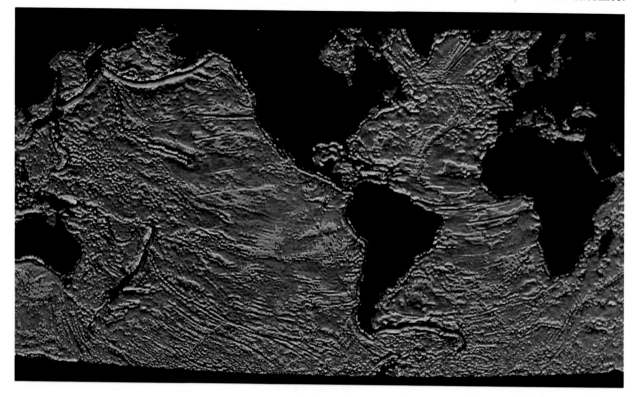

In three months (less time than it took some ill-starred Vikings to get from Norway to Greenland, cursing and bailing) *Seasat* made a thousand orbits of the Earth and 8 billion separate measurements of the sea surface. Then a massive electrical short-circuit blinded its eye and ended the useful life of *Seasat*. In 1982, a 31-year-old geophysicist named William Haxby, of Lamont-Doherty, was handed 24 computer tapes from the satellite and told to analyze them.

Haxby looked first at a small spot where the sea floor had not been well mapped by conventional echo-sounding techniques. A colleague of Haxby's, John LaBrecque, remembers the night when it became clear that Haxby was on to something big. "Bill was sitting at his terminal," LaBrecque told a reporter, "cranking in finer and finer contouring. We asked him to crank it up some more. He replied, 'Well, there might be a lot of noise in there.' But to everyone's surprise, more resolution emerged. It was like focusing a microscope. Things came out of the ocean floor that we never had hoped to see."

In a year and a half of computer hacking, Haxby surprised himself and his colleagues by arriving at a panoramic map of the bottom that was by far the most complete and detailed ever. The pictures his computer generated show the ocean bottom naked, as if someone had pulled the plug and all the water drained out. What had once seemed a single large seamount resolved into four smaller ones. New rifts and cracks and underwater mountain ranges sprang into view. Haxby even discovered fine ripples in the bottom of the Pacific that suggest the presence of currents of rock stirring in the mantle below the floor.

This was work at once solitary and cooperative, adventurous and safe. Alone in an office above the Hudson River, out of sight of the sea, Haxby, through *Seasat*, scanned the surface and floor of the whole ocean without moving from his armchair. It was a long leap from the Viking dragon ship to the satellite.

OF CURRENTS AND GYRES

Strangely enough, we now know the shape of the bottom of the sea better than the whirls, eddies, and currents at the surface. Turbulent liquid is much harder to keep track of—even with the help of satellites—than solid mountains and valleys.

One of the first to realize the currents' practical importance was the canny Benjamin Franklin.

Some years before the Revolutionary War, Franklin served as deputy postmaster general for the American colonies. While in London, he was asked by the lords of the Treasury whether he could help solve a nautical riddle. British mail pack-

*Benjamin Franklin—
a founding father
of oceanography.*

ets sailing from Falmouth, England, to New York were taking two weeks longer to cross the Atlantic than Rhode Island merchant ships sailing home from London to Providence.

It seemed odd to Franklin that there should be such a difference between Falmouth and London, or between New York and Providence, which were "scarce a day's run asunder." His cousin Timothy Folger, a Nantucket whaling captain, happened to be in London at the time, and Franklin asked Folger's opinion on the matter. Franklin gave the American Philosophical Society (as recorded in *The Transactions of the American Philosophical Society*, Volume 2, 1786) the following account of his conversation with Folger.

> He told me he believed the fact might be true; but the difference was owing to this, that the Rhode-Island captains were acquainted with the gulf stream, which those of the English packets were not. We are well acquainted with the stream, says he, because in our pursuit of whales, which keep near the sides of it, but are not to be met with in it, we run down along the sides, and frequently cross it to change our side: and in crossing it have sometimes met and spoke with those packets who were in the middle of it, and stemming it. We have informed them that they were stemming a current, that was against them to the value of three miles an hour; and advised them to cross it and get out of it; but they were too wise to be counselled by simple American fishermen.

The stream, Folger said, was strong enough to be important. While in it, mail packets were losing as much as 70 miles a day. Sometimes, when winds were weak, the stream was actually carrying the mails backward. So Franklin asked his cousin to sketch the path of the Gulf Stream, and he arranged for an engraver to add the current to an old chart of the Atlantic. Copies were sent down to Falmouth for the captains of the packets, "who slighted it however."

A full century passed before the first serious studies of the Gulf Stream. Franklin's great-grandson, Alexander Dallas Bache, was the superintendent of the U.S. Coast Survey. He ordered ships to crisscross the stream 14 times, measuring the depth and temperature of the waters. Lieutenant Matthew Fontaine Maury, a self-trained scientist who was head of the Navy's Depot of Charts and Instruments (and Bache's archrival), sent out his own department's research ship, the *Dolphin*, to study the Gulf Stream. Maury also asked sea captains to send him pages of their logbooks, to assist him in preparing better charts.

At first, sea captains were slow to comply. But in 1847, Maury published the first of his long series *Wind and Current Charts*, direct descendants of the Franklin-Folger map. Using them, some clipper ships racing from the port of New York to the California gold fields shaved 30 days from their trip. After that, ship captains from all over the world sent pages of their logs to the Depot of Charts and Instruments. Maury became famous as "the Pathfinder of the Seas." "For myself," wrote one Captain Phinney, of the clipper ship *Gertrude*, "I am free to confess that for the many years I commanded a ship . . . I yet feel that until I took up your work I had been traversing the ocean blindfold."

Ben Franklin made a chart of the Gulf Stream. This version was published in Philadelphia in 1786. According to oceanographer Phil Richardson, the engraver "added several decorative ships, one of which is stemming the Gulf Stream. Franklin must have been amused by this, and by the inset in the lower right corner, showing himself in discussion with Neptune." The engraving is also amusing for its Yankee frugality, Richardson notes. "The insert in the upper left-hand corner is a chart for the migration of herring."

Bache and Maury each claimed the Gulf Stream as his department's special territory—Bache because it touched the coast, and Maury because it extended into the deep sea. In the end, the world profited from their rivalry, which put wind in their sails. Through their research, the Gulf Stream emerged as a force to reckon with. Sailors learned not to slight it, and with good reason. The Gulf Stream carries 5,000 times as much water as the Mississippi River, 25 times the volume of all the Earth's rivers put together. At its fastest, where it jets out from the Straits of Florida, it can sweep a drifting boat north 100 miles in a single day.

The Gulf Stream looks like a warm, blue vein in the Atlantic, much warmer and bluer than the water around it, and its edges are frequently marked by schools of fish, pods of whales, turtles, wheeling flocks of seabirds, driftwood, flotsam, and jetsam. The break in color at its western boundary is often dramatic enough to be visible even from a ship, and from a plane or a satellite it is unmistakable. To the west of the stream is the relatively shallow water of the continental slope. To the east of the stream, in the center of the Atlantic, is the Sargasso Sea, a kind of floating desert of clear, hot, sluggish water in which only certain specialized creatures and plants have found a home—notably the sargassum plant that gives the place its name. Sargassum is a floating seaweed, also called "berry grass." Eighteenth-century sailors becalmed in the sea's still waters thought their ships were tangled in the masses of berry grass.

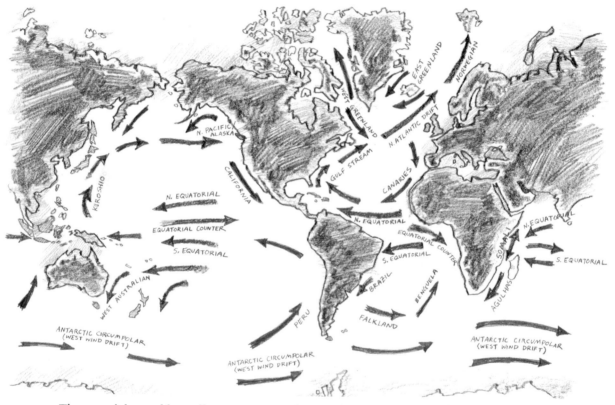

The seas of the world are all linked, and currents circulate between them. The Kuroshio, in the North Pacific, bears a striking resemblance to the Gulf Stream, in the North Atlantic.

The Gulf Stream's warm tropical water helps keep the British Isles from being as frigid in winter as the island of Newfoundland, which is just as far north. If it weren't for the warmth of the Gulf Stream, there might not have been a power in England capable of advancing Western civilization—or exacting tribute from American colonies. Without the stream, the poet Robert Browning would never have written the poem that begins, "Oh, to be in England now that April's there." In 1855, in his book *The Physical Geography of the Sea*, Lieutenant Maury wrote a paean to the stream:

There is a river in the ocean. In the severest droughts it never fails, and in the mightiest floods it never overflows. Its banks and its bottom are of cold water, while its current is of warm. The Gulf of Mexico is its fountain, and its mouth is in the Arctic Sea. It is the Gulf Stream.

Such eloquence helped draw many people into the study of the sea (and Jules Verne read and reread Maury's book before writing *Twenty Thousand Leagues Under the Sea*). But Maury was wrong about the stream. In 1885, the young Prince Albert I of Monaco (Prince Rainier's grandfather), who was rich from the gaming tables of Monte Carlo but whose life's love was the sea, sailed to the Azores in his yacht, the *Hirondelle*. There, with his mentor, Professor Georges Pouchet of the Paris Museum of Natural History, the prince threw more than 150 glass bottles, copper spheres, and beer barrels overboard. In succeeding years, he released more than 1,500 bottles and barrels along the path of the Gulf Stream. Messages in ten languages requested those who found the bottles and barrels to write to the prince at Monte Carlo.

From the replies he received, the prince deduced that the Gulf Stream forks in the northeastern Atlantic. Part of it heads northeastward, passes the islands of Ireland and Great Britain, the coast of Scandinavia, and at last dissipates in the North Atlantic. The second part of the stream heads south, passes Spain and Africa, and veers westward. Thus the Gulf Stream is really part of a *gyre*, a vast clockwise drift, in the Atlantic. Though we still call this current the Gulf Stream, and it still looks like a river in the sea, it really has neither head nor tail, beginning nor end. As Maury might have put it:

> There is a wheel in the ocean. Its western rim is near Florida, and its eastern rim is near the African Sahara. It is 13,000 miles around, fully three times the extent of the Nile, the Earth's longest river. It is so broad that a single revolution takes years. It is the North Atlantic Gyre.

With drifting bottles—and, more recently, with satellites—scientists have traced such gyres in each of the world's oceans (though, near the poles, they are rather small and cramped and their circulation is complicated). The gyres rotate clockwise in the northern hemisphere and counterclockwise in the southern hemisphere. North and South are divided neatly by currents that trace the equator.

The gyre in the North Pacific has a strong current on the western side that is strikingly like the Gulf Stream. This Pacific current bears warm water up from the tropics, sweeps against Japan, and then crosses the Pacific, where it helps warm the coast of California. The stream is called the Kuroshio, or Black Current, because its waters are a deep indigo blue.

These gyres are driven by winds. Strong, steady winds slant in toward the equator in each hemisphere of the globe, traveling from east to west. Because they have helped merchant ships ply their commerce down through the ages, they are known as trade winds. The trade winds push upon the water as they blow across the surface. Their friction sets currents in motion and keeps them going.

Besides the trades, there are two other belts of steady winds on the face of the planet. One belt flows from west to east in the midlatitudes; the second flows from east to west near the poles. If there were no continents, each belt of winds would set up a corresponding belt of ocean currents, girdling the Earth. But the continents are giant islands in these currents, and they interrupt the flow. Each current breaks up against the shores of a continent, or a shoal, or an island arc, and the current splits into separate streams.

Only in the waters around Antarctica does a current have free passage, and there it circumnavigates the globe, like a snake chasing its tail. This broad band of cold water isolates the southern continent from the rest of the world ocean and prevents warmer currents from reaching it; in this way, the current helps to make Antarctica the coldest place on Earth, with an icecap three miles thick. Only 100 million years ago, a mere blink in geologic time, there was little or no ice on Antarctica. It was still joined to the southern tip of South America. The thin and tenuous bridge of land that linked the two continents was enough to block the Antarctic current, to stir vast quantities of warmer water toward the South Pole, and to keep the climate there much milder. But when the two continents drifted apart, the cold current had an uninterrupted passage, and Antarctica's fate was sealed.

Besides wind and rock, a third factor twists the path of each current. It is the Coriolis force, named after the 19th-century French physicist who explained it first and best, Gaspard Gustave de Coriolis. This is not a fundamental force of nature, like gravity or electromagnetism. It is only a consequence of the spinning of the Earth. Its effect can be visualized in a thought experiment.

Spin a classroom globe and try to draw a line straight from the North Pole to the equator. Then stop the globe and look at the line. It is not straight; while the penpoint moved downward, the globe swept sideways beneath it, and the line the pen traced on the sphere was bent. In much this way, the great, spinning Earth bends the path of everything that crosses its surface, from winds to ocean currents to long-range ballistic missiles (whose trajectories are carefully adjusted to compensate for the Coriolis force).

This force helps to twist currents at the sea surface into gyres; and the force has surprising consequences below the surface, as well. Each surface current sets water moving in the layer of water just beneath it, by friction. The Coriolis force twists the motion of this second, lower layer, so that it flows at a slight angle to the water above it. The buried layer, in turn, sets in motion the layer of water beneath *it*, and this third layer is deflected by the Coriolis force, too. Thus, as one descends from the surface, each successive layer of seawater is twisted slightly farther, like steps in a spiral staircase. (This curious spiral pattern is called Ekman Drift, after the oceanographer who worked it out, Vagn Walfrid Ekman.)

The result is this: While water at the surface of each ocean circles in a gyre, masses of water below the surface are at the same time shunted inward, at right angles to the gyre; and this water piles up in the center of the ocean! The North Atlantic gyre is four and a half feet higher at the center than at the edges. It is, in effect, the hub of the great wheel. Indeed, the hill helps to perpetuate the motion of the gyre itself. Water flows downhill from the top of the hill to the bottom; but as it flows it is deflected by the Coriolis force into a circular path. The result is not a flow straight down the hill, but a wide, circular motion around it.

For years, scientists wondered why the North Atlantic gyre moves so much faster at the westward end, along the coast of Florida, than at the eastward end, along the coast of Africa. Clearly, the same amount of water must flow on both sides of the gyre, or the current would fall apart. In 1947, a brilliant young scientist at the Woods Hole Oceanographic Institution, Henry Stommel, solved this puzzle. He was fresh out of school and working as a technician—doing "slave labor," as he recalls it, for several scientists in Woods Hole—and he wanted to escape the drudgery. One day he went up to the office of a senior scientist, Raymond Montgomery, and asked him to recommend an interesting research problem. Montgomery mentioned the inexplicable speed of the Gulf Stream.

"If you had as empty a mind as I had," Stommel says now, "any kind of reasonably good-sounding question was very attractive. I couldn't think of anything else to do! So I started working on that." With advice and encouragement from Montgomery, the junior technician solved one of the most important questions in physical oceanography.

The hill of water in the gyre, Stommel said, is not right in the center of the Atlantic, as had been assumed. It is displaced to the west by the spin of the Earth as the planet rolls eastward. So the hub of the wheel is closer to Florida than to Africa. Thus, water flowing past Africa has room to spread out. It flows in a broad, slow, leisurely current. The same volume of water, in the westward part of the gyre, is squeezed against the coast of the Americas. Because its course there is narrow and compressed, the current rushes faster.

Hence the speed and power of the Gulf Stream.

THE RING SAGA

Even if one ignores the rest of the wheel and looks only at the Gulf Stream, which is the wheel's western rim, it still does not behave like a river in the sea, as Maury described it. It wanders with a wilder freedom than any landbound river.

On land, river courses often meander, especially on level plains. Once in a long while, they even skip from one bed to another. The Hwang Ho, or Yellow River, has changed course three times in the past 150 years, in each instance flooding so much farmland and killing so many millions of people that it has long been called China's Sorrow.

In the sea, a current is not confined by banks of sand or stone. It flows only through more water. So the Gulf Stream is free to change its path from day to day, week to week. The chart Timothy Folger drew for his cousin Ben Franklin was only an average, or approximation—the Gulf Stream wriggles like an eel. It is especially lively after heavy storms.

On land, when a river's path meanders, like the Yellow River's, a loop sometimes grows so wide and sluggish that the river finds a shortcut. It jumps its banks and bypasses the loop. Such a loop of sluggish water—a rejected detour—is called an oxbow lake.

In water, when a loop forms in the Gulf Stream, the result is more kinetic. The loop closes upon itself, buds off from the main stream, and wanders away, spinning fast. From above, it looks like a ring. It is a current moving in a circle, with a round core of quiet water trapped in the middle of it.

The existence of these strange rings was long suspected, but in 1950 Frederick C. Fuglister, an artist turned oceanographer, was the first man actually to observe a ring forming. Fuglister led a six-vessel expedition, Operation Cabot, out of Woods Hole in search of rings. He picked a likely meander and watched it closely. In the course of several days it split off from the Gulf Stream and went spinning away. Rings have since been discovered to accompany most strong ocean currents, including the Kuroshio, and the Agulhas Current of the Indian Ocean.

These rings are called "eddies." But that may be misleading, for the word suggests little whirlpools. Rings that form

The life and death of a ring in the Atlantic Ocean. This ring, called 82-B, was warmer than its surrounding water. It was tracked by oceanographer Otis Brown, of the University of Florida, Miami, and coworkers, using ships and satellites. In the first image in the series, on March 12, 1982, Ring 82-B (upper right center) is just several weeks old, and it is some 240 kilometers in diameter. False colors have been added to show temperatures: violet-blue is very cold water, two to 12 degrees centigrade; green water is 13 to 17 C; gold, 18 to 21 degrees C; and red water is warm, 23 to 26 C. In the second image, on April 23, the ring has wandered slightly, and cooled. To the southwest, another ring, 81-F, is visible near a meander of the Gulf Stream. In the third image, Ring 82-B is now three months old. A large Gulf Stream meander is visible (lower right). The second ring, 81-F, is being assimilated by the Gulf Stream, which is the fate of most rings in the Atlantic. In the last image, our hero, Ring 82-B, has bumped into the Gulf Stream, and it is vanishing from the face of the sea.

on the southern side of the Gulf Stream, in the deep Atlantic, are sometimes nearly 200 miles wide, larger in area than the whole state of Florida. They are, as one oceanographer has observed, "small only in comparison to the size of the oceans." In sea science jargon, rings are *mesoscale*—of middle size. They are bigger than the whirlpools in the wake of a ship but smaller than gyres. Oceanographers now speak of a "mesoscale revolution," the discovery that the sea is full of whirling eddies of this size.

A big ring south of the stream spins at an average of one or two knots, which is fairly fast for an ocean current (a *knot* is a nautical mile per hour—6,076.10 feet); the ring completes one or two revolutions a week. It can sometimes maintain a difference of as much as 10 degrees Fahrenheit between itself and the surrounding water. The ring current is strongest near the surface but extends down all the way to the bottom, several miles down. If we could view a ring from the side, we would see a sort of underwater cyclone or tornado. The rings are strong enough to tear lobster traps from their moorings (American fishermen used to blame the lost traps on Russian rivals fishing the same waters).

Some rings wander back into the Gulf Stream and disappear into it. Others last for months, even several years, before fading into the surrounding sea. As each ring moves away from the stream, it kidnaps billions of marine animals and plants and carries them off to waters that are hostile to them, such as the hot, watery desert of the Sargasso Sea. These exiles can survive in the Sargasso only as long as the ring protects them and the food holds out.

Biologist Peter Wiebe, of the Woods Hole Oceanographic Institution, has observed the fate of animals that are borne off into the hot Sargasso. As the cold water slowly warms up, captive creatures that require cool temperatures, like the little, shrimplike *Nematoscelis megalops*, are in trouble. Normally these crustaceans swim about near the surface and dine on microscopic plants. But as weeks pass, the surface waters grow inhospitable and the plants there thin out, like grass in a fenced-in, overgrazed pasture. There is no escape for *N. megalops* to the north, south, east, or west, for the Sargasso surrounds them, tepid and desolate. The animals move 1,000 feet, then 2,000 feet down, where the ring water is still cold. But in the dark depths, plants are even scarcer than at the surface. The ring is no longer a shelter, but a spinning prison. *N. megalops* starves to death.

Studying the turnovers of life within the rings may teach us much about the ways species flourish or falter as their environment changes. Such transitions are not easy to observe,

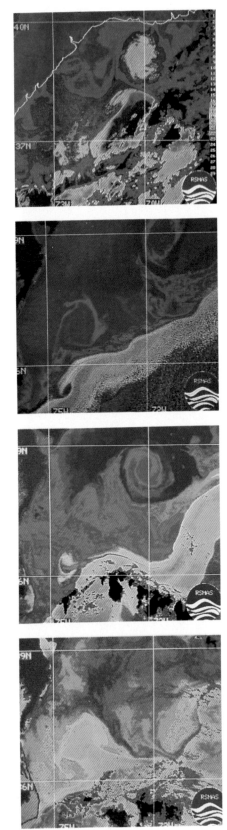

of course, because each ring covers as much area as the better part of New England. A single ship would soon lose track of a fast-moving ring. A whole array of ships and satellites is required to pursue it, sample its waters, and keep an accurate running census of its inhabitants—a myriad besides *N. megalops*. To Wiebe and others, the effort is well worthwhile. Wiebe has gone on a dozen Atlantic ring expeditions. "The opportunity is unprecedented in population biology," he has said. "An equivalent terrestrial experiment would require that an area the size of Massachusetts, New Hampshire, Rhode Island, and Vermont, with all its soil, forests, meadows, rivers, lakes, and animals, be monitored over a two-year period as it was moved toward the southern United States."

RACE OF THE RINGS

Rings also matter to sailors. Each year, in the month of June, a yacht race is held from New England to Bermuda. On even years, the Bermuda Race starts in Newport, Rhode Island; on odd years, in Marion, Massachusetts. The evening before the race, a hall near the marina is packed and steamy with 300 or 400 sweating yacht captains. They come to hear a briefing by Dane and Jenifer Clark, a husband-and-wife team from the National Oceanic and Atmospheric Administration in Washington, D.C. The sailors are so serious about the briefing that many of them tape it.

Speaking into clustered microphones like two chiefs of state, Dane delivers an up-to-the-minute weather report, and Jenifer gives a ring report. She outlines each ring on a map and predicts where it is headed and whether the Gulf Stream will sashay. Then she and her husband chart the route they believe will give the racers their fastest course.

The yacht captains know that catching a lift on a ring that is rotating in the right direction can carry a boat to victory. Getting stuck in a ring that is rotating the wrong way can sweep it backward and cost it the race. There are often more than a dozen rings in the Atlantic at any given time, and three or four rings near what is called the *rhumb*—the shortest, beeline course to Bermuda. The racers must dodge among the rings, remembering that rings to the north and south of the stream rotate in opposite directions.

Many of the captains prepare for the race months in advance by subscribing to the Gulf Stream Mailing List. They receive a stream and ring analysis prepared from satellite photographs three times a week by the National Oceanic and Atmospheric Administration. The black-and-white pictures are taken with infrared light, to pick up temperature differences at the sea surface. Warm water shows up in dark shades of gray,

These intricate spiral eddies were photographed from the U.S. Space Shuttle Challenger *by Paul Scully-Power, the first oceanographer in space.*

and cooler water in light gray; the Gulf Stream appears as a very dark—that is, very warm—ribbon of water.

On the morning of the race, Jenifer calls her office in Washington. There a colleague checks the latest satellite pictures of the Eastern Seaboard, plots the Gulf Stream and its rings, and lets her know if any last-minute changes have taken place. Her husband calls the Boston office of the National Weather Service and talks over their very latest forecast. The sailors get one last briefing, and they're off.

In 1984, some yacht captains steered close to the rhumb line, taking what seemed the shortest route, against Jenifer Clark's advice. They ran into a ring that had a record-breaking current of seven knots running against them, sweeping them backward. Seven knots is faster than many sailboats can go—and it felt to the yachtsmen rather as if they were driving a car on a treadmill spinning at 100 miles an hour. They lost. The captain of the *Pamir*, however, sailed 114 miles out of his way, caught a lift on the far side of the same ring, and won.

After the race was over, Jenifer and Dane collected the racers' logs, much as Maury collected ships' logs a century ago. The reports were useful feedback, helping the Clarks decide if meteorologists and oceanographers were interpreting the subtler details of satellite photos correctly.

The two scientists enjoyed being king and queen for a day, lords of the rings.

THE WATER COLUMN

If the ocean depths were truly stagnant, as was long believed, they would fill with death and decay; for the remains of all that lives in the sea fall toward the bottom in a slow and perpetual rain. Without deep currents to stir things up, noxious fumes would gather near the floor and kill all bottom-dwelling creatures. Slowly the Earth's own body heat would warm this foul black water until it was hotter than the water at the surface. Then, as oceanographer Tjeerd van Andel has written, "the unstable ocean would eventually turn over and vent the whole mess to the surface, with catastrophic effects on the fauna and flora of the surface waters and perhaps some poisoning of the atmosphere."

So it is lucky for us that the deep seas are not as quiet as scientists once thought. The deeps are, in fact, profoundly and majestically restless. Water is forever sinking from the surface to the depths, and slowly rising again to the surface.

This circulation is another instance of convection. It is the same sort of process as in a pot of soup on a stove, and—scientists believe—the process that stirs the mantle of the Earth itself. But in the seas, unlike the pot or the mantle, the driving

force is not in the depths but at the very top. Water chilled at the surface in polar seas is denser and heavier than water in the depths. As it sinks, it displaces deep water, which is forced up to the surface. (The journey from the surface to the bottom and back often takes more than a thousand years.)

Water near the poles is dense not only because it is cold but also because it carries an unusually heavy burden of dissolved salt. It holds the salt that icebergs leave behind—for water, on freezing, expels its share of salt, and the water around the ice must absorb it. (All icebergs are pure, fresh water—in fact, Prince Muhammad Al Faisal, of Saudi Arabia, has considered lassoing icebergs from ships and towing them south to fill his country's reservoirs and irrigate the deserts.) The Weddell Sea, in Antarctica, is the world's largest factory of cold, salty water. Other surface water "sinks" are in waters near Greenland: the Norwegian Sea and the Labrador Sea.

Ice floating at the surface of the sea helps to keep currents flowing across the bottom, from the poles of the globe to the equator.

Eddies and currents sometimes trap sea animals and plants, and whirl them far away from their native waters. Here the research vessel Atlantis II *drops a trawl to collect specimens for study.*

When this dense water sinks to the bottom, it advances slowly upon the equator, in a journey of centuries. Its presence in the tropics seems to have been noted first by a slave-ship captain. In 1751, Captain Henry Ellis, of the *Earl of Halifax,* bound from England to West Africa, discovered that a bucket of water hoisted up from a mile down was refreshingly chilly in the tropical heat. The captain used the water to cool his wine and his bath.

Eighteenth-century scientists reasoned that cold water near the equator could only have come from near the poles; and they believed the polar water must have spread out until it covered the whole ocean bottom on its long, slow crawl toward the equator.

In the mid-1950s, however, Henry Stommel, of Woods Hole, worked to develop more sophisticated mathematical models of the seas' circulation. Stommel was already famous in his field for explaining why ocean gyres are fastest along their western boundaries. Now he decided that the advance of deep, cold bottom water toward the equator could not be as slow and even as scientists had supposed. Instead, he said, the bottom currents—like the currents at the surface—must be channeled against the western margins of the continents by the spinning of the Earth. Thus, in the Atlantic, Stommel imagined a sort of negative or antithesis of the Gulf Stream—a countercurrent of freezing water moving south through the darkness at the bottom of the continental shelf.

In 1955, a British oceanographer, John Swallow, devised a simple but ingenious device that made it possible to test Stommel's hypothesis. Swallow weighted 10-foot lengths of aluminum pipe with just enough ballast to make them sink without reaching bottom. He fitted these pipes with acoustic transmitters, which emitted a high-pitched "ping" every few seconds. In that way the sunken aluminum floats could be followed easily by a ship on the surface.

In 1957, Swallow sailed to Bermuda on the British research ship *Discovery II.* Stommel met him there on the *Atlantis,* from Woods Hole. Together, American and British scientists dropped seven Swallow floats overboard. Some of these pipes were ballasted to float at fairly shallow depths, others at 9,000 feet. It was a sophisticated replay of Prince Albert's experiments half a century before—only now the currents of interest were far below.

The Swallow floats near the surface were drawn northward in the Gulf Stream. The floats in the depths drifted southward, pinging as they went. Stommel was right again.

There is, in fact, not only a western boundary current in the abyss, but a complete gyre; it runs counterclockwise beneath the warm clockwise gyre at the surface. Stommel's mathematical models predict the existence of such an abyssal gyre in each ocean basin, and also other horizontal currents at various levels of the sea. The more these models are elaborated, the more intricate the world ocean appears. The sea is layered like the pages of a book. Its structure has been compared to a bartender's novelty drink, the Zombie, in which several different kinds of alcohol are layered one on top of the next. In the layers of the sea (whose number is unknown), each sheet differs only very slightly from its neighbors in temperature and salinity. Yet there is surprisingly little mixing at the borders. Water can travel within its layer, undiluted, for thousands of miles. Handed a water sample, a chemist, with practice, can tell what part of the world a water sample came from, at what depth it was traveling, and for how long.

Swallow floats. Invented by British oceanographer John Swallow in 1955, the floats proved that the sea is restless and agitated far below the surface.

These stubborn layers greatly retard the rise of water to the surface. To replace water that sinks at the poles, an equal volume of water diffuses upward very gradually across the whole expanse of the oceans. Only under special circumstances does it well up quickly enough to pierce the horizontal layers. Such currents—upwellings—are bonanzas for life at the surface.

Along a continental shelf, for instance, if trade winds blow steadily from the coast toward the sea, the winds brush the surface water out to sea with them, and water wells up from below, near shore, to take its place.

This deeper water comes from the bottom, where blankets of dead organisms have rained down. The bottom is rich with decay, and the surface is rich in sunlight. Together, in an upwelling, the nutrients and sunlight make a potent attraction for life. *Phytoplankton*, which are microscopic floating green plants, bloom in the upwelling water, nourished by its phosphates and nitrates. Phytoplankton have been called the grass of the sea. They are grazed upon by tiny fish, which are eaten by bigger fish, and an entire food chain springs up, all dependent on the upwelling water, like nomads at a well in a desert oasis. Indeed, the surrounding water is a true desert, for without a mix of bottom water and sunlight, there can be no life in the seas. Water without nutrients is like soil without fertilizer. Nothing grows in it. The clear blue water of the tropics, which we often take to be a sign of health, is actually a sign of death—plenty of sun but no nutrients or plankton.

Upwelling waters teeming with life are found not only along some coasts but also under a variety of conditions in the open sea. Such waters are usually murky, tinted green or brown by the pastures of phytoplankton; and the more life present, the richer the hue of the water. Over millennia, albacore (a kind of tuna) and other big fish have learned to seek out such waters. In turn, deep-sea fishermen watch for the edges of green or brown bands at sea. As a sign of good fishing, a green band is almost as reliable as a wheeling flock of gulls.

Albacore are fast, and they migrate in schools across vast stretches of the ocean; fishing boats are slow. The West Coast tuna industry loses fortunes in fuel and valuable ship time hunting for their catch. Sometimes a fleet captain, in frustration, hires a helicopter pilot to survey the coastal waters from above.

Today, a special kind of remote sensor called the Coastal Zone Color Scanner (CZCS) is carried aboard some weather satellites, such as NASA's *Nimbus-7.* CZCS photographs of the Pacific are broadcast by NASA directly to the fishermen in a new, experimental program that is expected to pay for itself in savings to the fishing industry.

To take advantage of the program, albacore fishermen carry computers aboard their boats, which receive facsimiles of the satellite photographs over the radio and print them out for inspection. The pictures are in black and white, but each stripe and splotch is numbered according to a code. A fisherman at sea, following the code, colors in the facsimile in shades of indigo, blue, green, and brown—painting by number. When he is finished, he can survey the seas around him with what has been called "a God's-eye view."

It is a Space Age food chain of predator and prey. The tuna's eyes and the satellites' are both attuned to the color of the phytoplankton. The tuna catch the plankton; the satellites, the tuna.

EL NIÑO

In most years, there is good fishing off the coast of Peru. Trade winds blow steadily from South America out to sea and then west across the Pacific. The winds stir up whitecaps as they push the coastal surface waters westward. To replace the surface waters, cool, nutrient-rich water wells up from the floor of the continental shelf. Thus, near Peru, the sea is cool (one Peruvian meteorologist calls it "our national air conditioner") and full of murky greens and browns from pastures of phytoplankton. This is a paradise for anchovies, the little fish that have been—until recently—a mainstay of the Peruvian economy.

Every few years, however, the trade winds die, the cold upwellings cease and the waters grow hot and quiet. The blooms of brown and green phytoplankton dwindle and disappear, and soon so do the schools of fish, and with them the sea birds—boobies, petrels, cormorants, gannets. An episode like this in 1972 cut Peru's anchovy catch to one fifth its usual size. The industry and the country have not yet recovered.

After the winds die, feverish water spreads slowly, like a slow blush, until it covers half the equatorial Pacific, extending more than a quarter of the way around the Earth. Near Peru, the water is sweltering, in the 80s, as much as 15 degrees Fahrenheit above normal. The water is noticeably warmer even as far north as San Diego, California, and Seattle, Washington, driving off albacore and cold-water salmon and driving North American fishermen, too, upon hard times.

This heat wave in the sea is called "El Niño," Spanish for "The Child," because it usually appears off the coast of Peru around Christmastime. The most recent visit of The Child lasted from 1982 to 1983. It was one of the worst in history, and it signaled vast changes in the atmosphere's global circulation, alterations that made for strange weather around the world. There were torrential storms in parts of Ecuador, Bolivia,

School buses (left) mired in water and mud, a flood brought by El Niño. Yet (right) El Niño also meant drought and famine. Both these pictures were taken on the northern coast of Peru in the period between March and June, 1983.

Brazil, and Peru—some desert regions got 12 feet of rain. Flash floods and mudslides killed hundreds of people and evicted hundreds of thousands. In the United States, there were huge storms and rains along the West Coast, and even in Florida, causing more than $1 billion in property damage, and killing at least 100 people. The tranquil island of Tahiti, which hadn't seen a single typhoon in this century, was struck by one after another.

Meanwhile, in southern Africa, perturbations of the global weather, coming after two dry years, probably contributed to the terrible drought that has devastated Botswana, and also led to killing droughts in Indonesia, India, Sri Lanka, and Australia. There, in February of 1983, dry soil blew up into a vast, dark dust storm that choked the city of Melbourne with thousands of tons of earth.

All told, the El Niño syndrome is the largest disturbance oceanographers and meteorologists have recognized in the planet's weather. If scientists could predict the coming of The Child, they might be able to forecast bad weather months ahead in half the world. Given enough warning time, billions of dollars and thousands of lives could be saved. El Niño comes at irregular intervals, however; sometimes it is two years apart, sometimes ten. To see it coming, we must learn to recognize the ill winds that bear it.

Scientists know that healthy trade winds, by blowing from east to west across the Pacific, normally heap up surface water on the western shores of the ocean. Sea level near New Guinea and the Philippines is several feet higher than near Peru. It is as if the ocean basin were a large bowl of soup and the god of winds were puffing on it from one side.

Sometime before the onset of El Niño, the trade winds stop blowing, or even reverse themselves and blow from the other side of the basin. Then the warm water piled up off the coast of Asia sloshes back to the Americas. It spreads out over the eastern Pacific, making a ceiling of hot water, like a tin can's lid some 450 feet thick. When this happens, the cold, nutrient-rich waters from the bottom cannot penetrate the hot layer, and these cold waters no longer well up to the surface. They are sealed in.

For a variety of reasons, the hot water at the surface, by warming the air above it, prevents the trade winds from reasserting themselves. In a long chain reaction, the disruption of the atmosphere above the Pacific sets off series of storms and droughts elsewhere. As Eugene Rasmussen, chief climate analyst of the National Weather Service, has put it, "When one part of the atmosphere moves, another part feels the kick."

One link in this chain reaction was noticed in the 1920s by a brilliant Cambridge mathematician, Sir Gilbert Walker, while he was stationed in India. Walker was a man with an omnivorous curiosity. Besides his work in meteorology, he contributed to the study of electromagnetism, birds and boomerangs, and improved the design of the flute. Cambridge dons called him Boomerang Walker.

Walker was fascinated by the monsoon, whose sudden summer winds and rains bring life to India, and whose failures—which are all too frequent—bring famine. To learn what made the monsoon so fickle, Walker studied weather records from around the world. He documented a curious, global see-saw pattern in the atmosphere. When air pressure is high in the South Pacific, it tends to be low in the Indian Ocean. Every few years, the seesaw tilts: Pressure is low in the Pacific, high in the Indian Ocean. The unusual low brings torrential rains; the unusual high, drought. Walker called this seesaw the Southern Oscillation.

The Southern Oscillation was not much help in forecasting monsoons, but Walker was knighted for his work in India. He died at 90, in 1958, the year of a strong Southern Oscillation and a belligerent Child.

That was also in the International Geophysical Year. Jacob Bjerknes, one of a family of great Norwegian meteorologists, noticed the coincidence of the Southern Oscillation and El Niño. Observations made across the globe during the IGY made this the best-watched Child on record. Bjerknes took up and extended Walker's work, showing how the Southern Oscillation—the reversal of pressure centers and of trade winds—leads to the sloshing of warm water from New Zealand toward Peru. His work got modern oceanographers and meteorologists interested in what Bjerknes called "teleconnections"—the ability of unusual weather at one spot on the globe to affect weather far away. The warm water of El Niño has more teleconnections than any other freak of weather on the globe—apparently it occurs in what might be called a "pressure point" in the Earth's weather system.

But why do the trade winds fail in the first place? Jerome Namias, of the Scripps Institution of Oceanography in La Jolla, California, has observed that wind patterns in the Pacific often lead to large pools of abnormally warm or cool water in the open ocean. Called sea surface temperature anomalies, they are as much as 1,000 kilometers across and a few hundred feet deep. Though their temperature differs by only a few degrees from the water around them, the pools are so big that Namias thinks they may have significant affects on the passage of winds and the birth and death of storms at sea. Perhaps, he suggests, a pool somewhere in the Pacific, or even farther afield—in the Atlantic or the Indian oceans—causes the reversal of the Pacific trades. Since the pools are themselves born of winds, it is still impossible to disentangle the chain of cause and effect and say which comes first—a distempered wind, or a fevered sea.

In January 1985, an international team of investigators began a decade-long study of El Niño. The project is called by a name almost as unwieldy as the phenomenon: Interannual Variability of the Tropical Ocean and the Global Atmosphere (TOGA). With luck, 10 years should be long enough for the scientists to see one or two complete El Niños come and go and for the world to learn the full name of the program. TOGA, as its organizers freely admit, is a Byzantine example of international bureaucratic architecture. It involves numerous committees and subcommittees from many countries and disciplines. If it succeeds, we will know much more in 1995 than we do today. The phenomenon that begins with the death of an anchovy will end with a lesson of the very largest magnitude. Between sea and air, which is the master, and which the slave? Or do both evolve together?

"Serendipity," the oceanographer Tjeerd van Andel observes in his book *Science at Sea*, "is the opposite of orderly science. It is the lucky stroke, the great good fortune to tumble on something wholly unexpected and exciting, the great good fortune also to recognize what one sees as something important." One of the latest and most curious finds in the exploration of the Earth, the discovery in 1977 of vents and the bizarre life around them, was a classic in serendipity.

SECRET FOUNTAINS

Scientist-aquanauts had set out to settle a question about the midocean ridge. According to the theory of plate tectonics, the ridge is where red-hot basalt, extruded from the depths of the Earth, builds the sea floors. Therefore the nearer we go to the center of the ridge, the hotter the floor should be. By 1977, this prediction had been tested several times by scientists aboard research ships, who lowered *thermistors* on long probes three or four meters long, drove them into the bottom sediment, and measured the flow of heat. These measurements had confirmed the predictions of plate tectonic theory in all but one crucial place—the center of the ridge itself. There, where the floor should have been hottest, the curve of ascending heat abruptly leveled off. It was a thermal anticlimax. What was damping the fires at the ridge?

There was a second sea mystery, this one centuries old. All over the world, as James Hutton was the first to recognize, rains and rivers are forever wearing away the rock of the continents and carrying loads of silt and debris into lakes and down to the sea. This runoff is full of minerals, including salts (even fresh water is a little salty) and bicarbonate, a chemical produced in great quantities when rainwater weathers limestone (it is familiar in the kitchen as bicarbonate of soda).

Some lakes have inlets but no outlets, no escaping streams. Water can depart from such a lake only by evaporation, and in doing so the water leaves behind its load of minerals. Salts and bicarbonate accumulate. They create a Great Salt Lake, a Soda Lake, or a Dead Sea, in which virtually nothing can grow.

The world ocean itself is a sort of sunken, giant lake, all inlets and no outlets. (All roads lead to Rome; all flowing waters lead at last to sea.) Yet the ocean is not choked with bicarbonates; and though it is, of course, salty, its minerals are not in the ratios one would expect to find, given the chemistry of the waters that feed it.

This, then, was the second mystery: Why isn't the ocean a vast Dead Sea?

In 1965, when the theory of plate tectonics was taking shape but was not yet respectable, a British geologist, John W. Elder, made a shrewd suggestion. On land, he observed, there are places where magma lies pooled near the surface. Groundwater, seeping down, touches red-hot rock and boils back up to the surface. In New Zealand, such hot springs supply enough energy for a hydrothermal power plant, one of the first of its kind in the world. In the United States, in Yellowstone National Park, there are not only hot springs but also geysers, the most famous of which is Old Faithful.

Elder thought there might be hot springs in the deeps, too, along the midocean ridge. There, ice-cold seawater might meander down through cracks and fissures, meet magma, and explode upward in furious Old Faithfuls. Because the magma was cooled by this seawater, less heat would flow up through the sea floor's sediments. What is more, seawater, superheated in the fissures of basalt, would exchange chemicals with the rock. Bicarbonate in the water would fizz into carbon dioxide. The hidden fires and cauldrons would keep the seas' chemistry in balance. They would keep the seas alive.

In 1973, four years after the first men landed on the Moon, scientists in tiny submarines made it down for the first time into the rift valley at the center of the Mid-Atlantic Ridge. There they found frozen beds of basalt twisted in the same strange, swirling, ropy shapes that lava lakes make when they cool on land: eery fields of black, tormented stone that Polynesians call *panhoehoe*. This was a great discovery; it proved that eruptions do occur from time to time along the midocean ridge, as the theory of plate tectonics predicted. But the scientist-aquanauts did not see any hot water jetting up from the basalt. Apparently they had landed at a dormant spot in the long valley. All was cold and still.

In search of a live vent, scientists turned to the Pacific, since its ridge is livelier and more fiery than the Atlantic's. The scientists chose to dive at the Galapagos Rift, near the famous islands where, a century before, the young Charles Darwin, ashore from HMS *Beagle*, watched cormorants and sea lions and hitched a ride on the back of a giant tortoise.

On that voyage Darwin was the only scientist; there were some 30 scientists on this one, on two ships, the *Knorr* (which surveyed the area before the dives began) and the *Lulu* (which carried the submarine *Alvin*). John Edmond of the Massachusetts Institute of Technology; John Corliss of the University of Oregon; and Ralph Hollis, *Alvin's* pilot, made the first dive. They dropped for an hour and a half, straight down, through 7,500 feet of water.

Alvin's quarters, lined with electronic instrument panels, were too cramped for the three men to stand up. They squatted in *Alvin's* cold, tiny cabin, built of titanium to resist the enormous pressure at the bottom. Each man peered out a small Plexiglas porthole.

At first the three saw nothing at the bottom but more cold, dead basalt, stretching off into the darkness beyond their lights in a gentle, uphill slope. Like the basalt fields in the Atlantic, this was an underwater wasteland, a desert dotted here and there with a stray anemone, or a small crab. The scarcity of life did not surprise them. They assumed that precious little life could survive in that midnight of freezing temperatures and enormous pressures.

They stopped to pick up a rock sample—a basalt pillow—with one of *Alvin's* remote-controlled, mechanical arms. While the pilot wrestled with the manipulator, Edmond recalls, he and Corliss began to lose interest in the rock, their eyes unfocused, and at the same instant they both noticed the intervening water. It was *shimmering*, like air above a hot fire.

Instantly they dropped the basalt and went on up the slope. There they came upon a spectacle that no one, not even Elder, had expected. Spread out upon the basalt were dense masses of giant mussels, and clams the size of dinner plates. White crabs scuttled among them, and strange, colorful fish they could not identify. It was nothing less than an oasis.

"The people back on the ship thought there was something wrong with the submarine, because we were sort of raving at them from the bottom," Edmond recalls. "Communications from the sea floor aren't that easy, they're semigarbled under the best of conditions. So they were pretty worried. If anything goes wrong with the submarine's oxygen supply, the sub crew's first sensation is wild euphoria: 'rapture of the depths.' And then, of course, a coma. They were trying to prevent a coma, which was very good of them, but that wasn't what was actually going on!"

Following that first, delirious discovery, the expedition scientists made dive after dive in *Alvin*. They found five separate oases, which they dubbed Clambake 1, Clambake 2, Dandelion Patch, Oyster Bed, and the Garden of Eden. The sites were easy to spot now that the scientists knew what to look

RAPTURE OF THE DEPTHS

for—seen from above, the ring of white clams stands out against the black rock like a halo. At each site, hot, milky, shimmering water rose from vents and fissures in the floor. Shellfish clustered around the warmest vents, all but choking the flow of hot water. Feather-duster worms browsed among the shellbeds, along with brittle stars, and purple anemones with wavy fronds. A few black basalt pillows were draped with something white and stringy, which looked like masses of spaghetti (it was, in reality, another deep-sea worm). Above the heads of all these creatures swayed the strangest creatures of all. Giant worms, they looked like blood-red tulips four to ten feet tall, with stems white as chalk. The oases were a secret archipelago as strange and full of marvels as Darwin's beloved Galapagos.

"We couldn't leave that place without—if possible—having a sample of everything," Edmond says. "We had the whole ship's freezer full of clams and worms. People were climbing all over them, and they were slimy and horrible and everything else like that. They smelled, and they had a very, very high hemoglobin content, so there was dripping blood all over the place, slews of blood. It was wonderful. The *Lulu*'s freezer is built to hold several tons of food. That's a lot of clams. The cooks were not amused."

NIGHT LIFE   "I don't think there's ever going to be another discovery like this," oceanographer George Somero, of Scripps, exulted afterward. "It's sort of like discovering another planet, another form of life." The surprise is not just in the creatures' looks, but in the peculiar way they make a living.

Every other ecological community ever found on this planet, from tropical jungles to alpine lakes to coral reefs to New York boroughs, is run by the sun. Green plants are suncatchers. They use sunlight to drive the chemical factories within their cells. These microscopic factories, called *chloroplasts*, manufacture sugars and starches—carbohydrates—by *photosynthesis* (a word whose Greek roots mean, literally, "to put together with the help of light"). No human has ever designed a factory more efficient, or whose products are more in demand, than a chloroplast. Plants live on the carbohydrates, and so do virtually all their neighbors. Even carnivores get their carbohydrates from green plants, in one way or another. The wolf eats the deer that ate the grass.

But at the bottom of the sea there is no sun, there are no green plants. So the creatures clustered around the vents, unlike any other community on Earth, live on energy from the planet itself. They owe their lives, in a sense, to plate tectonics.

Water, after its encounter with the hot basalt beneath the sea floor, is rich in hydrogen sulfide (the sulphur compound that lends odor to a rotten egg). To us, hydrogen sulfide gas is a deadly poison. But to bacteria in the vents, it is the staff of life. They eat the sulfide, and use it in much the way that green plants use sunlight. With energy derived from splitting apart the compound, each bacterium's chemical factories make quantities of sugars and starches. They do this so effectively that

These giant tube worms live at the bottom of the sea, sustained not by the Sun but by the body heat of the Earth itself.

they multiply by the billions in the vent waters and turn them milky. From some prodigal vents, called *white smokers*, bacteria billow out as if from smokestacks.

The rest of the creatures at the dark vents depend upon the bacteria, just as we who live in sunlight depend upon plants. Small animals eat the bacteria, and bigger animals eat the small ones. Other creatures live with the bacteria in *symbiosis*, an intimate partnership of species. The giant tube worm *Riftia pachyptila*, for instance, is so dependent on bacteria that it is hard to say where the bacteria end and the worm begins. *Riftia's* body is stuffed with an organ called *trophosome*. The trophosome is stuffed with bacteria, which makes up most of the worm's body weight. These captive bacteria make carbohydrates, which enter the blood supply of the worm; in return, the worm provides the bacteria the shelter of its own body and the oxygen in its blood. This is clearly an ancient arrangement, a bargain struck long ago in evolution. The worm could not live without its tenants. It has no eyes, no mouth, no gut, and no anus. It couldn't eat if it tried.

Of all the extraordinary and improbable arrangements of life on this planet, none is as extravagantly unlikely as the creation of life itself. No one can yet explain how atoms and molecules first came together to make a living cell. Biochemists know that even the simplest molecular machinery in a cell is intricate, and has to be if the cell is to build duplicates of itself—that is, reproduce. How did inanimate molecules first arrange themselves into such complicated machinery? It must have taken more coincidental and fateful meetings than there are in the novels of Charles Dickens.

Yet life sprang up on Earth almost as soon as the planet cooled. Scientists are fairly sure, from the evidence of radioactive dating, that the Earth formed 4.6 billion years ago. The earliest geological traces of life are nearly 4 billion years old. For its first 500 million years, the planet was almost certainly too hot and violent a place for life. That leaves, for the Creation, only a few hundred million years—given the size of the job, almost no time at all. How did such an intricate marvel arise in so short a time? Can evolution really work that fast?

Strange to think that so much of our home planet—nearly three quarters of its surface—was glimpsed for the first time only in the past few decades. Even now, most of this territory remains unvisited and unexplored.

As Jack Baross and John Corliss, veterans of the Galapagos expedition, have noted, there were almost certainly vents beneath the seas of the early Earth, and they probably resembled today's vents. The heat, turbulence, and chemical energy in the vents would have made them a welcome environment for life to evolve. All the right chemical ingredients were present, including carbon, hydrogen, water, methane, and ammonia. No one knows the optimal temperature for a series of chemical reactions leading to life; but the vents provided a wide range—from the magma itself, which is hotter than 1,000 degrees centigrade, to the water beside it, which is some 600 degrees, to water just a little distance from the vents, a temperate 20 degrees.

The hot crust of the Earth, seamed with fissures and cracks, would have been like a vast set of interlinked test tubes, a near-infinite laboratory in which many kinds of reactions might be encouraged to take place, in many sequences, over and over, quickly. Given such a natural laboratory, say Baross and Corliss, rapid chemical evolution is almost inevitable. Here Earth may have taken its first steps toward life.

As parts of the midocean ridge rose above the sea, life would have been carried up to the sunlit surface and the world's first coasts. But in the very beginning, the healthiest place for fledgling life to grow up would have been the sea floor, in the shadow of the ocean. At the surface, in the early days, the Sun's ultraviolet radiation was deadly. Today living things survive in sunlight only because most of the ultraviolet rays are blocked by an umbrella of ozone (a form of oxygen) in the upper atmosphere. Life itself put up that umbrella—oxygen being one of the by-products of photosynthesis. And that took time. Thus life must have begun in the shade—beneath rocks in tidal pools, or in layers of clay, or in seawater a few feet below the surface. And what better shade than the bottom of the sea?

"This, of course, is a wild speculation," oceanographer Roger Revelle recently told a lecture audience, "and I hope you won't tell the newspapers about it. But it seems to me that it's something that may very well turn out to be true, in which case I won't have to eat broken glass."

Cyril Ponnamperuma, an authority on the origins of life, goes (albeit cautiously) one step farther. "The discovery of the hydrothermal vent is important," Ponnamperuma told a reporter from *Mosaic* magazine, "because it may mean that at last science has found a natural habitat like that existing at the beginnings of Earth. Here in the vents life may be arising anew—a kind of neobiogenesis. I believe this ought to be studied in greater detail."

John Corliss, who led the first expedition into the Galapagos Rift, is the most enthusiastic about their possibilities. "In my field," Corliss has said, "and I guess it's true in every kind of science, the great ideas are very, very simple. Plate tectonics! Continental drift! That was simple. And now the hot springs . . . "

The midocean ridge is 46,000 miles long and girdles the entire planet. So far we have visited only a few spots along it. No one even knows how many vents there are, or how many bizarre new species.

As Jack Donelly, a pilot of the *Alvin*, has said, "I like this job because you never know what may be out there, just beyond the lights."

The Climate Puzzle

*Fly into the heavens and contemplate the manifold shapes
of the clouds, the compacted power of the snow, and the source
of the morning dews; then examine the chambers of the hail
and the armouries of the thunderbolts. Let there be nothing
secret from you. . . .* JOHN MILTON

*Overleaf: Sunset clouds above the
Pacific Ocean, viewed from the
volcano Haleakala, on the Hawaiian
island of Maui.*

3 / The Climate Puzzle

We marvel at the exotic creatures that live on the floor of the sea; yet we are bottom-dwellers, too. We all eat, breathe, walk, talk, live, and die submerged in an ocean that is deeper than the seven seas combined. This ocean weighs some 5,000 million million tons, and it presses down upon each of our heads with a force of nearly 15 pounds per square inch. Our bodies are built to take the pressure. In fact, we can't survive without it. If we change depth too fast, our ears pop; and if we journey upward unprotected for too many miles, as some hapless early balloonists and aviators did, we die, like specimens of octopi, polyps, and sea anemones when they are trapped and dredged up from the great deeps that are their home. The air we breathe is a sea without shores; its currents are winds. As one meteorologist has observed, "We do not live on Planet Earth, but in it."

Our planet's transparent sea of gas and water vapor extends up from sea level more than 18,000 miles. It is thin and rarefied where it shades into outer space, and 99 percent of its mass is compressed into the lowest 50 miles. The roilings and churnings we call weather are limited to the bottom five or ten miles. Clouds, made of billions of microscopic water droplets, ice crystals, and bits of dust, are held aloft by the gas around them and rarely rise above that height.

The Earth's continents, mantle, and oceans are all restless, but much of the action is so obscure, so remote from human experience that we have only just perceived it. Only the atmosphere, which encloses the rest of our world, is as fitful and changeable as we are, and on the same time scale, and in the same places. Its moods shape our moods—its showers, mists, sunshine, sleet, snow, storms, floods, droughts, all the pageantry of the revolving seasons, impose themselves upon us in an endless parade, whether we like it or not. For those who live sheltered in cities, marching between office towers we call "skyscrapers," weather and seasons are the only daily reminders that Planet Earth is bigger than we are. (The tallest building in the world, the Sears Tower in Chicago, is less than half a mile high. Clouds sometimes descend that low, but they often float 10 times higher. The top of the sky, of course, shades off gently into the black space that surrounds us, so any talk of a ceiling is arbitrary. But whatever one picks as an outer limit, it will be tens, hundreds, or thousands of times higher than the Sears skyscraper.)

The atmosphere is in some ways the most delicate part of the living machine. Small changes in land and sea affect the air in dramatic ways. A slight drifting of the continents, a minor shifting of ocean currents may bring ice to one land and desert sands to another. The atmosphere's sensitivity to change has led modern investigators to wonder just how stable our climate really is. Climate is weather averaged out over years. Most people tend to assume, unconsciously, that the thousand lurches of weather, all the natural shocks of the seasons—mild winters and bitter winters, drought years and flood years— more or less balance out over time. Our faith in the steadiness of climate is as old as the Book of Genesis:

> While the Earth remaineth,
>   seedtime and harvest, cold and heat,
> summer and winter, and day and night,
>   will not cease.

Yet climate is not as constant and reliable as we like to think. Scientists who study present and past climate have arrived at many visions of rapid global change. They have read the dynamic record in lakebeds, in rocks, in ancient ice at the Earth's poles, in layers of ooze at the bottom of the sea. More and more scientists are devoting themselves to the climate puzzle— trying to deduce what paths Earth's climate has traveled in the past and where it is headed in the near future.

For those who live at the bottom of the sea of air, a change in climate—especially a sudden change—can mean catastrophe. Civilizations rise and fall to the pulsebeats of climate. The Anasazi Indians of the American Southwest and the Incas of Peru died off or moved on when rains failed. The green farms of England and Denmark may have suffered in the 14th century from too *much* rain.

Erik the Red, exiled from Iceland for murder, seems to have discovered Greenland at just the right moment. The climate in that part of the world was unusually warm 1,000 years ago. The name that Erik gave the new territory was not purely a real-estate scam, as one might think from looking at Greenland today. The band of Norsemen who followed Erik there in a fleet of 25 ships and settled on the coasts of the great island had a decent prospect of comfort; they raised the sheep

A vertical ghost town. The ancient Anasazi Indians built these cliff dwellings in Mesa Verde, southern Colorado. Then, in the late 13th century, they abandoned the cliff The Indians may have been driven from their homes by drought.

and cattle they had brought with them and even tried to grow grain. Around 1200, however, the weather began to turn bad, and the settlers became dependent on supplies shipped in from outside. As centuries went by, ice choked the seas, and the colonists were slowly cut off. Sometime in the 15th century, according to historian of climate C.E.P. Brooks, the world lost touch with the colonies entirely, and for hundreds of years, no one knew what had become of them. A modern archaeologist read their fate in an old Greenland churchyard near Cape Farewell. As Brooks writes in his classic book, *Climate Through the Ages*, the bodies were buried

> in soil which is now frozen solid throughout the year, but which, when the bodies were buried, must have thawed for a time in summer, because the coffins, shrouds, and even the bodies were penetrated by the roots of plants. At first the ground thawed to a considerable depth, for the early coffins were buried comparatively deeply. After a time these early remains were permanently frozen in, and later burials lie nearer and nearer the surface. Wood became too precious to use for coffins, and the bodies were wrapped in shrouds and laid directly in the soil. Finally, at least five hundred years ago, the ground became permanently frozen, and has remained in that condition ever since, thus preserving the bodies. The remains show a gradual deterioration in the physique of the colonists; their teeth especially are much worn, indicating that they lived mainly on hard and poorly nourishing vegetable food.

That was the pathetic end of the westernmost outposts of the marauding Vikings. The climate had turned so icy by 1400 that they could hardly bury their dead. Any culture, including our own, can be rudely upset by smaller climatic shifts than these. You change with it or it changes you.

Along the plains of the Indus River, which descends from the Himalayas to the Arabian Sea through eastern Pakistan, stand the half-buried ruins of a lost empire. There, 5,000 years ago, a diligent and enterprising people built 1,000 towns and villages and some of the world's first cities. The ruins of one of their greatest cities lay buried until this century; the hill that covered it over was known as Mohenjo-Daro, "Mound of the Dead."

The world remembers the Egyptians, who built along the Nile, and the Sumerians, who flourished along the Tigris and Euphrates. But these people of the Indus are forgotten, though their civilization lasted 1,000 years, and though their domain was vast, occupying a triangle 1,000 miles on a side. Their civilization's writings, preserved in clay tablets, have never been deciphered, and the very name of the people has been lost. Archaeologists call them Harappans, after another of the Indus cities, Harappa.

The story of the Harappans is as mysterious as that of the Etruscans, who ruled Italy before the ancient Romans and then disappeared. The Harappans domesticated animals, smelted bronze, traded widely in wood and ivory, and carved elaborate sculpture, though not many of their pieces survive. They also grew wheat, barley, dates, melons, and sesame, and they may have been the first people on Earth to grow cotton and weave cotton cloth. The granary in Mohenjo-Daro was huge—the area of its floor is more than 9,000 square feet. It must have been kept well stocked if it helped to sustain the 40,000 or 50,000 inhabitants who lived in the neatly laid-out grid of city blocks.

A ghost city. Once, 4,000 years ago, this was the capital of a great empire, Harrappa, whose people ruled the Indus Valley. But this immense ruin has been deserted for millennia. It is known today only as Mohenjo-Daro, Mound of the Dead. Reid Bryson believes the city was abandoned when monsoon rains failed.

Archaeologists once thought the Harappans had succumbed to Aryan invaders from the North. The Aryans lived for centuries in the mountains by the Caspian Sea and then suddenly went on the move, pushing into Mesopotamia to the east and the Indus Valley to the south. They spoke the Indo-European languages from which English and most other European languages are thought to descend. One of the most famous Aryan leaders was Zoroaster, also called Zarathustra. Their warlike story was an inspiration to Adolf Hitler; Nazi propaganda claimed the German people descended from Aryans.

It is now clear, however, that some 700 years passed between the decline of the Harappans and the arrival of the Aryans. These nomads' surge south did not overthrow the empire; something else did.

Any clues that may be hidden in their clay tablets we cannot read. But Reid Bryson, a climatologist at the University of Wisconsin, thinks he has deciphered the story of the decline and fall of the empire in another sort of clay: the dried-out lakebeds that are scattered across what was once the empire's proud domain.

Many of these lakebeds, and others around the world,

Downtown Bombay. Life in modern India still depends, as it did in the time of the ancient Indus empire, on monsoons. Too little rain, or too much, can mean disaster—or at least inconvenience.

are composed of *strata*, or layers, of sediment; the oldest layers are on the bottom, the most recent ones on top. Annual layers set down by lakes are called *varves*. "Stratified lake sediments," says Bryson, "are like a book in which the history of climate has been written. In such layers, each year, plant pollen, sand, and other detritus have blown in and accumulated. We now know how to look at that assemblage of pollen, charcoal, and sand and interpret it."

Sambhar Lake, in the ancient Harappan domain, is at least 10,800 years old. Today it is a salt lake, but Bryson can tell it was once fresh water by the cattail pollen in its older layers. Pollen remains of plants in each layer of the lakebed tell him how wet the climate was in the year when that layer was deposited. "Between 10,000 and 3,600 years ago," Bryson says, "rainfall was at least three times what it is now. Then, about 3,600 years ago, again judging by the pollen record, plants began changing from those characteristic of fresh water to those that grow around salt water. And then there's no lake at all—the lake dried up, and there's barren sand."

"That period lasted about 700 years and ended some 2,900 years ago," says Bryson. "That is a very long drought." All the vegetation in the region disappeared. Rainfall afterward increased, but never returned to the level it had reached in the heyday of the Harappans. Today Sambhar Lake is salt again. The former Harappan domain, which stretches across more than a quarter million miles of modern India and Pakistan, is now mostly desert. Much of Mohenjo-Daro, Mound of the Dead, is covered by centuries of sand dunes. It is visited only by an occasional archaeological field party and a few tourists.

Bryson believes drought caused the decline and fall of the Harappan empire. "The Harappan people had developed sophisticated methods of handling water in drainage and waterways, but in most of their area, they didn't develop agriculture based on irrigation," he says. "So they were totally dependent upon the monsoon rains. When, about 3,600 years ago, those monsoon rains failed and a long drought began, their agriculture, the economic base of their culture, disappeared."

There are other theories of the fall of the Harappan empire; one of them invokes earthquakes and repeated floods rather than drought. But Bryson's argument is plausible, in part because India today is terribly dependent on its summer rains, which are brought by the monsoon wind when it blows in from the South, laden with moisture from the Indian Ocean. The country gets much of its water in these rains. In modern times, when the monsoon has missed several years in a row, hundreds of thousands of Indians have died in the drought and famines that followed.

It is certain, says Bryson, that the Harappan lands dried up, the soil blew off with the winds, the floodplains became desert. When the Aryans came nearly 1,000 years later, they found ghost cities like Mohenjo-Daro already half lost in the dunes. The invaders built their villages elsewhere, closer to the shrunken streams. The name of that city and the name of the people who built it were lost. "These mute ruins are testimony to what can happen when climate changes," Bryson says. "It changed, and it changed rapidly, and it stayed changed for a long time. We must learn the lessons of climatic history, for the climate will surely change again."

THE WEATHER MACHINE

The lessons of climatic history begin with weather; individual weather events are the letters of the alphabet in which climate is written. We may not be used to thinking in terms of climatic change, but we are very used to variable weather.

One world's record for a quick weather change is held by Spearfish, South Dakota. At 7:30 on the morning of January 22, 1943, the temperature was −4 degrees Fahrenheit. Two minutes later, it was 45 degrees. Moments like that ensure that an interest in weather will always be our greatest global common denominator. Weather is the most popular topic of conversation when neighbors lean over hedges. Each year the American public places nearly 1 billion telephone calls to Dial-a-Forecast numbers—spending $100 million a year, a dime or two at a time, to decide whether or not to carry an umbrella. Americans spend another $100 million a year buying special radios to receive the continuous weather broadcasts of the National Oceanographic and Atmospheric Administration. Commercial television spends $500 million a year producing its weather reports—perhaps the best-watched part of the news. The federal government budgets about $400 million a year for the National Weather Service and its various branches, including pure research programs set up to improve our basic understanding of weather and climate.

Early weather forecasts were more art than science. Failures were more or less politely forgotten, and successes were enshrined in proverbs. In Brazil: "When donkeys walk crabwise, rain is on its way." In India: "As a dry cow bellows most, so a rainless cloud thunders most." In Japan: "When spiders weave their web by noon, fine weather is coming soon," and "When no clouds mask the Milky Way, it will be fine for a week and a day." In Iran: "Sheep stamp and butt before a storm." In Britain: "A yellow glare as the sun doth set foretells a night both windy and wet." In Arizona: "When the Apache scalplocks on the wall of the kiva feel damp, the rains will come."

A summer storm strikes Lake Powell, Arizona.

Such proverbs rely on correspondences and coincidences—spiders and sunshine. Modern scientists who study weather try to look deeper. They seek to understand the logic of cause and effect that governs the motions of the atmosphere. Though these motions are infinitely complex, they conform to the same physical laws that govern the rest of the universe, from the orbits of planets to the fall of apples from trees. The better we understand the atmosphere, the better our forecasting skills have become. That these skills are still notoriously inadequate is a measure of the atmosphere's complexity.

The ocean of air is like the kind of glass paperweight in which a miniature carved Eskimo plods across snow toward his igloo. Turn the paperweight over, right it again, and a blizzard of white powder swirls through the fluid in the glass and settles to the bottom.

The atmosphere churns like the snow in the paperweight, and the energy that stirs it comes from the Sun. Sunlight heats the planet's rocks, forests, fields, and seas, which then radiate some of this heat upward, warming the air from below. Just as hot air rises from an asphalt road in summer, or from a radiator in winter, air rises day and night from the sun-warmed Earth. Cooler air sinks to take its place, is heated, and rises. At night, the flickering and wavering of rising and falling air is made visible to us below in the twinkling of stars.

Because the Earth is round, the Sun's rays do not hit it

evenly. Sunlight beats straight down upon the equator, but strikes only low and glancingly at the poles. As a result, the belts of middle latitudes, the Tropic of Cancer and the Tropic of Capricorn (immortalized by salacious novels), soak up heat from the Sun faster than they radiate heat to the air, so they are warm. The poles radiate away energy more rapidly than it comes in, so they are cold.

The whole business of the atmosphere is, in effect, to strive tirelessly to cool the equator and warm the poles. Though the patterns of its circulation are highly complex, its motion is driven, at bottom, by the same fundamental process of convection that stirs the seas in their beds and sets continents wandering across the surface of the Earth. The trade winds are just one small part of the atmosphere's ceaseless efforts to bring the Earth's temperature into balance. Thus, windmills and tall ships are solar-powered: the Sun's uneven heating of the Earth drives the winds that fill their vanes and sails.

The lowest layer of the atmosphere, which convection perpetually mixes and overturns, is called the *troposphere* (the Greek word *tropos* means a turning). This is the weather sphere, the home of clouds and storms. Its ceiling is the *tropopause*. Above it is the *stratosphere*, a layer of air too high above the ground to be stirred directly by the warming of the Earth's surface. The stratosphere floats upon the troposphere with surprisingly little mixing, like layers of water in the ocean.

Hurricane Elena, seen from the Space Shuttle. One of the costliest hurricanes on record, Elena was fickle and unpredictable. At first, as it whirled in the Gulf of Mexico, the storm seemed about to hit New Orleans. Then it veered eastward, heading toward the Florida peninsula. Many thousands of Floridians evacuated their homes along the coast. But the hurricane stalled, retreated, changed course again, and made straight for the coast of Mississippi. Elena finally struck near Biloxi, Miss., on Labor Day, 1985, just after dawn. Property damage: more than half a billion dollars.

All air currents, like all ocean currents, are twisted by the spinning of the Earth, the Coriolis effect. This effect creates motion in the atmosphere as intricate as the great eddies and gyres in the sea. By giving a twist to every wind, the Coriolis effect creates the tight-whorled spinning winds, outlined in cloud, so prominent in weather satellite photographs. Eddies rotate clockwise in the southern hemisphere, counterclockwise in the northern. These cyclones (from the Greek *kykloein*, to circle around, whirl), moving slowly across the face of the planet, are often as large as 600 miles across. They are our biggest storms. They, too, help (on average) to transport heat from the equator toward the poles.

The equator is more than an imaginary line, an invention of cartographers. It divides the two hemispheres of air rather neatly (although not nearly as neatly, of course, at the line looks on a map). Notes atmospheric chemist James Lovelock, "Air from the north and south does not freely mix, as any observer traveling on a ship through tropical regions will readily perceive from the difference in clarity of the skies between the clean southern and the relatively dirty northern hemispheres."

In the first part of this century, the Norwegian meteorologist Vilhelm Bjerknes, working with his son Jacob and numerous students, studied the boundaries where cold and warm masses of air collide. Bjerknes did much of his research during the First World War, and he adapted the jargon of trench warfare. A mass of air sweeping down from the North Pole was a *cold front*. It "attacked" the mass of warm air to the south, which tried to penetrate its flanks and advance northward. Most storms, like most battles, Bjerknes observed, occur at the fronts. He charted fronts the way generals map battle zones, and he tried to forecast weather from the charts. Bjerknes saw that what he called "the rational solution of forecasting problems" required two things: First, one had to acquire a detailed knowledge of what the global atmosphere was doing; and second, one needed "a sufficiently accurate knowledge of the laws according to which one state of the atmosphere develops from another."

Early on, Bjerknes's philosophy inspired an imaginative British meteorologist, Lewis F. Richardson, to try to formulate the physical laws that govern all atmospheric motions— winds, fronts, cloudy eddies—in precise mathematical equations. If he could only take today's weather, Richardson thought, and translate it into the abstractions of numerical data, perhaps he could arrive at tomorrow's forecast by solving equations.

As a test, Richardson tried to predict the weather for a single spot on Earth. He chose Hamburg, Germany. In two hectic years, while working as an ambulance driver in World War I, poor Richardson was able to complete only one solitary six-hour forecast. "His manuscript was lost under a heap of coal during the Battle of Champagne in April 1917 but was recovered several months later," writes meteorologist Warren Washington. "His crude, hand-calculated forecast was hopelessly inaccurate and even discouraged meteorologists from pursuing his numerical approach."

Richardson kept trying. But the equations he used to describe the atmosphere took so long to solve that, no matter how he scrambled, the weather always advanced much faster than his arithmetic. He was in the position of the man who set out to write his autobiography and spent a year describing his first minute on Earth. At that rate he could never hope to catch up to himself. Richardson knew that, working alone, he would never get ahead of the weather. In those years there was still no thought of electronic calculators. Richardson dreamed instead of a "forecast factory" full of human mathematicians whom he called "computers."

> Imagine a large hall like a theatre, except that the circles and galleries go right round through the space usually occupied by the stage. The walls of this chamber are painted to form a map of the globe . . . . A myriad of computers are at work upon the weather of the part of the map where each sits, but each computer attends only to one equation or part of an equation . . . . From the floor of the pit a tall pillar rises to half the height of the hall. It carries a large pulpit on its top. In this sits the man in charge of the whole theatre; he is surrounded by several assistants and messengers. One of his duties is to maintain a uniform speed of progress in all parts of the globe. In this respect he is like the conductor of an orchestra in which the instruments are slide-rules and calculating machines. But instead of waving a baton he turns a beam of rosy light upon any region that is running ahead of the rest, and a beam of blue light upon those who are behindhand . . . .
>
> Outside are playing fields, houses, mountains and lakes, for it was thought that those who compute the weather should breathe of it freely.

Two decades after Richardson published this forecasting fantasy in his book *Weather Prediction by Numerical Process*, there was another world war. Out of it came the first modern computers: Colossus, in Britain, and ENIAC (Electronic Numerical Integrator And Computer) in the United States. Colossus was built to help crack Nazi secret codes. ENIAC was sponsored by the military in hopes of improving weather forecasts, which are of great strategic importance in wartime. Mathematician and philosopher John Von Neumann, at Princeton, became a prophet of ENIAC's peacetime potential. ENIAC (viewed from today's vantage point) was an ungainly dinosaur of a machine, with 17,468 vacuum tubes whose burning kept the room in which it was housed, and kept its teams of attendants, swelteringly hot. But Von Neumann knew the robot computer was a giant step toward Richardson's "forecast factory." With the late Jules Charney, Von Neumann managed to simplify the kinds of equations that Richardson had struggled with. Von Neumann and Charney fed ENIAC their new, streamlined equations. The results were primitive, but for the first time people had gotten ahead of the weather.

ENIAC, the world's first digital computer, was built during World War II in Princeton, New Jersey.

Today Bjerknes's two conditions for "rational forecasting" are met with the help of two kinds of machines. Satellites provide an instantaneous overview of the planet's cloud cover, and meteorologists can read into them a great deal about wind patterns and more. Supercomputers help organize and synthesize these data and take giant steps toward a forecast. In the United States, national forecasts are prepared in Camp Springs, Maryland, by the National Meteorological Center's new supercomputer, the Cyber 205A. It was built by Control Data Corporation for $15,997,906.

A TWIN EARTH

    Eighty million bits of weather data are fed the Cyber 205A each day from stations and satellites around the world—temperature, pressure, moisture, wind speed, and more. The supercomputer puts all that global data into a kind of three-dimensional map of the global atmosphere. To do so, it parti-

JAWS AND CLAWS

In 1975, an Eastern B-727 crashed on the runway of John F. Kennedy International Airport, in New York City, killing 112 people. In 1982, a Pan American World Airways Boeing 727 crashed as it took off from New Orleans. One hundred fifty-three people died. Both planes had run into sudden and peculiar shifts and reversals in the winds—called *wind shear.* So near the ground, the pilots had no time to recover. By 1985, when a Delta Airlines wide-body jet crashed as it tried to land at Dallas-Fort Worth Airport, killing 133 people, wind shear was immediately suspected as the cause of the accident. It had become clear that this quirk of weather is one of the worst hazards in modern aviation.

Windshear often begins high in the sky. A shaft of rain or snow falls from a heavy cloud. If there is hot, dry air just beneath the cloud—desert air, perhaps—the precipitation evaporates long before reaching the ground. Such abortive showers are called *virga*, from the Latin for a twig, or a streak in the heavens. Occasionally, virga is visible from the ground as a dark, slender shaft beneath a cloud.

This shaft of rain or snow drags air downward with it. The falling air, which is cool and damp, meets the warmer, dry air beneath the cloud. As its moisture evaporates, the falling air continues to cool, and it plummets faster and faster toward earth. It reaches the ground traveling at speeds as great as 150 miles per hour—a *microburst.*

Just as the stream from a garden hose, squirting straight down, splashes out in all directions when it hits the ground, so does the column of cold air. But the splash, since it is made only of air, is invisible. When a pilot takes off a runway, he has no way to know he is flying into one of these splashes. First he hits a strong, sudden headwind as the plane meets the outer edge of the splash. That's fine—pilots *try* to take off into a headwind, since the wind against their wings gives them extra lift. But in the center of the splash, the downdraft itself strikes the plane, shoving it downward. Then, just as suddenly, as the plane passes into the far side of the splash (which takes only a second) the pilot loses his headwind, and has a tailwind just as strong. Immediately the plane starts to lose lift, and altitude. If it is close to the ground, it may crash.

Meteorologists have made a study of microbursts at Denver's Stapleton International Airport, in Boulder, Colorado. During the Joint Airport Weather Studies Project (JAWS), in the summer of 1982, they scanned the air above the airport with *Doppler radar.* Traditional radar sends out a blip of high-pitched sound and "sees" objects by the echoes (the technique by which oceanographers have mapped much of the sea floor). Doppler radar analyzes the echoes to glean more information: it can tell whether the object is moving toward or away from the radar, and how fast.

Watching video monitors, the scientists at Stapleton Airport could see what pilots and air traffic controllers could not—the play of winds above the airport. The winds were displayed in contrasting colors, and the faster the winds were moving, the brighter the hues. Dangerous splashes of air showed up clearly.

In the summer of 1984, the scientists were back at the airport with a second experimental program, Classify, Locate, Avoid Windshear (CLAWS). By now it was clear that microbursts are much more common around Stapleton than anyone had suspected. "We had an enormous number of events," says meteorologist Jim Wilson. "In the 45 days of the experiment, there were major windshifts on 30 days, and on 20 of those days we had microbursts."

This was weather forecasting at its most urgent and immediate—more like "nowcasting." Time and again, the meteorologists were able to warn air traffic controllers of a dangerous microburst just minutes before a take-off. The scientists saved planes from running the gauntlet of the winds.

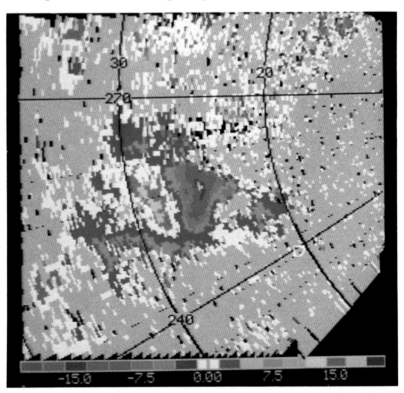

With Doppler radar, we can watch the invisible: the collisions of winds. This Doppler radar image shows dangerous microburst windshear at Denver's Stapleton International Airport, recorded during the Joint Airport Weather Studies Project (JAWS), on July 14, 1982. Blues, greens, and purples represent winds flowing toward the radar. Browns, oranges, and reds are flowing away from the radar. An airplane flying in a direction away from the radar would have encountered a 19-meter-per-second headwind, then a downdraft (which shows up in this image as white), then a 7.5-meter-per-second tailwind. If the plane was taking off, or landing, it might have crashed. This image is a zero-degree elevation scan: that is, it shows the winds at ground level, right on the runway.

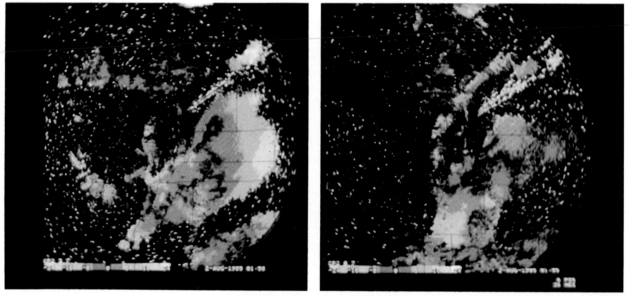

This is the view from the weather station of the future. In Boulder, Colorado, teams of forecasters are participating in a state-of-the-art, high-tech project called PROFS (Program for Regional Observing and Forecasting Services). At PROFS, a large network of robot weather monitors phone in reports every few minutes to a central computer. The computer digests this information, along with regional and national data from weather satellites. Sitting at computer consoles, weather forecasters can choose from a large menu of vivid displays of the weather world around them.

tions the atmosphere into neat parcels of air, imaginary boxes whose bases are roughly the size of the state of Kansas. Within each box, all the latest data for that piece of the atmosphere are plotted in and averaged out. If it is cool at the top of the parcel of air and sizzling at the bottom, the box in the computer becomes uniformly tepid. The model uses more than a dozen layers of these parcels, like invisible bricks, to build an up-to-the-minute model of the state of the global atmosphere.

Having organized and simplified the day's weather data, the computer is programmed to apply the laws of physics and figure out how each parcel of air is likely to affect its neighbors. Five equations are sufficient to describe these basic laws (though more equations usually are added as refinements). These five equations include Sir Isaac Newton's laws of motion, the third of which is: For every action there is an equal and opposite reaction. This is a fateful formulation, because *reactions* are what make the atmosphere's evolution complicated. Each motion in the atmosphere caroms and rebounds against others, like waves from one splash mingling with ripples of others in a great pond. The equations themselves are elegantly simple: All five can be written on the back of a postcard. But the sea of motion they describe is infinitely complex.

With so much to juggle, the supercomputer cannot figure out an entire day's weather at one time. Instead, it calculates just 10 minutes ahead and makes a 10-minute forecast. Then it takes the new atmospheric patterns from its forecast and calculates ahead another 10 minutes. In an hour or so it has completed a three-day forecast—a total of 150 billion arith-

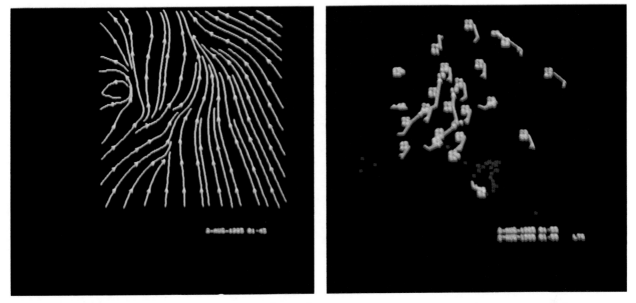

metic operations. It prints out a picture of weather patterns as they may look in three days. Meteorologists in Camp Springs relay these predictions to local weather forecasters around the country. In effect, there is a sort of model globe spinning within the supercomputer, a twin Earth, full of rains, snows, storms, and hurricanes.

Several supercomputers around the world are engaged in such daily forecasts: The best is the Cray-XMP at the European Centre for Medium Range Forecasts, in Reading, England. Those who run each supercomputer try to make their model, their twin Earth, as much like the real atmosphere as possible, and they try to program it with close approximations of the real Earth's laws of behavior. If they can design something close to an identical twin to the Earth's true atmosphere, then presumably it will proceed on a similar course as the real Earth's weather—at least for a run of a day or two.

So far, all supercomputers enjoy mixed results. They make decent one-day predictions, from which local weather stations get their local forecasts. They generate modestly successful three-day forecasts of national precipitation patterns. Coarse, six-day predictions of worldwide wind-flow patterns have been achieved, but the predictions are so general and abstract that they are of little practical use. When the computer is pushed beyond these limits, the errors with which the machine began its forecast multiply so wildly that they destroy all semblance of reality. The twins are just not identical enough.

Clearly, if the finest detail the computer can handle is a box of air the size of the state of Kansas, then small winds

Here, a forecaster zeroes in on an area 150 kilometers in diameter in northeastern Colorado. Screen 1 shows wind velocity near the surface, as seen by a Doppler radar. Blues and greens indicate winds coming toward the radar; yellows, browns, and reds are winds away from the radar. Screen 2 covers the same territory as Screen 1, but shows winds at mid-levels in the atmosphere. In Screen 3, the computer offers a graphic sketch of this wind flow. The wind is blowing in the direction of the arrows. The closer together the lines, the faster the wind. Screen 4 shows the same area, but it includes, in symbolic form, the latest observations of 22 automated monitors. Each N or P indicates a lightning stroke that hit the ground in the previous five minutes.

and eddies, and even large clouds and thunderstorms, are too small to show up. But these are the sorts of local details that matter to the man and woman on the street. Those who work with these *General Circulation Models* often wish they could increase resolution by doubling, tripling, or quadrupling the number of boxes of air in the twin Earth. With smaller boxes, the computer could work in finer details, like an artist who switches to a smaller brush. Right now, however, doubling or tripling the number of boxes would bog down even the best and brightest supercomputer. So meteorologists wait impatiently for each new advance in Silicon Valley.

It sometimes seems odd that we have mapped out the elliptical orbits of the nine planets around the Sun and guessed the paths of stars billions of light-years away, yet we still cannot predict the precise motions of the currents in our own sea of air. The reason for the difficulty is that there are more turbulent gestures even in a little glass paperweight than there are in all the orbits of the solar system put together. The slightest disturbance in the air can have large and unpredictable effects. It is conceivable, meteorologist Edward Lorenz of the Massachusetts Institute of Technology has suggested, that the flap of a butterfly's wings in Brazil can start a tornado in Texas. Even if we could build a twin Earth that was like the real Earth right down to that last butterfly, but if the two butterflies flapped their wings at different moments, Lorenz has proven mathematically that the paths of the twins would soon diverge. There would be almost no resemblance between them in a month's time. Of course, the best twin Earth in today's supercomputer isn't nearly detailed enough to include a butterfly. So errors swamp it early, sometimes after only hours.

In geology, the greatest lesson is *time*—that in the vast backward and abysm of time, enormous works can be achieved by small, humble, and patient means. In meteorology, the greatest lesson is *feedback*—the unimaginable complexity that results from the elements of air, earth, and water interacting, their influences feeding back upon each other. When the zephyr stirred by a butterfly's wing can be magnified by feedback into a wind, or even a tornado, prediction will always be difficult.

The Geophysical Fluid Dynamics Laboratory (GFDL), in Princeton, New Jersey, is part of the National Oceanic and Atmospheric Administration. Workers at GFDL use two supercomputers to try to refine the Global Circulation Model and teach it to cope better with detail and with the innumerable feedbacks that bedevil the atmosphere. Their Cyber 205s are just down the street from where Von Neumann and his colleague Jules Charney performed their first primitive weather forecasts with ENIAC.

This is the peak of Mount Rainier, in Washington, capped with clouds, and churning the wind. Multiply this peak by a thousand, and you have a mountain range. A range can alter wind and weather over a large part of the face of the Earth.

Theoretical meteorologist Raymond Pierrehumbert is trying to find equations that will describe more accurately the effects of mountain ranges on oceans of air. That is how far we are from describing the effects of butterflies. In the spring of 1982, feeling the need to get a taste of mountain wind (as Lewis F. Richardson said, "those who compute the weather should breathe of it freely"), he joined a field project called ALPEX (Alpine Experiment). He found himself flying through the agitated air of the Alps in a Lockheed Electra, an old passenger service plane. The Electra weathered the world's worst turbulence, and Pierrehumbert, after months struggling to understand winds as numbers on paper, reveled in the real thing.

Pierrehumbert made some of his measurements high above the little Yugoslavian walled town of Split, in the Denaric Alps, where the Roman emperor Diocletian built a palace. Split is set on a steep slope leading down to the Adriatic Sea. Waterfalls of wind rush down the slopes and through the town. The people of Split call this wind the Bora. It is cousin to the fierce Foehn wind in Bavaria, and the Chinook, which spills down the eastern slopes of the Rocky Mountains. The Bora tears through Split at 100 miles an hour when it is really blowing, and the townspeople have had to set ropes along the sidewalks as handrails.

Before ALPEX, the Bora had been measured only on the ground, by meteorologists with their coattails flapping. Pierrehumbert helped make some of the first upper-air observations of the Bora. Now, back in Princeton, using the supercomputers' twin Earth, he is studying larger-scale distortions that the Alps cause, eddies many hundreds of miles across that whirl away downwind. He is also trying to find equations to describe the jagged shapes of the peaks.

"You are continually going back and forth between the real world and the image of the real world in the mathematical equations," says Pierrehumbert. "That's what makes the field both so difficult and so interesting: You need a feeling for the weather *and* the mathematics.

"I'm not as much a weather nut as some. I don't make weather observations at home, or that sort of thing. There's a forecasting game here at the laboratory, where people look at weather maps and place bets. I haven't ever tried doing that.

"Still, understanding something is a little like making it your own. It brings a feeling of satisfaction. Sometimes I feel like I've conquered a little corner of the universe. It's not the sort of thing that happens to you every day; but once in a while, you look at some phenomenon—the way clouds form over a mountain, or the Bora when it's really blowing—and you really understand it. And that gives you a good feeling—a grasp of some of the forms of the world."

CLIMATE BY PROXY

Those who study climate wish they had centuries of weather reports on file. But detailed and accurate weather records have been kept only for the past few decades, and then only for parts of the globe. This is probably too short a time in which to discern trends. To see where our climate is tending, and make climate forecasts for the near future, scientists try to extend the record backward through detective work. All sorts of antique odds and ends are made to testify about past climate. These odd clues are called *proxies*. They are first used not for forecasting but for hindcasting.

One example of hindcasting is the way modern archaeologists interpret the melancholy Norse graveyard near Cape Farewell. The graves are proxies that tell a story of progressive climatic decline. Bryson's varved lakes near the Mound of the Dead are another kind of proxy.

Hindcasting can also be a more cheerful business. Once, for instance, art critics believed the 17th-century Dutch masters Rembrandt van Rijn, Frans Hals, and Jan Vermeer had used poetic license in painting their famous winter landscapes, which feature spectacular snowdrifts, frozen canals, and skaters everywhere. But Huug van den Dool, of the Royal Netherlands Meteorological Institute in De Bilt, has studied the old canal records. The canals were built in the early 17th century to link the Netherlands' biggest cities, and records of barge trips were kept beginning in 1633. It seems that during many winters in those days, the canals really were frozen and impassable, sometimes for as long as three months. Hans Brinker had plenty of time to practice for the Silver Skates. There were 17 extremely

cold winters in the 17th century; in our century there have so far been only five. The great painters did not lie.

The general chilliness of that century in Europe is corroborated by another sort of proxy. For the past 500 years, French winemakers have kept detailed books describing the quality of each grape harvest. The grape-growing season extends from early spring to early fall. If it is warm and sunny, grapes ripen fast; if it is cold and cloudy, the harvest is late and poor. These facts are pregnant with meaning in both climatology and gastronomy. A noted French historian of climate, Emmanuel LeRoy Ladurie, has spent years visiting winemasters in their cellars and poring through their old record books. Ladurie has found that the years from 1617 to 1650 were abnormally cold, just as they were in Holland. For the Grand Cru wineries of Bordeaux, those were bad years.

Judging by this and other evidence, a long, uneven cold spell seems to have visited much of Europe in the 17th century, and for some decades before and after. This period has been called the *Little Ice Age*. The Little Ice Age also troubled North America, where a record of severe winters has been discerned in old tree rings, and also in history books (during the Revolutionary War, for instance, cast-iron cannons were trundled across the ice of Long Island Sound). It may have been the long, slow onset of the Little Ice Age that did in the Norse colonists in Greenland. No one knows what caused this cold

The Dutch master Jan-Abrahamsz Beerstraten painted "The Village of Nieukoop in Winter" in the mid-17th century. Today, the canals of Holland rarely freeze over, but in Beerstraten's time—the period we now call the Little Ice Age— winters were severe.

spell, but it happens to have coincided with an unusual period in the life of the Sun, during which astronomers remarked on the unusual scarcity of sunspots. Since warmth in the atmosphere comes ultimately from the Sun's rays, some scientists have posited a connection between the century of ice and the blank face of the Sun. According to some estimates, there is a 10 to 30 percent chance of another Little Ice Age within the next century.

Go back farther in time and there are no canal records to guide us, no ruins to scan for clues. Before the dawn of the human animal, there is only the record of the Earth itself and the impressions made upon it by the comings and goings of early life. Yet climatologists have found many respectable proxies for climate before the coming of humankind. "Nature has recorded an awful lot of its own history," says Reid Bryson. "What we have to be smart enough to do is learn the language in which it was recorded."

New Zealand's big North Island is riddled with limestone caves from one end to the other. Geologists clambering in these caves, their miners' headlamps lighting their way, have discovered remarkable climate records in the limestone. *Stalactites*, the stone icicles that hang from cavern ceilings, and *stalagmites*, the pillars that grow up from the floor below, are built drop by drop by rainwater. Water is forever seeping through the limestone ceiling of the cave, dripping down each stalactite like beads of wax on a candlestick, and evaporating. Each drop leaves a slight residue of limestone at the bottom tip of the stalactite and at the top of the stalagmite below. The stone rods grow in patterns as neat as the rings of a tree or the varves of a lake.

All rainwater comes originally from the sea, and the certain subtleties of the sea's composition change slowly with time. Notably, seawater's ratio of two isotopes, O_{18} and O_{16}, varies in ways that experts can use to infer something of the climate in which the stalactites and stalagmites grew. The ratio of the isotopes is preserved in the limestone of the caverns, and the order of its change is preserved in the neat layers of the cavern decorations. Slicing open a stalagmite and analyzing the isotopes in its layers of limestone, one can construct a rough climatic history of a large part of the world outside the cave.

New Zealand stalagmites suggest to geologist Chris Hendy that temperatures in this part of the southern hemisphere were chilly in the 17th century. The match in the data is remarkable, given that Europe and New Zealand are at opposite ends of the Earth and that the kinds of proxies that have been assembled as evidence are so different. Hendy's find feeds curiosity about the cause of the Little Ice Age because it suggests that the chill was, if not global, at least widespread.

A diary of the Earth, hidden in New Zealand's Waipuna Cave. These stalactites and stalagmites contain a history of the world's climate.

Hendy has sliced through one granddaddy stalactite he found in a cave on the western shore of North Island. "When we cut through it," he says, "we found that we had a record of 100,000 years, with the last 25,000 years compressed into the last three centimeters. The stalactite was still growing at the time; beads of water were still dripping down it. So the record extended right to the present day. This gave us a very good chance to look at major climatic changes for all of New Zealand—and for the whole world, in fact."

Such long natural histories, volume upon volume of ancient weather journals, record events that make the Little Ice Age seem balmy.

THE COMING OF THE ICE

Toward the end of the 18th century, the Scottish genius James Hutton visited the Swiss Alps. There he was puzzled to see, lying in valleys and perched on slopes, boulders that did not

Louis Agassiz, the outspoken Swiss naturalist. After the great ice age controversy of his youth, he immigrated to the United States and taught biology at Harvard University. His lectures were charming and often hypnotically powerful. He became the most celebrated scientist of his time in America.

Louis Agassiz published this study of the Glacier de Viesch, in Switzerland, in 1840. He was struggling to convince his colleagues that glaciers once ruled the world, in a great ice age.

seem to belong—since they did not match the native rock of the mountains around them.

Hutton hiked to the margins of *glaciers* in the heights of the Alps—great seas of ice, in some places thousands of feet thick. Glaciers can last almost as long as the lofty mountain peaks on which they lie; the ice melts a little each summer but is replenished by fresh snows each winter. Hutton noticed boulders embedded in the ice of some glaciers, and more boulders lying on the slopes just below them, rock and rubble that the ice had apparently picked up from the ground as it grew, and then dropped again when it shrank. Hutton put two and two together. Some of these Swiss glaciers, he decided, must once have flowed down from their eminences and filled more than a few Swiss valleys. The glaciers must have plucked up thousands of boulders as they traveled forward and then dropped their loads when they receded, the way a tide strews pebbles on a beach—hence the misfit boulders lying in the valleys, far from any modern glacier.

This insight, like many of Hutton's finest, was unpopular in his lifetime. Misfit boulders, or *erratic blocks*, had long been considered to be irrefutable evidence of Noah's Flood. They were supposed to have been tumbled up hills and down dales by the churning biblical waters. In those days, many people felt as if a dark crack were slowly widening between the world as explained by science and the world as revealed in Holy Writ. Any hypothesis that threatened to widen the crack was frightening. A theory that both geologists and theologians could respect was accepted with gratitude and relief. So the Flood theory prevailed, and Hutton's was ignored.

Over several decades, a long line of shrewd and independent thinkers arrived at the same conclusion as Hutton—including a Swiss minister, a German professor of natural science, a chamois-hunter, a highway and bridge engineer, a woodcutter, and the director of a salt mine. They noticed the misfit boulders, and they observed valley bedrock that had been strangely scoured and polished, as if a rude and massive carpenter's plane had been run over it, back and forth, many times. This, too, seemed the work of glaciers rather than floods.

But these clever observers convinced almost no one. They lacked the prominence, or the force of personality, to seize the world by the lapels and force people to *look*.

On July 24, 1837, a brilliant Swiss naturalist, Louis Agassiz, then only 30 years old, delivered the opening address at a meeting of the Swiss Society of Natural Sciences in the town of Neuchâtel. Some of the most distinguished geologists in Europe were present. Agassiz welcomed them all graciously to Neuchâtel; then he made a surprise announcement. He had

come to the conclusion, after long talks and walks with one Jean Charpentier (the director of the salt mine), that it was not Noah's Flood that had rolled the erratic blocks, but mountain glaciers. The valley in which they stood, Agassiz declared boldly, had once been buried in ice a mile thick. Agassiz went even further. Glaciers had once descended from the mountains and spread across most of Europe, killing everything in their path.

The august members of the society were furious with their young president for ambushing them like this, and with such a wild idea. The meeting almost broke up. But with infinite pains, Agassiz persuaded them to follow him outdoors and see the evidence for themselves. Two days later, early in the morning, the assembled scientists rode out of town in a procession of horse-drawn carriages and wound their clattering way into the Swiss countryside. Two of the world's most famous geologists, Leopold von Buch and Jean Baptiste Elie de Beaumont, rode with Agassiz in the lead carriage, which was pulled by four white horses. The silence in the carriage was glacial. In his authoritative history *Ice Ages: Solving the Mystery*, climatologist John Imbrie quotes one observer who joined Agassiz's little expedition.

> In general, I was convinced by my short acquaintance with the leading scientists of the party that a great amount of jealousy and egoism existed between them. Elie de Beaumont was, during the entire trip, as cold as ice. Leopold von Buch was walking straight ahead, eyes on the ground, mumbling against an Englishman who was talking to Elie de Beaumont on the Pyrenees while we were in the Jura, and complaining rather offensively about the stupid remarks made by some amateurs who had joined the group. Agassiz, who was probably still bitter about the sharp criticisms made by von Buch of his glacial hypotheses, left the group immediately after departure and was walking a quarter of a league ahead all by himself. . . .

This expedition won Agassiz a few converts; and after a long, hard, international campaign, the young scientist carried his point. Virtually every student of the Earth came to accept that glaciers do move and that there have been times when ice covered a significant portion of the planet—as much as 11 million square miles. That is much more ice than there was on Earth in the 17th century, or at any other time in human history.

Agassiz called such a monstrously wintry period an *Eizeit*, an *ice age*. He set up a research station beside the Unteraar Glacier, southeast of Bern, that became famous all over Europe and

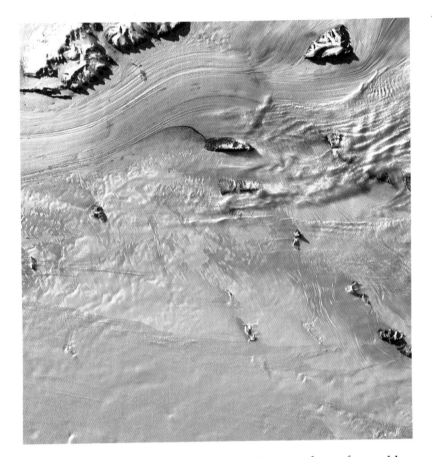

The Lambert Glacier is part of the East Antarctic ice sheet, which is the largest in the world. The glacier flows into the Amery Ice Shelf. This satellite image covers an area of about 24,300 kilometers.

America. It was a rude stone house whose roof was formed by the jutting overhang of a gigantic erratic block. From this base camp, which he called the Hôtel des Neuchâtelois, he carried out extensive studies of the 1,000-foot-thick Unteraar Glacier and established the modern science of *glaciology*.

As Agassiz helped to show, glaciers form when mountain snows pile up about 100 feet thick. Snow crystals at the bottom are packed and compressed together into solid ice. Over the years, as more and more snow piles on, a thick and solid sea of ice forms. It grows so massive that it can outlast human generations and seems to those who live beneath it virtually a part of the mountain. In the blue ice of one of their largest glaciers, the Swiss have carved long passageways with branching corridors, vaulted chambers, and a souvenir shop at one end. Tourists pay to wander through.

Despite their solidity, glaciers constantly ooze and flow under their own weight, the way a blob of Silly Putty spreads out if left on a tabletop. Usually the motion is only a few inches, or feet, a winter. Occasionally, however, a glacier has been known to surge. On January 10, 1962, a glacier on Peru's Mount Huascarán surged, and the lowest part of the ice broke off and avalanched into the valley below, killing 4,000 people in nine villages. More recently, on June 9, 1983, the lower part of the Variegated Glacier, in Alaska, was clocked moving 210 feet a day. A calamity like this was recorded by 17th-century tax collectors during the Little Ice Age, who saw it strictly in terms of the bottom line. According to the records of the Chamber of Accounts of Savoy for May 2, 1605, "In the villages of La Roziere and Argentier seven houses were covered by glaciers, whose ravages continue and progress from one day to the next. . . . Because of all this ruin the tithe was greatly reduced."

A mountain glacier behaves like a reverse thermometer. It grows in the cold and contracts in the heat. If the climate changes, a glacier may grow miles longer, extending down its mountain and into the valley below. When the climate changes back, the glacier melts and retracts. During thousands of years of this kind of back-and-forth, a glacier wears the walls of the valley into a smooth, deep, rounded "U." Such U-shaped valleys are found in many of the world's mountain ranges, and they are in a sense giant proxies. They speak of variability—of climates that have changed over and over, and sent the great ice back and forth many times, like a carpenter's round-bottomed file.

If the climate stays generally cold year after year, ice sheets may extend far down the mountains, and ice sheets floating upon the sea may grow as well. At the height of the last ice age, ice sheets covered about a third of the Earth. That most recent ice age lasted at least 20,000 years, and it ended less than 10,000 years ago. Human beings were chipping flint spearheads to kill the last woolly bison and carving flint sickles to work the world's first rude farms at the time the ice withdrew from Europe and North America. "The whole of human history has been lived in the shadow of the Ice Age," noted historian Norman Pounds. "And oblivious to it, one might add," says solar scientist and climatologist John Eddy. It is curious that the ice was not recorded in our myths. Some mythographers have wondered if the story of the Flood, which is found in one form or another in cultures around the world, might be a sort of dim and confused memory of the great ice sheets. If that is true, then Agassiz was only setting our collective memories straight.

The height of the last ice age was about 18,000 years ago. Ice was more than a mile thick over Boston, and two miles thick over the Gulf of Bothnia, between Finland and Sweden. It reached as far south as New York and London. Rather like a bulldozer, it pushed heaps of earth before it. At its southernmost margins, and along the line of its retreat, it deposited not only boulders but all manner of rocky rubble, called *glacial till*, along with much finely ground soil. Since the great yellowish-brown drifts of soil were dry, and since they had no roots and vegetation to hold them in place, they were as loose as the dunes of deserts. Cold winds that howled about the margins of the blue-white glaciers picked up the soil and scattered it for thousands of miles around. The rich farm belt of the American Midwest was laid down in this way. It is a paradox of history that the continents owe some of their most verdant soil to their periods of deepest cold. Geologists call this type of soil *loess* (from the German for "loose").

Nineteenth-century geologists digging in glacial till turned up something important. In places they found the remains of ancient plant life sandwiched between layers of till. This suggested that there had been times when the ice retreated, the climate warmed up, and plants grew on the heaps of till; and that the ice afterward came back and buried the plants in more till. In the American Midwest, someone found the remains of a whole forest preserved between two layers of till. There had to have been a very long interval between the visits of the ice if a mature forest had time to grow there. This sort of evidence led to the inescapable conclusion that the world has endured not just one but *many* ice ages.

WHAT MAKES ICE AGES?

The word "science" derives from the Latin verb *scire*, meaning to discern, to distinguish, to know. Yet scientists are always more interested in what they don't know. Like detectives, they move from mystery to mystery. Having convinced themselves of the reality of ice ages and having explained the nature of misfit boulders, till, and loess, the great question became not whether but why. Why did glaciers come sweeping down out of the North to overrun the continents? What makes ice ages?

Generation after generation of investigators has attacked this question. The problem is more than academic. Not only is the phenomenon one of the most dramatic events in the history of the Earth, and therefore fascinating in its own right, but also we have to know why it happens if we can hope to predict whether the ice will come again.

One ice age theory was proposed in 1842, just five years after Agassiz spoke in Neuchâtel. It was published by Joseph Alphonse Adhémar, a French mathematician who supported himself as a tutor in Paris.

Adhémar knew that the Earth's axis is not perpendicular to the plane of its orbit around the Sun. It is tilted at an angle and looks almost as if it were about to fall over, like a spinning top. A schoolroom globe's stand holds it tipped at this fixed angle, which is 23.5 degrees.

Since the planet is tilted as it revolves around the Sun, sometimes the northern hemisphere is tipped toward the Sun, and sometimes away. When the hemisphere is leaning inward toward the light, it is summer there. When it is leaning away from the Sun, it is winter there (and summer in the southern hemisphere). The poet John Milton was aware that humankind suffers through winters because of the tilt of Earth's axis. He assumed this tilt to be part of the general planetary decline that ensued when the first man and woman were expelled from the Garden of Eden. An angry God, Milton wrote in *Paradise Lost*,

> bid his angels turn askance
> The poles of Earth twice ten degrees and more
> From the Sun's axle . . .

Furthermore, Adhémar knew that the North Pole of the Earth does not point always in the same direction in space, though it changes too slowly and leisurely for us to notice in our brief lifetimes. Right now the North Pole points almost straight at the star Polaris (which is why we call it the Pole Star). But 2,000 years ago, while Julius Caesar was conquering Gaul, the North Pole pointed to the stretch of sky between the Little Dipper and the Big Dipper. In fact, the axis slowly revolves upon a circular path and completes one full revolution every 26,000 years.

Adhémar also knew that the Earth's orbit around the Sun is not a perfect circle but an ellipse, as the astronomer Johann Kepler demonstrated in the 17th century. Kepler proved that half of the Earth's elliptical orbit is slightly farther from the sun than the other half.

In 1842, after calculating the ways in which these subtle cycles in the Earth's orbit might interact, Adhémar published his conclusions. Earth, he said, enters an ice age whenever a hemisphere enters winter while it is at its farthest possible remove from the sun. According to his calculations, this event should occur every 11,000 years, when—Adhémar thought— a series of abnormally cold winters would allow snow and ice to build up and would pitch the globe into an ice age.

Adhémar's basic premise was interesting, but the details of his work were flawed, and the astronomical approach to the ice age riddle was discredited. A few years after Adhémar published his calculations, however, an astronomer discovered another cycle in the Earth's orbit. Because of the gravitational tug of the other planets in the solar system, Earth's orbit is slowly but continuously changing shape. Sometimes it is more elliptical, and sometimes more nearly circular. This discovery aroused the curiosity of a remarkable Scot named James Croll, a poor man who had taught himself mathematics, astronomy, physics, and geology and who came up with some of his best ideas while working as janitor at a school museum in Glasgow.

Croll knew that the orbital variations he was analyzing were extremely subtle. He wondered if such slight alterations in the Earth's journeys around the Sun could really cause a dramatic deluge of ice. This worry led him to one of his most original ideas. He knew that snow reflects most of the sunlight that falls on it, while dark soil absorbs more sunlight than it reflects. If tiny orbital variations caused just a little extra snow to fall, Croll reasoned, the snow would cause the surface of the planet to absorb a little less sunlight; it would cool, and so would the air above it. In cooler weather, more snow would fall—which would reflect more light, and cool things off even more. Thus snow could give rise to more snow, and more, and more. A slight effect could trigger a big reaction. This is a classic example of what we now call *positive feedback*. (Today the amount of light a planetary surface reflects is called *albedo*, from the Latin *albus*, whiteness. A planet covered in ice would have a high albedo. A planet covered in soot would have a very low albedo.)

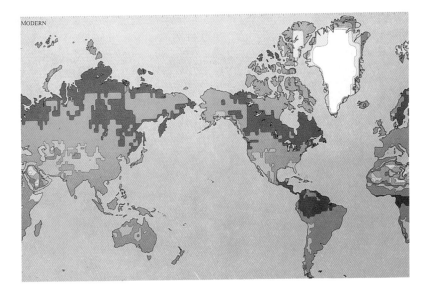

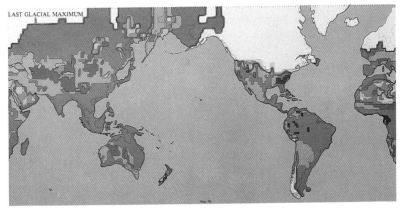

We live in a lull between ice ages. These maps show North and South America today, and as they were 18,000 years ago, during the last glacial maximum. The ice will come again.

Croll reexamined the astronomical approach to the ice age question, and in 1864 he, too, predicted a cyclic series of global winters. According to his calculations, the last ice ages should have occurred about 80,000 or 100,000 years ago. His idea, which aroused international interest, could be tested by dating the debris of the ice ages. Nineteenth-century geologists could not do this very accurately; they tried, by various means, and concluded that the last ice age had been quite recent in the life of the Earth—it seemed to have come perhaps 10,000 years ago. Thus Croll looked way off. After tremendous brouhaha and controversy, his work was shelved, like Adhémar's.

In 1911, a young Yugoslavian mathematician, Milutin Milankovitch, drank three bottles of wine with a friend in a Belgrade coffee shop. They were celebrating the publication of his friend's book of patriotic verses. Flushed and exuberant, the poet vowed to write a national epic. Not to be outdone, the mathematician vowed to tackle a "cosmic problem." He would reopen the ice age question and settle it once and for all.

A further astronomical subtlety had meanwhile been discovered. The Earth's axis is not *always* tilted at 23.5 degrees. Sometimes the angle is a degree or so more, sometimes a degree or so less. Milankovitch included this fact in his calculations. He labored with his "cosmic problem" for the next 30 years. At last he concluded that there are *three* cycles of ice ages—at 100,000, 41,000, and 22,000 years. Having solved the problem to his own satisfaction, he wrote a wonderful memoir, *Through Distant Worlds and Times: Letters from a Wayfarer in the Universe*, and then he died.

The best way of testing this new orbital theory was, once again, to date past ice ages to see if they fit the predictions. But during Milankovitch's lifetime, ice ages were still difficult to assign dates to. The snows of yesteryear are gone. As one ice age follows another, it erases many traces of those that came before. Earth is what artists call a palimpsest—a canvas that has been painted over many times. It takes ingenuity to distinguish the ghostly outlines of the first and second paintings beneath the work in progress, and it takes more ingenuity to tell just when each of the old paintings was made. When scientists finally learned to date objects by the state of decay of their radioactive isotopes, they won a chance to solve some of the most stubborn riddles of the past.

In the 1960s and 1970s, geologist Wallace S. Broecker of Columbia University, and coworkers, examined ancient coral along the shores of Eniwetok Atoll, the Florida Keys, the Bahamas, the Hawaiian Islands, and New Guinea. Broecker knew that sea level had dropped during each ice age, when water was locked up in glaciers on land. Sea level had risen markedly

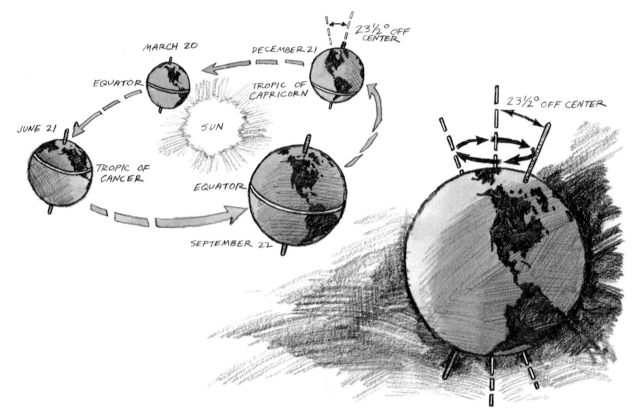

when most of the ice melted and water returned to the ocean. Coral grows only near sea level, and fluctuations in sea level sometimes leave terraces of coral along an island's shores—a picturesque staircase of terraces running up the island, each of which grew when the sea stood at a different height.

Broecker could determine the age of the ancient coral in each terrace by radioisotope dating. From this, Broecker could tell how sea level had varied on the shores of the islands, and hence he could help indirectly to assign dates to the beginnings and endings of ice ages. The coral terraces Broecker and his colleagues examined tended to be 20,000 years apart. Thus the terraces supported one of Milankovitch's predictions, the 22,000-year cycle.

This tentative evidence aroused interest. Now several scientists combined forces to try a novel approach to the ice age problem.

Research ships such as the *Glomar Challenger* had spent years drilling at sea and bringing up samples of ooze and rock in long cores. Each such core holds a record of hundreds of thousands of years in the life of the seas. Pioneering ocean-floor geologist Maurice Ewing had the foresight to store great numbers of these cores in vaults at Columbia University's Lamont-Doherty Geological Observatory. There they wait for ingenious researchers to come up with new ways of reading them.

Earth has seasons because its axis is tilted at an angle relative to the plane of its orbit around the Sun. When a hemisphere is tilted toward the Sun, it experiences Summer, and when it is tilted away from the Sun, it experiences Winter. The planet's axis is always tilted by the same amount (within a degree or so). But the direction in which the axis points does change slowly over the millennia, following a circular path, as shown at right. (Based on diagrams in Ice Ages: Solving the Mystery, *by John and Katherine Imbrie.)*

James D. Hays is an expert at reading the Lamont core library. He specializes in the study of tiny sea animals called *radiolaria*, and he uses radiolaria skeletons in deep-sea cores to trace the vicissitudes of the world's climate. Certain species of radiolaria are known to live only in cooler water, and others in warm. Hays cuts a core into wafer-thin slices, and studies each slice through a microscope. By identifying each species of radiolarian, he can deduce the average temperature of the water at the sea surface at the time that particular layer of radiolaria lived, died, and drifted to the bottom. Making slices of a core from the top to the bottom, he can learn something of how climate has changed over hundreds of thousands of years.

The sea's ooze also holds the shells of microscopic sea animals called *foraminifera*, and these shells provide another way to learn about ancient climate. Like coral, or the stalagmites and stalactites of caverns, these tiny animals build their shells of *calcium carbonate*. All calcium carbonate is composed of calcium, carbon, and oxygen; but which variety, or isotope, of oxygen goes into each foraminiferan's shell depends partly upon how much water is locked up in glaciers on the continents. Growing glaciers tend to absorb Oxygen 16, which takes some of this isotope out of circulation; so seawater grows a little poorer in Oxygen 16 when global ice sheets expand, and seawater grows richer in it when ice sheets dwindle. Thus, remarkably enough, microscopic shells at the bottom of the sea contain a nutshell history of the volume of glaciers on land.

To test the ice age question, Hays looked for a long core that was full of both radiolaria and foraminifera, and had especially thick, well-preserved layers. After an exhaustive search, he found one appropriate core in the Lamont vaults, and a second one in a core vault in Florida. Both cores had been raised from the southern Indian Ocean; taken together, they provided a continuous record going back 450,000 years.

Painstakingly, Hays studied the radiolaria skeletons in these two cores, and he asked Nicholas Shackleton, of Cambridge University, to measure the oxygen isotopes in the cores' foraminifera (a technique Shackleton had helped to perfect). Then Hays gave all their results to John Imbrie, of Brown University, who subjected the data to a rigorous and sophisticated statistical analysis, which helped draw a clear graph of ancient climatic trends.

The three men were thrilled to discover clear-cut ice age cycles of 100,000, 43,000, 24,000, and 19,500 years, extending back in time nearly 500,000 years. The first two cycles were very close to what the old mathematician Milutin Milankovitch had concluded after his lifelong analysis of the orbit of the Earth. The latter two cycles had been predicted independently by

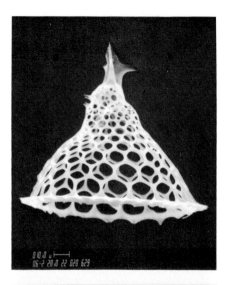

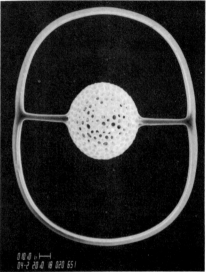

Creatures smaller than grains of sand helped to solve the riddle of the ice ages. Top: the radiolarian Theocalyptra bicornis *(Popofsky), magnified 500 times. Bottom: the radiolarian* Saturnalis circularis *(Haeckel), magnified 300 times. Their tests, or skeletons, are made of pure silica—the chief ingredient of sand and glass. Left: A foraminiferan. It is built not of silica but of calcite. Calcite skeletons like this, piled one on top of the other over eons, and then raised from the bottom of the sea, made the White Cliffs of Dover.*

several modern astronomers, who had just redone all the necessary mathematical analysis of the Earth's orbit with the help of modern computers. Theory and evidence fit like lock and key.

On December 10, 1976, Hays, Imbrie, and Shackleton published a triumphant account of their findings in a long lead article in the journal *Science*. They titled their article "Variations in the Earth's Orbit: Pacemaker of the Ice Ages." Most geologists and climatologists were immediately impressed and—after several studies confirmed the results—they were convinced. At last we have a good idea of what triggered the ice ages that have come and gone in the past million years of Earth history. We know when they have happened in the past, and it is a simple matter to calculate (although the date is still very approximate) when the next ice age is due.

"This is where we stand right now," says James Hays. "We have just come out of a very large glaciation, which culminated about 18,000 years ago and was one of the biggest: All the cycles came together to make a very cold period. We have emerged from that, and we've gone through an interval of time that was unusually warm—*only 10 percent of the last million years has been as warm as we are now*. We have passed the peak and are now moving back toward cold. The next glaciation will not be as extensive as the one we just went through. But there will be substantially more ice around than there is now, probably in a few thousand years."

THE GLOBAL HEAT WAVE

If the Earth was an icehouse 18,000 years ago, it was a hothouse 100 million years ago. In those days, there was not a speck of permanent ice anywhere on the planet; at least, geologists have found no trace of it, even at the poles.

This was the *Cretaceous* period, when dinosaurs ruled the Earth, browsing among steamy swamps and tropical forests and along the shores of warm, shallow seas. Winters seem to have been so mild then that trees grew near the earth's poles. On icebound Greenland, where Alfred Wegener lost his life, geologists have found the fossils of alligators. "Unless alligators had fur in those days," jokes climatologist Eric Barron of the National Center for Atmospheric Research, "it must have been a much warmer climate than today."

Geologists think weather in the Cretaceous period was balmy even at the poles. On a global average, temperatures were warmer by something like 6 to 12 degrees centigrade. That is an extraordinary contrast between then and now—the greatest difference in global climate ever documented. In the Little Ice Age of the 17th century, winters averaged only about

2 degrees centigrade cooler than today's. Even during a major ice age, the global average temperature was only cooler than today's by about 5 degrees centigrade. Thus the hothouse was much hotter than the icehouse was cold. The planet ran a high fever.

Until quite recently, most scientists assumed the extraordinary climate of the Cretaceous period was caused by its geography. Lands and seas were not where they are today. Pangaea was still breaking up, and the shattered continents were drifting rapidly apart. Large areas now land were then under water; in North America, a shallow sea extended from the Gulf of Mexico to the Arctic Basin and from Colorado to Kansas. Investigators could not spell out precisely how these alterations might have tweaked the global climate. But it seemed safe to guess that the geography of those days made *some* difference.

Over the past five years, Eric Barron has run a series of global experiments to investigate the hothouse question. He has shifted the seven continents to their ancient positions and flooded millions of acres of land, spilling salt water over the whole of the American Midwest and the Canadian heartland, from Fort Worth and Dallas to Saskatoon and Moose Jaw, Saskatchewan. He has released the world's winds and allowed them to play about on the altered landscape while he observed the

One hundred million years ago, dinosaurs basked and baked in a planetary warm spell. What turned up Earth's thermostat? And is man turning it up again?

path each trade wind took and waited to see if the globe heated up. Barron did all this planetary remodeling using the twin Earth in the supercomputer of the National Center for Atmospheric Research.

When Barron plugged the ancient geography into his computer model of the Earth, the global climate began to warm up as expected. Oceans soak up more heat from the Sun than lands do (that is, the seas have a lower albedo). So the shallow seas in his twin Earth heated up and helped to warm the planet. However, because they were warmer, the seas also evaporated faster, and more clouds formed overhead in the imaginary skies of the twin Earth. Clouds reflect a great deal of light (they have a high albedo). They blocked sunlight, shaded the surface of the planet, and kept things from getting as warm as geologists had expected. In the end, the twin Earth warmed up only about one third as much as Barron needed. Apparently geography alone could not explain the hothouse temperatures of the Cretaceous period.

While Barron puzzled over this failure of the established theory, a few other investigators hit upon a new idea. They knew that when Pangaea was breaking up, oceans were opening, and new sea floor was being manufactured at a great rate. In fact, it is estimated that sea floors were spreading about twice as fast then than they are today. That means sea floor was also being *destroyed* twice as fast. ("Since the size of the Earth is not changing," Barron explains, "if you create new crust, you've got to destroy crust somewhere else.")

We have trouble today with volcanoes and earthquakes, but the dinosaurs had double. The creation and destruction of so much sea floor meant vast quantities of molten rock and hot gas were spewing from deep within the Earth, releasing, among other substances, a great deal of carbon dioxide. Perhaps, a team of investigators suggested, this extra carbon dioxide made the Earth a hothouse.

There is very little carbon dioxide in the atmosphere— a fraction of a single percent. Lately, however, the power of this gas has been making headlines around the world.

One atom of carbon joined with two atoms of oxygen make one molecule of carbon dioxide. For living things, as earth scientist Roger Revelle has observed, this stable and invisible gas is possibly the most important substance on the planet. When the gas is inhaled by plants and broken apart, the carbon atom becomes a principal building block in virtually all the molecules that make up living creatures. (So intimate is the association between carbon and life that by tradition any molecule containing carbon is termed "organic.") From each broken carbon dioxide molecule, plants discard the two atoms of oxygen and release them into the atmosphere. Animals, in turn, inhale the oxygen and use it in a kind of internal combustion to power their metabolic engines. *They* exhale carbon dioxide, which plants promptly reuse. It is a global symbiosis. More carbon and oxygen are cycled and recycled by inanimate land, sea, and air. The global paths and wanderings of carbon are complex and vital, but the details of the *carbon cycle* are still poorly understood.

While it is in the airborne part of its wanderings, carbon dioxide helps to warm the life below. For this effect, the gas is often compared to the glass of a greenhouse.

Carbon dioxide is transparent to the visible light streaming down upon us from the Sun. Sunlight passes through virtually undiminished, as if through a windowpane, and falls full strength on the surface of the planet, which it warms each day. The Earth's rocks, deserts, trees, and seas radiate some of this heat back into the atmosphere. What they radiate is *infrared energy*, the band of radiation that lies just below red in the spectrum. If our eyes were designed differently, we would see infrared light as a band beside red in every rainbow; and we could see by its dim light after sundown—though landscapes and people would seem to be lit from within. In fact, we cannot see infrared radiation without special instruments, though we feel it on our faces when working in front of a stove. Satellites record the Gulf Stream using infrared radiation because the stream's warmth makes it stand out against the cool water around it.

The planet's surface, warmed by the Sun's rays, radiates a good deal of infrared energy. If there were no atmosphere, most of this radiation, as it streamed from the Earth, would be lost to outer space. But carbon dioxide absorbs some of the radiation. It warms up, and it reradiates the energy in all directions. Some of its infrared rays shoot right back down to Earth, further heating the planet's surface. Thus energy from the Sun is trapped, locked in between air and ground, bouncing between them, and warming both of them over and over again.

Technically, the greenhouse analogy is flawed. A greenhouse holds in warmth because the glass keeps hot air from rising and blowing away. Carbon dioxide is part of the air itself and holds in warmth because it keeps *radiation* from getting away. Nevertheless, the term has stuck; the action of carbon dioxide has for years been called the *greenhouse effect*. And it is true that we live in a global greenhouse, a hothouse planet in the cosmic winter night. Without the greenhouse effect, the oceans would be solid ice.

One hundred million years ago, when the volcanoes

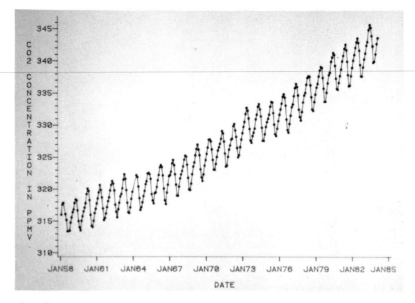

The level of carbon dioxide in Earth's atmosphere is rising, step by step, year by year.

that loomed around the dinosaurs vented vast quantities of carbon dioxide into the atmosphere, and the gas rose from vents and seams in the sea floor, did that make the ancient Earth a hothouse? Eric Barron found this suggestion appealing. He cranked up his computer model of the Cretaceous period, added more carbon dioxide to the atmosphere, and ran his experiments over again. Immediately the global climate heated up. "I've now shown in my climate models," says Barron, "that four times to ten times the present carbon dioxide level will reproduce the tremendous warmth of the Cretaceous." This finding does not *prove* carbon dioxide was responsible for the events of the past, but it strengthens the hypothesis, and it provides geologists with a ball-park figure for the amount of carbon dioxide that the evidence of the Cretaceous hothouse requires.

Visions of a global icehouse and hothouse make our planet's climate feel less secure and hospitable than it once did. Some earth scientists argue that the human population itself may now be powerful enough to tip the global balance in one direction or the other. Without quite realizing it, we may be forcing a global change in climate.

THE GREENHOUSE OF GREENHOUSES

In 1958, Charles David Keeling of the Scripps Institution of Oceanography began carefully measuring the amount of carbon dioxide in the atmosphere. He knew that the steady winds for which Hawaii is famous arrive there after crossing 2,000 miles of nothing but open sea. So he set up his instruments at 11,000 feet on the slopes of the Hawaiian volcano Mauna Loa. In his first year of testing, Keeling found there were about 315 parts per million of carbon dioxide in the air. Each year since, the

The greenhouse at Kew Gardens, in London.

quantity has increased by about 1½ parts per million. By 1984, there were 344 parts per million. Keeling's observations have been checked by stations as far north as Point Barrow, Alaska, and as far south as the South Pole. Each station has gotten similar results.

The increase is a by-product of the Industrial Revolution and the population explosion. The burning of fossil fuels—coal, oil, natural gas—sends 500 million tons of carbon dioxide into the atmosphere each year. At the same time, the Third World is now clearing its forests at a staggering pace (as the First and Second Worlds already cleared theirs). Millions of acres of trees that could have taken in carbon dioxide from the atmosphere are being felled and burned (in what is known as *swidden*, or slash-and-burn agriculture), and smoke from the fires is throwing yet more carbon dioxide into the air.

In effect, the global balance of the carbon cycle is now skewed by our phenomenal success as *Homo sapiens*, human beings. We are filling the atmosphere with our exhalations. An estimated 230 billion tons of carbon have been poured into the atmosphere since 1860, when the fires of the industrial revolution really began to smoke. Not all of these billions of tons of gas have remained airborne—much was absorbed by plants and dissolved in the seas. Nevertheless, enough has remained in the atmosphere to raise the amount of the gas there by perhaps 17 percent since the decade of the Civil War.

When Charles Keeling plots the increase in carbon dioxide on a graph, the line is not smooth and steady. Each year it swings up and down by a few percent: highest in the spring and lowest in the fall. The measurements are low in the fall because plants' foliage has been absorbing carbon dioxide all

ACID RAIN, ACID SNOW

Acid rain, in the past half decade, has been added to the technological world's litany of fears. Like carbon dioxide, it is an unintended by-product of the Industrial Revolution. Evidence strongly suggests that pollutants in the atmosphere are acidifying rains, lakes, and streams.

The problem is not well understood. It is not even well named. The words would sound less sinister if it were commonly known that all rains and all snows are naturally acidic. A substance's acidity is measured on the pH scale, in which 7 is perfectly neutral, neither acidic nor alkaline. Speaking very roughly, the average pH of rain in nature—though it varies from place to place on the globe—is thought to be 5.6, which is slightly acidic.

In many parts of the industrial world, however, and in forested country far downwind of factory country, the pH of rains and snows is much lower. Rainfall in the eastern United States is currently estimated by the Environmental Protection Agency to be about pH 4.5. The pH scale is logarithmic, which means that as one counts down the scale, each integer is 10 times more acidic than the one before it. So rains and snows of pH 4.5 are about 10 times more acidic than normal. And they often come worse. "One long rainfall in the autumn of 1978 holds a dubious national record," environmentalist and writer John Luoma reports in his book *Troubled Skies, Troubled Waters.* "Instruments registered values less than pH 2, a level six to eight times more acidic than vinegar and some five thousand times more acidic than normal rain."

The pollutants responsible for this increase are chiefly sulfur dioxide and the oxides of nitrogen. Swirled and cooked together with other gases and chemicals in the atmosphere, they can combine to form, among other things, sulfuric acid, which then falls on our country's soil and gathers in our lakes.

Those lakes most at risk are in territory that was scraped clean of topsoil during the last advances and retreats of the ice age. In the great chain of wilderness lakes that extends from northern Minnesota into Canada; in the Appalachians; and in much of Scandinavia, the ice scoured right down to the bedrock, and the new soil that has collected there is still quite thin. These regions are poor in the kind of natural alkaline rock, like limestone, that elsewhere helps to neutralize acid rain. Many of their lakes have been greatly acidified, altering their chemistry in complex ways that are only beginning to be understood. Fish in these lakes have died off. The water is eerily clear and clean, because in it so little life survives.

Ironically, part of the problem is an engineering feat that was once seen as the problem's solution. Coal-burning plants such as Kyger Creek, and the General James M. Gavin plant, both in Cheshire, Ohio, have built huge smokestacks (Gavin's is over 1,000 feet high) to loft their emissions of sulfur dioxide and nitrogen oxides high into the atmosphere and keep these wastes from sickening their neighbors in Cheshire. The gases are borne extraordinary distances in the upper atmosphere, where they have plenty of time and space to recombine into sulfuric acid, which then falls thousands of miles from Kyger Creek and Gavin. Tall stacks help convert acid rain from a local to an international problem.

Environmentalists and industrialists agree that acid rain is poorly understood and must be studied further. But they disagree about what to do in the meanwhile. Some argue for several kinds of preventive action now. For instance, expensive "scrubbers" could be installed immediately by plants such as Kyger Creek and Gavin to clean sulfur dioxides from the stacks' emissions. But many other people—including most of those who would have to pay to install the scrubbers—think the expense premature. The issue has as many sides as any in climatology. Some of the chemical emissions in question even make good fertilizer. Notes climatologist Reid Bryson of the University of Wisconsin, "It may be the old saying about a silver lining to every cloud—but here in Wisconsin, when they cleaned up the sulfur emissions from one of our local power plants, the farmers in the area had to start adding sulfur to their fields."

Though the debate continues, Jon Luoma says, "the difficulties in the way of reducing acid rain are not so much scientific as political."

Robin Heid of Denver parachutes from the top of the 1100-foot smokestack of the Gavin Power Plant in Cheshire, Ohio. Heid's jump was part of a protest by the environmentalist group Greenpeace against acid rain. Giant smokestacks like Gavin's are supposed to "solve" pollution problems because their smoke and noxious chemicals are blown away on the winds. But what goes up eventually comes down.

spring and summer. The measurements are high in the spring because during the preceding winter most plants have slowed down, and animals breathed out more carbon dioxide than plants were inhaling. In this annual, stepwise fashion, the line on the graph climbs steadily upward.

If we continue to burn fossil fuels and strip forests, by the year 2040 we will double the current CO_2 level, and reach 600 parts per million. And if climatologists are right, by 2040 that increase will drive up temperatures, averaged across the globe, 2 degrees Centigrade, or 3.6 degrees Fahrenheit.

"This is a huge warming in terms of what it will do to us," according to Walter Orr Roberts, president emeritus of the University Corporation for Atmospheric Research. He believes the poles could heat up by as much as 10 degrees Centigrade, or 18 degrees Fahrenheit. If so, the polar ice caps would begin to melt, and the sea level would rise—perhaps a few feet a century, perhaps more. Hundreds of the world's largest ports could be flooded. The sea level is already rising some 1.5 millimeters a year. If the western Antarctic ice cap were to break apart, the seas could rise quite suddenly 16 to 20 feet, flooding the streets of Miami, New York, and Tokyo and drowning Venice. Saving even a single port city would cost society hundreds of billions of dollars.

On the other hand, it is thought that the tropics would become only slightly hotter than they are today. So the global contrast in temperature between the equator and the poles would be diminished. Since that contrast drives the atmosphere's great convective winds, global circulation patterns would change. Today, moisture-laden air rises from the tropics and settles in the midlatitudes, bearing rains and snows. By 2040, those rains could fail. "This is very bad news for the corn and wheat belts of the United States," Roberts writes. ". . . If the greenhouse warming produces the effect that I consider the most probable, in spite of the uncertainties, the Dust Bowl of the 30s may seem like children's play in comparison with the Dust Bowl of the 2040s . . . . The soils will desiccate, and the winds will lift them to the skies."

"If you warm up the planet," says Stephen Schneider of the National Center for Atmospheric Research (NCAR), "you help those areas worried about freezing and hurt those with hot summers. A place like Dallas, to me already unlivable, in the summer would become *totally* unlivable. A few degrees would increase the probability of 100-degree weather, we calculate, by a factor of two! Instead of a one-third chance of a heat wave, they'd have a two-thirds chance. What does that do to the urban poor, without air conditioning?"

Bristlecone pines are the oldest living things on the planet—some of them live as long as 5,000 years. This windswept specimen stands on Sheep Mountain, in Inyo National Forest, California.

In what has been called the *runaway greenhouse*, there would be "winners" and "losers." Canadians might buy beachfront real estate. Texans might want to buy Maine. But many of the worst side effects and negative consequences are difficult to see in advance. In our present climate, Schneider notes, scourges such as malaria, schistosomiasis, and elephantiasis are confined to the tropics because the parasites that transmit them cannot survive northern winters. However, a few decades from now, New York, Rome, and Paris may be just warm enough for the comfort of the malaria mosquito. "So warming may sound great to those of us freezing our tails off in the winter," says Schneider. "But we forget what the winter does for us with regard to eliminating tropical diseases."

Though a two-degree warming now seems likely, no responsible climatologist will swear it is coming. Too many issues remain unsettled. Already, for instance, Arizona dendrochronologists have noticed that the annual rings of their bristlecone pines are widening. The pines are fattening on CO_2, which acts on plants like a chemical fertilizer. If the world's foliage grows sufficiently lush, the greenery might inhale enough gas to check the greenhouse effect.

The oceans, like the forests, may absorb excess carbon dioxide from the atmosphere, and help avert a planetary disaster. But how much gas the world's waters will take in, and how quickly, depends on how fast the oceans are stirring—how fast water from the abyss rises to the top, and water from the surface sinks into the depths. No one knows these figures with any precision, and what is worse, no one knows how ocean currents might be affected in the future by a global warming. The interaction of sea and air remains beyond our powers of prediction, even with supercomputers.

Clouds are another unknown factor. If the planetary warming caused an increase in cloud cover, that might add to the greenhouse effect by absorbing and trapping infrared radiation; or it might cancel the effect and cool the Earth by blocking sunlight from reaching the planet and reflecting it back out to space. Clouds already do both these things—but no one is sure of their net effect. If clouds were to block out even 1 percent more of the Sun's energy, they would suffice to wipe out the warming effect of doubled CO_2. Even a fine wisp of cirrus, which some call mare's tail, too wispy to show up in satellite pictures and too fine a detail to model, can strongly affect incoming and outgoing radiation. According to one earth scientist, a 1 percent error in our understanding of cloud cover could spoil all our greenhouse forecasts.

Says Warren Washington of NCAR, "It's one of the biggest uncertainties in the CO_2 question." And he adds, summing up, "Our observations are flawed, and our models are flawed." Says Syukuro Manabe of GFDL, "CO_2 *is* increasing. Only this is certain. Nothing else is certain."

Unfortunately, there are other gases in the atmosphere that act like greenhouse glass; many believe these gases will dramatically amplify the greenhouse effect, doubling the speed of its onset and the degree of warming. This fear has led to a new and curious controversy in the annals of atmospheric research.

Several years ago, Pat Zimmerman of NCAR joined an expedition to Guatemala to measure gas emissions from volcanoes. There, in the Guatemalan rain forest, he saw colonies of termites living in massive arboreal nests. One day, Zimmerman trimmed the branches around one nest, put a teflon bag over it, and watched. The bag filled with methane gas.

Entomologists had known for some time that termites produce methane in the course of digesting wood. But no one had ever thought of termites or their digestive systems as threats to the global atmosphere. The methane interested Zimmerman because after nitrogen, oxygen, water vapor, and carbon dioxide, methane is the fifth most abundant gas in the atmosphere, and it is, like carbon dioxide, increasing. According to some climatologists, it has doubled in the past 150 years and is continuing to climb at a rate of nearly 2 percent a year. And methane, like CO_2, is a greenhouse gas.

Zimmerman began chasing termites. He traveled to Kenya with Joan Darlington, a British entomologist, to look at African termite mounds, some of which look like chimneys, or miniature volcanoes. There he found more methane billowing up: "You can actually feel moist gas coming out the top."

Zimmerman estimates that there are 200 quadrillion termites in this world, three quarters of a ton of termites—mostly in the tropics—for every human being on Earth. They thrive on slash-and-burn agriculture, and whenever an acre of rain forest is axed, the termite population explodes. Since an area of forest about the size of Connecticut is cleared from the planet each year, this is a good time to be a termite. If Zimmerman is right, they are giving off more than 100 million tons of methane each year, perhaps a quarter to a half of the methane annually released into the atmosphere.

Zimmerman's figures are controversial; some say there are nowhere near that many termites. But methane is unquestionably increasing in the atmosphere. Cows eat cellulose, too, notes Zimmerman, and once every 30 or 40 seconds, the cows have to break wind. There are 17 cows per human being on the planet (up 50 percent in the past few decades). Rice paddies give off methane, too (also up 50 percent), as do swamps

Pat Zimmerman collects air samples from vents of a Macrotermes termite mound in Kenya. Zimmerman thinks termites may be altering the world's atmosphere by pumping out methane. Methane, like carbon dioxide, is a powerful greenhouse gas. As global polluters, termites may even rival people.

("swamp gas"). Methane seeps out from leaky natural gas pipelines, as well.

Zimmerman and others are now studying the problem from NCAR headquarters in Boulder, Colorado. They have imported a termite colony to his laboratory and established a rice paddy on the roof.

And there are still other greenhouse gases to monitor. The chlorofluorocarbons (CFMs) from aerosol cans could have a warming effect, too—some say they will cause nearly 40 percent as much as the warming from CO_2 doubling. For this reason, the United States is discouraging the use of aerosol cans; but in other countries their use is still growing, so CFMs are still increasing in the atmosphere. And feedback effects from these gases could release still others, as Roger Revelle has noted. "There's something called methane hydrate, or methane ice, contained in the mud under the sea floor. It is stable only at low temperatures and high pressures. If you raise the temperature of the seawater, this stuff becomes unstable and escapes, which adds to the methane in the atmosphere. You don't have to add very much to achieve the same effect as you would by doubling the CO_2 level."

"People say that within 10 years we'll know," Revelle said in a recent Omni magazine interview. "On the other hand, you might have had many grandchildren by the time it happens." Mankind, in spite of itself, is conducting a great experiment—"probably the greatest geophysical experiment ever conducted."

The polar ice caps are more sensitive and changeable than one might think. They grow mightily each winter, and dwindle each summer. This is the southern ice cap, monitored by the weather satellite Nimbus 5. In these false-color images, waters that are more densely packed with ice are green, brown, red, and purple.

THE CAMP AT ICE STREAM B

If the global climate does begin to warm up in coming decades, especially at the poles, will masses of polar ice collapse into the

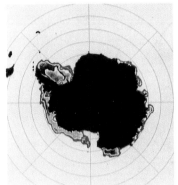

FEBRUARY 1974

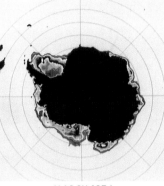

MARCH 1974

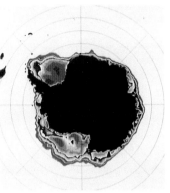

APRIL 1974

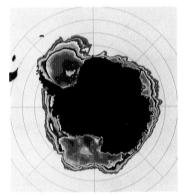

MAY 1974

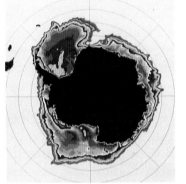

JUNE 1974

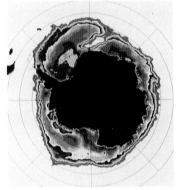

JULY 1974

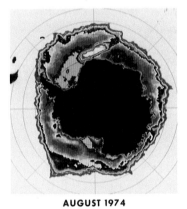

AUGUST 1974

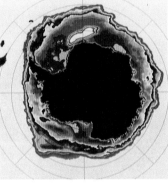

SEPTEMBER 1974

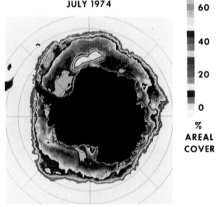

OCTOBER 1974

100

80

60

40

20

0

%
AREAL
COVER

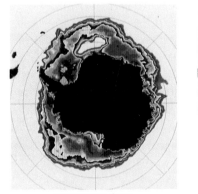

NOVEMBER 1974

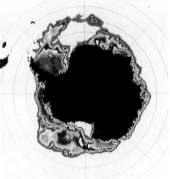

DECEMBER 1974

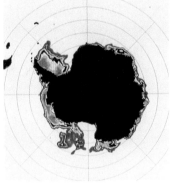

JANUARY 1975

sea, flooding the world's coasts, spoiling harbor after harbor, and causing a trillion dollars' worth of damage? Most climatologists don't think so, and many have condemned the headlines that trumpet such doomsday predictions. But the Earth's white ice caps do affect global climate; they are powerful and influential parts of the living machine, and the details of their influence are still poorly understood.

It is the ice of West Antarctica that has aroused the greatest interest and concern. This ice seems to be delicate—even fragile. It does not rest on solid ground, but on rock that is far below sea level. It is fringed by *ice shelves*, which jut out across the surface of the sea, floating, though pinned here and there by islands. The East Antarctic ice sheet is anchored more simply and sturdily. It rests on ground that is above sea level. If all the ice in Antarctica were to melt, there would be land in the East but only scattered islands in the West.

Thus the East Antarctic ice sheet is firmly fixed to its rock floor, but the West Antarctic ice sheet is capable of rapid change because the ice there can spread out over the open water on either side. "Rapid change" could be rapid indeed. Indirect evidence suggests that this ice sheet may have collapsed at least once in the dim past, and it may have taken as little as two or three centuries to cave into the sea—which is, in the life of the Earth, hardly time enough to blink. If all the ice in Antarctica melted, it would raise sea level worldwide some 200 feet. If the West Antarctic ice sheet melted, it might raise sea level suddenly about 15 feet. Even that would be a global disaster.

It was once assumed that an ice sheet flows steadily and slowly outward toward the sea, the outermost edges calving off icebergs. But 10 years ago, a scientist looking at images of the Antarctic made from high above the ice noticed striking bands of large fissures known as *crevasses* (French for "crevice") running through the ice sheets and out toward the sea.

Studies soon showed that between these lines of crevasses the ice sheet is moving relatively quickly, while the surrounding ice sheet remains more or less motionless. Each stream is 10 or 15 miles broad and flows between banks of ice down to the sea. These *ice streams* are, in effect, rivers of ice within the ice, as the Gulf Stream can be loosely described as a river of water within water. The streams are an important and hitherto unsuspected part of the dynamics of the polar ice sheet, and a wild card in global climate, because we do not know how they would respond to a general warming or cooling.

There are five ice streams in West Antarctica, and they have been assigned the pedestrian names A, B, C, D, and E. Glaciologist Ian Whillans, of Ohio State University, has established a camp at Ice Stream B. His team has inserted great numbers of stakes—steel pipes—at intervals along the stream and is monitoring the way the rows of pipes are deformed by the surface motion of the ice. Whillans has also littered the ice with a number of enormous black panels, 10 feet on a side, which show up clearly against the white ice in aerial photographs taken from 23,000 feet up. For good measure, his team has layed out satellite receivers on the ice, and is tracking their motions using polar-orbiting satellites. The experiment has just begun and Whillans feels it is too soon to say whether the motions of ice streams A through E are changing fast, or remaining stable. But there is some evidence, Whillans says, "that they are in the middle of a major event right now."

Geophysicist Charles Bentley is also studying Ice Stream B—not the surface, but the hidden depths. It is sometimes said that geologists look *at* rocks and geophysicists look *through* rocks. Bentley looks through the ice stream with radar, which bounces radio echoes off the rock bottom. He also drills shot holes in the ice, sets off small explosive charges, and records the echoes with small *seismic geophones* strung out thousands of feet along the ice. He hopes to map the complete contours of the ice stream's bed and deduce why this portion of the ice is flowing while the ice around it is standing still. The zone where the ice meets its rock bed, deep below sea level, is of particular importance to this question, because there may be muddy pools of melted water that lubricate the passage of the ice streams and allow them to glide along.

If theory is correct, this boundary zone of water or muck could be influenced indirectly by extra snowfall at the surface, because, oddly enough, the thicker the ice piles up, the warmer it becomes at the bottom. It is heated at its base by friction, and also by the warmth of the Earth itself, the planetary body heat that diffuses upward from the mantle. Ice is cold, but it is also a good insulator and acts like a blanket (which is why Eskimo families can stay warm in igloos). The thicker the blanket, the warmer it is underneath, says Whillans. If world precipitation patterns changed, more snow fell at the poles, and ice thickened, it would melt more at the bottom, and it would flow faster. "Some people," Whillans says, "have postulated a catastrophe in consequence."

For investigators, ice streams are a window on the ice ages. "If you want to see what the glaciated regions of the Earth looked like back 20,000 years ago, just go anywhere where the ice sheet is now," Whillans says. "Nobody—including us— would be able to tell the difference. You set us down in the middle of the ice sheet someplace, we don't know whether we're on the current ice sheet or on the Pleistocene ice sheet. It's going to look the same. And we believe that ice streams were flowing even then. We don't think they're a current phenomenon. Ice streams were there before we were."

Whillans and his field teams, who work on the ice streams with Ski-Doos and Sno-Cats full of equipment, drive very carefully. Many of the crevasses that border the streams are filmed over with a thin bridge of ice, which makes them hard to see. Such hidden crevasses are as dangerous as land mines. Other crevasses are in plain sight. "They could take several tractors—and their drivers," Whillans says. Some of Whillans's assistants are interested in descending into these crevasses, on ropes, to inspect the walls. Bentley's team has a certain interest in the crevasses, too. "Our main interest is in staying out of them," Bentley says. "You don't go into one of those on purpose (except very carefully), and we hope we don't go into one by mistake."

"Within your lifetime, if not my lifetime," Bentley recently told a youngish visitor, "it will be possible to predict what's going to happen, in a general sense, to the ice sheet in the next 10,000 years. . . . Of course, in order to predict what may be happening to the ice sheet in the future, we have to know what's happening to other parts of the climate system. We can't predict it all by itself."

Meanwhile, however, all predictions are premature. Says Bentley, "It is a gross oversimplification to assume that climatic warming is definitely and rapidly going to cause an

Ice shapes the fate of the Earth's climate in ways we are only just beginning to guess. This is Beardmore Glacier, in Antarctica.

inundation of the coastal cities. In the first place, we don't even know whether the immediate effect of climatic warming will be to cause the ice sheet to melt, or cause it to grow. One possibility is that the rate of snow accumulation on the surface will increase—that is, that the precipitation rate will increase as the climate gets warmer. It is quite possible that, given enough time and enough climate warming, the West Antarctic ice sheet will disappear on a reasonable geologic time scale— let's say 10,000 years. It is entirely unreasonable to think it could disappear within a century. The critical question is: What is the fastest that the West Antarctic ice sheet could possibly be expected to disappear, in an extreme case? My own feeling is that the fastest is about 500 years."

TERRAFORMING—THE FUTURE?

Headlines these days make it sound like bad news that the Earth's climate system is sensitive and that humankind can perturb it. Yet if we learn to know the climate system well enough, its exquisite sensitivity may become a blessing to us. We may then be able to make selective improvements in the climate, or arrest its decline.

Today the Industrial Revolution is modifying the weather, and probably the climate, without our meaning it to. Thus, in the short run, the climate's sensitivity really is bad news, since we don't yet understand it and since we are changing it much faster than we are learning how it works, or even finding out just what we are doing to it.

Aeolus, the wind king, once gave Odysseus a magic bag of winds. With the winds secure in that leather bag, he could have sailed wherever he wished. But while he slept his men opened the bag to see if there was gold inside it, and the fury of the winds exploding from the bag drove most of the crew to their deaths.

Someday, if we can win an understanding of weather and climate, we may be as powerful as Odysseus. If we do not undo the thong and unleash the winds upon ourselves too soon, there may come a time when humankind drives climate, instead of being driven by it.

One of the best ways we can gain perspective on the planet and come to understand more deeply the mechanisms of the living machine is to visit other worlds. There are nine planets in our solar system. In the past quarter century we have gotten to know some of these near neighbors. Vistas of enormous danger and unparalleled oppportunity have opened out around us. We had been rather provincial. There are more things in heaven and earth than are dreamt of in our philosophy.

Tales from Other Worlds

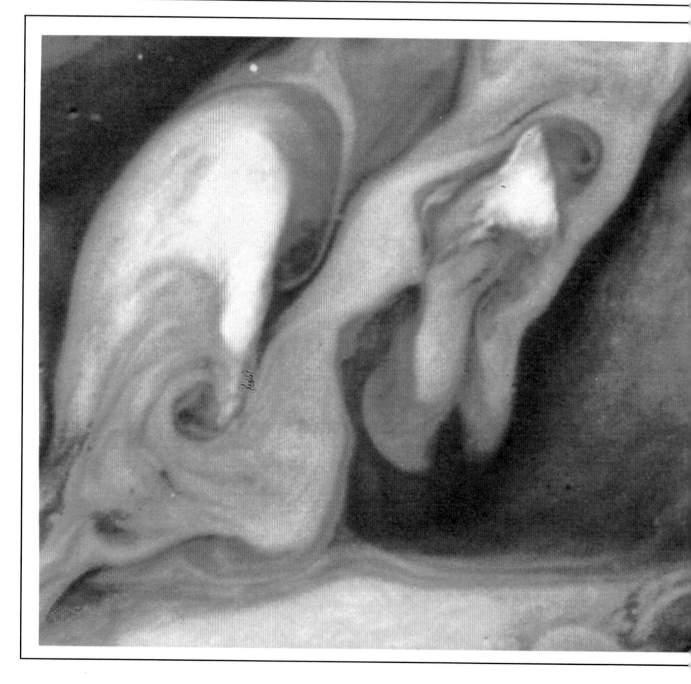

Where wast thou when I laid the foundations of the world? Declare, if thou hast understanding. . . or who laid the corner stone thereof; when the morning stars sang together, and all the sons of God shouted for joy?

THE BOOK OF JOB

Overleaf: Jupiter's Great Red Spot
is thought to be a vast storm.
It is big enough to swallow several
Earths, and has raged for more
than three hundred years.

4 / Tales from Other Worlds

• *From giant telescopes in mountaintop observatories across the globe, astronomers are searching the nearest stars for a new solar system.*

Using an instrument called a coronagraph, *the astronomers can block a star's light, to catch the dim glow of dark matter that may surround it.*

Around a small star called Beta Pictoris, in the constellation Pictor—the Painter's Easel—they have glimpsed a faint cloud of dust and gas. Fifty light-years from Earth, a planetary system may be forming, with worlds like our own.

• *In a natural crater in the hills of Arecibo, Puerto Rico, scientists have built a 1,000-foot white bowl. It is the biggest, most powerful radio transmitter and receiver in the world.*

There, astronomers from SETI, the Search for Extraterrestrial Intelligence, have sent messages to the globular cluster M13, a gathering of stars 25,000 light-years away. The astronomers are listening, with the great cupped ear of Arecibo, for voices from the stars.

• *In Pasadena, California, investigators wearing clothes of white nylon, capped and gloved as if for a surgical operation, are working in chambers they like to call the Lunatic Asylum.*

With exquisite instruments, they are examining rocks that have traveled to Planet Earth from the dark outer edges of our solar system.

These rocks are older than the oldest on Earth. In them, the scientists are reading stories once thought to be lost forever—tales of the cataclysmic birth of the nine planets.

This has been an extraordinary quarter century for life on Earth, a whirlwind tour of the solar system, with glances outward into the greater universe. Until recently, we could not visit the other planets with which we share the light of the Sun. We could only stand and stare. It is still hard for us to believe that we now have the power to follow our eyes and travel to other worlds.

We took our first steps into space in the International Geophysical Year, with the launch of the satellites *Sputnik* and *Explorer*. A mere decade later, in 1969, men walked on the Moon and helped learn secrets of its earliest days.

In 1976, the robot *Viking 1* landed on the Red Planet, Mars, and we peered through its remote-controlled eyes at the rubble of the Martian desert. Some scientists believe there may once have been life in those barren wastes. They also think there is a connection between strange markings in the Martian desert and a catastrophic flood 15,000 years ago on Earth.

Robots landed on Venus, too, and gave us a brief glimpse of its scorched terrain, the hottest of the nine worlds, where temperatures rise to the melting point of lead, beneath acid skies. Using the radar dish at Arecibo, investigators back on Earth penetrated Venus's thick cloud cover and began mapping the planet's terrain in surprising detail. It looks as if the Venusian nightmare world, and our planet, may once have been very much alike.

In 1979, with the two *Voyager* spacecraft, we traveled 1 billion miles from Earth, with the Sun, our star, receding behind us; and we arrived at the giant among planets, Jupiter—a failed star, with monstrous storms and a family of strange moons. On the weirdest of its moons, Io, we discovered huge erupting volcanoes—the only ones ever seen outside the Earth. The *Voyagers* also flew by Saturn for a close-up look at its lovely, shining rings. *Voyager 2* is now on a course that will take it out of the solar system entirely, on a long path to the stars.

From all this exploration have come new theories about our own planet, visions of where we come from and where we are going. One controversial hypothesis links the life on our planet with violent impacts from space. Did the dinosaurs vanish in a global catastrophe that strikes here every 26 million years?

A new field has arisen, *planetology*, uniting the study of Earth with the study of space. In an era of increasing specialization, planetologists strive, through a sort of Renaissance teamwork, to synthesize a dauntingly broad range of disciplines, from astrophysics to zoology. Planetologists are trying to sum up what we have discovered of the worlds in our solar neighborhood—their distances from the Sun, their atmospheres, climates, mountains, plains, and poles—and explain what makes Earth so different from the rest. How is it that we alone have blue seas of air and water? Why do we alone have a gentle climate? Why are we the only world in this solar system (so far as we know) that is a home to life?

The evidence suggests that all nine planets and their many moons were born at roughly the same time, while caught up in the same vast swirl of matter. Venus, Earth, and Mars, neighbors in space, probably started out pretty much alike. Why is each world so different now? The poisonous atmospheres and alien deserts we have visited in recent years may be lessons for us, *memento mori*, showing what tragedies can befall a living planet. Tales from outer space are teaching us to see Earth as a small place, a world amid innumerable worlds, and a home that is still—after all these years—unfamiliar ground.

A temple of ancient astronomy, El Caracol was built by the Mayan Indians in 317 A.D. It is the oldest known observatory in the Americas.

Our kind wondered about the planets before we knew we were on a planet ourselves. Squatting in the mouth of a cavern, by the embers of a dying fire, we stretched out a hand toward the stars and pondered what the lights in the sky might be, and how far away they were, and how they fit with the rest of our world—with the hills, streams, and fields, the herds of caribou, and with our tribe. A few among the stars seemed steadier than the rest; they did not flicker like torches in a wind. Night after night we watched for these strange ones, and we noticed how they traveled in the sky, slowly, from month to month and season to season, now shining in one constellation, now in

THE FIRST WHO
WATCHED THE NIGHT

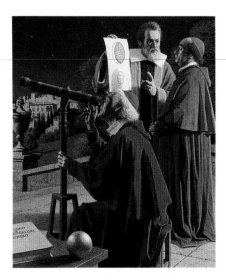

In 1609, Galileo Galilei built one of the world's first telescopes and saw that the Moon's face is pockmarked and mountainous. The news disturbed those who believed the heavenly spheres were perfect, crystalline, and nothing like Planet Earth.

another. The Greeks gave these lights the name we use today—the planets, the wanderers. The wanderers were studied not just by Greek philosophers but also by every people with a view of the night.

In the jungles of Yucatán, archaeologists have found temples and ruined pyramids built by the ancient Maya. Three thousand years ago, and 600 years before Aristotle, the carved stones' alignments with the risings and settings of Sun, Moon, and planets allowed Mayan priests to plot the changing seasons. It is the earliest known observatory in the western hemisphere (and, built on such an ambitious scale, it must have represented for the Maya what our own space program does for us).

Across prehistoric Europe, peoples without writing or skill in masonry planted circles of rude, uncut stones as their observatories. Nine hundred of these circles have been found so far, of which the most famous is Stonehenge, on England's Salisbury Plain. Until 1965, the lost people who built Stonehenge were presumed to have been "howling barbarians." But in that year, British astronomer Gerald Hawkins found precise sighting lines (looking out through spaces between the stones as if along the sights of a gun) to 32 positions of the Sun and the Moon.

In Mecca, near the Red Sea, stands a windowless, roughly cubic building, the Kaaba. Embedded in its walls are sacred stones, of which the most holy, the Black Stone, may be a meteorite, a little chunk of iron, 30 centimeters in diameter, that fell from space and landed in western Arabia. Ever since the death of Mohammed, the Kaaba has been the holy focal point of all Islam. But some scholars, including Hawkins, believe that before it was adopted by Mohammed's followers, the Kaaba served the same sorts of purposes as stone circles and Mayan pyramids. The Kaaba's corners and faces and Black Stone are aligned with motions of the heavens and with the Arabian winds, the *shamal*, from the north, and the *yamin*, from the south. It, too, may once have been an observatory.

Hawkins, having discovered the astronomical lore concealed in Stonehenge, often wonders about "the spirit that animated the Stonehenge builders, and that which inspired the creators of the Parthenon, and the Gothic cathedrals, and the first spacecraft to go to Mars."

"This is only the beginning," he says, "and no one can predict the outcome."

Despite the ingenuity of the ancients, there were limits to what could be learned about the heavens with the naked eye. Modern astronomy may be said to date from the year 1609, when Galileo Galilei, a professor of mathematics in Padua, heard that a certain Dutch spectaclemaker was building magic tubes "by means of which distant objects could be seen as distinctly as if they were nearby." Galileo spent a night thinking through everything he knew about optics, and he deduced the Flemish fellow's trick. In a few days' time he put together a spyglass of his own. It was a tube of sheet metal wrapped in crimson sateen, with a glass lens at each end, one lens being concave and one convex. On top of the Tower of St. Marco in Venice, Galileo demonstrated this invention to the senators of the city, who promptly doubled his salary to 1,000 scudi. Then Galileo turned the glass on the stars.

Some 3,600 stars are visible to the naked eye, and until that moment most people had assumed that was all there was to see. Through his simple telescope, Galileo peered up at familiar constellations, Orion, the Big Dipper, the Little Dipper, and the Pleiades, and saw many lights no one else had ever seen before. The Milky Way, that broad, dusty road of light across the zodiac, resolved upon his inspection into innumerable thousands upon thousands of faint stars.

Looking at the bright light of the planet Jupiter, Galileo discovered several dim lights beside it. On the night of January 7, they looked like this: * * ● *

On January 8,   ● * * *

On January 9, the night was cloudy. On the 10th, he saw: * * ●

And on the 13th: * ● * * *

Reading between the lines, Galileo deduced that Jupiter has moons revolving about it, one or two of which, on an average night, are hidden from view behind the planet.

Turning his spyglass to the Moon, Galileo discovered that its surface is not perfectly smooth and spherical, as most philosophers then believed the heavenly bodies to be, "but that, on the contrary, it is full of irregularities, uneven, full of hollows and protuberances, just like the surface of the Earth itself, which is varied everywhere by lofty mountains and deep valleys."

From these discoveries, Galileo arrived at startling ideas about Planet Earth. Most of his contemporaries still interpreted what they saw of the world around them according to the traditions of Greek philosophers. Stars were supposed to be decorations, according to Aristotle, jewels placed in the heavens purely for human enjoyment. If so, argued Galileo, why were so many stars too small to be seen with the naked eye? Apparently mankind was not, after all, the reason the universe was made. Stars had their own reasons for being.

The Andromeda Galaxy is the Milky Way's nearest full-sized neighbor. Like the Milky Way, Andromeda is a whirling, spiral disc, each of its long arms made of billions of stars. And like the Milky Way, Andromeda has two small companion galaxies.

Aristotle said the sky was the realm of absolute, crystalline perfection. But Galileo showed the Moon's face to be battle-scarred and pocked. He could see with his own eyes that the worlds in the sky were no more perfect than the Earth.

Aristotle said all the heavenly bodies, the Sun, the Moon, the stars, and the planets, revolve around the Earth. How, then, Galileo asked, could Jupiter have its own moons whirling around it? If Jupiter was the center of *some* celestial motion, then Earth was not the sole and absolute center of the cosmos.

A revolution was aboiling. Copernicus had shown that the seemingly erratic motions of the wandering planets could be explained if they were all assumed to be orbiting not the Earth but the Sun. Johann Kepler worked out the mathematics of their orbits; not only do they travel around the Sun, he said, but also, their paths in space are not circular (as the Greeks assumed, since circles were their idea of perfection) but elliptical, egg-shaped.

Anyone who listened to such talk with an open mind found himself excited, disoriented, and a little scared. Natural

The Whirlpool is a spiral galaxy, like the Milky Way and Andromeda. But from our vantage point in the universe, we see the Whirlpool face-on, rather than at an angle. Note the long, spiral arms with their dark lanes of dust, and the Whirlpool's small companion.

philosophers were on the brink of the modern vision of space. They had discovered a fact we sometimes (caught up in day-to-day affairs) lose sight of even today, that Earth and sky are one single realm. Everything on Earth and in the heavens is part of a vast, far-flung, troubled kingdom we call the universe. Each world in the universe is made of more or less the same stuff as the rest, though mixed in different proportions, and every world is ruled by the same set of physical laws that apply to us here on Earth.

For Galileo, in a few nights of stargazing, the scope of the universe was "enlarged," he said, "a hundred thousand times beyond the belief of the wise men of bygone ages." Yet there were many people for whom the old beliefs were sacred. If the ancients said Earth was immovable, then Earth was immovable. Roman inquisitors forced Galileo, in his old age, to kneel in the Vatican and deny that our world journeys through space. "*E pur si muove,*" he muttered afterward (or so legend has it)—"Still, it moves."

The Moon is one of the most badly battered objects in the solar system, and most of its scars date from a primeval episode of terrible violence, the Great Bombardment. This is a composite photograph of two "half moons," the first- and third-quarter phases. The composite, prepared at the Lick Observatory, highlights craters near the center of the Moon that normally look flat during a full moon.

THE FLIGHT OF APOLLO

Over three centuries later, on July 15, 1969, the world prepared to make a leap as great as Galileo's when he pointed his spyglass at the Moon. *Apollo 11* sat on a launch pad at Cape Kennedy. Our progress from the first, frail, open-cockpit biplanes to that mammoth missile and spaceship had been so rapid that pioneering aviator Charles Lindbergh was still alive to see it. He had thrilled the world by crossing the Atlantic solo in the *Spirit of St. Louis*, flying on a prayer and a sandwich. Lindbergh dined with the Apollo astronauts the night before the launch, shaking his head, feeling a little like Rip Van Winkle.

The lift-off, on the morning of July 16, was perfect. In three days, astronauts Neil Armstrong, Buzz Aldrin, and Michael Collins traveled a quarter of a million miles and stared down at the pocked and cratered face of the Moon from 62 miles above it. Then Armstrong and Aldrin left the mother ship, the *Columbia*, in the lunar module, the *Eagle*, and began descending toward man's first contact with a world not his own.

During the trip down to the Moon, the computer overloaded and went into a state described afterward by its engineers as "dither." Armstrong, 38 years old and a veteran pilot, coolly took the controls from the computer and piloted the module by hand. At 4:17 P.M. on July 20, he radioed, "Houston: Tranquillity Base here. The *Eagle* has landed." The two men had touched down on their target, a vast and desolate plain, the Mare Tranquillitas—the Sea of Tranquillity. These dark patches on the Moon were mistaken by early observers for oceans, or, in Latin, *maria*, but they are really bone dry. Our satellite has neither air nor water; its gravitational pull is only one sixth the Earth's, too weak to hold onto an atmosphere.

Seven hours passed as the astronauts readied their equipment and made sure they would be able to blast off again to rejoin the *Columbia*. Then Armstrong started a small television camera and climbed down the nine-step ladder. At 10:56 P.M., he lowered his foot from the last rung, and carefully stepped away from the *Eagle*. "That's one small step for a man," he said, "one giant leap for mankind." He and Aldrin found that in the weak gravity they could walk comfortably and even bound about despite the encumbrance of their space suits. The dusty ground was much darker than it looks from Earth and stuck a little to the soles of their boots. They felt as if they were walking on cocoa. The two men set up scientific instruments, planted an American flag, joked a little with Mission Control, and filled two boxes with rocks.

For earth scientists waiting back home, that was the key event of the pageant. Holding their breaths at the NASA television monitors, they watched the astronauts prospecting in the Sea of Tranquillity. Perhaps among the rubble, they thought, was a trophy dating back to the birth of the solar system. Genesis rock.

Earth has destroyed all its Genesis rocks. Wind, rain, and weather, drifting continents, restless sea floors, and the great wheel of the revolving seasons have destroyed all the original rock that was here when our planet was born. Virtually everything we see around us has been ground to dust, melted down, and recast at least once—and sometimes tens of times. The oldest object ever found on Earth is the *Isua formation* of Greenland (Isua means, in Eskimo, "far out"). The Isua rock is 3.8 billion years old, as measured by the state of decay of its radioactive isotopes. That is certainly old; yet between Isua and the birth of the planet lie 1 billion years of which there is no trace on Earth.

We suspect our world was a very different place in its first billion years. Probably there were no seas and lands. The crust was thin, and most of the globe was molten. The air was unbreathable; the sky was lurid and strange. But since we have no earthly records of those times, it is hard to say for sure what our world was like or how it became the friendlier place we know today. "If you ask, 'What was the Earth like in the beginning?' the answer is, 'We just don't know,'" says planetologist Jim Head. "It is like trying to read a history book in which the first few chapters are ripped out."

Scientists once hoped to find out about our planet's first days by dredging up rock from the bottom of the sea. They thought the floors of the great deeps had lain silent and undisturbed since the beginning of time. But the rocks in the abyss proved to be not the oldest but among the youngest on the planet. Now, to find the missing first chapters of our corner of space, scientists had turned to the Moon.

One clue to the Moon's history had already been found in a strange and lunar landscape on Earth.

A century ago, a Philadelphia mineralogist named A. E. Foote visited a desert plateau east of Flagstaff, Arizona, a spot known then as Coon Butte. There was a famous hole in the ground at Coon Butte. It was one mile across, three miles around, and nearly 600 feet deep. Geologists thought it was the crater of an extinct volcano.

On the crater's rim and in the desert around it, Foote picked up more than a hundred nuggets. They were a distinctive alloy of iron and nickel—meteorites. Foote examined the nuggets through a microscope, and he saw tiny diamonds.

When Grove Karl Gilbert, chief geologist of the U.S. Geological Survey (USGS), heard about the meteorites and the diamonds, he wondered if people were wrong about Coon Butte. It certainly looked like a volcanic crater. But what if a meteorite of unheard-of dimensions had blazed through the skies and smashed into the Earth? Foote's nuggets might be bits of it, and his microscopic diamonds might be evidence of the terrible violence of its impact. Normally, diamonds are formed only in the depths of the Earth, when carbon is compressed for eons by the great weight of the millions of tons of rock above. Perhaps Foote's diamonds had formed almost instantaneously in the tremendous heat and pressure of the collision.

To Gilbert's colleagues this sort of talk was ridiculous. Many of them had a meteorite or two in their collection cabinets. They considered such nuggets to be curiosities, freaks of nature—nothing with which to explain a hole in the ground big enough to hide the Washington Monument.

Gilbert, however, thought meteorites might be important in the cosmic scheme of things. He had a vision of giant

Arizona Meteor Crater is a mile across, three miles around, and almost 600 feet deep. It is a small memento of the kinds of collisions that can destroy, or create, a planet.

hailstorms of rock falling on the Moon and gouging its craters. If such a thing had ever happened on Earth, it would support this lunar theory. Gilbert went to Coon Butte and made careful magnetic measurements there; but he found no sign of a buried mass of iron.

Then Daniel Moreau Barringer heard about Gilbert's speculations. Barringer was a wealthy Philadelphia lawyer and mining engineer. He drilled dozens of holes and dug a few mine shafts in the crater, hoping to find a lode of nickel and iron. He found hundreds of feet of *breccia* (rock that has been pulverized and cemented together) in the crater floor, and this encouraged him to hope that a giant heap of alien metal lay buried just out of his reach. Barringer sank 30 years and most of his fortune into the crater, but with no luck. In 1929, the stock market crashed, and he knew he would no longer be able to raise money to keep drilling and digging. That year, he died.

There the matter rested for decades.

"If you were around there in 1957 and asked a geologist if they thought a stone fell out of the sky and onto the Earth, you would have gotten a big horse laugh," says Eugene Shoemaker of the USGS. In 1957 Shoemaker, then a graduate student, camped out in the Hopi buttes and studied the crater from all sides. The rock layers in the rim walls are arched and peeled back, as they would be if a great meteorite had struck.

The rocks that were once where the hole is now are scattered across the desert for miles around. "They have been thrown out," he says, "almost as though a flower were opening and the petals were lying back." The young geologist descended into Barringer's old mining shafts. "The crater's underlain by a deep lens of broken rock, going down about 600 feet," Shoemaker says. "The lowest 50 feet contain microscopic droplets of the melted meteorite itself, now frozen into glass, which is a shock-melted rock."

Shoemaker concluded that he was looking at "our best exposed example on Earth of a young impact crater." Coon Butte—now called Arizona Meteor Crater—really *was* carved by a meteorite. Gilbert and Barringer's only mistake was in the way they pictured the impact. Today, Peter Schultz, of Brown University, can illustrate the sequence of events with a high-tech cannon called a *vertical light gas gun*. The gun, at NASA's Ames Research Laboratory in California, is three stories high, and it can fire a pellet downward at any angle at meteoric speeds of 25,000 miles per hour. For targets, Schultz arranges small plots of soil, rock, and powder, and he records each collision with an extremely high-speed camera.

The impact of the pellet re-creates a giant collision in miniature. The bullet heats up so much when it strikes the

As they explore the Moon, and other nearby worlds, planetologists are beginning to see the Earth in a new and cosmic perspective. How was the solar system born? Why is our world so different from the rest? Why is Planet Earth alive?

target that most of it melts and a small fraction of it vaporizes; the ground where it strikes is partly melted, pulverized, and thrown up and out. Schultz can demonstrate, among other things, that an increase in the projectile's speed affects dramatically the size of the crater. Investigators calculate that if the Arizona meteorite were traveling at 45,000 miles an hour, it need only have been about 100 feet in diameter (much smaller than Gilbert imagined) to blast open a crater a mile wide. The impact probably released about the same amount of energy as a very large hydrogen bomb.

The object that fell in the Arizona desert was not a behemoth, and it did not survive the impact. All that remains of it are the tiny droplets of glass that Shoemaker found in the walls of Barringer's tunnels, and nuggets like the ones Foote picked up in the desert. Barringer struck his meteorite with the first holes he drilled. There was not much more to find.

After Shoemaker convinced his colleagues that Coon Butte is a meteor crater, they looked again at the pocked face of the Moon. Most geologists came to accept Gilbert's old idea that the Moon had been bombarded. Shoemaker was asked by officials at NASA to guide the first Apollo astronauts around Arizona Meteor Crater before they went to the Moon, to teach them about the bizarre geology of explosive impacts. During their tour, the astronauts found a meteorite.

The startling fact is that stray chunks of matter from outer space collide with Planet Earth every day. Most of them burn up as they fall through the atmosphere and never reach the ground. The bright, fiery trails of their passage are what we call *meteors*. Often a single large meteorite shatters from the violence of its fall through the atmosphere, and the fragments burn up in the air and drift to the Earth as dust.

This dust rains steadily down upon our heads. About one hundred tons fall into our atmosphere *each day*. "These particles are in the air we breathe, the food we eat, and the water we drink," says astronomer Donald E. Brownlee. They are called *micrometeorites*, and they are so small that, Brownlee calculates, the average outdoorsman is "hit" by a few of them a week without knowing it.

In 1982, a six-pound meteorite crashed through the roof of Robert and Wanda Donahue's home in Wethersfield, Connecticut, and landed in the living room, where they were watching *M*A*S*H* on television. They were unhurt. A decade before, another meteorite had struck a Wethersfield house a mile away.

But meteorites have crashed near human habitations rarely enough that until the dawn of the modern age thoughtful people were not sure whether such a thing had ever really happened. There were ancient reports of fireballs that went flashing through the night sky and crash-landed in farmers' fields, smoldering. Pliny the Elder, the Roman naturalist, writing in the first century A.D., called the falling rocks "thunderstones," because, he said, they made a great roar when they dropped from the sky. But Pliny also wrote that pearls are the offspring of shells made pregnant with dew; that a hawk at certain seasons of the year becomes a cuckoo; and that human beings have had love affairs with dolphins and whales. In the late 17th century, at the dawn of modern science, French astronomers of the Enlightenment reviewed Pliny's writings and all the other thunderstone stories they could find and decided there was probably no such thing.

A spectacular meteorite shower promptly fell in L'Aigle, 70 miles west of Paris. A Parisian astronomer was sent to investigate and found townspeople trading thunderstones in the streets. After that, no one could doubt any longer that rocks do fall from the sky.

At the turn of this century, a fireball was seen by the townspeople of Vanavara, in the wastes of Siberia. The people of Vanavara said the thunder of the fireball's passage, and the explosion that followed, had cracked windows in their village and knocked jars out of their cupboards. A Soviet scientific expedition made its way into the Stony Tunguska Forest to

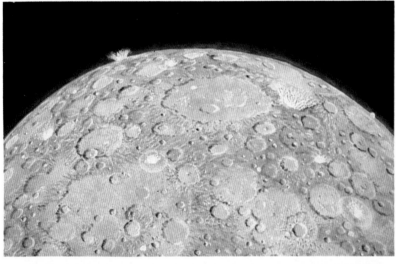

This is the story of the birth of the Moon, as scientists understand it today. Four and a half billion years ago, amid the reeling maelstrom of the young solar system, planetesimals fell together, and quickly built up the red-hot, molten Moon. Then, after a last, furious bombardment four billion years ago, the Moon began to cool, and its oceans of lava hardened into mares, *dark lunar seas. Unlike the Earth, the Moon's surface has changed but little from that day to this, save for the odd impact of a stray asteroid or comet. One of these latterday collisions may have been witnessed by five monks in Canterbury, England, on June 25, 1178. There was a bright new moon that night. The monks swore under oath that suddenly, on one horn of the new moon, "a flaming torch sprang up, spewing out fire, hot coals, and sparks."*

investigate. The members of the expedition found that *several hundred square miles of trees had been knocked down and burned.* The trees' scarred trunks all radiated outward as if from the epicenter of an explosion—a point 40 miles from Vanavara.

For decades, the event at Tunguska was wrapped in mystery and obscurity. Today it seems likely that a meteorite exploded in midair above that lonely spot in the Siberian forest.

The Arizona crash, too, may have been witnessed by human beings, for Stone Age hunters from Asia had already found their way, by a land bridge, across the Bering Strait and wandered south across the American Southwest. Even from scores of miles away, the hunters, letting fall their flint spears, would have stared at the fireball arcing across the desert sky amid claps of thunder. They would have seen a flash of fire many miles away and a giant mushroom cloud rising miles into the air, precisely as clouds were to rise in the desert from atomic bomb tests in our time. God knows what omen the Stone Age hunters made of it.

Lunar Rover on the rim of Shorty Crater, which is 110 meters in diameter. The Moon is pocked with craters of all sizes, from microscopic to monumental.

Armstrong, Aldrin, and Collins returned safely to Earth, bringing home 45 pounds of Moon rocks, which they handled like jewels ("as, in a sense, they are," said Collins). The three astronauts were held in quarantine for weeks, while white mice, cockroaches, algae, fish, and quail were exposed to them, and to bits of Moon rock, to see if Apollo had brought home an alien plague. The rest of the lunar treasure was sealed off in aluminum chests and vacuum chambers.

During this quarantine, Terry N. Slezak, a NASA photo technician, was working late one Friday night in the Lunar Receiving Laboratory, and he unpacked a roll of 70mm film with his bare hands. Suddenly he noticed a fine black powder clinging to his fingers. Apparently Armstrong had dropped the cartridge in the lunar dust and never brushed it off. "I just looked and thought, 'My goodness! There it is,'" Slezak said afterward. "The dust was very black. It looked and felt very dry, but it was not as fine as talcum powder." Slezak and the five others in the room with him immediately stripped, sealed all their clothes in plastic bags, and rushed to the showers.

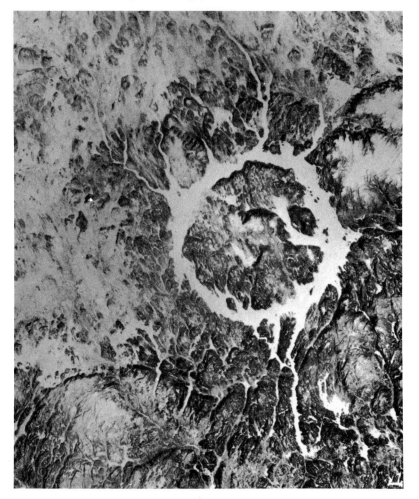

Manicouagan Reservoir, in Quebec, seen from space. Some 41 miles wide, it may be the scar of a big meteorite's impact. Such ancient, weathered scars on the Earth's surface are sometimes called ghost craters, *or* astroblemes.

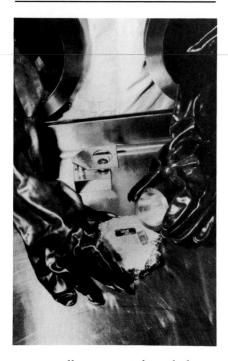

Apollo astronauts brought home many treasure boxes full of Moon rocks. To preserve them from contamination, the rocks are sealed away from Earth's atmosphere and they are never touched by human hands.

The quarantine ended without further incident, and the gray, ginger, and cocoa-colored rocks were sent out to be analyzed in special laboratories such as the Lunatic Asylum in Pasadena, California. Five successive Apollo missions brought back Moon rocks, bringing home a total of 2,000 separate specimens.

From the astronauts' observations and careful dating of the lunar rocks they brought home, we now have some sense of the Moon's first billion years. It seems to have been a period of furious, almost unimaginable bombardment, a blizzard of stone like nothing we have ever seen, and it lasted millions of years. The cocoa powder in which the astronauts planted their footprints was pulverized rock, or *regolith*. It lies in some places as deep as 60 feet. The pounding of meteorite after meteorite formed this regolith; the Moon was like a mortar beneath a million pestles.

A few stray lunar fragments happened to escape the bombardment, and these rocks are older than the Isua formation on Earth. Some may be as old as 4.6 billion years, and thus they apparently date from the Moon's first years. But these relics are very rare. Most of the basalt that fills the Moon's dark maria is between 3.1 and 3.8 billion years, roughly as old as the Isua rock of Greenland.

This is how many lunar experts read the story: The Moon probably formed some 4.5 billion years ago, about the same time as the Earth. Its surface was heated by furious successive impacts and then began to cool.

Four billion years ago, a second, late bombardment took place. Huge impact craters, hundreds of times larger than Arizona Meteor Crater, destroyed most of the earliest rocks on the Moon's surface—making the first chapter of the solar system almost as hard to read on the Moon as it is on Earth.

For the next few hundred million years, lava welled up through the weakened crater floors, flooding great stretches of the surface. These lava seas hardened into maria.

When the last of the lava hardened, the Moon had evolved as far as it would ever go. Three billion years later, it is virtually unchanged—except for, here and there, a fresh impact crater. Meteorites continue to fall on the Moon to this day, as they do on Earth, but at perhaps one ten-thousandth the rate at which they fell in the beginning.

In retrospect, the exploration of the Moon has proven like the exploration of the bottom of the Earth's oceans. Neither of these exotic places showed us precisely what we were looking for—a complete set of pages from the missing first chapters of the solar system. But the events that erased the records have proven to be dramatic in their own right. The ocean floor helped us see the creation and destruction of the Earth's surface—the story of plate tectonics. The Moon shows us the creation and destruction of whole worlds—it speaks of a titanic episode of primordial violence that has come to be known as the *Great Bombardment.*

As our space probes visit other, more distant worlds, they have sent home more and more evidence of the Great Bombardment. The planet Mercury, nearest to the Sun, appears to have been as battered as the Moon; so was Mars; so were the moons of Jupiter and Saturn, more than a billion miles out from the Sun. Our home in space began not with a whimper but with bang after bang. The discovery has implications for early life on Earth, and perhaps for the future of life, if we understand it correctly. In the most desolate place on Earth, scientists are now catching glimpses of the events that led to the Great Bombardment.

THE BIG BANG

In 1969, a Japanese scientific expedition was trekking near the Yamato Mountains, in the region of the Antarctic icecap that lies directly south of Africa. The Japanese found nine dark meteorites lying close together on the surface of the ice.

Given meteorites' scarcity, the expedition leaders assumed that the nine samples they found were fragments of a single large specimen that had broken apart in its fall to the ice. To their amazement, however, they soon discovered that their finds were all of different types and chemical compositions. They were not pieces of one rock. They had not even formed in the same region of the solar system. This was thrilling: The convergence of nine separate thunderstones at that single spot implied that the ice sheet itself was somehow collecting these rarities of nature and sweeping them together.

The wastelands of Antarctica are the best places on Earth to look for meteorites. These relics from space hold clues to the origin of our world and of the entire solar system.

The Japanese mounted more expeditions to the Yamato ice in 1973, 1974, 1975, and 1979, and they were rewarded with a grand total of 3,000 meteorites. Every year since then, during the brief Antarctic summer, international expeditions have converged on the Japanese rock gardens. Each small meteorite is photographed where it lies and then nudged gingerly into a teflon bag, which is an awkward procedure when performed with thick mittens and in deep subzero cold, with the stone skittering on the ice. Once bagged, each specimen is shipped home and studied in an antiseptic laboratory, using the same sorts of apparatus built to study Moon rocks. The sample is never touched by human hands.

Meteorites have been called the poor man's space probes: They are fragments of the solar system that came to us. They are of priceless value to science, because many of them have not been melted down and transfigured since the birth of the solar system. That makes them fossils of the Creation, as valuable as the bones of Lucy, thought to be the oldest hominid ever found. These are the Genesis rocks we sought and missed at the bottom of the sea and on the surface of the Moon. We can read in these homely shards from space bits of the Story of Stories—how our corner of the cosmos came to be.

The story is, and may always be, speculative, and it is subject to change with each new piece of cosmic evidence. But the tales the meteorites tell scientists at the Lunatic Asylum are helping to make the story more solid and substantial.

The *very* beginning of this tale is told not by earth scientists or planetologists but by astrophysicists and cosmologists, who work mostly with equations rather than rock samples. They

A scientist prepares to collect a small iron meteorite in a plastic bag.

believe that between 10 billion and 20 billion years ago, all the matter in the universe was concentrated in a single, small spot and exploded in a Big Bang. A vast, formless cloud hurtled outward in all directions. As it flew, the cloud collected into clumps, which evolved into stars. The universe is full of great groups of millions and billions of stars, gatherings we call galaxies. It is thought that every galaxy in the universe is still flying apart from every other, from the force of the primordial Big Bang. Certain extremely faint radio background radiation, first detected in the 1960s, may be energy that lingers in space even today from the cataclysm in which our universe was born.

Perhaps 12 billion years ago, the galaxy we call the Milky Way took shape among the rest. It is a collection of more than a hundred billion stars, and it is known as a *spiral galaxy* because its bright stars are clustered in graceful spiral arms. Viewed from the outside, a spiral galaxy has the shape of a child's pinwheel. The vast pinwheel of stars slowly spins in space. A star near the center of the pinwheel of the Milky Way takes about 20 million years to make one revolution. A star at the outskirts takes 200 million years. The Milky Way is part of a local group of a dozen galaxies, all composed of billions of stars and spinning as they hurtle through space.

After the Milky Way galaxy had formed, stars were born in it and other stars died, sometimes in sudden and terrific explosions that spewed out quantities of radioactive debris; for a few days, each dying star gave off as much energy as the light of a whole galaxy. Such an explosion is called a *supernova*. The debris from each supernova drifted off into space like dust clouds from an atomic bomb, and eventually some of the dust fell together again to make another star. Thus even stars have life cycles and go from dust to dust. Amid sagas of birth and death, peace and violence, billions of years passed in the Milky Way.

Now we come to the epoch for which planetologists and Earth scientists can contribute evidence and clues. Around 4.6 billion years ago, in the outskirts of the Milky Way, in one of its spiral arms, a cloud of dust and gas began to condense, to fall inward upon itself. The cloud was, possibly, the debris of a supernova, or of more than one supernova. Indeed, its collapse inward may have been triggered by the violent death of a nearby star. Tiny compared to the size of the whole galaxy but still billions of miles across, this dark cloud collapsed into a flat, spinning disc. It looked like a miniature model of the galaxy itself. Within the cloud, bits of dust and gas collided and stuck together, and these clumps grew larger and larger as more debris stuck onto them. The center of the disc thickened and darkened as it drew in more and more matter from the outskirts by its growing gravitational attraction. When the disc's center reached a critical mass, it lit up—another star was born.

The same sort of thing had happened already innumerable times in the universe and many billions of times in the Milky Way; it was a humdrum event (if anything celestial can be called humdrum). But that particular birth has special significance for us as we peer back in time. The radiant heart of that cloud was to be our Sun.

As the center of the cloud lit up, an observer a safe distance away would have observed it to be swaddled in dark dust and gas. Not all of the cloud had been drawn into the center, to light up in thermonuclear reactions. The dark matter that was left over had stayed dark. It, too, collected, clumped, knotted. The composition of each clump was governed by its distance from the blazing fire in the center of the disc. Far from the disc's center, Jupiter took shape—a giant mass of gas. Its gravitational field swept up any gas and dust nearby. Closer in, volatile elements were driven off by the Sun's heat. Here the rocky planets formed.

The dark cloud was swirling with huge, rocky, and metallic *planetesimals*, some as large as our Moon. These worldlets were so crowded, and their orbits so chaotic, that they collided with each other, piled against each other, and pummeled the growing planets, which gained in size with each collision. Each young planet's gravitational pull drew more planetesimals inward toward it. It was a celestial demolition derby.

A succession of such collisions built the planet we call the Earth. Perhaps one last immense impact spun off a lump of matter from which the Moon formed. The infant Earth began its transformation into the world we inhabit today.

Thus, what we have called the Great Bombardment was only the tail end of a vast, creative process. Some worlds, like the Moon, which have hardly changed since, still carry the wounds of the final saturation bombing. But Earth has long since healed.

There are millions of shards in our solar system that never collected into worlds, and are still whirling around the Sun. Fortunately, most of them are confined to two zones, far away from Earth. *Asteroids* are chunks of rock and metal ranging from the size of Rhode Island to the size of a golf ball and are in orbits between Mars and Jupiter, the *asteroid belt*. *Comets*, thought to be "dirty snowballs," rocky ice, are believed to circle the Sun far out beyond the orbit of the farthest planet, Pluto. There are probably trillions of comets in the outer limits of the solar system, in a great, dim cloud of ice.

Many of these asteroids and comets are in orbits that cross those of the planets, so random collisions are possible, indeed inevitable.

Each collision seems to us on Earth an aberration of nature, a bizarre and violent episode. Yet it is part and parcel of the process that made our galaxy and made our solar system—the infall of matter. Craters are far more important in the life of worlds than we ever realized. They still shape the surfaces of most of the worlds in our solar system; they would be prominent on ours today if Earth's wind, water, and weather did not hide the scars from us.

Says Shoemaker, "Impact is the most fundamental of all the geological processes."

THE RUNAWAY GREENHOUSE NEXT DOOR

Ours will be remembered as the time of the first Grand Tour of space, an age of exploration perhaps greater than the era of Columbus, Magellan, da Gama, and the Cabots. Everywhere our reconnaissance missions have taken us, toward the Sun or away from it, we have found traces of the Great Bombardment. On worlds with atmospheres, we have found signs of climatic change and disaster that make our own Earth's stormy weather look like the Garden of Eden.

The planet Venus, named for the goddess of love, was once known to us only as the morning and evening star, because it is brilliant enough to be visible even when the sky still is half lit by the Sun. Venus is bright partly because it is near Earth—it is the closest of the other planets—and partly because it is cloaked in thick white clouds, which glare in the light of the Sun. When Galileo first peered at Venus through a telescope in 1609, it appeared to him without spot or blemish, a blank white disc. He could tell he was looking at a sphere, because it waxed and waned in phases like the Moon, but he could see nothing of its surface. Neither could three centuries of astronomers who followed Galileo. Until just a few years ago, science fiction writers were free to dream that the world beneath the clouds might be a paradise.

Venus is shrouded in thick clouds, which hide its surface from our view.

Of all the nine planets, it is ironic that Venus should have been so hard to get to know. It is similar to Earth in size and weight, in its inheritance of chemical elements, and in its distance from the Sun. Astronomers call it Earth's sister.

To get through the clouds, the Soviet Union and the United States have sent a dozen space probes and robots down to the Venusian surface. Many of them suffered the fate of spies in a war zone—destroyed before they could get a message home. Among the probes were those dropped to the surface by *Pioneer Venus 2*, in 1978. Jules Verne would have liked those probes. They were small, heavy spheres shielded against the heat and pressure by walls of titanium, with a few tiny windows of diamond and sapphire. Nevertheless, one of the probes

A glimpse of the Venusian surface. This is the first image radioed to Earth from the Soviet robot lander Venera 14. The rocks are at hundreds of degrees Fahrenheit. That the robot survived long enough to radio home its report was a triumph of the Space Age. The terrain in this image is remarkably bare of dust or soil. It resembles certain lava flows on Earth, including those that cover the Earth's ocean floor in many places.

burned up almost as soon as it entered the Venusian atmosphere. Two others died upon reaching the ground. The last robot sent home radio messages for 68 minutes before its circuits failed.

The harsh fate of these probes, and the messages they managed to send back, did help us put together a picture of Venus. It is no paradise; it is more like Dante's Inferno.

We now know that its clouds are not water vapor but droplets of sulfuric acid. They are racked with storms, riven by thunder and lightning, and they shed perpetual downpours of acid rain. The air beneath the cloud layer is almost all carbon dioxide. It is so soupy that the atmospheric pressure at the surface of Venus is as great as the pressure 3,000 feet beneath the Atlantic Ocean!

The clouds never part to let a ray of sunlight touch the ground, so the surface is dusky even at noon. It is a somber desert of brown, dun, and burnt ocher, and it shimmers like tarmac on a hot day. If Arizona Meteor Crater is the closest thing on Earth to a moonscape, then Death Valley, one of the hottest places on our planet, is one of our better approximations of Venus. Recently Venus expert Jim Head went to Death Valley to give himself a taste of the Venusian climate. "It's nowhere near as hot as the surface of Venus," he says. "Even though temperatures in Death Valley on a really hot day can exceed 120 degrees Fahrenheit, on Venus they get up regularly to 900 degrees Fahrenheit. In fact, it's hot enough on the surface of Venus to melt lead." That is much too hot for rain to fall; the acid rains from the clouds boil, turn to vapor, and rise again long before they reach the desert. At night, the rocks may glow a dull red in the dark. If Death Valley were only half as hot as Venus, this book, dropped on its rocks and sand, would burst spontaneously into flames.

When space probes first showed us this inferno, planetologists were baffled by it, for the Venusian clouds reflect 98 percent of the light from the sun back into space, and only 2 percent filters down to the ground. It seemed strange that 2 percent of the Sun's light should be enough to keep a whole world hotter than an oven. Instead, with its skies so cloudy, the planet should be quite cool. True, Venus is closer to the Sun than we are, but not enough to explain its temperature. We now know that even Mercury, the world nearest to the Sun, is not as hot as Venus.

At first, some investigators thought the answer might be Venus's spin. Venus takes 243 Earth days to complete one rotation, which is remarkably sluggish for a planet. The direction of its rotation is also unusual; on Venus, the Sun rises in the west and sets in the east. Perhaps Venus originally rotated normally, and a titanic collision early in its history sent it reeling backward. (Oddly enough, Venus's upper atmosphere swirls around the planet at more than 200 miles per hour. Though Venus is moving very slowly, it is wrapped in a whirlwind.)

However, climate modelers have studied the effects of Venus's rotation, and they do not believe the slow spin can account for the planet's temperature.

Carl Sagan was the first to suggest that the answer might be Venus's carbon dioxide. On our planet, most of the heat from the Sun is radiated back out into space. Some of this reradiation from Earth is blocked by the carbon dioxide in our atmosphere and by other greenhouse gases; this blanket of gas helps to warm the Earth. On Venus, Sagan noted, the very dense atmosphere is almost all carbon dioxide, and it probably makes an incredible greenhouse, trapping the heat beneath the cloud layer and keeping it there.

More of Venus's story has come from maps of its terrain. It was surveyed from above by an orbiting robot, the *Pioneer* Venus spacecraft, and it is currently being charted in 50 to 100 times more detail by astronomers at the world's largest radio telescope, in Arecibo, Puerto Rico. Investigators at Arecibo bounce radio waves off the surface of the planet and then catch the echoes—the rebounding waves—in the great white-glazed aluminum dish. A computer analyzes the echoes and prints out maps of the contours of the distant terrain. It is similar to the technique that oceanographers use to map the floors of the oceans on Earth—only in mapping Venus, the echoes return to us across 26 million miles.

The global layout of the Venusian terrain is not unlike

Earth's. Investigators are mapping mountain ranges higher than the Himalayas, on broad, high plateaus the size of our continents. Earth's seven continents would appear much the same if all our seas were drained. "It looks as if Venus may have had oceans hundreds of millions of years ago," says planetologist Jim Head. If so, Venus would have been much more like Earth. Its continents may have enjoyed rivers, streams, puffy white clouds, and pleasant weather. It is even conceivable that in those early days of the planet, life began much as it did here on Planet Earth. But then, says Head, "the temperatures got so hot that the oceans boiled away, leaving Venus the hot, bone-dry place it is today."

If this tale is true—and it is supported not only by the dry basins but also by subtle chemical evidences in the Venusian atmosphere of a vast episode of evaporation in its past—why did the oceans evaporate on Venus, but not on Earth? Quite possibly, the planets' positions in space made all the difference. Venus, being just slightly nearer the Sun than we are, would have been slightly warmer. Daily, a little more water would have evaporated from its seas than from our own. The added water vapor in the atmosphere, according to this scenario, created a greenhouse effect—for water vapor, like carbon dioxide, is a greenhouse gas. As the Venusian surface grew warmer and warmer, the oceans evaporated faster, which heated the planet still more. Gradually the hot, steamy atmosphere leached carbon from the bare Venusian rocks until the whole atmosphere was nearly pure carbon dioxide. Venus had turned into a runaway greenhouse, and the last drop of water in the ocean basins boiled away.

Until recently, we have been lucky. Earth has just as much carbon as Venus, but most of it is still locked away harmlessly in rocks—mostly limestone. Today, however, visions of the Venusian desert, with its hot, vacant basins, disturb many earth scientists. Just how frail is a living world? Can a little thing tip its climate and ruin it forever? We have been burning more and more fossil fuels since the dawn of the Industrial Revolution, taking carbon out of rocks and putting it into the atmosphere as carbon dioxide. We know we are doing this faster than the stirring of the Earth's spheres can remove it. If we keep this up, is it possible that we will someday destroy Earth's good health and turn our home into a runaway greenhouse? Will the human volcano heat Planet Earth until all the seas go dry and lead melts in the sunlight? Are we already on the downhill path to Venus?

We simply do not know enough yet about Venus, or even about Earth, to be sure of the answer. But judging by our neighboring world, we are playing with fire.

Venus may help us assess the dangers not only of the greenhouse effect but also of acid rain. One of the great environmental debates of our time turns upon the acidity of our rains and snows. Scientists are investigating whether strongly acid rains are a natural or a man-made condition on Planet Earth and whether they are dangerous.

Venus is a simpler world, and it has a striking acid rain cycle that would repay study. Its lower atmosphere is laden with the chemical compound sulfur dioxide. Winds loft some of this sulfur dioxide above the clouds and into the sunshine, where the harsh ultraviolet rays of the Sun split the compounds' chemical bonds, and they recombine with water vapor. Sulfuric acid forms, and drops of acid rain fall downward through the clouds. In the hot lower atmosphere, the rain evaporates, breaks apart into water and sulfur dioxide, and once again wafts upward above the clouds. Thus acid rain never stops falling but never touches the Venusian desert.

Where does Venus's sulfur dioxide come from? Perhaps from the eruptions of giant volcanoes. The radio telescope at Arecibo reveals great circular ridges that look like the rims of volcanic calderas. There is also a strikingly long valley on Venus, with rifts running up the center of it. This valley looks very much like a famous rift in East Africa, where forces are pulling the crust apart. The great rift on Venus has a massive

An artist's vision of Venus's acrid and poisonous clouds. Of all the worlds in our solar system, Venus is the most like Dante's Inferno.

volcano jutting up from one of the major faults; the cone appears to have filled in part of the valley and sent lava flowing out across the plains on either side of the valley. This Venusian volcano reminds planetologists of Mount Kilimanjaro, a giant volcano that is an outgrowth of the East African Rift.

Perhaps, then, Venus owes its acid rains to the sort of global vulcanism that comes with plate tectonics. We don't know the Venusian terrain well enough yet to be sure if plates were ever in motion there; it is possible that the plateaus of Venus are drifting even now, like our continents. Maybe plate tectonics gave Venus acid rain.

In just a few years of exploration, the planet we named for the goddess of love has gone from a fantasy island to an island of nightmares. But, as Sigmund Freud observed, we can learn even from nightmares.

THE STRANGE LIFE OF A RED PLANET

At 8:00 P.M. on the night before Halloween in 1938, on CBS Radio, Orson Welles and his *Mercury Theatre on the Air* performed a clever adaptation of the British science fiction writer H. G. Wells's novel *War of the Worlds*. The actors presented their show as a series of flash news broadcasts, announcing that Martians had landed in New Jersey and were headed for Manhattan, killing everything in their path with heat rays and poison gas.

At least 6 million listeners tuned in to *Mercury Theatre on the Air*, and many thousands, having missed the show's lighthearted Halloween introduction, were terrified by what they heard. ("Those who have never seen a living Martian can scarcely imagine the strange horror of its appearance. The peculiar V-shaped mouth with its pointed upper lip, the absence of brow ridges, the absence of a chin . . . "). On the East Coast, people exchanged frantic phone calls with family, friends, and neighbors, then scrambled into their cars, pointed the wheels away from New Jersey, and fled.

The extent of the panic says something about the mood of the country in those years; Americans were still shaken from the Great Depression. But their readiness to believe what they heard also shows how many people felt Mars was really alive. Martians were old and well-established bogeys. They had gotten their start 60 years before—with a mistranslation.

In 1877, the Italian astronomer Giovanni Schiaparelli, having studied the Red Planet closely through his telescope, announced that its surface was crisscrossed with *canali*. In Italian, *canali* are channels. But the English-speaking press reported Schiaparelli had seen *canals*, and the word suggested hydraulic engineers directing platoons with shovels. Readers imagined Mars as a red, global desert in which an ancient civilization clung to life in a webwork of dying cities. Vast canals carried water to the cities from the melting polar ice caps and kept the desperate Martian race alive.

One American who was stirred by visions of *canali* was a wealthy and aristocratic astronomer, Percival Lowell, of Boston ("where the Cabots talk only to Lowells, and the Lowells talk only to God"). Percival's brother Abbott and sister Amy were famous poets, and he was a romantic himself. In 1894, he left Boston to build a first-rate observatory on Mars Hill in Flagstaff, Arizona, from which to watch the Martians. He filled his notebooks with maps of the spidery canals.

Lowell could see the polar caps of Mars growing each Martian winter and dwindling each summer. Color changes swept the planet, which he took to be seasonal changes in vegetation. He described all this in his book *Mars as the Abode of Life:*

> To the thoughtful observer who is privileged to see them well there is nothing in the sky so profoundly impressive as these canals of Mars. Fine lines and little gossamer filaments only, cobwebbing the face of the Martian disc, but threads to draw one's mind after them across the millions of miles of intervening void.

The Martian question could not be entirely resolved until half a century after Lowell's death and one century after the observations of Schiaparelli.

In July 1976, in a triumph of human engineering, pluck, and luck, *Viking 1* landed safely in a Martian plain, the Chryse Planitia. *Viking's* camera had been designed by the planetologist Thomas Mutch of Brown University at a cost of $16 million. If it worked, it would provide our first close-up view of the surface of the mysterious Red Planet.

The first close-up look at the surface of Mars— Viking looks at its own footpad.

An image of the russet Martian terrain from the robot lander Viking 2.

There was a short but agonized pause as the camera filmed one of its own footpads ("In case it were to sink into Martian quicksand," Carl Sagan has explained, "we wanted to know about it before the spacecraft disappeared."). The camera absorbed the scene before it slowly, like a young scholar reading Chinese, scanned in long vertical columns, and sent the message back to Earth dot by dot. The system was working perfectly, and the NASA control team at the Jet Propulsion Laboratory (JPL), watching the picture unfold, cheered wildly when they saw that the footpad, with every rivet showing clearly, rested on sandy, pebbly, solid ground. One NASA director, Gentry Lee, wept with joy.

For Mutch, the impact of that very first picture of his dream planet was so great that he was transported. "I could feel myself walking out on the surface of Mars," he said later. Radiant in the JPL control room, he exclaimed, "It's just incredible to see that Mars is really there."

But for many people, the robot's panoramic pictures were melancholy and disappointing. The Martian desert in which Viking had landed looked less promising than the Arizona landscape around Lowell's observatory on Mars Hill. They confirmed the pictures other robots had taken of Mars from orbit high above. So much for the dreams of Wells and Lowell.

What happened to the canals? Lowell was a good astronomer, whose zeal and enterprise ultimately led to the discovery of the ninth planet, Pluto, after his death. But alas, his canals were merely optical illusions, fictions of overeager eyes straining to see beyond the resolution of the telescope. "Lowell always said that the regularity of the canals was an unmistakable sign that they were of intelligent origin," writes Carl Sagan. "This is certainly true. The only unresolved question was which side of the telescope the intelligence was on."

Looking at those desert panoramas, people gave up on their favorite Martians and turned away. Science fiction writers dream now of more distant realms of space: In recent years, alien visitors like Mork, E.T., and the messianic Star Man (whose rescue ship landed in Arizona Meteor Crater) tend to come from other solar systems or distant galaxies, not from our neighboring world.

Yet planetologists have quietly gone on studying Mars, and they are reading surprising messages in its red deserts.

Like Venus, Mars's terrain suggests it may once have been livelier than it is today. Among the most intriguing photographs of the *Mariner* and *Viking* robots we see fine, fingerlike beds of streams and rivers crisscrossing great stretches of the Martian desert. There is no water in the beds now, of course—any water would evaporate instantly in the low pressure of the Martian atmosphere. Yet the sinuous riverbeds show that Mars was once, at least briefly, a wet world and a very different place.

The long, sinuous channels on Mars fan out from highlands and disappear into lowlands. There are no signs of lakebeds along them; the rivers that cut the channels seem never to have pooled in standing water but to have flown along quickly and evaporated quickly, the way flash floods do in deserts on Earth. The walls of the Valles Marineris look as if they have been eroded after the same fashion as the walls of the Grand Canyon, not gradually but abruptly, in landslides set off by the rare torrents.

The pattern of erosion suggests that there was once not only *some* water on Mars, but deluges greater than the Flood of Noah. Geologists looking at Martian terrain have found a striking resemblance between the surface of Mars and the Scablands in southern Washington State. The Scablands are one of the strangest geological formations on our planet. Some 13,000 years ago, during the last Ice Age, a deep lake backed up behind glaciers in mountains now on the border of Idaho and Montana. The lake they formed was as much as 2,000 feet deep and 3,000 miles broad. When the ice dam broke, a wall of water perhaps 30 stories high roared all the way to the Pacific Ocean. The flow was perhaps 10 times greater than that of all the rivers in the world today combined. Wherever the torrent went, it gouged away a layer of soil and rock between 100 and 150 feet thick and ripped up and carried off rocks the size of houses. Canyons and buttes that normally would take millions of years to form were carved in less than a week. Land in three states was scarred by the flood. One of the biggest channels it dug was the Grand Coulee, where the Columbia River now flows and where modern engineers have built the famous dam.

The Scablands are the closest we can come on Earth to this sort of Martian terrain; but our catastrophic flood in Washington was dwarfed by the deluges on Mars. The Scablands are smaller than a postage stamp compared to the flood plains of Mars.

How could a desert planet have had such floods? Where has all the water gone? Some scientists think vast, dark seas of frozen water are locked deep beneath the crust, as a layer of *permafrost* several miles thick. Perhaps volcanic eruptions or the collisions of asteroids have now and then cracked the surface, melting and unleashing billions of tons of water.

Mars is only one third the size of Venus or Earth, but, according to planetologist Vic Baker, "Almost everything on Mars is bigger, whether it's volcanoes, mountains, landslides, flood features. You name it—it's bigger on Mars. Not just because gravity is lower on Mars, but also because on Mars, erosion is much slower. Rare catastrophic things that happen to it get preserved."

The robot *Mariner* found a huge gash, which we call the Valley of the Mariner (in Latin, *Valles Marineris*), cutting across the Martian equator. It averages two miles deep (in some places, four), and it is as long as the United States is wide. Compared to this valley, the Grand Canyon is a gulch.

Northwest of the long valley, *Mariner 9* photographed a volcano that rises three times higher than Mount Everest— 17 miles from surface to summit. In guessing at the age of this volcano, which is called Olympus Mons (Latin for Mount Olympus), astronomers have counted the number of meteoritic impact craters on its flanks, rather as Captain Ahab judged the age of the Great White Whale by counting its harpoon scars. The more craters, the longer the lava has been exposed on the surface. Crater-counting shows that some slopes of the volcano are hundreds of millions of years old, with a few smooth, relatively uncratered stretches that probably represent fairly recent lava eruptions. So it is possible that the planet was alive (in the geological sense, at least) quite recently.

And what of biological life? "Even though Lowell was totally wrong," says planetologist Toby Owen, "the idea that life could exist on Mars is a very powerful notion. And many of us thought it was credible even as recently as some 10 years ago. It was one of the prime motivations for the Viking project to send landers to this planet and look for any evidence of life that we could find. Not Lowell's life; but life even at the microbial level would have been a great discovery."

Accordingly, the *Vikings* each took along a tiny traveling laboratory, a box just one foot on a side. Using a scoop, each robot dug a bit of dirt, dumped it in the box, and ran a series of three experiments to test for the presence of Earth-like microbes in the Martian soil. The results of the experiments were ambiguous. The Martian sample behaved in some ways as it might have if teeming with microscopic organisms; on the other hand, tests showed the soil contained none of the complex organic molecules that are the chief building blocks of all life on Earth.

It is possible that the experiments were misconceived, or misinterpreted. But most planetologists now agree, given all the evidence, that Mars probably is a dead world. Its atmosphere is more than 100 times thinner than our own and made mostly of carbon dioxide. By day, temperatures hover around 0 degrees Fahrenheit, and at night they plummet to 150 degrees below, which is colder than the Earth's record low in Antarctica. It is so cold that its polar caps are made not just of water ice but also of dry ice—frozen carbon dioxide.

Says Owen, "To get a feeling for what Mars is like today, you might think of yourself being there on a camping expedition, and your job is to try to make a fire and boil an egg. The first thing you discover is that there's no fuel on Mars; there's nothing on the surface of the planet that will burn. Not only no life, no organic material. The second thing you discover is that even if there were fuel, it wouldn't burn, because there's only a tiny trace of oxygen in the Martian atmosphere. And finally, if you chipped some water off the polar cap (there is some water ice, buried under that dry ice) and put it in a little pan that was fueled by an electric heating device, you'd discover that the ice wouldn't melt into water. It would simply begin to disappear into gas—because liquid water can't exist on Mars today; there isn't enough atmospheric pressure to allow it to remain in a liquid state. So that's Mars as we find it now: a dry, cold, desertlike planet with no possibility for life as we know it to exist there."

Nevertheless, Owen believes Mars had a thicker atmosphere in its early days, a blanket of gases to trap the Sun's heat, like the atmospheres of Venus and Earth. "Looking at Mars today," he says, "we can convince ourselves that volcanic activity was widespread on that planet about 4 billion years ago. . . . At that period on Mars, there could have been a dense atmosphere produced by this volcanic activity. That atmo-

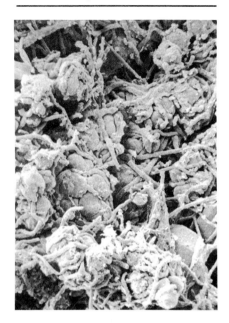

These microscopic creatures are magnified 20,000 times. They live in one of the most hostile environments on Planet Earth— inside rocks in the dry valleys of Antarctica. Future expeditions to Mars will probably search for traces of such microscopic, hardy life on the Red Planet.

sphere would have been rich in carbon dioxide, which is a very good gas for holding heat in, once the planet gets warmed up. It would have exerted enough pressure—just about twice as much as we experience on Earth—to allow liquid water to exist on the surface. And the surface temperature on Mars in those days would've been about room temperature on Earth—about 68 degrees Fahrenheit or so. Under those conditions, it's easy for liquid water to exist and run across the landscape, carving riverbeds and forming standing ponds and lakes.

"So you have a warm temperature, a high pressure, liquid water, and all the elements that you need to get life started: nitrogen, carbon, oxygen, hydrogen. We have all the basic conditions that life would need to begin on Mars. The only question is: Did it happen? And what did it produce?"

If astronauts someday explore on Mars, Owen says, they will look for the fossils of extinct Martians. The fossils, if there are any, are unlikely to be large. In the course of evolution, life has to start very small—microscopic, in fact—and only gradually build up to big projects like dinosaurs, crocodiles, and human beings. Evolution on Mars would have been nipped in the bud when the planet cooled. "Mars with life," says Owen, "would look very much like Mars without life. . . . That means that our job, in trying to find evidence of past life on Mars, is going to be a very difficult one. We have to go back with some very sophisticated machinery that will allow us to maneuver our way into spots where we think fossils may have been laid down. And these fossils are not going to be that easy to detect."

Still, if we find them, we will know that we have not always been alone; that at least one of our two nearest planetary neighbors started on the road with us and traveled a little of the way.

Mars today is an icy wasteland. It is too cold, and its atmosphere too thin, for running water. But some Martian terrain appears to have been scoured by titanic floods. Scientists are not sure where the floodwaters came from; perhaps Mars's climate was once as gentle as Earth's.

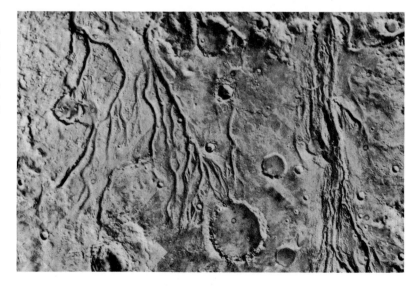

In the summer of 1977, two spacecraft, *Voyager 1* and *Voyager 2*, set out toward the far reaches of our Sun's realm to visit Jupiter and Saturn. It was our most ambitious journey through space, carrying us past the dark, revolving road of rubble that lies beyond Mars, the asteroid belt.

Jupiter and Saturn are something more than planets. Each is, in its own right, a miniature solar system. Between them, they have many more moons than the Sun has planets. Jupiter is the largest object in our corner of space, besides the Sun. Its diameter at the equator is 88,980 miles, which is 11 times the Earth's, and its inner core alone weighs 20 times as much as the Earth.

The two worlds are huge gasbags, made up mostly of the same light elements as the Sun, hydrogen and helium. They are lighter than water (as astronomer Jay Pasachof has said, Saturn would float in a bathtub, though one would have to do something about the ring). Jupiter is a failed star—that is, it is not big enough for the matter in its center to start the thermonuclear chain reactions that light the universe. Endowed with more mass, it would have lit up like the Sun. Then we would enjoy two sunsets each evening instead of one (if we had come to exist at all in such a solar system). Indeed, the majority of the stars in our galaxy are twins—*binary stars*.

Neither Jupiter nor Saturn has a crust, only layer upon layer of gas, each layer compressed by the weight of the gas above it, until the gas liquefies. Near the center the pressure is many tens of millions of times the pressure of our Earth's atmosphere at sea level. There it may be compressed into a solid. Because the atmosphere is so deep, it obeys rules we have not fathomed. The phantasmagorical yellow, brown, pink, and red bands we see in Jupiter are signs of its extraordinary weather. Our planet has only one layer of weather, the troposphere, and only one *kind* of weather, caused by the circulation of water in its several phases, solid, liquid, and gas. Jupiter is thought to have three active layers, each with its own kind of weather. The first and outermost is a cloud deck of ammonia; the second, a cloud deck of ammonium hydrosulfide; the third, a cloud deck of water ice crystals.

Jupiter is so hot that it radiates about 1.5 times as much energy as it receives from the Sun. Despite its size, the planet also rotates very quickly—once every 10 hours. Its inner heat and its spin keep its gases turbulent. The colored bands change shape and pattern from week to week. Despite its mercurial weather, the face of the giant planet has been marked for more than three centuries by a single furious storm, the Great Red Spot. This is a raging vortex of cosmic dimensions: Two or three Earths could easily fit within it. The Italian astronomer

Gian Domenico Cassini first looked into this angry red eye more than 300 years ago, and it is by far the longest-running storm in meteorological history.

Perhaps the Great Red Spot has lasted so long because there is so little beneath to slow it down. There are no coasts and mountains on Jupiter to break up the winds. No solid surface limits their depth. Earthly storms are pancake affairs, because the troposphere is thin compared to the diameter of the solid Earth. But the Great Red Spot has nothing underneath it but gas; it may bear its rage far down into the depths.

It is conceivable that some strange, gaseous, and spineless form of life is afloat in the heavy, swirling atmosphere of Jupiter. It is not even impossible that there is something analogous to Earth's hydrothermal vents in the planet interior, with primitive creatures living in the dark, feasting and multiplying on chemical energy. Such talk is only speculation—but, having seen the unexpected and bizarre animals at the vents at the bottom of our own seas, scientists believe it is valid speculation. However, it is far more likely that life, if there is any out there, is hidden on one of Jupiter's extraordinary moons.

Galileo saw only the four largest of Jupiter's moons, Io, Europa, Ganymede, and Callisto, named for lovers of the Roman god Jupiter. They are all big places. The largest of the four, Ganymede, is half again as big as our Moon and almost as large as Mercury; the smallest, Europa, is only slightly smaller than our Moon. In 1979, while passing Jupiter, the *Voyagers* beamed back images of three new moons, known at first only as 1979J1, 1979J2, and 1979J3, and now as Metis, Adrastea, and Thebe. And in 1980, when the *Voyagers* flew by Saturn, they added to Saturn's nine known moons (Mimas, Enceladus, Tethys, Dione, Rhea, Titan, Hyperion, Iapetus, and Phoebe) eight new moons, 1980S1 through 1980S8. With each new moon, corks popped from champagne bottles at JPL, just as Sir Charles Wyville Thomson and his crew aboard HMS *Challenger* toasted each strange new species they had dredged from the great deeps.

Scientists had been sure that moons this far from the Sun must be cold and dead—worlds without histories, with nothing for us to read in their faces but the terrible record of the Great Bombardment, and an occasional falling rock. But each of Jupiter's moons has its own personality and its own lessons to teach.

Io is the most remarkable, one of the biggest surprises of our entire Grand Tour of the solar system. Torrence Johnson, a member of the *Voyager* imaging team, recalls, "As we got closer and closer to Jupiter, Io began to look stranger and stranger to us. We thought we'd start seeing very large impact basins,

The giant planet of the solar system. Jupiter and a few of its many moons, seen in a montage of images from the Voyager *space probes.*

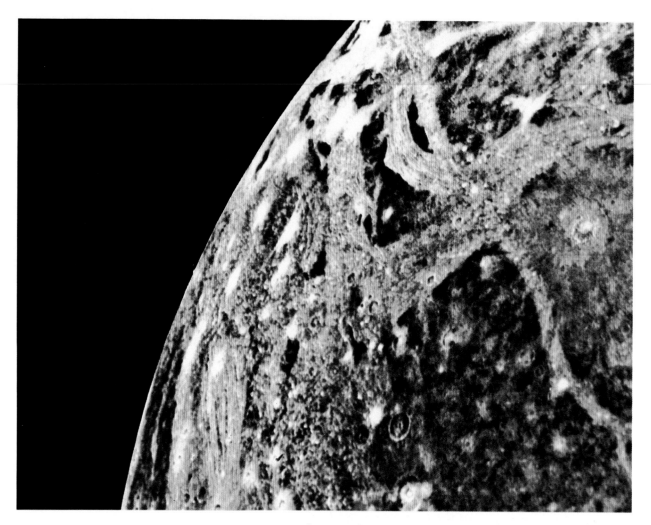

*Ganymede,
Jupiter's largest moon.
Its surface is icy, pocked
with craters, and scarred by
long, parallel grooves.*

craters such as we'd seen on the Moon, Mercury, and Mars. We could see strange markings, but no signs of craters. We couldn't fully interpret what we were seeing . . . but what we did know was that we were looking at a geologically very young surface and that the surface must be renewing or resurfacing itself in some manner." Io is mottled, yellow-gray, and ill-looking. During computer enhancement of the *Voyager* images, false colors were added to make details stand out clearly, and much of Io became the hue of the deep-red dye known to the ancients as "dragon's blood." Bradford Smith, head of the Voyager imaging team that processed the first close-up pictures, had an overwhelming first impression. "I've seen better-looking pizzas," Smith said.

Processing one of the *Voyager* images, Linda Morabito, of the *Voyager* navigation team, spotted a small glow on the horizon of Io's southern hemisphere. Fiddling with the computer to enhance the picture, she was amazed to see this glow resolve into a gauzy cloud. The spot of light was an enormous

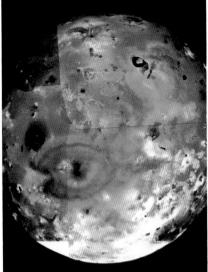

Io is the liveliest moon in the solar system. Left: on Io's upper horizon, a volcano hurls plumes of sulfur dioxide more than 100 miles into space—the first eruptions ever seen on another world.

volcanic eruption, the first alien eruption ever observed. Crystals of sulfur dioxide, or perhaps of pure sulfur, were spewing out to a height of more than 150 miles! *Voyager 1* found seven more violent eruptions in progress upon Io (three of the liveliest were named Prometheus, Loki, and Pele, fire gods on Earth). Four months later, when *Voyager 2* flew by, seven of its eight known volcanoes were still alive and kicking.

Thus a moon we had assumed to be cold and dead proved to be seething. Io is the most active body in the solar system, even more restless than Earth. It covers itself over each year in as much as 10 millimeters of sulfur dioxide. We have said that Earth is like a kettle near boiling; Io *is* boiling. It is a world literally turning itself inside out.

But why? Where could all that energy come from, on so small and dimly lit a world? "We really weren't prepared to find a body as small as our own Moon still actively popping off with active volcanoes," says Johnson. "It implied an energy source that we had not encountered on the other planets, which are mostly driven by heat from radioactive decay."

The explanation: a bizarre consequence of gravity.

Io is the moon closest to Jupiter. Trapped between the giant planet and Europa, the next moon out, Io's orbit is distorted, and the whole moon is stretched and squeezed between Jupiter's and Europa's gravitational fields. Just as the tug of the Moon raises tides on Earth, the tug of Jupiter raises tides of solid rock on Io, bulges of stone 300 feet high. The constant flexing heats its interior to the melting point, and as this heat escapes, it makes the dazzling pyrotechnic displays discovered by *Voyager*.

Until recently, no one thought such a source of heat could be enough to heat a world. Planetologists had usually considered just three sources of heat: the original heat left over from the infalling of planetesimals, when the world first came together in space; the heat generated by the decay of radioactive elements trapped within it; and the heat of the Sun's rays upon its surface. All three of these heat sources are important on Planet Earth. None of them is especially significant on a place like Io, which, being small, contains only a minor amount of radioactive matter, has long since radiated away its original heat, and is too far from the Sun to be warmed much by it. The new idea of heating by gravity tides (which planetologist Stanton Peale had postulated just days before *Voyager's* arrival at Io) means we will have to look more closely at the moons of the giants. They can be much livelier and more interesting places than we had ever supposed.

Knowing about gravity tides makes the moons of giant planets seem more promising as abodes for life; it gives them a whole new energy source. We will be exploring such moons more closely in the future. Sounds cannot carry through space; but if we could listen to Io, we might hear, between the cannon volleys of Io's giant volcanoes and the thunder of its moon-quakes, the murmers as of a ghostly galleon in a storm, its hull, ribs, and decks groaning with the strain.

Saturn's surface is quieter than Jupiter's, and so far none of its moons seems to be as wild as Io. But its rings still catch the imagination like nothing else in space. They circle it as if for emphasis—as if to say, like the ghost of King Hamlet, "think upon me; remember me." Our quarter century of exploration has shown us that rings are more common in the solar system than we ever suspected. Jupiter has a faint ring, and Uranus has at least nine narrow, dark ones. But none is as glorious as Saturn's. These mysterious rings have fulfilled one of the informal maxims of planetology, that the closer we get the lovelier each world looks. In 1610, Galileo saw the rings as two blurry moons.

In 1655, Christian Huygens saw them as a solid disc; in 1675, Gian Domenico Cassini saw two separate, concentric rings (the dark space that divides them is called Cassini's division). In the

THE FAIREST OF THEM ALL

The closer we get to Saturn, the more beautiful and mysterious it looks.

late 1970s, with the *Voyagers*, the JPL imaging team saw seven major divisions and so many hundreds of thousands of subdivisions that the rings at last took on the appearance of a phonograph record. They begin at about 70,000 kilometers from the planet's center and extend out more than 135,000 kilometers. Yet they are probably much less than a kilometer thick. That makes the rings, as one observer notes, "thousands of times thinner than razor-thin," and their particles are so dispersed that starlight can shine right through.

The rings, gleaming in the sunlight, appear to be made of ice: they are chunks of all shapes and sizes, from grains to pebbles to boulders, all herded together closely in their orbits. According to one current theory, nearby moons do some of the herding: The gravity of *shepherd moons* helps to give ringlets their sharp and well-defined boundaries.

Two ghostly and evanescent phenomena were recorded in the rings by the *Voyagers*. First, dark, fast-moving spokes appeared in the rings, changed shape as they went around and disappeared again, as if Saturn's rings were a great spinning wagon-wheel seen dimly by moonlight; then one narrow ring looked for a time as if it were three or four ringlets braided together. Neither of these curious effects, spokes or braids, fits what we expect of the neat elliptical orbits predicted by Kepler and Newton, and they have yet to be satisfactorily explained. (On either side of the braided ring were tiny moons; perhaps these shepherds somehow twisted the braid.)

What made the rings? They may be remains of a moon torn apart by Saturn's gravity, or, perhaps, bits and pieces that have strayed into Saturn's orbit from interplanetary space and been captured. It is also possible that the rings are debris left over from the birth of the planet and its moons—ice scraps and shards that never assembled. If so, their study should teach us something more about the way this miniature solar system called Saturn first came together, and we may learn more about the birth of the solar system itself. Fragments plucked from the rings, like meteorites from the ice sheets of Antarctica, could help us learn the sequence of events by which the solar nebula collapsed and the Sun and the nine worlds were born.

Of Saturn's many moons, the most interesting to us is Titan, one of the largest satellites in the solar system. When the *Voyagers* approached it, scientists at JPL were startled to find, 1 billion miles from Earth, that it is yet another small globe with a thick atmosphere—60 percent more dense than Earth's!

Titan is very cold—its surface temperature is −295 degrees Fahrenheit. Around that temperature, methane, sometimes called "marsh gas," is found simultaneously as gas, liquid, and solid. "Titan's methane thus might act the way water does on Earth near 32 degrees Fahrenheit," says planetologist Clark Chapman in his book *Planets of Rock and Ice.* "The view on Titan's surface at this 'triple-point' of methane would be richly varied but weird. A Titanian inhabitant might peer across an arctic sludge-scape, dully illuminated by a blood-orange sky. The 'rocks,' made of methane and ammonia ices, would be mostly buried beneath a gooey layer of soil, accumulated over eons from the continual settling of tiny dust specks of tarry smog, formed near the top of the atmosphere. Titan's soupy lakes and oceans of liquid methane would often be hidden by choking mists of methane ice-fog. High overhead, through the slightly hazy air, the Titanian resident would see reddened clouds of liquid methane droplets." Many planetologists hope to send a probe to its surface to see this strange land. It is terribly cold, concedes Carl Sagan. "But with abundant organic matter, sunlight and perhaps volcanic hot spots, the possibility of life on Titan cannot be readily dismissed." As Sagan notes, the astronomer who discovered Titan in 1655, Christian Huygens, also believed it might be inhabited. Huygens wrote, "It is impossible but that their way of living must be very different from ours, having such tedious Winters."

So far as we know, we are alone in the universe; but we have hardly begun looking for company. Someday, not very long from now, an astronomer at Arecibo may receive a coded message from the stars, or a space probe may find some new and alien form of life. The recent discovery of other solar systems around distant stars proves that our own is not a freak event in the universe. And the surprises of the *Voyager* missions encourage us to wonder what curiosities we may yet find in remote and unpromising corners of this single solar system. Surely, with the many billions of solar systems that are likely to exist in the universe, and with such myriad and various worlds in each, life has arisen in many times and many places besides Planet Earth.

Astronomers hope to learn more about the variety of worlds in our solar system when NASA mounts Project Galileo. In this project, long planned and often postponed (launch dates missed so far include 1982, 1984, and 1985), a robot inspector will be launched from the Space Shuttle by a specially designed booster and set into orbit around Jupiter. It will bring us views of Io and the other Jovian moons—close-up pictures 10 to 100 times more detailed than we have seen so far. And it will drop a probe into the Jovian atmosphere; the probe will send back messages for an hour as it descends on a parachute through the clouds and disappears into the vaporous planet.

Saturn's rings—a close-up view.

In 1985, NASA announced that it would launch *Galileo* in 1986 and that the space probe would make a detour on its course to Jupiter, to visit, for the first time, an asteroid in space. In late 1986, according to this plan, *Galileo* will pass near a giant asteroid called Amphitrite, one of the cold, dark giants of the asteroid belt between Mars and Jupiter. Amphitrite is 135 miles in diameter.

Meanwhile, the *Voyagers* journey on. Beyond Saturn are other worlds still unexplored: Uranus, with a peculiar, upright band of rings; and more distant yet, Neptune, with its moon, Triton (another moon with an atmosphere). At last, the *Voyagers* will leave all the nine planets behind. As they venture into interstellar space, they will pass through the last outpost of our solar system—the Oort Comet Cloud, a halo of cosmic, icy debris left over when the planets formed.

There was a time, not so long ago, when the remote and exotic Oort Cloud was of interest only to specialists. Now, quite unexpectedly, it begins to seem that the debris of this distant realm may have shattering effects here on Planet Earth.

There have been dark times in the history of the Earth when almost every kind of living thing went extinct all across the planet. About 440 million years ago, a vast number of animals then living in the sea vanished. Two hundred fifty million years ago, perhaps 96 percent of all animal species that lived in the sea or on land were killed off. The last of the primitive shelled creatures we call trilobites disappeared; so did all of the Earth's ancient corals, 75 percent of its amphibian families, and 80 percent of its reptiles. Paleontologist Stephen Jay Gould calls these sudden, mass extinctions the *Great Dyings*. They are moments when life on Earth hung by a thread.

The most famous Dying, the one that has made the deepest impression on the human imagination, is the one that felled the mighty dinosaurs 65 million years ago. The death of the dinosaurs may have taken a few thousand years, or it may have happened, as some have suggested, on a weekend. But they all exited the Earth's stage more or less together. With them went species of sea turtles; crocodiles; and ammonoids, whose lovely forms looked much like the shell of the modern nautilus. The passing of this extraordinary menagerie marked the end of the geological period known as the *Cretaceous*.

Dinosaurs were not only giant in size (one of the biggest, Brontosaurus, was 90 feet long from head to tail) but also in the length of their rule on this planet. They dominated it for 145 million years. That is longer than the mammals' tenure has lasted so far and perhaps 30 times as long as man has existed (depending on what date one chooses). Compared to the dinosaurs, then, we human beings are tourists here, mere arrivistes.

What killed off the kings of the reptiles? For decades, paleontologists have tossed out many scenarios, most of which have died more quickly than the dinosaurs. Perhaps, one scientist suggested, the dinosaurs simply got too big for their own good and could no longer mount their mates. (But not all dinosaurs were gigantic, and some of the largest apparently got along just fine, thank you, for tens of millions of years.) Perhaps, proposed another authority, the dinosaurs were poisoned by eating flowering plants, which first blossomed on the planet during their reign. As evidence, this scientist pointed to the contorted limbs of some dinosaur fossils, which are reminiscent of the writhings of victims of strychnine poisoning. (But there is a simpler explanation: The contraction of ligaments, rigor mortis, often contorts bodies after death.) Perhaps, then, said a third expert whimsically, flowers did not poison the dinosaurs but gave them a fatal case of constipation. After surveying such theories, the satirist Will Cuppy wrote that "the Age of Reptiles ended because it had gone on long enough and it was all a

According to the controversial Alvarez theory, falling comets destroyed the dinosaurs.

mistake in the first place. The bats," he added, "are going to flop, too, and everybody knows it except the bats themselves."

The death of the dinosaur is still perhaps the grandest whodunit in evolutionary history. And like all good detective stories, the latest chapter has begun with a startling twist and a serendipitous discovery—one that sends our gaze upward, to the stars.

In 1978, Walter Alvarez, a geologist at the University of California at Berkeley and working in Italy, inspected a thin layer of clay in a deep gorge near Gubbio, a tiny medieval village halfway between Rome and Florence. The reddish clay layer was just a half inch thick but stood out clearly, because below it the limestone gorge was white, and above it, grayish-pink.

The clay, Alvarez noticed, was right at the boundary between the Cretaceous and the period that followed, the Tertiary. That meant it had been laid down just at the time the dinosaurs died. Most species of *foraminifera* (forams for short), which are the microscopic marine creatures whose shells make up limestone, went extinct at that time, too. Below the clay are a myriad of different species, while above it one can see that only a single species of foram survived. In the clay itself there are no forams at all.

For years, Alvarez had been looking for a good project to share with his father, Luis Alvarez, who won the Nobel Prize in physics in 1968 for studies of subatomic particles. Luis Alvarez's wide-ranging and passionate interests have often led him to jump outside the realm of his specialty, the quantum world of leptons and quarks. Luis once devised a way of using cosmic rays to explore one of the pyramids of Giza for secret chambers; he designed an electronic indoor golf trainer that corrected a golfer's swing with a photoelectric eye; he invented a foul-weather landing system for airplanes; and he searched for high-energy particles in the upper atmosphere with a balloon flown 100,000 feet in the atmosphere. Walter told his father about the clay layer, and Luis was intrigued.

"This was the first rock that I'd looked at seriously for about 45 years," Luis says now. "I had one geology course in college, and then I'd completely forgotten everything. So when Walt showed me his rock and said, 'Dad, right here, when this clay was laid down, that's when the dinosaurs disappeared,' that really got my attention."

Luis ("practicing geology without a license") hit upon a way to find out precisely how long the clay had taken to accumulate, as a small step toward solving the dinosaur whodunit. "When meteorites enter the atmosphere, most of them burn up—they're shooting stars," he explains. "When they burn up they turn into meteoric dust and the dust settles down on the surface of the Earth. It's just as though you went around with a salt shaker and shook meteoric dust all over the Earth at a certain constant rate. So my basic idea was that you could tell how fast the clay layer was laid down by observing how much this special kind of salt, if you will, was sprinkled all over the Earth by the meteoric dust coming down."

Thus Luis suggested measuring the amount of iridium, a rare relative of platinum, in the clay layer. Iridium is rare on the surface of the Earth, because in our formative years, when the planet was still molten, most of our share of iridium sank into the core (with most of our iron) and was buried there. However, the dust of meteorites holds much higher levels of iridium than our native rock—as much as 10,000 times more. If the clay held a lot of iridium, then that might mean it had taken a long time to form.

It was a clever idea, and they put it to the test. Walter, Luis, and two physical chemists, Frank Asaro and Helen Michel, measured the iridium in the clay. They were flabbergasted. It contained iridium in huge and unexpected amounts, about 30 times more than they could account for by the salt-shaker theory, the rain of cosmic dust. They checked sediments of the same age at Stevns Klint, a sea cliff in Denmark, and there they found even more iridium, 160 times normal. Where could all this iridium possibly have come from?

Luis, by his own account, sat around for weeks concocting one crazy scheme after the other and scrapping them. Finally he realized that the iridium might have been brought in by an asteroid or comet that collided with the Earth. The impact, he speculated, cast up a huge cloud of dust that rapidly encircled the planet. The dust was so thick that it kept sunlight from reaching the ground for months. The shadow of the cloud caused the Great Dying: In the darkness, photosynthesis ceased and green plants died. The food chains were broken at their first, vital links, and the whole chain of animals and plants collapsed. The dinosaurs and three quarters of all living things died of starvation, and their kind went extinct. It was a miracle that any life at all managed to scavenge and survive.

As the dust settled over the gray, somber, silent Earth, it formed the thin layer of clay.

This was an extraordinary and unexpected story—a dramatic death for the dinosaurs. It was also instantly controversial. Though other workers soon confirmed the existence of the iridium layer—it has been detected in the Netherlands, in Spain, and as far away as New Zealand—most geologists did not care for the Alvarez interpretation.

"Geologists, like all folks, have their prejudices," Stephen Jay Gould has noted wryly. "They prefer causes emanating from their own domain, the Earth."

The impact of the comets, according to the Alvarez hypothesis, would have caused a dark, planetary winter 65 million years ago.

The impact theory is troubling for many reasons; it touches upon deep feelings we all have about life on this planet. For one thing, it stirs prejudices we have against change. Psychologists sometimes draw up charts of stress, itemizing the sorts of events that make for a difficult year. The collision with Earth of a rock the size of Providence, Rhode Island, apparently is off the scale. A change like that affects us even when it is only experienced at great remove, taking place eons in the dark past of our planet. We want to feel that our homes rest on solid foundations and that the blue sky above us is a benevolent firmament. "What good is a house," said Thoreau, "if we haven't a respectable planet to put it on?"

It is possible that Alfred Wegener's vision of continents adrift angered his colleagues because it seemed so lurid and violent. It smacked of what earth scientists used to call, with some contempt, *catastrophism*. Today, now that earth scientists have accepted Wegener's vision of shattered and sundered continents, it is easier, perhaps, to contemplate other catastrophes in the record: the sudden onset of ice ages, the nightmare notion of the runaway greenhouse, the monstrous flooding that carved the Scablands. It is only recently that such rude shocks to the Earth have entered the domain of sober and respectable discussion in the forum of scientific journals. It is interesting how much of our thinking about the Earth is shading toward catastrophe theories, as Clark Chapman notes in *Planets of Rock and Ice.* Once, for instance, we spoke of the Grand Canyon as having been eroded by wind, weather, and water, day by day and grain by grain. But some time ago, Eugene Shoemaker, the man who proved Arizona Meteor Crater to be a meteorite impact (a catastrophe theory if there ever was one), retraced the route of the first scientific expedition through the Grand Canyon, and he rephotographed all the outcrops and cliffs from the same point of view the 19th-century scientists had used in making their meticulous etchings. Shoemaker was surprised to find that in most places the Grand Canyon's walls were essentially unchanged by the passage of 100 years. But here and there, in a sudden, rare torrent, a whole façade had caved in. He concluded that the Grand Canyon is not carved so much grain by grain as landslide by landslide. Catastrophism again.

Paleontologists Stephen Jay Gould and Niles Eldridge have proposed a similar revision of Darwin's vision of evolution. Darwin assumed that species evolve smoothly and gradually. He saw the development of species in much the way that one of his mentors, the great geologist Charles Lyell, saw the development of the Earth, as a process of slow, smooth change proceeding at a uniform rate. "Nature does not make jumps," Darwin said. But the fossil record does not really bear this out.

Try as they might, Darwinists have found very few fossils that show smooth transitions from one form to another with hundreds of small, intermediate steps, as the master expected. Perhaps nature does make jumps. Many species stay more or less the same for long stretches, and then undergo relatively sudden bursts of evolution in perhaps only a few hundred generations—too short to have left a continuous record in rock layers. To describe what they see in the record, Gould and Eldridge speak of "punctuated equilibrium." Life stays pretty much as is until something disastrous happens, and then life changes fast. Catastrophe theory yet again.

In our new vision of Planet Earth, change is imperceptibly gradual most of the time and shockingly sudden some of the time. As the British geologist Derek Ager once put it, the story of the planet is like the life of a soldier: long periods of boredom alternating with brief periods of terror.

"There is no catastrophe greater than the collision of worlds," says Clark Chapman.

Thus the Alvarezes' hypothesis, often called their *Cretaceous Extinction Theory*, was timely, though so spectacular that it was bound to stir controversy. Some paleontologists argued that the dinosaurs and their doomed contemporaries died out slowly—so slowly that one didn't need a catastrophe to explain it at all. Other critics attacked the clay layer. Perhaps the iridium might have been laid down by stupendous volcanic activity, which brought up the iridium from deep within the Earth and spread it out in dust and smoke and ashes—meanwhile doing in the dinosaurs.

This latter was a strong rival hypothesis. To test it, geologist Bruce Bohor, an expert on volcanic ash with the U.S. Geologic Survey, decided to examine the clay layer—the same layer Alvarez had inspected in Gubbio. After a search, he and a coworker, Don Triplehorn, found the layer at Brownie Butte in Montana, not far from a spot early settlers named Hell's Gate. It is a transition as striking as the one at Gubbio. Below the clay layer are fossils of all sorts of life; above it virtually all of them have disappeared, and new forms of life have taken their place.

Bohor intended simply to take a sample of the clay and test it for volcanic properties. Though he was no dinosaur expert, he felt he could at least resolve that part of the debate. Back in the lab in Denver, he and his team painstakingly sifted through the clay—and they found something altogether unexpected. Within the clay were silt-sized grains of quartz, which under the microscope seemed to be cracked and strained. Bohor had never seen anything like it before, but other scientists had. Apollo missions had returned rock much like this from the

Moon. Bits of such quartz, with their surfaces seamed by strain, had been discovered amid the debris ejected from lunar craters. The same peculiarly-featured quartz had been found in two other places on Earth: near meteorite craters such as Shoemaker's in Arizona, and at the sites of nuclear bomb tests. Such quartz can be formed in only one way: It must be shocked, subjected to the kind of instantaneous heat and pressure generated only by an extremely powerful explosion.

Bohor's discovery strengthened a hypothesis as catastrophically lurid as any in the old pulp days of science fiction— that 65 million years ago a huge object, hurtling in from outer space, had smashed into Earth and extinguished the dinosaurs.

This thin layer of clay in a limestone quarry in Gubbio, Italy, caught the eye of geologist Walter Alvarez. The clay layer formed at precisely the time that the dinosaurs, and many other living things, went extinct. Alvarez believes the clay is the fallout of a collision from outer space.

Meanwhile, J. John Sepkoski, Jr., a paleontologist at the University of Chicago, was engaged in a vast and encyclopedic effort to pull together and synthesize thousands of published studies of extinctions. He had compiled a list of all the families of marine animals known to have gone extinct over the past 600 million years. By assembling the data, he hoped to get a more complete picture of the patterns of living and dying on the planet across time.

When these labors were partly finished, Sepkoski teamed with David Raup, a paleontologist, head of the geophysics department at the University of Chicago, and an expert statistical analyst. To cope with the long and unwieldy lists of species, hundreds of thousands of births and deaths, they put all their data into a computer and began to analyze the data.

The analysis turned up more Great Dyings that had until then gone undetected. Though some mass extinctions were much more devastating than others, they showed an unexpected and regular pattern. Over and over again, a period of slow, steady proliferation of species was followed by a brief episode during which an extraordinary number of species disappeared. Slowly, over a period of millions of years, life on the planet recovered, until the next Great Dying. They looked at the graphs printed out by the computer. The mass extinctions took place *every 26 million years*. What was their reaction?

"Horror!" says Raup. They had never expected to see "this very, very regular pulsing of extinction. It's not a pleasant thing, with our background and training, and let's say brainwashing, to think about. . . . It sure did violence to my world view." Extinctions were supposed to happen because a lot of things got bad at once, he says. The Great Dyings were thought to have resulted from a random coincidence of minor-league disasters, one after the other, the last of which was the straw that broke the dinosaurs' backs. But if the Great Dyings occurred regularly, that implied a single, powerful, and awesome cause, recurring like clockwork.

"We said to ourselves, it can't be regular, this must be some sort of statistical fluke," Raup says. "We went through the summer of 1983 spending a great deal of time trying to think up things wrong with it, trying to kill it. And first one of us, and then another would come in in the morning with a new idea, a new explanation for this as an artifact [that is, a false result stemming from the way they handled the data]. Many mornings, we thought we had killed it. I think we hoped it would go away. But it went on and on, and ultimately we got to the point of sufficient confidence where we decided to publish it—which doesn't make it real, but is some threshold in our confidence, at least."

What gears could drive this deadly clockwork? As far as we know, none of the grand cycles of rock, sea, and air have a period of 26 million years. Not even the ice age cycles repeat at such an astronomically long interval. The clockwork, the springs and ratchets and gears—if they can be found—must lie beyond the Earth, in the vasts of space.

Back in Berkeley, Luis Alvarez challenged a young colleague, astrophysicist Richard Muller, to find a plausible explanation for the cycles. Muller came up with many ideas, from solar flares to supernovae, and scrapped each of them in turn. At last, working with two colleagues, Marc Davis and Piet Hut, he devised a working model.

Most stars in our galaxy have companions: Stars are more often born as twins than as solitary suns. Muller hit upon the daring idea that our own sun might have a companion, a fellow traveler that astronomers had never spotted because it is small, dark, and far off. Suppose this companion star orbits our Sun every 26 million to 30 million years, Muller said. Just once on each orbit, the star passes close enough to disrupt the outermost objects that orbit our Sun—the cloud of icy comets called the Oort Cloud, named for their discoverer, the Dutch astronomer Jan Hendrik Oort, who also helped to map the spiral arm structure of the Milky Way.

Muller and his colleagues prepared a computer simulation of this new vision of the solar system. A dark circle in the center represents the Sun. Small, black dots orbit around it like a swarm of bees, representing just a few of the many, many comets circling the Sun. Off in the distance is a large, black dot, the companion star. It travels very slowly when it is far from the Sun, and it has very little effect on the swarm of comets then. But every 26 million years, it sweeps around closer to the Sun, coming in among the comets, disturbing their orbits, and sending a large number of them showering toward the Earth and the Sun. A few of them collide with the Earth and lead to mass extinctions every 26 million to 30 million years, in the regular pattern found by Raup and Sepkoski.

Muller, Davis, and Hut published their speculation in the British journal *Nature* in April 1984. "If and when the companion is found," they wrote, "we suggest it be named Nemesis, after the Greek goddess who relentlessly persecutes the excessively rich, proud, and powerful. We worry," they added, "that if the companion is not found, this paper will be our nemesis."

Walter Alvarez thought of one way to test the Nemesis idea, and got together with Muller to analyze it. If comets collide with the Earth every 26 million years or so, we ought to find impact craters dating from those catastrophic periods. Do craters on Earth, and elsewhere in the solar system, occur at random times, or are they clustered every 26 million years?

On the Moon and Mercury there is such a welter of overlapping craters that any such pattern probably is lost. On Earth, there are far fewer impact craters. Geologist Eugene Shoemaker, after his work at Arizona Meteor Crater, along with other geologists, searched the face of the Earth for more craters. More than 40 likely scars have been discovered in the United States and Canada alone. The Serpent Mound, a vast earth sculpture by Indians in Ohio, is on a crater. The bed of Lake Bosumtwi, the sacred lake of Ghana's Ashanti tribe, is a meteorite crater. One spectacular crater is the odd, circular lake called Manicouagan, in the heart of Quebec. The lake is 60 miles across, with a circular island in the middle. Manicouagan is thought to be the much-eroded crater of an impact that occurred about 210 million years ago. The central island disguises the crater. Shoemaker believes the island formed when the glaciers of the last Ice Age swept rock into the crater.

Why aren't there more meteorite scars on the planet? Partly because smaller meteors burn up in the atmosphere, but perhaps more importantly because Earth is so restless. Glaciers probably have flattened and filled countless craters besides the one at Manicouagan. The collisions of plates, and the upheavals they cause, have doubtless destroyed many others. Wind, water, and weather wear away each crater rim, the soil on the slopes washes down to the bottom, and the hole fills up. Arizona Meteor Crater, only 25,000 years old, already has 100 feet of lakebed sediments at the bottom. If Earth preserved its craters, it probably would be as pocked as the Moon.

Even among the hundred or so impact craters still visible on the face of the Earth, many cannot be dated precisely. If a crater's age is not known to within about 20 million years, one can't tell which extinction cycle it might belong to. Still, among those craters whose dates are accurately known, Alvarez does see some evidence of a cycle. Every 26 million years or so, there is at least one crater, and sometimes a cluster of craters, on the face of the planet.

What is more, Alvarez claims, the two cycles are in synchrony. The craters arrived at about the same time as the mass extinctions.

These ideas are still hotly contested. They are at the cutting edge of science, where shouts of "Eureka!" are heard in shower stalls, and shouts of delight, or hoots of derision, interrupt scientific meetings. But if Muller is correct, on its third-to-last pass 65 million years ago, the Death Star rammed the Oort Cloud. One or more of its comets struck the Earth, enveloping it for months in a huge cloud of dust. The dinosaurs died in the darkness. The way was cleared for our mammal ancestors, tiny, scurrying creatures the size of shrews, to take over the continents, and for our own human species to emerge into the light. (We still don't know what saved the shrews.)

The theory is still far from winning total acceptance. Many astronomers think the orbit Muller describes would be too unstable to allow the Death Star to return so many times; they think it would long ago have flown off into interstellar space, or crashed into the Sun. Many geologists still think the Alvarezes' iridium layer was more likely laid down by volcanoes than by an extraterrestrial impact. Many paleontologists think the mass extinction at the end of the Cretaceous period happened too gradually to have been caused by something as sudden as the whomp of a falling comet. And many scientists simply find the whole comet idea too sensational and lurid to be plausible. One paleontologist, Dewey McLean, has called it "science gone absolutely bonkers."

Still, even if the theory is eventually disproven, it has made a cosmic point. As Sepkoski says, it teaches us, in a nutshell, that "We are not alone. We can't consider the biosphere as a closed system that has a history independent of the Earth, and the Earth's extraplanetary environment. If we want to understand the history of life, we have to understand the history of the solar system as well."

Luis Alvarez says of the controversy, "You'd be surprised how many scientists were simply scandalized by the very thought of mass extinction being caused by the impact of a large object. I think probably a lot of people just don't like to think that big rocks can fall out of the sky. Many people—especially paleontologists, who had actually been out in the field collecting fossils—just didn't like this idea at all. On the other hand, there were other groups of scientists who were quite willing to accept it: people who had studied the Moon and the planets and who knew how important impacts were in the history of the solar system. They said, 'Sure, why not? That's a perfectly reasonable thing to have happened.'"

NIGHT WATCH

On a hilltop near Berkeley, Richard Muller and his colleagues are now searching for the dark star. If it exists, it will not be easy to find.

Nemesis should be a red or a brown dwarf—a star much smaller and dimmer than the Sun. Red dwarfs are among the commonest stars in the galaxy. There are thousands of them in the star catalogues of astronomers. The scientists have selected about 5,000 stars from these catalogues and are examining each one in turn.

Such an exhaustive star search can be managed only by computer. A computer has been programmed to direct the telescope to photograph each target star in turn. The system is so fast that in theory the entire sky can be surveyed in this way in just 20 hours.

Muller's team will photograph the positions of all 5,000 stars as rapidly as possible. Then they will wait six months and photograph them again, the computer guiding the telescope through the entire survey. They can then compare the two positions of each star. A star that is a long way away from us will not have moved perceptibly. But a nearby star, such as Nemesis, will have moved enough for us to notice.

Says Muller, "I estimate that my chances of finding Nemesis are probably one in three. I think those are great odds. Without these periodic catastrophes, we might never have developed. The mammals were around for a long time, but they were never able to take the Earth away from the dinosaurs until the dinosaurs were wiped out by something external. The whole picture that we have of where we came from and where we're going is affected by this. I find it exciting; it's not just astrophysics, it's biology, it's evolution, it's paleontology, it's a question of—why are we here?"

From his Arizona observatory, Percival Lowell thought he could see "canals" on Mars. Today, we smile at his visions of an advanced, but doomed, Martian civilization. Yet it is often difficult to sort out hypotheses that are marvellous, but false, from hypotheses that are both thrilling and true. Currently, astrophysicist Richard Muller is scanning the night skies for a Death Star. Will posterity regard this romantic quest the way we look back on Lowell's? Whether or not the Death Star exists, it is clear that impacts and collisions from outer space have fundamentally shaped the worlds in our solar system—including Planet Earth.

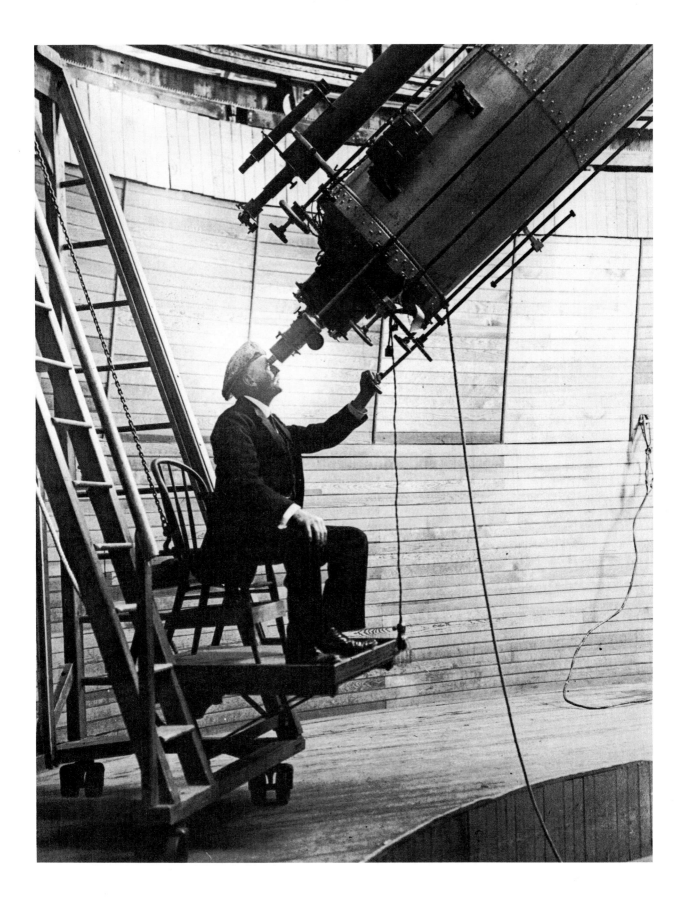

The Solar Sea

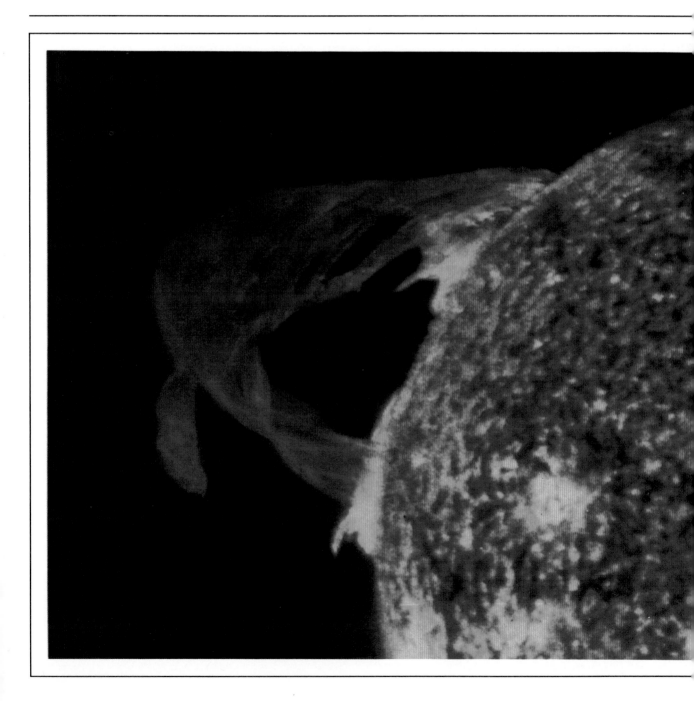

*It is reasonable to hope that in the
not too distant future we shall be
competent to understand so simple
a thing as a star.*

ARTHUR S. EDDINGTON, 1926

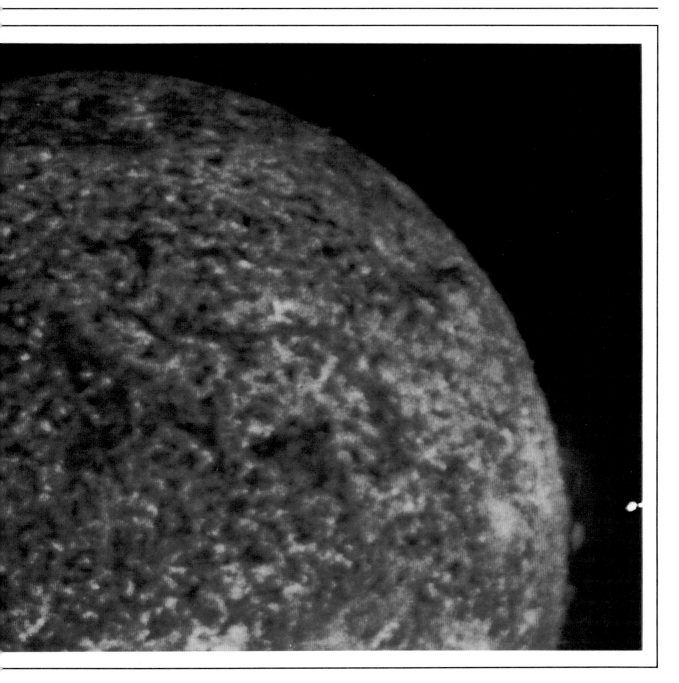

Overleaf: A cataclysm on the Sun sent up this arch of incandescent gas, a giant prominence. *The arch extends thousands of kilometers into space. If our small planet were added to this picture for scale, it would be a speck the size of a grain of sand.*

5 / The Solar Sea

Each day, before the Sun rises on the holy city of Varanasi, Hindu supplicants gather at the western bank of the Ganges River. They stand in the dark by the thousands—sometimes by the tens of thousands—bare-legged in the tepid water. As the eastern horizon brightens and the Sun rises through the mists of the sacred river, the pilgrims shout greetings. They ring bells and beat drums. Hundreds wade waist deep, cup their hands, and offer water to the Sun with outstretched arms as a modest thanks for the light of day.

"Nowhere in the world," a Western traveler to Varanasi has said, "is the Sun received daily with such celebration." But at one time or another, sunrise seems to have been a cause of jubilation wherever the Sun touches the planet. On the coast of Norway, for instance, the fishing village of Tromsø, which is farther north than any other permanent settlement in the world, does not see the Sun for two solid months in the middle of winter. The villagers call this interval *mørketiden*, the murky time. It is said that crime rates rise, liquor sales rise, and spirits sink. The village suffers from late November to January 29, which is *Soldag*, Sun Day. On that morning, according to one visitor's account, school is closed and the children parade through the streets. The Sun rises shortly after 11:00 A.M., always between the same two hills, and crowds of townspeople cheer as joyfully as pilgrims at the Ganges. Tromsø villagers are said to have their own customs. Children press their hands against a wall touched by the Sun's first light. Some of their parents let a Bible fall open, and they read the first verse that catches their eye. Those words color the new year.

Ancient Egyptians, Babylonians, Mayans, Aztecs, and Incas all worshiped the Sun; they kept track of its rising and setting points and its paths across the sky. In the American Southwest, Indians carved circles, spirals, long-tailed lizards, and stick figures on the walls of caves. These carvings were once thought to be simple pieces of cave art. Recently, however, astronomer Robert Preston of the Jet Propulsion Laboratory in Pasadena, California has found that many carvings bear a secret

This feather tunic was woven by the Incas of Peru between A.D. 1100 and 1400. Rows of feathers were knotted on cords and stitched to handwoven cotton in a marvelous praise of sunrise.

Two centuries ago, Jai Singh, the maharaja of Jaipur, in Northern India, built several observatories to track the Sun's progress across the sky. This one, in Jaipur, still is used today for calculating the Indian calendar. As a maharaja, Jai Singh considered himself a direct descendent of the Sun.

The Cave of Life, in Arizona's Petrified Forest. Here, a wedge of orange sunlight points to the center of a mystic cross. The cross was carved in the cave wall in prehistoric times by the Anasazi—the same tribe that built the cliff dwellings of Mesa Verde. "Anasazi" is the Navajo word for "the Old Ones." No one knows why the Old Ones arranged this meeting of Sun and stone in the Cave of Life.

relation to the path of the Sun. One of the most striking is in the heart of the Petrified Forest in Arizona, in a place called the Cave of Life. There, on one stone wall, the Indians carved a mystic cross. Two days out of each year, the setting Sun's last light casts a red dagger on the wall of the cave. As the Sun sets, the dagger fades; it dies pointing at the center of the cross.

This light appears on the cave wall 45 days before and after the *winter solstice,* when the North Pole is tipped farthest away from the Sun and the northern hemisphere has its shortest day of the year. On just those days, many miles from the Cave of Life, near Gila Bend, Arizona, in a place called Painted Rocks, a ray of the Sun touches the center of *another* cross carved in a cavern wall; and another ray of the Sun strikes yet a third ancient carving, that of a long-tailed lizard.

No one knows what the Indians meant by arranging these alignments of Sun and stone. Probably they served the Pueblo and Anasazi Indians as calendars; farming in the desert was precarious, requiring a sure sense of the time to plant and the time to harvest. Possibly the sun daggers meant something more. Since the ancient Indians left no written word, we may never know. Today each red ray in the caverns seems as purposeful and precise as the pointer of a lecturer in a darkened hall; but the hand that arranged the lesson has been gone from the desert for 1,000 years.

Recently, solar astronomer John Eddy of the High Altitude Observatory in Boulder, Colorado made his own pilgrimage to India and squinted into the rising Sun at the Galta Sun Temple in Jaipur. "From earliest times and on every continent," he said, "man has worshiped it, rising to greet it at the dawn, praising it with bell and drum, bowing down before it. And for what a practical reason! We depend upon it utterly for light and heat, for all the food we eat, for the air we breathe (oxygen is replenished by photosynthesis). Without it there would be no life on Earth and very little poetry. No day, no blue of the sky, no rushing brook, no rainbow."

In the past few centuries, however, and especially in the past few years, we have vastly extended the work of the world's ancient sun worshipers and astronomers. We have done what they could only dream of doing—we have gazed long and deeply upon the blinding face of the Sun. Thanks to careful precautions and ingenious instruments, we have not been blinded in the process, even during prolonged sun-watching sessions out in space, above the thin blue veil of the Earth's atmosphere.

In these investigations, we have been impelled toward visions that would have shocked the ancients—and have startled the astronomers. The Sun, as revealed in the past few years, is more awesome than even an impassioned mystic could have imagined. Distance makes it seem peaceful. But viewed more nearly, its surface heaves and tosses, and its smallest gesture dwarfs our scale of existence as the Sphinx overshadows the sand. The Sun's violent fire erupts sometimes in great flares, hoops of fire in which dozens of Earths could be stacked one on top of the other. These gargantuan storms stir our planet and touch our lives.

New observations from solar observatories and from telescopes launched out into space show that our two worlds— one of fire and one of stone—are bound more closely than we ever thought. The links are many and intricate. Sun and Earth are now seen to comprise, in the words of a recent NASA report, "an energetic and dynamic system, fluctuating, vibrating, changing shape, and interacting in rhythms that vary from minutes to millennia."

Indeed, we never realized until quite recently how near the Sun is, day and night, through emanations both visible and invisible. Our whole planet is waist-deep in the Sun, like a pilgrim in the sacred river.

For the Ancient Egyptians, the Sun was God, and pharaohs were the sons of God. Egyptian artists put a small, tender hand at the end of each ray of the Sun, caressing the Earth and all that lives upon it. In this bas-relief, on a balustrade at Tell el-Amarna, King Akhenaton and Queen Nefertiti make an offering to the Sun God. 1370-1353 B.C.

The best way to get a sense of the Sun's enormous size and power is to consider how far it is from the surface of the Earth to the surface of the Sun. Though the bright disc in our sky

GREAT BALL OF FIRE

looks near and feels warm on our upturned faces, it is about 93 million miles away, more than 400 times the distance from the Earth to the Moon. A jet plane travels west from New York City to San Francisco in five hours; if it could fly to the Sun through outer space at the same speed, the trip would take more than 20 years. The fastest-moving object in the universe, a particle of light, travels at 186,282 miles per second and makes the journey from the solar surface to the Earth in eight minutes, 20 seconds.

Because the Sun does not look that far away, it is hard for us to appreciate how big it is. There is nothing in view to give us the true perspective. By a variety of calculations, astronomers have determined that the Sun is 864,000 miles in diameter, as wide as 109 Earths. A million Earths could be packed inside it with room left over. It has a third of a million times more mass than Earth, and it is 745 times more massive than all the planets combined, including the two giants, Jupiter and Saturn. The Sun is almost half a million times brighter than the full Moon. If you lit 1 octillion (1 followed by 27 zeroes) candles, their light would be only a third as bright as the Sun's.

Once, notes solar physicist Robert Noyes, people made no connection between the Sun we see in the daytime and the stars we see at night; sunlight and starlight seemed literally as different as day and night. "What a grand surmise it must have been," Noyes says, "for the first stargazer who realized that the Sun and stars were the same and that the universe was teeming with distant suns!" The idea seems to have dawned a few hundred years ago and to have taken hold among educated people by about the year 1600.

Today we know that the Sun really is a very ordinary star, of middling size and middle age, and that it outglares the rest of its kind only because it is so much the nearest—just as a small mountain campfire looks much brighter, to those huddled around it, than the far-off lights of a city in a dark valley below. Our Sun is classed as a yellow dwarf—somewhere between a red giant and a black dwarf. It is spinning in a backwater of our galaxy, far from the center, where most of the cosmic action is. It is just one star among a hundred billion others; and even the Milky Way is just one among a hundred billion galaxies in the universe.

For those of us on Planet Earth, the Sun is the most important star in existence, but to an astrophysicist, it is interesting chiefly because it is the only star near enough to be studied in detail, and hence it provides us with a sort of keyhole through which we can see something of the lives of all stars. We have the Sun in perspective when we remember that it is one star among multitudes—the only one near enough for us

The face of the Sun, viewed close up, is far more violent and storm-ridden than the ancients supposed. It is seen here through a solar telescope of the National Oceanic and Atmospheric Administration, in Boulder, Colorado. In the foreground is a rocky ridge, and a mountain climber cheering on the Sun.

to see as more than a pinpoint of light. The next nearest star to us is Alpha Centauri, and it is 275,000 times farther away. A beam of light from Alpha Centauri takes not just minutes but 4.4 years to reach us.

THE SUN'S TRUE COLORS

The Hindus call the Sun "Maker of Knowledge" because it shows them the face of the Earth. Yet sunlight hides the face of the Sun itself. Ancient peoples worshiped it, but they could hardly see it. One wonders how many people over the millennia went blind trying. Even today, in spite of widely broadcast warnings, there are casualties during each solar eclipse. Looking straight at the Sun for even a few seconds can damage the retinas. Five or ten minutes can cause blindness. Sunglasses are no protection, and neither are the lenses of cameras, binoculars, and telescopes—in fact, they focus many times more sunlight upon the eyes, like magnifying glasses.

If the Sun were not so painfully difficult to look at, one ancient misconception might never have arisen. The Greek philosophers of the fourth century B.C., who founded the Western scientific tradition, saw the Sun as a perfect circle of perfect power. In medieval Europe this idea became dogma, because it was endorsed by Aristotle. Occasionally, when the Sun was dulled by thick smoke or clouds, or sank low on the horizon, people glancing at it would notice what looked like small black blotches. Such observations were recorded many times in many places (even by a pupil of Aristotle's). But no one seems to have thought the Sun was blemished. People dismissed the spots as clouds or planets silhouetted against the Sun.

Early in the 1600s, Thomas Harriot, in England, and Galileo, in Italy, pointed the new "spy-tube" at these spots (risking blindness much as Benjamin Franklin, with his kite and key, would later risk electrocution). Galileo saw that the spots really were on the face of the Sun itself. Soon he learned to use his telescope safely. He held up a white card behind the eyepiece and focused the image on the card. Staring at a pool of light on a piece of paper was much easier on the eyes than glancing furtively through the telescope. Making a careful series of drawings and observations, he discovered that the spots usually appeared in pairs. They rotated slowly from the left-hand side of the Sun to the right—the first indication that the Sun was spinning. The spots meandered and changed shape from week to week; some of the larger ones lasted months before decaying. Each spot had a dark center, which Galileo called the *umbra*, or shadow, and a lighter rim, the *penumbra*, or partial shadow.

The Sun, Galileo decided, was no more perfect than

the Earth, or the pocked Moon. But though he was quick to publish his observations of the Moon, he brooded about his discovery of sunspots for a long time. Perhaps Galileo himself was awed to realize that the Sun is imperfect; or perhaps he feared a public outcry might follow his announcement. He wrote later, "Certain discoveries of mine that depart from popular opinion have been denied, obliging me to hide in silence every new idea until I have more than proved it."

In any case, Galileo made enough discoveries for a dozen scientists. He could spare one of them. For the German scientist Johannes Fabricius, who arrived independently at this particular observation a few months after Galileo but published it first, the day he found a sunspot probably was the brightest of his life. Not believing his own eyes, Johannes called his father, and they marveled at the inky splotch on the Sun (using the safe white-card-and-telescope approach) until sundown. "Thus passed our first day," wrote Fabricius in 1611, "and our curiosity oppressed our night, as we lay wondering whether the spot was truly on the Sun or beyond it." The next morning, to his great joy, he found the spot again right away. It wasn't a cloud. It was a blemish in the face of the celestial fire. The Sun would never be the same to us again.

As years passed and the quality of telescopes improved, sun-watchers made more and more detailed drawings of the umbra and penumbra, puzzling over the thousands of strange filaments that gave each spot the look of sheaves of wheat. Even after 200 years of meticulous observations, however, they still had no idea what sunspots were. Most astronomers assumed the spots were black clouds. Others spoke of storms, bubbles, mountains, meteorite impacts, or volcanic slagheaps. In 1801, the astronomer Sir William Herschel, who discovered the planet Uranus, suggested the spots might be *holes* in bright clouds. He thought astronomers were looking down through these holes at the Sun's real surface, which, he said, was solid and "most probably also inhabited, like the rest of the planets, by beings whose organs are adapted to the peculiar circumstances of that vast globe." (It was one of the wildest guesses in the history of science.)

In studying the Sun, the telescope was not as much help as one might expect. Astronomers could see more of the Sun's features but had no way to explain what they saw, except by wild guesses like Herschel's. John Eddy says the numerous fanciful sunspot theories that competed for attention just a century ago "reveal the limitations of astronomy without physics: of pictures and visual observations without the benefit of accompanying measurements and deductions of physical quantities, such as temperature, density, velocity, and chemical composition."

A meticulous engraving of a single sunspot, made by the 19th-century American scientist Samuel Langley.

The invention that made these crucial measurements and deductions possible was not the telescope but the *spectroscope*. This instrument had its beginnings during a few sunny days in England in 1665, when Isaac Newton closed the shutters of his study and held a piece of glass in one of the shafts of sunlight that streamed in through the slats.

"The Sunbeams, passing through a glass prism to the Opposite Wall, exhibited there a Spectrum of divers colours," Newton later wrote. He was the first to call the seven colors of the rainbow the *spectrum*. At the time and for long afterward, the word "spectrum" meant "specter," "ghost," "apparition." Newton's choice of this word suggests how eerie an experience it must have been, in his lonely chambers, to break apart a ray of sunlight and study the bewitching colors dancing on his wall and ceiling.

By careful experiments, Newton demonstrated that the prism had not altered the nature of the light. What we call "white light" is really this whole array of colors blended together: violet, indigo, blue, green, yellow, orange, and red.

Newton was studying optics at the time. But his trick of bending light was, in retrospect, the first step in one of the most extraordinary achievements of modern science—the discovery of the secret code hidden in every beam of starlight.

In 1802, another English physicist, William Wollaston, despite a handicap—he was partially blind—noticed something curious about the spectrum that Newton had inexplicably missed. Instead of a window slat, Wollaston was using a fine slit to narrow the beam of light entering his prism. He saw that the spectrum is not the smooth and continuous rainbow Newton reported. It is crossed by dark, vertical lines, as if there were strands of black piano wire running through the rainbow. He counted seven lines: two in the red, three in the yellow-green, two in the blue-violet. A decade later, a Bavarian optician, Joseph von Fraunhofer, refined this work and counted 500 fine lines. He labeled each line and mapped its place on the spectrum. In honor of this meticulous work, they are called *Fraunhofer lines.*

Eventually, investigators set aside the prism in favor of a *diffraction grating*, a fine grid that splits light into the spectrum more sharply than a prism does (an ordinary phonograph record can serve as a diffraction grating—hold it slantwise to sunlight, and rainbows play in the grooves). With good diffraction gratings, thousands of Fraunhofer lines show up in the spectrum.

For nearly half a century, the meaning of these dark lines remained unknown. Then, in 1859, the German chemist Gustav Kirchhoff, with coworker Robert Bunsen, cracked the code, with the help of a new invention of Bunsen's. The two men looked through a spectroscope at the flame of a Bunsen burner. They discovered that the Fraunhofer lines they saw in the spectrum depended solely upon what they had burning in the burner. The chemical element hydrogen created the lines Fraunhofer had labeled C and F. Vaporized iron made Fraunhofer's E line.

In effect, the two men realized, the Fraunhofer lines were like artists' signatures. The C and F lines could be read as, "I, hydrogen, created this beam of light." The E line meant, "Cast by iron."

This simple technique is now used in laboratories all over the world to determine the composition of an unknown chemical compound. With a Bunsen burner, a spectroscope, and patience, one can itemize every last element in a bit of rock. One has only to burn a small piece of the sample, inspect the spectrum of the glowing flame, and find the Fraunhofer lines. Looking up the lines in books of tables, one can tick off the signatures of all the elements in the rock, one by one.

Kirchhoff and Bunsen immediately saw their discovery's celestial possibilities. Bunsen wrote to a fellow chemist in England:

> At present Kirchhoff and I are engaged in an investigation that doesn't let us sleep. Kirchhoff has made a wonderful, entirely unexpected discovery in finding the cause of the dark lines in the solar spectrum . . . a means has been found to determine the composition of the Sun and fixed stars.

In 1665, Sir Isaac Newton split sunlight into the colors of the rainbow—and termed the array of colors the spectrum. *The spectrum is like secret writing—deciphered, it tells tales of the Sun and stars.*

THE DANGEROUS SUN

This extraordinary 19th-century painting, entitled *Regulus*, hangs in the Tate Gallery in London. It depicts a sunrise in the ancient African city of Carthage. The artist, Joseph W. M. Turner, devoted years to the scientific study of light and color, and here he rendered the sunrise so vividly that the paint dazzles. But in *Regulus*, Turner was not trying simply to glorify the Sun. He concealed in the canvas a darker message of awe and danger.

The title was one of those classical allusions a 19th-century artist could rely upon his audience to know. Regulus was a Roman consul and general who played a part in Rome's interminable war with Carthage and was captured. To punish Regulus, the Carthaginians cut off his eyelids and tied him facing east at dawn. As an art historian, Valerie J. Fletcher has noted, "none of the tiny figures in the harbor scene actually depicts the condemned man. Rather, in looking at the painting the viewer assumes the role of Regulus being tortured by the searing light."

"Regulus," by Joseph W. M. Turner.

This is the spectrum's secret code: fine, dark, vertical lines that streak the rainbow. They are Fraunhofer lines. Without them, we would not know what the Sun and stars are made of. At bottom left, the first dark line is the signature of hydrogen.

Of course, he and Kirchhoff couldn't put a piece of the Sun in a Bunsen burner. But the two men didn't have to—Nature had done that for them. The Sun was already on fire, and the scientists had only to read its Fraunhofer lines to find out what it was made of.

Using this technique, the signatures of more than 100 elements have since been found in the spectrum of sunlight. The strongest signature, by far, is hydrogen's: The Sun is about 90 percent hydrogen. There are also traces of the elements that are building blocks of our own bodies—carbon, nitrogen, and oxygen—and in the same order of abundance as in the human body. This kinship is no coincidence. We ourselves are the stuff of stars; the raw materials of which each of our bodies is made were condensed from the hot cloud around our young Sun.

After hydrogen, the most abundant element in the Sun is helium. Indeed, helium was discovered in the Sun, through its Fraunhofer lines, 30 years before it was found on Earth. Scientists believed for those 30 years that the element was special to the Sun. It is named for the Greek sun god, Helios.

Ironically, just before Kirchhoff and Bunsen's discovery, the French philosopher Auguste Compte wrote a treatise on the scope of human knowledge. Casting about for an example of something humanity could never know, he thought of the stars. We can never visit them, he wrote, and "never, by any means, will we be able to study their chemical composition."

Only three years after Compte died, human beings had found the means. They could split a star's rays into a rainbow and read the rainbow. Not only can modern scientists use Fraunhofer lines to find out precisely what the Sun and the other stars are made of, they also have learned how to read between the lines, as it were, to determine the temperature of the excited atoms that sent the light, how fast the atoms are moving relative to us, and much more. Even in the single, thin ray of light from a star a million light-years away, scientists can now read volumes. An experiment that began with a simple glass prism and a window shutter has led to a miraculous expansion of the known universe.

WHY DOES THE SUN SHINE?

The Sun is not, as people once believed, simply a sort of floating bonfire in space. If it were, it would have burned out long ago, despite its size. What we on Earth call fire is a chemical process in which energy is released by making or breaking the ties that bind atom to atom. The Sun has a source of power that is far more awesome than this and far more efficient. In a process we have come to understand only in the 20th century, the Sun releases the energy latent in the atoms themselves.

The key to the Sun's energy was stated by Einstein in his famous formula $E=mc^2$ (the only mathematical formula in Bartlett's *Familiar Quotations*). Ever since Einstein, matter and energy have been understood to be like two sides of a coin, alternate identities of the same cosmic stuff. E is energy; m is mass (that is, a given amount of matter); c is the speed of light. The amount of energy stored in a bit of matter, then, is equal to its mass multiplied by the speed of light squared.

There are two profound surprises in this equation. The first is surely the equal sign: for who would have dreamed that energy could be equated with matter at all? The second is the innocent-looking c. The speed of light multiplied by the speed of light is a huge number. When multiplied so greatly, the mass of even a single twig of kindling translates into a fabulous wealth of energy. As solar physicist Robert Noyes writes in his book *The Sun, Our Star*, "The energy equivalent of a spoonful of water could send a steamship a thousand times across the ocean, and the energy equivalent of the mass of the Sun could make it shine for 5,000 solar lifetimes."

The core of the Sun is at a temperature of millions of degrees, and under such enormous pressure, hydrogen gas is 11 times denser than lead. In these extraordinary conditions, hydrogen is turned into helium. It is a complex chain of atomic reactions, and the hydrogen that goes into the reaction has slightly more mass than the helium that comes out. Each sec-

According to Albert Einstein's famous equation $E=mc^2$, a tiny amount of matter can become an astonishing blast of energy.

A hydrogen bomb, says astronomer Carl Sagan, "is essentially the physics of the center of the Sun, brought near the Earth." This test explosion, on May 20, 1956, at the Bikini Atoll, was code-named Cherokee. The nuclear fireball was photographed from an airplane 50 miles away, flying at an altitude of 12,000 feet. Cherokee was the first air-dropped hydrogen bomb, and its power was equivalent to several megatons of dynamite.

ond, the Sun turns about 700 million tons of hydrogen into 695 million tons of helium. The five million tons of matter that are lost in the process are converted into energy. It is this energy that makes the Sun shine.

Because hydrogen nuclei are fused together to make helium, the reaction is called *fusion.* Theoretical physicists predicted the existence of such reactions in the 1930s, and later, in particle accelerators, experimentalists proved that under the right conditions they really do happen. The same sorts of reactions also take place in a hydrogen bomb, which (unfortunately) works very well, too.

According to our current model of stellar anatomy, fusion does not take place throughout the body of the Sun but only in its core; only there is matter sufficiently hot and compressed for these thermonuclear reactions to take place. The Sun's core is thought to be about the size of the planet Jupiter, and its temperature is estimated at about 15 million degrees centigrade.

The gas just around the Sun's core is slightly cooler than the core itself, though this zone of the Sun, too, is superheated and supercompressed. Conditions there are sufficiently milder that fusion reactions do not take place, and the dense gas in this zone is thus more opaque than transparent. This region of the Sun might be called the solar doldrums, because as each particle of light, a *photon,* rushes out from the core, it can travel only a fraction of an inch before it runs into an atom of the surrounding gas. The photon loses a little energy in the collision and rushes off again—to another collision. Each photon rebounds backward as often as it caroms forward, making its journey from the core outward agonizingly slow.

By retarding the passage of each photon, this immensely thick layer of the Sun, technically called the *radiative*

The underground viewing room at the McMath Solar Telescope, at Kitt Peak, Arizona.

interior, alters the quality of the core's radiation, which would otherwise be lethal for life on Earth. Photons as they depart from the core are dangerously high-energy gamma rays, but after suffering innumerable collisions in the radiative interior most of the photons are less energetic. They have become ultraviolet light, and also certain wavelengths of light that carry even less energy than ultraviolet and that are the only kinds of radiation our limited human eyes can detect: the rainbow colors of the visible spectrum.

Yellow is the predominant wavelength of light emitted by the Sun. So it is no accident, observes Jack Eddy, that we put our children in yellow raincoats. Our kind has evolved beneath a yellow star, and our eyes are specially adapted to be strongest in that wavelength.

Each second, the Sun and the other stars are emitting a much wider range of radiation than our eyes can see, from X rays to gamma rays to ultraviolet rays to infrared rays to radio waves. We can detect this radiation only with the help of instruments. Newton called visible light the spectrum, but these other ranges of radiation are truly spectral, or ghostly. We are surrounded all our lives by invisible worlds.

But we are getting ahead of our photons. They do not pass directly from the solar doldrums to the surface. When each photon reaches the outer limits of the radiative interior, it enters the equivalent of a zone of storms. Here, about two thirds of

the way out from the center of the Sun to the surface, gas is boiling madly. Great bubbles hurtle toward the surface, cool, sink into the depths, and rise again, all at speeds of several thousand kilometers per hour (much faster than a photon can travel in the radiative interior). This is the *convection zone*, and it is as turbulent as a kettle on a stove. Once a photon reaches this zone, it is guaranteed a quick trip to the surface. Innumerable photons are ferried up to the surface in each giant bubble.

Through a good telescope, we can actually watch the Sun boil. The McMath Solar Telescope, on the summit of Kitt Peak, near Tucson, Arizona, is the largest of its kind in the world—300 feet long. The mountain on which it stands belongs to the Papago Indians, who at first refused to allow astronomers to build there, because it is the sacred dwelling place of their god Eel-ol-top. But a group of astronomers invited the Papago tribal council to view the Moon through a telescope, and the Indians were moved. Eel-ol-top, the tribal leaders said, is the guardian of the heavens, and the mountain god and the astronomers probably would get along. The Papagos have leased Kitt Peak to scientists ever since.

The McMath Solar Telescope casts an image of the Sun on a large table in a dark underground chamber. The solar disc is almost a yard in diameter, and it is so bright that it can be studied only with dark sunglasses, or welder's glasses. Seen on the solar table, the Sun's broad surface looks grainy, like

The corona of the Sun is millions of degrees centigrade, which is far hotter than the layers of gas immediately below it. Its extraordinary heat is one of the mysteries of solar physics. In this image, false colors have been added to show temperature differences. The picture was taken by a coronagraph aboard the Solar Maximum Mission satellite, launched by NASA in 1980 and repaired by Space Shuttle astronauts in 1984.

millions of wheat kernels viewed from the top of a silo. Watch a single kernel fixedly, and in a few minutes one sees it slowly disappear. Each dark grain is a giant bubble of gas 1,500 kilometers across that has risen from the depths, to burst or subside in minutes. Solar astronomers playing films of the Sun in fast motion are reminded of a pot of boiling rice.

The bubbling, boiling realm we see with a telescope is called the *photosphere*. We speak of it as the Sun's "surface," and it does look like one. In fact, however, there is more gas above it, in two outer layers, the *chromosphere* and the *corona*. These layers are normally invisible to the naked eye, because in visible wavelengths of light they are powerfully outshone by the radiant photosphere beneath them. Without special filters we can catch glimpses of the chromosphere and corona only during total eclipses of the Sun, when the Moon blocks out the light of the main body of the Sun.

The chromosphere is the deep red of blood, or rubies. It is visible briefly when the Moon's shadow obscures all but the rim of the Sun—then its brilliant color startles even a seasoned eclipse-watcher. After that crimson flash, as the Moon blocks out the whole disc of the Sun, the sky darkens, and stars appear in the sky. At the moment of *totality*, a halo suddenly springs up around where the Sun had been. It looks like a set of great, white rays, as in a young child's drawing of the Sun. This is the *corona*, the Sun's large and gauzy outer atmosphere. Like starlight, the corona is too faint to be visible in the blue sky of ordinary daylight; but the rays are out there every day nonetheless. Children's drawings of the Sun are more accurate than their parents imagine.

It takes a photon a long time to get from the core to the bubbling, boiling surface, the photosphere. Some estimate the length of the journey at 10 million years. Once at the surface, however, the photon is free at last. The chromosphere and corona are too thin to delay its passage. It flashes outward into space at the speed of light and reaches us eight minutes later.

INTO THE DEPTHS

The heart of a star is surely, as one writer has observed, one of the most inaccessible places in the cosmos. We can never descend into the solar depths as we have into our own seas. No manned submersible could penetrate the surface without vaporizing. We cannot *see* beneath the surface, either, for the only light that reaches us is what radiates from the topmost layers of the Sun. Yet to avoid making wild guesses like Herschel's, we must find ways of exploring the heart of the Sun. We have two curious and indirect ways of peering into it.

One by-product of the fusion of hydrogen into helium

is a ghostly subatomic particle called the *neutrino*. Like photons, neutrinos are formed in great quantities in the Sun's core every second. Unlike photons, however, neutrinos rarely interact with matter. So they are not trapped in the thick layers of Sun. They shoot straight out from the core to us at the speed of light (overtaking and passing energy that has been struggling outward for thousands of millennia). Neutrinos are the free spirits of the universe. Physicist Enrico Fermi called them "the little neutral ones." If stellar theory is correct, about 70 billion of them are passing through every square centimeter of the Earth, and of our own bodies, at this moment. We can't see them, of course; they go right through our retinas as easily as they penetrate everything else. But if we could somehow devise a neutrino detector, we could look straight into the Sun's core.

In 1968, physicist Raymond Davis of the Brookhaven National Laboratory built a vat in the bottom of a gold mine. The vat is 20 feet round and 48 feet long, and it holds 100,000 gallons of perchloroethylene, which is ordinary cleaning fluid. The vat sits 4,900 feet down in a tunnel of the Homestake Mine, under the Black Hills of South Dakota.

Nothing from outer space but a neutrino can penetrate that deep into the Earth and reach the vat. Most neutrinos go right through the cleaning fluid without leaving a trace. But with so many neutrinos passing through and so many atoms in the tank (the best estimate is 1 nonillion—1 followed by 30 zeroes), theory predicts that each day about six neutrinos should be stopped by atoms in the tank. In the collisions, six chlorine atoms should be changed into atoms of radioactive argon.

Davis, after herculean labors, is actually able to find and count the argon atoms in his tank and thus to measure the number of neutrinos reaching the Earth. The results have confounded all expectations. Davis is catching only one or two neutrinos a day, where he should catch six or seven. No one knows what has happened to the missing neutrinos. Something is wrong, either with the experiment or with our understanding of the nuclear engine in the Sun's core.

Many ingenious suggestions have been made to explain the discrepancy. It has been proposed, for instance, that neutrinos may have mass after all—not constantly, the way a cannonball has mass, but *briefly*, in a manner peculiar to creatures of the subatomic zoo. Then some neutrinos might decay and disappear on their way from the Sun's core to Earth. This suggestion has vast implications, for there are so many neutrinos in the cosmos that if even a small number of them have mass even a fraction of the time, they would greatly increase the total mass of the universe. In fact, if neutrinos have mass, then the universe, which (according to theory) has been expanding ever since the moment of its creation in the Big Bang, should someday stop expanding, pause in space, and begin to fall back inward upon itself because of the added gravitational attraction of all those neutrinos. It would fall until it could fall no farther, in a cosmic collapse that has been called the "Big Crunch." Then there might be another cataclysmic explosion, a "Big Bang, Part Two." Eventually, another Big Crunch. In this vision, the cosmos would be born and die and rise again from its own ashes, over and over. Our universe would be only one in an endless series, as in Hindu philosophy.

It is curious to think that not only people, nations, species, and stars, but even the universe may be born, live a while, and die. If so, absolutely nothing we can see around us is eternal. "Nations die," says an old Japanese proverb; "Rivers go on; mountains go on." But as the Scotsman James Hutton saw, rivers carry whole mountains down to sea, and mountains sometimes rise to halt a river. Neither goes on forever. In the last quarter century we have learned that the ceaseless shifting of plates alters the very shapes of the oceans, opening and closing their beds like books; and on our nearest planetary neighbor, Venus, all the oceans seem to have boiled away. Beyond our solar system, even the stars of our galaxy, and the other hundred billion galaxies, and the very laws of physics, which we are proud to believe are universal, someday may all decline together, to collapse in the Big Crunch.

However, not everyone agrees that neutrinos have mass; there are other neutrino theories, each of them controversial. It has seriously been suggested that there are so few neutrinos because the core of the Sun is *dying*. If the core has just gone on the blink, we could not tell the difference yet by looking at the surface of the Sun, which is all ancient light anyway. (The energy that reaches us in eight minutes' time, remember, took an estimated 10 million years to travel from the Sun's core to the surface.) For a long while we would know there was trouble in the Sun's core only by a tapering off of neutrinos.

Most astrophysicists think this hypothesis unlikely, judging by what we know of the behavior of stars. But if the Sun's core is dying, we on Earth are all like wartime sweethearts, still getting bundles of mail from a fallen soldier long after the fateful telegram has arrived.

SUNQUAKES   No one has solved the case of the missing neutrinos. Meanwhile, there is a second trick by which we can hope to see beneath the Sun's surface.

In the early 1960s, careful measurements of portions

of the Sun's surface by Robert B. Leighton of the California Institute of Technology revealed that small patches of the photosphere—the solar "surface"—were slowly heaving, like swells on a sea, taking about five minutes to rise and fall.

Some years later, in 1975, Robin Stebbins and Tim Brown of the National Center for Atmospheric Research (NCAR) and Henry Hill of the University of Arizona were attacking a separate problem, using a superb 250-ton solar telescope on Mount Lemmon, near Tucson, Arizona. "We were trying to test Einstein's General Theory of Relativity," Stebbins explains. "The test relies on knowing whether the Sun is exactly round or not. In measuring the diameter of the Sun to one part in a million, we discovered that the Sun is not constant in size at all but is *pulsating*."

Serendipitously, they had helped to make an amazing discovery. The motions Leighton had seen were actually part of a global pattern. "It now seems clear," says Stebbins, "that the entire globe of the Sun is vibrating mechanically in and out, very much as a musical instrument vibrates when it makes a sound." The whole Sun is shaking and quivering, or *oscillating*. It is ringing like a bell!

A range of oscillations has now been detected in the surface of the Sun, with periods from 5 to 70 minutes long. Some investigators say they have measured even slower vibrations, in which it takes the Sun several hours to go through one cycle of rising and subsiding—trembling in extreme slow motion.

Planet Earth shakes, too, of course, during earthquakes. Seismologists have learned how to use quakes to "see" into the interior of the planet. Sound waves from each quake race through the rocky layers of the Earth at different speeds, depending on how hard the rock is, how hot it is, and other factors. It was a careful analysis of such waves that revealed to us the deep layers of which the Earth is made—its inner core, outer core, mantle, and crust. Someday, the detailed and colorful pictures that Don Anderson and colleagues are making with the help of supercomputers may even show us the convection of the Earth's mantle, the vast, dark, and ponderous motion that is thought to push continents across the surface of the Earth.

Subjected to the same sort of computer analysis, quakes may prove useful in the study of the Sun. One of those engaged in such work is Martin Pomerantz, an astrophysicist at the Franklin Institute's Bartol Research Foundation in Newark, Delaware. "The technique of solar seismology, as we now call it," says Pomerantz, "may give us information about what the Sun looks like, from the surface down to the center."

Over the next few years, solar seismic data may bring

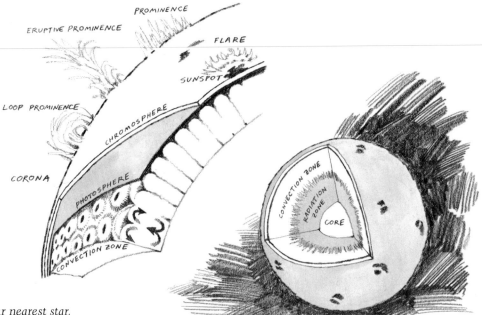

Anatomy of our nearest star. Details remain speculative. Just how thick are each of the Sun's inner layers—the core, the radiative zone, and the convection zone? How fast are each of these layers of gas moving, and in which directions? What makes the Sun a magnet? What stirrings in the interior create the fireworks at the surface—such as sunspots, prominences, and flares?

Solar observatories have been established in camps near the South Pole. During the summer months the Sun does not set for weeks on end.

about a revolution in our understanding of the Sun's interior—and, by extension, of the hearts of all stars. The tool may prove almost as revolutionary as spectroscopy. Analysis of the waves may someday reveal the dimensions of the Sun's various layers, their temperatures, the rates at which they are moving, the size of the core, and its ratio of hydrogen to helium. When we know as much about the interior of the Sun as we do about the interior of the Earth, we may even be able to find the missing neutrinos.

So far, though, our knowledge of these waves is very imperfect. The waves are confusing to follow because they are perpetually crossing each other, overlapping and interfering, like busy swells and ripples in open sea. Even with sophisticated mathematical analysis, it is hard to sort them out. And each day, at sundown, an observatory loses track of the wave patterns it has been monitoring; astronomers there have to wait until morning and start over. Solar astronomers wish it were always daytime (just as conventional astronomers sometimes wish it were always night). Their dream has been to observe the Sun around the clock, 24 hours a day. For these reasons, Pomerantz, Stebbins, and others have recently set up small solar observatories at the South Pole. There summer begins in September, and for six months the Sun never sets.

"Great God, what an awful place!" the explorer Scott exclaimed at the South Pole in 1912. "Evidently," Pomerantz says cheerfully, "he did not appreciate the astronomical potential." For those who are "listening" to the Sun, the South Pole is almost paradise.

We do not actually hear the Sun because the gas between the star and our ears is too thin to support the passage of sound waves. Also, the frequencies at which the Sun vibrates are very, very far below the lower limit of human hearing.

If we *could* hear the Sun, though, we would have a deeper sense of its awesome power. We would have to endure, day and night, a roaring as of a million jet engines, created by the turbulence of the Sun's convection zone. We would hear and *feel* (as we feel strong vibrations beneath the range of the human ear) the incessant wild heaving of the solar sea. And far beneath this tumult, we might detect, using electronic microphones, a profound, almost pure tone, more than a dozen octaves below the lowest note on a piano. Someday, perhaps, an imaginative solar astronomer will use a Moog Synthesizer to translate the rhythmic solar quakings and shakings into music audible to the human ear. It might prove to be, as someone once said of Beethoven's Fifth Symphony, "the most sublime noise that ever penetrated the ear of man."

THE FIERY DYNAMO

In the story of scientific discovery, serendipity is almost the rule rather than the exception. In the early 1800s, a German apothecary and amateur astronomer named Heinrich Schwabe kept track of sunspots, hoping to find among them a new planet silhouetted against the face of the Sun. In 1843, after 33 years of fruitless searching, he realized that his records contained a discovery he found even more exciting than a planet. "I can compare myself to Saul," he said, "who went out to find his father's asses and found a throne!"

The number of sunspots, Schwabe announced, wax and wane in fairly regular cycles. He said 10 years; we now estimate the average cycle at 11.2 years. At times of sunspot maximum, there are as many as 100 spots visible from Earth on the face of the Sun. At times of sunspot minimum, a month may occasionally go by without a single spot. The last sunspot maximum was in 1979–80, and 1986 is a sunspot minimum.

The discovery of the sunspot cycle helped point toward a fundamental factor in the life of the Sun. Since Schwabe's discovery, astronomers have learned, through a variety of observations, that the Sun is a powerful magnet. Sunspots are points where its magnetic forces are concentrated.

The process that turns an entire world into a magnet is still poorly understood; but in our solar system, Jupiter, Earth, Mercury, and the Sun are each known to have a magnetic field. The Sun is assumed to be magnetic by virtue of the motion of its gases. The Sun rotates at more than 4,000 miles per hour at the equator. Its swirling and bubbling masses of gases generate

This giant prominence began as an eruption near the surface of the Sun. Here, a mere twenty minutes later, it has rocketed more than half a million kilometers in space. That is almost as far as Apollo astronauts travelled on their journey to the Moon and back.

its magnetic field in long, looping lines of force, something like those traced by iron filings around a bar magnet. In the Sun, however, instead of iron filings, hot, charged gases trace the lines of force. Somehow these gases get "locked into" the lines of force, forming long magnetic tubes and pipes. As the Sun turns and churns, the tubes are stretched and broken, and some of them get twisted into knots and braids. The Sun's magnetic field becomes as tangled as pasta in a pot.

This *magnetic dynamo* is believed to be the source of most of the Sun's storms and disturbances. When, for instance, a loop of magnetic pipe pokes out of the Sun, its strong magnetic field quells the boiling of the convection zone at the place where the tube breaks the surface. This spot, under the spell of the concentrated magnetic field, grows cooler than the sea of bubbles around it and, being cooler, the spot emits less light. A big loop of magnetic tubing, protruding from the Sun like a handle, breaks the surface in two places and thus makes two dark spots on the Sun. These are sunspots.

It is because they are almost always found at the bases of such loops that sunspots generally appear in pairs. One is magnetic north, the other south. These pairs tend to line up parallel to the equator; and in each hemisphere, the polarity of the sunspot pairs follows a fairly consistent pattern in relation to the spinning of the Sun. In the northern hemisphere, for instance, it may happen that all the leading sunspots are magnetic north and all the trailing sunspots are south. In the southern hemisphere, the order is reversed: Leading sunspots are south, trailing sunspots north.

Once every 11 years or so, this pattern reverses. The south poles lead in the northern hemisphere, and the north poles lead in the south. And 11 years after that, when the pattern reverses again, the whole dance returns to its starting point. Thus there are at least two sunspot cycles—an 11- and a 22-year cycle.

These cycles are presumed to be caused by flip-flops of the Sun's magnetic dynamo. The Earth's magnetic field (which is as poorly understood as the Sun's) also flips occasionally, exchanging north and south magnetic poles. Our pole flips can be traced in volcanic rock; and a quarter century ago, the pole-flip record was used ingeniously to prove that continents are drifting (see Chapter One). But the Earth's dynamo is much weaker and slower than the Sun's. The last flip of the Earth's poles was about 700,000 years ago. We are overdue for another, and some scientists think it is coming soon—in 3,000 years.

The fusion reactor in the Sun's core, its thermonuclear engine, sends us light. But the magnetic dynamo, together with the blazing gases of the outer Sun, sends us something more: invisible storms.

On September 1, 1859, in Surrey, England, at precisely 11:18 A.M., amateur astronomer Richard Carrington was in his private observatory mapping that day's sunspots. The existence of sunspot cycles had been discovered, by Schwabe, only the decade before, and Carrington hoped to learn whether these events on the Sun had any cyclic effects upon the Earth. Suddenly, as he was sketching a sunspot on a piece of white paper, he saw something no one on Earth had ever seen before: Two patches of light broke out on the Sun. The patches were, he recorded later, "intensely white and bright."

THE STORM THAT FELL
FROM THE SUN

> I thereupon noted down the time by the chronometer, and seeing the outburst to be very rapidly on the increase, and being somewhat flurried by the surprise, I hastily ran to call someone to witness the exhibition with me, and on returning within 60 seconds was mortified to find that it was already much changed and enfeebled. Very shortly afterwards the last trace was gone. . . .

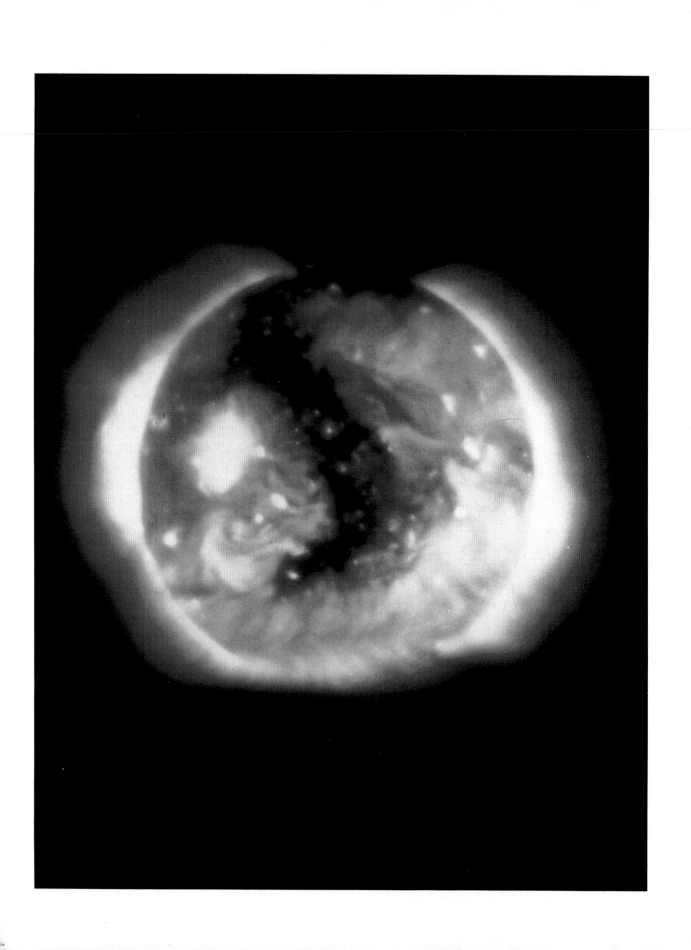

Just two minutes later, at 11:20 A.M., instruments at Kew Gardens—not far from Carrington's home in Surrey—detected strange waverings in the Earth's magnetic field. Before dawn the next morning, at 4:00 A.M., these waverings became more marked. Delicately suspended compass needles pointed not due north but trembled a few degrees to either side, like weather vanes in a storm.

That night the sky was lit from horizon to horizon with eerie, shifting lights of red and green, as if great, ethereal silk curtains were blowing in the breeze of an open window. All over Europe, people woke each other to stare at the lights. In Kansas, pioneers on their way West, camped beside covered wagons, watched the sky and marveled. So did Hawaiians in Honolulu, and sheep ranchers in the Australian outback.

Meanwhile, telegraph wires all over the world, from Canada to Australia, went crazy. Some stations had to shut down; operators stared while the telegraph keys tapped out incoherent messages—patterns of dots and dashes no human being had sent and no one could decipher. On the other hand, for two hours there was so much current flowing in the telegraph wires between Boston, Massachusetts, and Portland, Oregon, that operators could send messages without using batteries: they needed only the electricity that seemed to have fallen into the wires from the sky.

Soon afterward, at a meeting of the Royal Astronomical Society, Carrington reported what he had seen. It seemed possible, he said tentatively, that the effects of the disturbance he witnessed on the Sun had traveled 93 million miles in a flash and wreaked havoc upon the Earth's magnetic field.

A man more easily flurried than Carrington probably would have felt certain of that. But Carrington knew the power of a good coincidence; he knew how easily the mind perceives cause and effect where there is none. It was *conceivable* that disturbances in the Sun stir the Earth. However, being a disciplined scientist and possessing that sobriety for which English country gentlemen are famous, Carrington cautioned the society against leaping to conclusions. "One swallow," he said, "does not make a summer."

By the middle of the 20th century, it was clear that the mild derangement of compass needles and telegraph keys, together with magnificent displays of the northern lights and the southern lights—the *aurora borealis* and the *aurora australis*—were not coincidental. They do occur together more often than not. It was also clear that they were most frequent at certain points in the 11-year sunspot cycle. But no one knew why.

In the early 1950s, physicists made a few calculations

Much of the Sun's life is hidden from us—first, because our eyes cannot see its ultraviolet and X-ray radiation, and second, because most of these rays are blocked from reaching Earth by our atmosphere. Out in space, however, using special instruments, we see a strange new Sun. The astronauts aboard Skylab took this X-ray photograph of a hole in the corona, shaped rather like the Boot of Italy. Coronal holes are gaping chasms in the outer regions of the Sun. Through these holes, solar winds pour out at high speed.

Comet West looped sunward in the mid-1970s, its tail blown back and dishevelled by the solar wind.

that seemed equally puzzling. The first concerned the corona, which is visible during total eclipses. Spectroscopic analysis had proven the corona to be amazingly hot, nearly 2 million degrees centigrade. If the corona was so hot, calculations suggested the gas would expand so greatly that the Sun's gravity would be too weak to hold it. The thin gas in the corona should therefore be escaping in all directions far into outer space. (Strangely enough, the corona is much hotter than the surface below it. How can the Sun's surface, at 5,000 degrees, heat the corona to 2 million degrees? One might just as well expect an ice cube to boil water. The corona's heat remains one of the Sun's outstanding mysteries. Many astrophysicists think the long loops of magnetic fields that poke above the Sun's surface and out into the corona heat it somehow.)

Independently, physicist Ludwig Biermann noticed an odd fact about comets. Astronomers had long observed that as comets orbit around the Sun, their tails (made of dust and vapor) always point away from the Sun. Most theorists assumed the tails were being blown back by the force of sunlight, like a ponytail in a gale. But light is composed only of photons. Biermann made some calculations. Even the vast numbers of photons that stream from the Sun, he said, would not be strong enough to blow back a comet's hair. Heavier particles must be flying out from the Sun, too.

In 1958, a theoretical physicist, Eugene Parker of the University of Chicago, put two and two together. The corona must indeed be expanding, he said. The breeze that stirs the comets' tails is the corona itself! He could not determine how fast it flows—as a mild breeze, or as a powerful wind.

This matter could not be investigated further here on Earth. Our planet's magnetic field repels most charged particles that stream toward us from outer space. The Earth's invisible force field is like a shield, and it shelters us from stray atomic particles even better than our atmosphere protects us from falling meteorites. Only space probes far out beyond Earth's magnetic field, journeying through in the black near-vacuum that surrounds us, could check for solar breezes and prove or disprove Parker's theory.

In 1959, some of the first Soviet spacecraft, as they left the Earth's magnetic field, detected a flying wind of charged particles. So did the U.S. *Explorer 10* satellite in 1961. And in 1962, when the United States' *Mariner 2* headed toward Venus (which is, of course, sunward of us), the probe ran into a headwind gusting to 1 million miles an hour. There really is a solar wind. It is a kind of continual buckshot of electrons, protons, and atomic nuclei.

Far from being empty, the region between the Sun and

Skylab astronauts discovered the comet Kohoutek (visible in this coronagraph) as it traveled toward the Sun. Its tail is being blown back behind it by the solar wind.

the Earth is filled with star stuff—fragments of the Sun itself in the form of hot gases of charged particles, a state of matter called *plasma*. Plasma is the lifeblood of the universe—the most common form of matter. It flows through all of interplanetary space. When Apollo astronauts arrived on the Moon, they unrolled banners of aluminum foil, facing into the Sun; before leaving, the astronauts rolled up the banners and took them home. Careful laboratory analysis found atoms of hydrogen and helium embedded in the foil—bits of the Sun itself. And mingled in the lunar dust the astronauts brought home was more stardust, borne to the Moon on the strong winds of the day star.

When Richard Carrington reflected upon the strange eruption he had witnessed on the Sun, he decided it might have been the splash of a meteor plunking into the ball of fire like a pebble into a pond. But such a splash would not cause nearly as much disruption as Carrington saw in the Sun. What Carrington actually observed was a *solar flare*, one of the most dramatic events in the life of the Sun.

    Flares are very rarely visible on the photosphere; they are much more commonly seen in the red chromosphere. There they are normally invisible from Earth (being outshone by the photosphere), but seen with the proper instruments they make a dramatic sight. Often, says John Eddy, they look like a pool of gasoline that has suddenly been ignited.

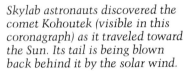

HOLES IN THE SUN

The scientist-pilot of *Skylab*'s third and last mission, Edward Gibson, was anxious to see the genesis of a flare. He hoped to watch one through his powerful Gatling gun of instruments, the Apollo Telescope Mount, or ATM, which allowed him to film the Sun simultaneously in more than one wavelength of light, and view what was happening in different layers all at once. Toward the end of Gibson's mission, as he floated before the control panel (one needs no chair in outer space), he was disappointed to realize that neither he nor any of the others had succeeded in catching a flare and recording its earliest stages. Flares burst out of the Sun too quickly; by the time anyone had taken aim with the ATM, they were already in full flame. Gibson said afterward:

> So, as the active region shown on my TV display seethed with small energy fluctuations, I practiced the exact control panel procedures I would use if a flare erupted. (I had done this many times before, but to no avail.)
>
> Suddenly, a small bright point appeared right in the center of my screen. As I started the instruments taking data rapidly in their flare modes, I was elated to see the bright point blossom into a full-blown flare.

Flares often erupt from *active regions*—zones of intense magnetic activity. When the magnetic field lines get twisted, they store energy, like rubber bands; if they are twisted one time too many, they snap, and the release of energy leads to a flare. A large flare, like the one seen by Gibson, can release the same amount of energy as 10 million hydrogen bombs. Gas in the explosion often reaches 20 million degrees—hotter than the center of the Sun. If flares weren't so short-lived, their incredible temperatures might set off fusion reactions in the corona. A big explosion there, without the great mass of the Sun to muffle it, could be a catastrophe for life on Earth. We are lucky that flares are brief.

Solar flares are most frequent when there are the most sunspots; during such times, as many as 12 flares are observed in 24 hours. Flares are rarest when there are fewest sunspots; then only one or two small flares may be observed in a whole month.

The occurrence of geomagnetic storms tends to follow the 11-year sunspot cycle, because gusts of solar matter are hurled outward by flares, and when this matter reaches Earth, it leads to the kinds of disturbances noted by Richard Carrington, and the scientists at Kew Gardens. Thus Carrington was right: There is a link between flares, and storms that fall from the Sun. That accounts for the 11-year cycle of geomagnetic storms on Earth, a cycle linked to sunspots. But geomagnetic storms sometimes recur on a 27-day cycle, too. Every once in a while, for a few months running, auroras and magnetic disturbances recur at 27-day intervals. The same pattern was detected by *Mariner 2* on its way to Venus.

Since 27 days is the period of the Sun's rotation, the gusts were presumed to emanate from some undiscovered feature on the face of the turning Sun. For years, these hypothetical features were simply called M-regions (M for Mysterious).

X-ray and ultraviolet photographs of the corona, taken from space with better detail than ever before by *Skylab* astronauts, show the M-regions to be large and strange. An M-region turns out to be a hole or chasm that cleaves the corona nearly in two. The Sun often looks as if it were about to crack open, like a hatching egg.

Skylab's detailed observations of these M-regions, now called *coronal holes*, proved their profound influence upon the Earth. Each hole is far larger and often lasts much longer than the average sunspot, taking three months or more to heal and close up. It rotates, like the rest of the Sun, roughly once in 27 days. From the hole pours a steady and extrapowerful stream of solar wind. As the Sun turns, the stream rotates through space, rather like a lighthouse beacon. Every time a coronal hole is, from our vantage point, in the center of the Sun—that is, pointed straight at us—Earth gets magnetic storms. Solar astronomer Art Hundhausen of NCAR calls this discovery "the triumph of the *Skylab* era."

In the winter of 1974, for instance, the last *Skylab* crew, before abandoning the space station, photographed a new coronal hole, off to one side of the Sun's face. Then, as the hole rotated, an old *Explorer* space probe, far out in space, came into the line of fire and was struck by a strong solar wind. Astronomers, alerted by *Skylab* and *Explorer*, trained their telescopes on Comet Kohoutek and saw its tail grow disheveled as the gusts of wind from the coronal hole swept across it. Four days later, according to a NASA report, the rotation of the Sun aimed the coronal hole straight at Earth "like the nozzle of a garden hose." The extra solar wind gusted against our planet, and there was a strong magnetic storm.

The solar wind itself is invisible. But its effects on our world are not. Besides causing geomagnetic storms, the wind helps to create one of the most beautiful and mysterious phenomena on Planet Earth. Until modern times, no one knew that this awesome effect, which we call the *aurora*, or the northern lights and the southern lights, was connected with storms on the Sun. But to many people it hinted of a cosmic disturbance with dimensions far beyond the scope of life on Earth.

The northern lights are commonplace near the Arctic Circle, but they are very rarely seen farther south—so rarely that when they did appear in ancient times, they inspired holy dread, and descriptions of them were passed on from generation to generation. When the lights appear far from the poles, they are generally a deep red, and the surprise, combined with the ominous color, makes them stupendously frightening. "Under Tiberius Caesar," according to the Roman historian Seneca, "the cohorts ran together in aid of the colony of Ostia as if it were in flames." When the soldiers arrived, they found the Ostians unharmed; the fires they had seen were farther off—seemingly among the stars. "The glowing of the sky lasted through a great part of the night, shining dimly like a vast and smoking fire."

On the night of January 12, 1570, lights were seen over much of central Europe. According to a medieval broadside, the good people of Kuttenberg, Bohemia, saw

Norwegian Arctic explorer Fridtjof Nansen liked to stroll from his ship after dinner to admire and sketch the aurora borealis. In this woodcut, Nansen shows the lights arcing like a great rainbow above his ship, the Fram.

many burning torches like tapers and among these stood two great pillars, one towards the east and the other due north, so that the town appeared illuminated as if it were ablaze, the fire running down the two pillars from the clouds like drops of blood. And in

order that this miraculous sign from God might be seen by the people, the night-watchmen on the towers sounded the alarm bells; and when the people saw it they were horrified and said that no such gruesome spectacle had been seen or heard of within living memory.

Eskimo tribes, on the other hand, saw the play of the northern lights almost every night, and they were accustomed to them. The Eskimos believed the colored bands were spirits of the dead playing ball with a walrus skull. This legend is remarkably uniform, found in tribe after tribe, around the Arctic Circle—although somehow, according to Alaska writer Dorothy Jean Ray, "The Eskimos of Nunivak Island had the opposite idea, of walrus spirits playing with a human skull."

Eskimos of Point Barrow, Alaska, thought the lights were evil. At night they kept knives at the ready, in case the long arms of fire reached down from the sky. They threw the frozen offal of their dogs at the lights to keep them far away.

William Tyson is an Eskimo who grew up in Point Barrow and now lives in Fairbanks. "We had a lot of medicine men that claimed to have power on other things, like on wood,

Because they live near one of Earth's magnetic poles, Alaskans are often treated to light shows like this.

or trees," he recalls. "But somehow, they never had anything to say about the northern lights. All they told us was, they're scared of them, and they respect them."

One night, Tyson has heard, a man was sitting on a walrus skin. "He had kids with him, he was baby-sitting them. Then the aurora came down and took them and brought them up, and the man, and the kids, with the walrus skin, disappeared. They never found them no more.

"We used to have a lot of TB [tuberculosis] and a lot of spitting blood," he says. "A lot of people died of that TB. Anytime we saw the aurora get red in winter, they used to say that's a sign people are going to die of spitting up blood.

"But then, before the Second World War, all winter long, we sat there, and anytime we'd see the aurora, it'd start getting red from the west end, up almost halfway, and then change color again. That happened all winter long, and then, in the fall, the war broke out. Then my grandmother told me, 'Now, I've been telling that anytime the aurora gets red, there's gonna be a lot of bloodshed. Now you see that! There's a war going on down, there's a lot of people going to die, and a lot of people are going to bleed to death. That's what the horizon, the aurora, told us.'"

Tyson himself once had a bad encounter with an aurora, and in a recent conversation, he seemed on the verge of confiding the story to a visitor. But the sight of a glow on the horizon, which might have been the aurora, or might have been the rising Moon, made him edgy. "I don't like to talk about it," he said. "It happened to me in person, but I don't believe it, and I don't want to believe it. But still it happened. And I don't feel like talking about it."

The scientific vision of auroras is as wild in its way as the Eskimos' walrus skulls. Auroras are, scientists believe, caused by clashes between the solar wind and the Earth's magnetic field. The upper atmosphere has been called a battleground between the Sun and the Earth.

If there were no wind from the Sun, the Earth's magnetic field would resemble more closely the field around a simple bar magnet. But the solar wind blustering against Earth's field blows it back into a kind of comet shape, with a long tail. It extends 40,000 miles toward the Sun but perhaps 1 million miles downwind (or rather, "downsun"). This phenomenon was predicted before the Space Age by physicist Sydney Chapman and his graduate student Vincenzo Ferraro. Later, in the late 1950s, Chapman was named president of the International Geophysical Year, the huge scientific project that launched the Space Age. During the project, Chapman had the pleasure of seeing his early prediction verified by some of the first satellites.

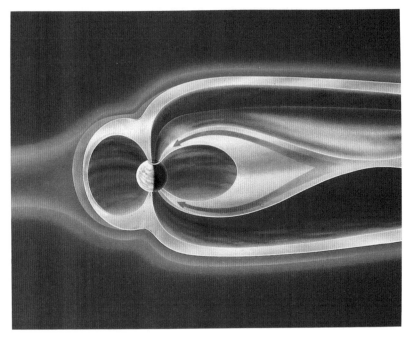

The Earth's magnetic field is still called the *magneto-sphere*, but we now know that, as Chapman and Ferraro predicted, it is really far from spherical; it looks, one writer has observed, like "a celestial tadpole."

We now know that the solar wind, blowing against the magnetosphere, gives us auroras; but just how the wind and the shield interact to give us such extraordinary light shows is still mysterious. One who is fascinated by this question is the geophysicist Syun-Ichi Akasofu. He fell in love with the northern lights while traveling as a young man, and he left his native Japan and settled in Alaska for one reason only: He could not see the lights from his home country. Akasofu has devoted his life to the study of the aurora.

The solar wind, Akasofu explains, is plasma, and the motion of its electrons through space is an electric current. It also carries magnetic fields blown loose from the Sun's corona. When it crashes into our planet's magnetic field, the two fields merge in a complex way, and the magnetosphere, Akasofu believes, "becomes a natural electrical generator," generating as much as 1 million megawatts. This power *accelerates* those particles of solar wind that manage to penetrate the Earth's magnetic force field, and these particles hurtle toward Earth.

They spiral inward toward the polar regions, following the lines of the Earth's magnetic field, which are shaped like funnels, one over the vicinity of each magnetic pole. As the solar particles collide with atoms and molecules in our upper atmosphere, these atmospheric particles are ionized—that is, lose electrons—and emit light. Low-energy solar particles reach

Outer space is not as empty as we once imagined. Instead, space in our neighborhood is full of extraordinarily intricate magnetic force fields, and it is torn by gusty winds of plasma from the Sun. This is a model of the Earth's magnetic field, or magnetosphere. If there were no solar wind, the magnetosphere would be much simpler than this: it would be shaped more or less like iron filings around a bar magnet. But the solar wind buffets and distorts the magnetosphere. On the sunward (or day) side of the planet, the solar wind compresses the magnetosphere, while on the night side, the wind extends it, blowing the magnetosphere far out into space, and giving Earth a long tail rather like a comet's—the magnetotail. Scientists are now studying this model of the magnetosphere to figure out what makes the northern and southern lights. According to current theory, gusts of solar wind strike the Earth, setting off a complex chain reaction and sending plasma particles flowing back upwind, toward the night side of the Earth. There, the particles' collisions with the gas of Earth's atmosphere creates the lovely glow of the auroral lights.

an altitude of about 150 miles; when they hit oxygen atoms there, the atoms emit a red light. High-energy particles penetrate farther, as low as 60 or even 50 miles. Because they have more energy, they strike oxygen atoms harder, and the atoms give off a pale green light. Atoms and molecules are ionized by solar ultraviolet radiation and X rays, so this zone of the atmosphere is called the *ionosphere*. Fifty miles up is 10 times higher than clouds, and that is the lowest an aurora ever descends—though, viewed from the ground, the lights sometimes look *as if* they brush the Earth. (This information would reassure Eskimo William Tyson, if he believed it.)

Stray particles of solar wind are forever spiraling inward toward the vicinity of the magnetic poles, and they cast a glowing ring around each of them. From below we see rippling arcs and sheets, the aurora; from above, satellites see a halo sitting atop the planet, as if Earth were graced by the Sun.

Curiously enough, many auroral scientists believe, the magnetosphere *hoards* vast amounts of electrical energy from the solar wind in its tail, rather than releasing this energy in a steady trickle. Every few hours, the magnetosphere releases this energy in what amounts to the lashing of the dragon's tail—an auroral *substorm*. That is why the polar lights come and go through the night.

When a strong gust of solar wind streams from a flare or a coronal hole, and particles from it accelerate along the Earth's magnetic field lines, they drive this halo down from the Earth's polar regions so that it girdles the middle latitudes. Only at such times can people at those latitudes see the lights, which are generally blood-red. Auroras in Egypt, Italy, and Bohemia really did signify terrible violence—but it was 93 million miles away, on the hidden face of the Sun. When we watch the northern lights, we can contemplate the Sun's upheavals from the relative safety of our home planet, rather as we watch the evening news.

Indeed, Akasofu has observed, the aurora and the cathode-ray tube in a color television have much in common. Each is lit from behind by a stream of electrons, which are pointed by shifting magnetic fields. In nature, the stream of electrons comes from the solar wind; the guiding magnetic fields are Earth's; and the fluorescent screen is the polar upper atmosphere. Our planet, Akasofu says, has "a giant television tube, which has as its face the Earth's atmosphere." The aurora is the world's first color TV show; and it will always be the most beautiful, though silent, picture. (Indeed, using TV cameras in orbit and on the ground, Akasofu and his group at the University of Alaska have recently managed the difficult feat of filming the aurora simultaneously from above and below.)

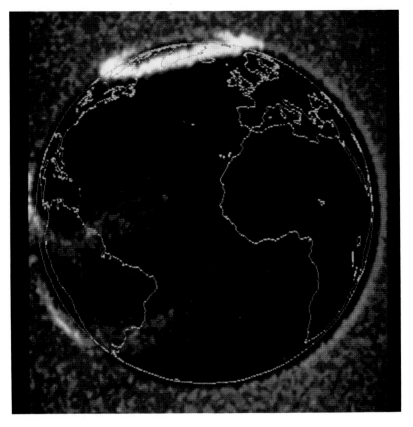

Seen from below as we stand on Earth, auroras look like broad, rippling arcs and sheets. But when Earth is viewed from out in space, each of the planet's magnetic poles looks like it is crowned with a halo of light, a sort of cosmic wedding ring. When the solar wind gusts, the two rings dance in unison, one on the top of the Earth and one on the bottom.

Only 25 years ago, most people thought of space as a vacuum. The solar wind was one of the most important discoveries of the 1960s, a vital link between the Sun and the Earth. Today an international team of scientists is creating its own comets to study how the solar wind penetrates the Earth's magnetosphere. The project was conceived by Tom Krimigis of Johns Hopkins University and Gerhard Haerendel of the Max Planck Institute for Extraterrestrial Physics in West Germany. It involves three satellites, launched in 1984. The first is a West German spacecraft, which wears a kind of cartridge belt of scuba tanks, converted to hold barium and lithium gas. These gases, when released into the solar wind, can be traced downstream; the scientists can throw a dye into the cosmic plasma and watch its motion, just as one might pour a dye in a river, or in the currents of the sea. Two satellites—one British and one American—monitor the paths of the tracers in the Earth's magnetosphere. Each time a canister ejects its tracer into the wind, it makes a momentary comet, as the solar wind tears the mass of atoms into a long streamer. After a few minutes it is, as Krimigis says, "gone with the wind."

The project is called by the unlovely name AMPTE (Active Magnetospheric Particle Tracer Explorers), but it is a beautiful series of experiments. AMPTE allows scientists to study the heavens by getting right into them, rather than merely observing and speculating from below. The logistics are forbidding, however. This is perhaps the first scientific experiment to require excellent weather not only on Earth (where observatories watch the artificial comet from the ground) but also in space (where a sudden gust of solar wind can pulverize the comet and confuse the data). Two days after Christmas in 1984, for instance, the scientists created a comet. The solar wind was mild, and they hoped their comet would last as long as an hour. But the solar wind gusted, blowing the comet away in six minutes. Space weather is proving as hard to forecast as weather here on Earth.

IS THE SUN STEADY?

Architects of the Bauhaus School thought of a house as a "machine for living." Planet Earth, too, is a machine for living; and the Sun alone keeps it that way. We owe the Sun everything. Scientific inquiry only deepens our sense of its power.

Not only was our planet born in the solar cloud and warmed by its rays, but almost every source of energy on the Earth today is solar. All food comes from the Sun, since the chain of life depends upon photosynthesis. Oil, wood, and natural gas are ancient gifts of the Sun. A shiny black shard of anthracite coal is stored sunlight. The new, hybrid fuel known as gasohol—gasoline and alcohol—is sunlight drawn from two separate taps. Even windmills and watermills are powered by the Sun, which drives the winds, and keeps the waters journeying down to the sea, up into clouds, down onto mountains, and back again to sea.

As the Earth spins around its axis and revolves around the Sun, the changing angles and varying dosages of sunlight bring us day and night, the four seasons, even the comings and goings of glaciers and ice ages.

If the Sun went out, every drop of water on this planet would freeze over; the seven seas would be solid ice miles thick. Earth's very air would chill to liquid, and lie in shallow seas, pools and puddles on the black and frozen ground.

Given this power (which is so vast that, as one solar astronomer has written, "it is hard to find the word to name it; it is more than mere control and dominance"), it is natural to wonder what subtler influences the Sun may have upon us, effects of which we may not yet be aware. We know how the Earth's orbit varies—but when the Sun itself varies, what does it do to our relationship? We have discovered the Sun to be wavering, spotted, explosive, and variable. Does all that alter our climate?

Can the Sun blink and thus change the weather?

The level-headed British astronomer Richard Carrington was working on such questions when he witnessed his great September flare; and the great auroras and geomagnetic storms that follow such disturbances on the Sun are, to this day, among the most clear-cut and dramatic terrestrial results of the Sun's variability. Many other links have been sought between Sun and Earth—some sensible and some nonsensical. Few scientists in this field of inquiry have shown Carrington's restraint.

The distinguished astronomer Sir William Herschel (who believed there were people living in the Sun) followed the London stock exchange in his old age. Herschel reported in 1801 that the price of wheat had for a few decades gone up and down with the number of sunspots. This correspondence did not seem entirely farfetched to him, since fluctuations in the Sun might conceivably affect the weather, and hence the harvest, and hence the price of wheat on the open market. For a while Herschel thought he had found, in the Sun, a way to predict seasonal weather—and to make a fortune besides. But after 1801, the correspondence vanished.

Astronomers have also thought they discerned the influence of the sunspot cycle in monsoons in India, hot spells in tropical rain forests, booms and busts in England's large population of rabbits, and the annual catch of polar bears in southern Greenland. The classic case, notes John Eddy, the rueful historian of this troubled field, was the claim made early in this century by British climatologist C.E.P. Brooks. Brooks knew that the water level in Lake Victoria, which is the largest lake in Africa, fluctuates with the seasons; its height is a measure of the average rainfall over a large part of the continent. Based on two decades of careful records, Brooks found that Lake Victoria's ups and downs were in perfect synchrony with the sunspot cycle. The more spots, the more water; the fewer the spots, the lower the lake. It seemed to Brooks an unimpeachable instance of sunspots altering weather, at least in Africa. Alas, says Eddy, "Soon after Brooks's paper was published the connection that seemed so clear vanished, like the Lost Chord, never to repeat again."

In 1894, a young Harvard man named Andrew Ellicott Douglass went West, to Flagstaff, Arizona. There he helped world-famous astronomer Percival Lowell set up a new observatory, from which Lowell hoped to map the canals of Mars.

In his spare time, Douglass got interested in tree rings. He noticed that trees held similar patterns of wide and narrow rings. They grew more in damp years than in dry years, and the annual ring of growth they laid down was correspondingly fat or lean. Not many people would have cared; but Douglass saw in this simple fact two lifetime opportunities.

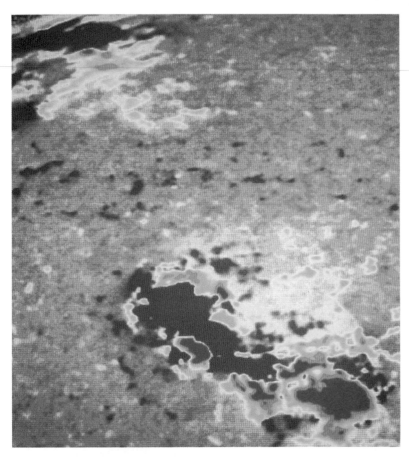

*Sunspots—
a computer-enhanced image.
Kitt Peak, February, 1978.*

First, by comparing enough trees, young and old, Douglass was able to put together a continuous record in tree rings running back many hundreds of years. If an archaeologist showed him an old timber from an abandoned pueblo, Douglass could locate the sequence of wide and narrow on his chart and determine the year the tree was cut that made the timber. For the first time, archaeologists could date hundreds of old ruins with precision. The science Douglass founded, *dendrochronology,* is still a powerful tool of archaeology (the field's name derives from the Greek words *dendron,* tree, and *chronika,* annals).

Second, Douglass thought he could discern in the patterns of wide and narrow rings an 11-year cycle matching the sunspot cycle. This excited him more than the dating of ruins. He was sure he had proof of a connection between the Sun's variability and the Earth's seasons, extending back not merely decades, like the studies of Herschel or Brooks, but centuries. The evidence was never quite conclusive, however. As modern solar astronomer Robert Noyes explains, "He just did not have enough data, or the high-speed computers to analyze them, to establish that the correlation was meaningful." By 1962, when

Douglass died in Tucson at the age of 94, many scientists ranked his pet project beside that of his old mentor, Lowell, who dreamed of canals and advanced civilizations on the Red Planet.

In 1976, John Eddy reopened yet another of these lugubrious case histories, one that had been gathering dust for a century. It seems that late in the 19th century, the German solar astronomer Gustav Friedrich Wilhelm Spörer collected records of old sunspot sightings. He was startled to discover that for about 70 years, beginning around 1645, sunspot sightings were great rarities. Apparently the Sun was, for this strange interlude, virtually spotless. (This period coincided, as it happens, with the reign of Louis XIV of France, known as the "Sun King." The Sun was virtually without blemish as long as Louis sat on his throne. It is one of the few Sun-Earth correspondences that has *not* been trumpeted by an excitable investigator.)

A Victorian astronomer, E. Walter Maunder, who studied sunspots from the Royal Greenwich Observatory in England, double-checked the historical record and saw that Spörer was right. But scientists are only human. In the 1600s, they had been reluctant to accept a blemished Sun; when they finally had to, they decided that the Sun was at least constant. In the 1800s, they hated Schwabe's announcement of a variable Sun. When they swallowed that at last, they decided that the Sun was at least consistent—that is, varying in a regular and reliable cycle. After that, says Eddy, "no one seemed to question again the universality of the 11-year sunspot cycle or whether it had always been a dominant feature of the Sun." The way one tries to bury a bad dream, astronomers forgot about the strange interlude when the Sun shed its spots. No one listened to Spörer or to Maunder, either.

Eddy was curious about the case of the missing sunspots. "When I first read these early accounts of Walter Maunder's, saying that sunspots had almost disappeared for 70 years in the past, I did not believe it. It went against the grain of everything I had been taught, and that I believed, about the behavior of the Sun. It challenged the regularity of the star. And it seemed so long in the past, written in such old and dusty records, that one could hardly believe it. Frankly, I thought it would be good to lay this skeleton to rest."

So Eddy triple-checked Spörer and Maunder—and soon decided they were right to trust the quaint records of the early astronomers. "Rare old books published more than three centuries ago give us a direct record of what the Sun was like in the past, and one that we can believe," says Eddy. "One of them was written by Christopher Scheiner, a Jesuit priest, and published in the year 1630. He was a contemporary of Galileo, and one of those who was awed by the new discovery that the Sun was covered with spots. It must have been hard for him to imagine that this celestial fire *changed*. His book is entirely about sunspots, and it's 784 pages long, written entirely in Latin. If you think that a book entirely about sunspots 784 pages long and written in Latin is a boring book, you're absolutely right—it is. I think it bored the people of the day and may well have squelched interest in sunspots for a while. But Scheiner's drawings of the face of the Sun are as good as any that are done today. It was his book more than any that convinced me that we could trust the astronomers of the early and middle 17th century when they showed us that the Sun, at the time, was undergoing a major period of change."

Looking at these old volumes, Eddy began to suspect that Spörer and Maunder were right—that the Sun had episodes of misbehavior in its past. "This led us to look farther back in history for similar changes. That search has taken us, among other places, into old Chinese records, dynastic accounts that go back as long as 1,900 years." Careful Chinese astronomers kept a watch on the Sun, as they did on all the sky, using the naked eye, and they carefully recorded in handwritten diaries what they saw.

Eddy and colleagues combed more records than had Spörer and Maunder. "We were able to add new lines of evidence," Eddy says, "ways of looking at the Sun that were not available to the solar astronomer of the 19th century—most important, the record written in tree rings; for tree rings are compulsive diarists, and they only know how to tell the truth. In the radiocarbon records of trees is a direct record of how the Sun behaved in the past. And in those tree rings, laid down during the years from 1645 to 1715, is an undeniable account of a period of very unusual behavior of the Sun. It matches exactly the record that we find in the books. The fact that the record is both in trees and in books also gave us a way of looking farther back in time, for this was a kind of Rosetta Stone in

Three ways of looking at a sunspot. On the left, a false-colored image of the Sun's magnetic field, colored to show north-south polarity. Sunspots usually come in pairs, one magnetic north, the other magnetic south. In the center, the same sunspots are shown in visible light. On the right, colors have been added to reveal motion—what's coming toward us and what's receding are depicted in contrasting colors. Skylab was equipped to view the surface of the Sun in all these modes at once.

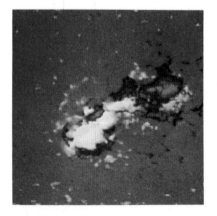

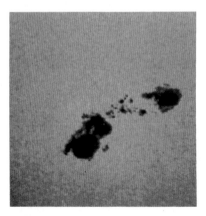

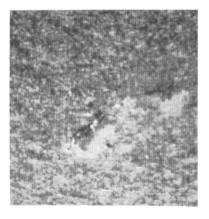

which we could read the same story in two languages—one in Latin and one in tree rings. That led us to interpret the much longer history of the Sun that trees record, for the oldest trees are several thousands of years old, and in the bristlecone pine, you can read the history of the Sun back 7,500 years."

The Sun was quiet indeed in the reign of the Sun King, Eddy concluded. Many astronomers of the day had noted the fact with puzzlement. In 1684, the astronomer royal of Great Britain, John Flamsteed, saw a single spot and was so impressed he wrote a paper about it. "These appearances," said Flamsteed, "however frequent in the days of . . . Galileo, have been so rare of late that this is the only one I have seen in his face since December 1676." Auroral nights, a strong indicator of solar activity, were also rare, and much missed by astronomers. Eddy named this period the *Maunder Minimum*. Eddy also turned up another strange solar interlude from about 1460 to 1550, which he calls the *Spörer Minimum*. "Until recently," he concluded, "both the Sun and climate had been assumed to be either constant or regular in their variation. It is now known that both have changed significantly, and perhaps in erratic or irregular ways, in the time of modern man."

Curiously enough, the Maunder Minimum coincided neatly with the Little Ice Age, when northern Europe's winters were a series of deep freezes. The Thames River, the English Channel, and the canals of Holland iced over year after year— in our time, rare events—and Hans Brinker raced for his silver skates (see Chapter Three, "The Climate Puzzle"). Was the Sun's strange behavior somehow connected to the Little Ice Age? In the late 1970s, Eddy was excited enough by the coincidence to argue the connection; but afterward, recalling the bad luck of Herschel, Brooks, and others, Eddy bit his tongue. He still sees the link as exciting but is not sure, without more research, whether there is a real correlation.

Eddy's work revived the hunt for Sun-Earth connections and gave it fresh respectability.

A few years ago, Charles W. Stockton and David Meko of Tucson's Laboratory of Tree-Ring Research (founded by Andrew Ellicott Douglass, the world's first professional tree-ring reader), examined the drought cycle of the American West and the Great Plains. It was a project that tree-ring experts had undertaken before; but this time the researchers looked at many, many tree-ring sites simultaneously—choosing some 60 sites across the United States, all west of the Mississippi. Sorting tree-ring data with a supercomputer, Stockton was able to construct a series of maps showing the extent of drought conditions in North America for every year in the past three centuries.

These studies confirmed the popular belief that the Great Dustbowl of 1934, chronicled by John Steinbeck in his novel *The Grapes of Wrath*, was one in a long and regular series.

When climatologist J. Murray Mitchell heard about Stockton's work, he asked permission to analyze the data. "So we sent the data," says Stockton, "a large box of cards, to his office in Washington, D.C. And about two weeks later, we got a call from him. He said, 'Yes, there's a significant 20-year cycle in the data, and I've already taken the liberty of comparing it to the solar cycle, and the two match up very, very well.'"

For 300 years the cyclic occurrence of drought has been followed by the double sunspot cycle (the time it takes for the dance of the sunspots, and the solar dynamo, to run through one complete waltz and return to the starting point). The tree-ring team has traced this 22-year cycle all the way back to 1600. It is strong evidence that the two cycles are intimately linked.

Andrew Douglass missed this evidence only because the drought jumps from place to place. A single tree, or even a single forest, may have been struck by only a few severe dry spells; but when records are gathered from forests all across the region, from Montana to Nebraska to Oklahoma, the pattern grows more and more regular. It is a shame the old man did not live to see this discovery. It has cast his career in a new light, for the correspondence between the Sun's cycle and the drought cycle has stood up to very stringent statistical analysis—and is considered one of the strongest Sun-Earth correlations ever found. "As hitherto avowed agnostics with regard to many previous claims of Sun-climate relationships," the three men wrote in their report, "we find ourselves somewhat unnerved by our own data."

Soon Stockton hopes to take his project around the world to see if the 22-year signal matches the solar cycle all over. Meanwhile, the notion of a link between sunspots and climate remains one of the most controversial topics in science.

THE INCONSISTENT SUN

John Eddy gave the keynote address at an international symposium on Sun, Earth, weather, and climate, held in Boulder, Colorado, in 1982. He took a long, rueful look back at all the false starts and wrong turns of the past 100 years. "Critics will say, and some have, that as a discipline, Sun-weather studies have never really departed from the course that William Herschel set: deductions drawn from little more than the similarity of two records, without the buttress of a testable mechanism—a search guided as much by hope as by reason and with very little light from physics. . . .

"I think a lot of progress has been made," he said,

Dust bowl days: An abandoned farm in the Coldwater District, near Dalhart, Texas. Photographed in June 1938 by Dorothea Lange.

"chiefly in the slow, hard work of laying the physical foundations of what it is from the Sun that really varies, and what in fact fills the 93 million miles that separate the Sun from the lower troposphere of the Earth." What we need now, Eddy argued, is a *mechanism* by which the Sun may jostle the Earth. But we cannot hope to find such a mechanism without making careful and costly measurements right down the line, from Sun to space to solid ground. "In the process," he said, "we might move the tattered question of Sun-weather studies—traditionally the 'poor relations' of solar-terrestrial relationships—into the 20th century, where it belongs.

"It seems to me," Eddy concluded, "that some questions in science, however appealing or pressing, must wait for the appropriate time and technology for their resolution." Perhaps Sun-weather studies had to wait for the Age of Space.

In search of the missing mechanism, for instance, Earthbound astronomers have tried for a century and a half to measure the *solar constant*—that is, to determine precisely how much solar radiation travels across space to our orbit in space, an average of 93 million miles away. If this amount varies even slightly—if the solar constant is not constant—it could have enormous effects on our climate. Calculations suggest that even a .05 percent change could dramatically alter the world's weather. A 1 percent change over centuries could cause a Little Ice Age. If the solar constant could be shown to vary, the missing mechanism (or a good candidate for it) might be found at last.

This crucial measurement is hard to make from the ground, however, because the Sun's rays are so tattered by the time they get through our atmosphere. Most of the ultraviolet and X-ray radiation is blocked, and so is much of the infrared; dust and vapor cut into the energy that reaches us in the visible spectrum. In 1837, a measurement was made at high noon in Cape Town, South Africa, using a simple apparatus consisting of a thermometer, a little can of water, and a black umbrella. It was accurate only to about 10 percent—pretty good, considering, but not good enough. Refinements, some of them exquisite, were made as time went by, and in the first half of this century measurements of the solar constant were carried out with painstaking care from carefully chosen mountaintops around the planet. But these experiments still failed to prove whether the solar constant was constant. It was like trying to detect minute fluctuations in the wattage of a lighthouse beacon through miles of swirling fog. And the precision of the instruments used in these measurements was never fine enough, given how small the variations the solar astronomers were looking for.

On St. Valentine's Day in 1980, the *Solar Maximum Mission*, fondly known as *Solar Max*, was launched by NASA. It carried an instrument designed by Richard C. Willson, who had been trying for years to measure the solar constant from balloons and rockets. He called the instrument the Active Cavity Radiometer Irradiance Monitor (ACRIM). "Under normal conditions," Willson says, "ACRIM produces one solar-constant measurement every two minutes with an error of about 0.005 percent, or 50 parts per million."

The Sun was at the maximum point of its cycle in that year (hence the name of the mission), and its face was splotchy. *Solar Max* found the long-sought answer almost immediately—thus, as Eddy notes, "realizing a goal that had eluded seven generations of scientists." The solar constant varied with how much of the Sun's face was covered by spots. The more sunspots, the less energy reached *Solar Max*. The largest dips in energy, Willson reported, were 0.3 percent variations.

So we are at last on the track of a physical mechanism by which solar variability can influence Earth's weather and climate. By the year 2002, when the Sun has been watched from space through 22 years, or one complete double-sunspot cycle, we will have a better idea of the range of the Sun's fluctuations. We may learn, for instance, whether this variability causes the pattern of droughts in the Midwest. Stay tuned. There is some suspense involved, since the fluctuations since 1980 have tended downhill on average. In June 1984, Willson reported the solar constant had been declining continuously at the "substantial rate" of .004 percent per year. "It is unlikely that this trend will continue for many years," he said. "If it continues declining at this rate, we could anticipate another episode like the Little Ice Age within a century."

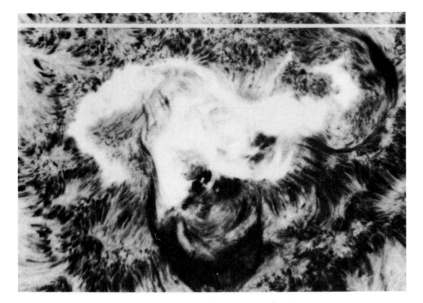

*The Sun's magnetic field creates
on its surface extraordinary,
tangled patterns that we are only
just beginning to understand.*

HIDDEN MECHANISMS?

The search is on for other ways in which the Sun's slight variations might influence Earth's weather and climate.

We know, for instance, that the Sun's ultraviolet and X-ray emissions are radically variable. During a sunspot maximum, the Sun can give off 30 or 40 percent more ultraviolet than normal and many times more X rays. An astronomer watching the Sun only in these wavelengths would conclude that the Sun is a highly variable star. Actually, this radiation makes up such a small part of the Sun's total energy output that the increase makes little difference to the solar constant. But these emissions might still affect the Earth. The height of the troposphere—the layer of the atmosphere stirred by weather—varies with the seasons. It averages about 16 kilometers above sea level, rising about one kilometer when Earth is closest to the Sun and receives the most sunlight. Its height may also vary with the sunspot cycle. Some investigators believe the troposphere rises another .5 kilometer at times of sunspot maximum. A variation that size could subtly affect global wind patterns.

It could have dramatic effects as well. It caused one of the media events of 1979. "When the last astronaut left *Skylab* in 1976," explains Herbert Friedman of the National Academy of Sciences, "it was thought that the spacecraft was in a safe parking orbit where it could await a visit by an early Space Shuttle flight, which would push it to a higher orbit for safekeeping until it could be refurbished and reactivated. Unfortunately, the plan was frustrated by a delay in the Space Shuttle's schedule and by a rapid rise of solar activity toward sunspot maximum. With high sunspot activity came a hotter and denser atmosphere at *Skylab*'s altitude, which increased the drag and caused the orbit to decay much faster than anticipated." The great, patched, abandoned space observatory came atumbling down. Thus, says Friedman, Skylab fell victim to sunspots. The lab we sent up to study the Sun was cast down by it.

Another subtle mechanism by which the Sun may influence our atmosphere is through the regular alternations of its magnetic fields. Of all the candidates now in the running for "missing mechanism," this is perhaps the best-studied and most respectable.

The first satellites to detect the solar wind also found that the wind striking Earth reverses magnetic polarity, from north to south to south to north, usually about four times with each rotation of the Sun. Apparently the solar wind streaming in all directions from the Sun is divided into quadrants—four wedges of alternate polarity. One might picture the solar wind as a daisy with four petals, alternately black and white. As the Sun turns, these petals brush by the Earth—black, white, black, white. (Actually the shape of the wind is much more rippled, curved, and elegant. It has been likened to the pleated tutu of a whirling ballerina.)

Each time the Earth lies in a boundary between two petals—called *sectors*—there is a brief lull in the solar wind. Then, two days later, we're in the next petal; solar wind rises again, sharply, and so does geomagnetic activity on Earth. Compass needles tremble. Auroras dance around the poles.

Walter Orr Roberts, meteorologist Roger H. Olson, solar astronomer John Wilcox, and others have found that the sectors of this daisy wheel seem to cause a change in the weather, too. On average, the boundaries in the solar wind are followed by a lull in strong cyclonic storms on Earth. The area covered by large low-pressure storm systems drops by about 10 percent, then climbs back to normal. A few years ago, a young Harvard undergraduate, Philip Duffy, working for Wilcox at Stanford, looked closely at records of the winter storms born in the Gulf of Alaska. Duffy found that storms born in positive sectors of the solar wind tended to be larger than average; those born in negative sectors, smaller than average.

By what physical mechanism might the solar wind, which is blocked in the ionosphere, 40 miles up, touch thunderstorms down in the Gulf of Alaska? So far the most promising theory involves what is called the *global circuit*. The ionosphere carries an electric charge. The solid Earth below is reversely charged. Current flows between them partly through the planet's thunderstorms, which not only carry electricity but also generate it. The flow of electric current between air and land makes a global circuit.

Ralph Markson of the Center for Space Research at the Massachusetts Institute of Technology thinks this is a way in which weather on the Sun could change weather on Earth. Solar flares, and fluctuations in solar wind, may alter the flow of electricity in the global circuit, affecting the birth, life, and death of thousands of thunderstorms worldwide. This thesis is new and still controversial. But the mechanism Markson is proposing is attractive, partly because it is *fast*—changes in the solar sectors affect our planet quickly, and electrical influences upon the ionosphere reach the ground quickly. In this way, storms on the Sun could have a hot line to storms on Earth.

Herschel, Brooks, and so many other scientists sought correlations between Sun and Earth, but they had no physics to back up their stories, which, in consequence, sometimes floated off into fairy tales. Now sunwatchers have found three plausible correlations on three scales of time: days to weeks (the daisy wheel and the global circuit); decades (the sunspot cycle); and centuries (the solar constant). The search goes on.

THE SUN IN THE STONE

A geologist stands in a creekbed in Flinders Range, a belt of folded rock in a desolate corner of South Australia. His name is George Williams, and he works in the exploration department of The Broken Hill Proprietary Company Limited, an international resources company based in Australia.

Generations of Australian geologists have come to study these rocks, says Williams, because they hold evidence of sharp swings in climate. The siltstone and sandstone cliffs along the creekbed where he stands are finely layered, or banded, like pages of an enormously thick book. Today Flinders Range is dry and the summers are very hot, with many days over 100 degrees Fahrenheit. But long ago, the beautifully layered rock tells him, this was a neighborhood of glaciers.

"I believe the layers are annual deposits," Williams says. "They were laid down at a rate of one a year, about 700 million years ago." Each spring or summer, nearby glaciers melted a little, and the turbid, muddy meltwaters fanned out on a lakebed. Each year left a single layer on the bottom of the lake. Now the glaciers and the snows and the lake are long gone, and only the layers remain. You can touch 900 years in the life of the Earth with the palm of one hand.

"The fascinating thing about these rocks is the regularity of the banding," Williams says. There are darker, clayey bands spaced about half an inch apart; between them lie paler, more sandy bands in bundles of about a dozen. "The regularity is so conspicuous that I believed when I saw these rocks that it couldn't be attributed to normal, random Earth processes. I thought that there must be some astronomical control of the regularity. And to test that idea, I collected rocks from the

This rock from the Flinders Range, in South Australia, is almost one billion years old. According to George Williams, its bands are a clear record of the 22-year cycle of the Sun.

creekbed here and took them away for study and counting of the bands."

Williams soon decided that he was looking at the story of the ancient Sun written in stone. Wide bands were laid down when warmer summers caused a lot of melting and a large amount of sediment to be washed into the lake. Thinner bands formed during cooler summers when glaciers didn't melt as much. The bands therefore record year-by-year climatic variations, as do tree rings; but the banded rock formed long, long before the first tree grew on Earth and before life crawled out of the sea. The rock holds a continuous record of about 18,000 years of solar history no one had ever hoped to see, when the Sun was nearly a billion years younger than it is today.

"It would seem that the ancient glacial lake was acting as a solar observatory, faithfully recording the cyclic fluctuations of the Sun in Precambrian time, many hundreds of millions of years ago," Williams says. "The cyclic patterns that the rocks display match very closely the cyclic variations observed in the Sun today." The darker bands, he concludes, were laid down at times of fewest sunspots; the paler, thicker bands at times of most sunspots. The bands in between show the same sorts of progressions we see in the carbon 14 record in tree rings and in the solar cycle today: Both the 11- and the 22-year cycles are visible in the rock.

It may seem surprising that solar cycles should have so striking an influence on the buildup of silt and mud at the bottom of a lake. Perhaps the Earth's climate in Precambrian times was more sensitive to solar fluctuations than it is today. Yet even now, weather in the area seems tied, to an unusual degree, to the sunspot cycle. A well-known chart of annual rainfall in Adelaide, the capital of South Australia, for the century from 1844 to 1944 looks convincingly like a chart of sunspot numbers for the same interval.

Williams's findings are still quite new, and not everyone is convinced by his interpretation. If Williams is right, however, this single dusty creekbed may revolutionize the study of the Sun, as the record it contains is so much older and longer and more detailed than anything to be found in tree rings or the journals of ancient Oriental sunwatchers. Solar astronomers like John Eddy, scanning the stone diary of many thousands of years, would hope to learn how common or rare are sunspot famines like the Maunder Minimum.

The rock record suggests that the deepest sunspot minimums in the strength of the 11-year cycle recurred every 275 to 335 years. If there *is* a connection between the Maunder Minimum and the Little Ice Age, children may soon be skating again on the canals of Holland. The evidence suggests to Williams that "another solar (and climatic?) minimum is due near the start of the 21st century, some three centuries after the Maunder Minimum." We could be on the brink of another Little Ice Age.

But the fundamental message in the rock is profoundly reassuring. It suggests that the Sun has behaved, in recent history, much as it has for nearly a billion years. "It would appear that the Sun has remained a relatively constant star," says Williams, "though it is undergoing minor flickering, or cyclic changes. And this gives us confidence, I feel, that the Sun . . . will continue to flicker along, as it has done for hundreds of millions of years."

If the Sun's dynamo has run smoothly for so long, solar scientists can relax a little, and so can we all. The disconcerting discoveries made since the time of Galileo, many of them within the past few years, cause much less anxiety when viewed in this long perspective. The Sun varies, but it does so very reliably. We have that written in stone.

"In the past 15 years," says Jack Eddy, "our discoveries about the Sun have been unprecedented. We have seen it from space, showing us faces that we have never seen before, some of them angry and violent. We've learned that one of the long-held tenets of the Sun—that if it wasn't constant, it was at least *regular*—is simply not true.

"We've learned that its surface shakes and wiggles like a bowl of jelly and gives us a way of looking into the interior of the star, a place we thought we could never see.

"In spite of all the variation that we see in the Sun, the long record of the Earth attests that over its long life, the Sun has never been so hot that it has boiled away the oceans, or so much dimmer that they have frozen. And I think it will continue to burn in much the same way in the next 5 billion years. It is, after all, a star we can depend on."

Gifts from the Earth

Geology controls our lives.

JACK OLIVER

6 / Gifts from the Earth

What is the Earth's first gift to us? Simply its location in space, warmed by the fires of a nearby star. It is a stable foundation on which life can build. What is the Earth's second gift? The blue of its sky and sea, which, together, make the planet a fit home for our kind of life—the only hospitable place we know in the universe (though voyagers someday may find another blue world beneath another yellow star). And what is the Earth's third gift? That its crust is rich, with nearly a hundred naturally occurring elements in thousands of chemical combinations. This is the gift of variety. Without it, life's possibilities would be infinitely constrained. With no lime for our bones, iron for our blood, and salt for our tears, we would not be here to stroll along the seashore, beneath the blue sky, in sunlight.

Human history has been shaped from the beginning by the rich gifts of the crust. The ages of civilization are named for what we have found there, beginning some half a million years ago in the Old Stone Age, when a rudely chipped hand ax was high technology. Around 10,000 years ago someone found that a certain gleaming red metal was easier to hammer into shape than flint; the Age of Stone gave way to the Age of Copper. Copper chisels quarried the great stone blocks of the pyramids.

Ancient smiths discovered that copper could be strengthened by mixing in a little tin. This mixture of metals, or *alloy*, was bronze. The new swords could pierce copper shields, and the Copper Age gave way to the Bronze.

Sometime around 2000 B.C., Hittite nomads who settled in the hills of Anatolia learned to mine rock containing iron ore. They heated the ore in bonfires to separate the iron from the rock and then hammered the iron until the metal was workable and more or less pure (hence, from all the hammering, the term *wrought iron*). For a while, ironsmithing was a Hittite secret and helped them conquer Turkey and much of western Asia. When the secret got out, the entire Mediterranean region entered the Iron Age. Because of their power to shape iron—

This Chinese broad ax, from about 1000 B.C., is thought to have been hammered from an iron meteorite. Some of the first iron in the Iron Age came from outer space.

and the fates of nations—early blacksmiths were seen as magicians, alchemists, very nearly priests. Their methods, according to the historian of mining Cedrik Gregory, "were rather weird. One school of swordmakers believed that the best sword blades had to be quenched by plunging them when red-hot into the body of a Nubian slave."

Then, abruptly, in the past 300 years, people who had relied largely on their own elbow grease, or on the blood, sweat, and tears of slaves, or on the brute strength and patience of pack animals discovered new ways to use the gifts of the crust: as fuels to *power* their tools. There followed in quick succession the Ages of Coal (from about 1750), Oil (from 1850), and Uranium (from 1950), all of which comprise the Industrial Age. Combining metals and energy from the crust in elaborate machines has so multiplied our power that the human population has increased as never before. We are taking more and more from the Earth with each passing year. Our race has now become a geological force. And we are entering an age that seems almost as surprising to us as our own era would have been to those huddled around a Stone Age campfire. We have reached the Age of Limits.

COPPER ISLAND At the turn of this century, a young engineer by the name of D. A. Gunther scouted the mountains of the American Southwest, looking for red and yellow hills that might hold copper. But the Southwest had been pretty well explored by then, and Gunther found nothing new to report to his boss, mining man Seeley Mudd.

Disappointed, Gunther went home to his family in Brooklyn and consoled himself with Broadway shows. One night his date was late to their meeting place in the stacks of the New York Public Library. As miner Ira B. Joralemon tells it in his book *Copper,*

> Gunther passed the time looking over the books on the shelves near the meeting-place. He had an inquiring mind, and out of curiosity picked out the books that looked as though they had never been read. One of them was a treatise on archaeology. As he turned the pages, a reference to the use of copper by the Phoenicians caught his eye—and his mind. Where had these ancients found their copper?

The young man sat through the show that night in a haze of excitement that had nothing to do with Broadway. The next morning he wrote to Mudd proposing that they stop looking for a new copper mine and hunt down an ancient one, where there might be plenty of treasure left. Mudd agreed, and he financed Gunther on a romantic search in the Mediterranean. First Gunther led a camel train on a series of strenuous treks around Mount Sinai. This ended in failure—Gunther found the slag heaps of ancient mines, but nothing on the grand scale he and Mudd had hoped for.

From ancient Greek and Latin texts, Gunther had learned that some of the world's first copper mines were on the island of Cyprus. Copper ore was mined there probably as early as 3000 B.C. Copper ingots in the shape of oxhides and marked with the stamp of Cyprus were shipped out to Egypt, Crete, Syria, and Anatolia. The great mines were held, in various epochs, by Phoenicians, Persians, Assyrians, Greeks, and Romans. The island's wealth of copper played a large part in man's emergence from the Stone Age. Our very word "copper" comes from the Romans' *cuprum*, which they got in turn from the Greek Kyprios—Cyprus. Copper Island!

So Gunther sailed to Cyprus. He headed for the ancient village of Skouriotissa. (He was prospecting by place names. *Skouris* is Greek for slag. Why not start looking in Slag Village on Copper Island?) Arriving at sunset at the top of a ridge overlooking the village, the young man saw the hills of Skouriotissa gleaming with brilliant reds and yellows in the day's last light. They were the colors he was looking for. "The world was his," says Joralemon.

The first tunnel he dug broke into a Roman mine. Ancient earthenware oil lamps still rested in their niches, where they had once lit the way for thousands of panting slaves. "The workings were still open and in fair condition," Joralemon says. "Only the openings to the surface had been filled with earth and hidden by vegetation in the 16 centuries during which the mines had been abandoned."

This was a thrill—but another financial failure. The Romans and their slaves had picked the tunnels pretty clean. There was not much copper left for Mudd and Gunther.

Still Gunther did not give up. After a year of drilling and hard work, he found a hill of ore the Romans had missed. Then it was another 10 years before Cyprus Mines, Inc., went into production. But today, the island, after a lapse of more than a thousand years, is once again a mining center. Each year it exports (besides some iron and chromite) hundreds of thousands of tons of copper ore.

Gunther's tale misses having a Hollywood ending on two counts: He never married the girl at the public library; and he died in Cyprus before the mines became really successful.

The Cyprus deposits he rediscovered are rich in cop-

This ingot god protected the copper mines of Cyprus. The statue was found on the island at an ancient sanctuary in Enkomi. It is cast in solid bronze, and stands on a base shaped like a bronze ingot of the day. It dates from the 12th century B.C.

Cyprus meant copper to the ancient peoples who built Western civilization, and today the ore of Cyprus is being mined again. Here, a modern pit mine has uncovered the gallery of an ancient Roman mine. The mouth of the Roman tunnel is at left center.

per and also bear some gold, silver, zinc, iron, lead, and other metals. They are part of a rock formation called the *Troodos Massif.* Seen in cross section, this formation shows four broad zones. At the top is a layer of sediment. Just below that is a layer of basalt, much of it in the shape of bulbous pillows. Beneath that are tall, vertical basalt sheets and pillars. These three layers span about six kilometers from top to bottom. Under them lies the fourth layer, masses of a hard rock type called *gabbro,* which forms the *basement* rock of the region.

All the metal is in the upper three layers—the sediment and the basalts. Most of it is mingled among the pillow lavas. At Skouriotissa, where Gunther first struck it rich, the ore averages 2.25 percent copper, 43 percent iron, and nearly 50 percent sulfur. This high concentration of sulfur is important, because it makes the metals relatively easy to process—that is, to separate from the rock. When metals bind chemically to sulfur, forming *sulfides,* the ties can be broken apart. Most of the minerals in the Troodos Massif are made even easier for mining because they are massed in large clumps. They are *massive sulfides.*

Having discovered—or rediscovered—the Troodos Massif, geologists had a second mystery to crack: Why was this great patch of ore sitting on a small island in the middle of the Mediterranean? What made these massive sulfides? The clues were all there in the rock, exposed in the sunlight for anyone who had eyes to see them. But the answer came from an unexpected quarter.

Today, these dark stone pillows bake beneath the strong sun in a Cyprian sheepmeadow. But once, they lay at the bottom of the sea. The stones are clues to the remarkable process that created the treasures of Cyprus.

In the mid-1960s, a small fleet of oceanographic research vessels headed out from ports in the Mediterranean Sea and passed through the Suez Canal, bound for the Indian Ocean. The project was called the International Indian Ocean Expedition and was intended to survey that ocean's floor. Rather than waste valuable ship time en route, however, the scientists in the expedition used their sophisticated echo-sounding equipment to survey the bottom of the Red Sea, too.

Echoes from the deep waters lying just above the Red Sea floor were peculiar and aroused curiosity. Water samples were taken. There proved to be a number of very warm pools at the bottom, lying in basins on the long axis of the Red Sea. The water in these pools did not mix much with the ordinary seawater above them, because the great load of minerals dissolved in the hot water made it heavy. Each pool contained high concentrations of salt, sulfur, and a number of metals, including copper, zinc, and silver. The pools were dredged, and the muck and mud at the bottom were also found to be rich in salts and metallic sulfides, with some gold.

At about this time, the theory of plate tectonics was becoming widely accepted, thanks partly to oceanographers' careful surveys of sea floors. Scientists took a fresh look at the Red Sea. They noted that if the sea were closed, Africa and Arabia would fit together as neatly as two pieces of a jigsaw puzzle. The two shores, they realized, must be spreading apart. A great rift is slowly opening between them, like the rift that long ago split Africa and South America. Within this new rift, magma is welling up from deep below, and as it hardens, it is creating fresh ocean floor on the bottom of the Red Sea (though in the narrow sea, all the action is hidden, covered over with mud from nearby shores). The Red Sea is an Atlantic or a Pacific in embryo: If it spreads long enough, it will be the Red Ocean!

Some earth scientists took this reasoning a step farther and used it to explain the rich minerals at the bottom of the Red Sea. They imagined water seeping miles down into cracks in the ocean floor and being heated there by the magma below. Hot, salty water leaches metals from rock; so as seawater percolated through the rock, it would dissolve many metals; and rising to the surface, it would carry the dissolved metals up with it and drop its load in the oozes of the sea floor. Water would keep circulating down through the bedrock and bringing up metal. Where sea floors were spreading rapidly, as in the Pacific, the superheated water might even gush up from the floor in underwater *geysers*, fountains of superheated water laden with minerals. The Red Sea floor, and other ocean ridges, might be, in the words of geophysicist Peter A. Rona, "a perpetual metal factory."

This theory was so novel and spectacular that it inspired a series of descents in tiny submarines to search the sea floor for geysers. It was during one such dive a few years ago that geochemist John Edmond and others discovered bizarre oases of life at the bottom of the Galapagos Rift (see Chapter Two). Edmond and other adventurous scientists were thrilled by the strange life-forms they saw in those cold, black, abyssal deserts—the blood-red tubeworms 10 feet tall; the masses of giant white clams weighing several pounds each; the agile, spidery crabs. But the scientists were disappointed that they saw no geysers. There was plenty of warm water rising from the bottom, and it was laden with sulfur and other minerals; indeed, it was the rich mineral content of the water that sustained the life of each oasis. However, the water apparently was not hot enough to create the dramatic fountains that theory predicted might be down there. Maybe there were no geysers to be found. Maybe geologists' imaginations were getting overheated.

In April 1979, John Edmond, oceanographer Bob Ballard, Bill Normark of the U.S. Geological Survey, and others descended in *Alvin* to investigate another spot in the Pacific. They were southwest of the southern tip of Baja California, at latitude 21 degrees North, where two plates are pulling apart. There, at a depth of 9,000 feet, in blackness never before penetrated by light, human eyes saw the Earth creating itself. Roaring from the bottom of the sea was a great, violent, hot, dark fountain—a *black smoker*. It jetted from a tall, beetling mass

This black smoker, like a chimney stack, is belching superheated, mineral-laden water at the East Pacific Rise. Photographed in 1979 from the small sub Alvin—*part of which is visible in the foreground.*

of dark rock—a *chimney*. The load of minerals in the jet made it as black and grimy as the smoke over old Pittsburgh.

In the searchlights of the little sub, the sediment around the chimney's base gleamed tawny yellow and orange from the incessant rains of metallic sulfides that settled from the fountain. Looming in the shadows around the chimney were the bulbous shapes of pillow lavas, frozen in all the grotesque and eerie forms that magma takes when it oozes up from the depths of the Earth and meets ice-cold water.

The photographs and samples that *Alvin* returned to the surface (having found nearly two dozen black smokers) electrified the scientific world. The geysers of the deeps were real. Not only had a radical theory been proven, but the process was going on *now*. For geologists, who focus so much of their attention on events millions and billions of years in the past, it was an extraordinary moment.

Scientists were eager to see if they could find black smokers elsewhere along the bottom of the sea. In 1983, the tiny submarine *Pisces IV* sank slowly to the floor of the Pacific, off the coast of Oregon. The sub's target was the crater of an undersea volcano that, judging from seismic records, had recently been acting up. The pilot of the sub was Keith Shepherd, the observer at the port window was Dick Chase, and geologist Steve Scott was at starboard. Scott hollered into an acoustic telephone to keep "Surface" appraised of their progress. In his hand he held a small cassette recorder, which he turned on whenever he wanted to make himself a memo about the geology of the abyss. A transcript was later made of the tape.

"This looks promising!" Scott shouted (the acoustic telephone had a bad connection). "There's a bit of a scarp [cliff]

Model of a strange new world—black smokers and swaying tubeworms.

to the starboard side. . . . Straight ahead, it's just absolutely oblivion, and off to the port side, I don't see anything, either. This is a very deep fissure we're coming to. It's worth exploring. Whew!"

The sub maneuvered down into the deep canyon, or crevasse, it had found. "Still in this same crevasse!" Scott shouted after a while. "It's obviously very big. Looking down I can't see anything. Looking ahead I see nothing. Looking left and right I see nothing. We're in a very big crevasse. Now Dick says off to the left he can see a wall coming up."

A pause. "This is an *elephant*. It's well worth exploring." Long pause. "Uh, we're still going down. The depth is 1,584 meters. . . . What'd we hit?" Their stern had glanced against the face of the cliff that ran due north, the same direction the submarine was facing. "I've taken two more pictures with the stereo camera, although probably too far away to get anything. . . . Keith is trying to maneuver us around. . . ."

Suddenly Scott's tape becomes a medley of wild voices. "Wow! Where? Take—there's one—a black smoker! Surface, we have—we're taking pictures. Oh, my God! And we've got a smoker! Ahead of us! Take lots of pictures. Take lots of pictures. Just bang them off. Just bang them away. . . . Right exposure. Got it? Look at the size of this thing! It's a chimney! It's a chimney! . . . Our first smoker! Oh, hell, I've got my tape [cut]."

Scott had suddenly noticed that his tape recorder was running and had turned it off. Only later did he realize that he had accidentally recorded the most exciting moment in his scientific career. He and his two crewmates had been privileged to discover a new place where the waters of the deep are mining the gifts of the Earth. Thanks to bold scientists such as Ballard, Edmond, and Scott, one of the most imaginative hypotheses in recent memory has been proven correct in every detail. The sea floor really is a "perpetual metal factory." As Scott said that day off the coast of Oregon (in a slightly calmer moment), "How about that! Geology works!"

Now it is clear why there are rich metals in the muds of the Red Sea, since the sea floor is spreading there just as it is in the Pacific. Finding hot water and metallic oozes in both the Pacific and the Red Sea helps to confirm that our new, global theory really does apply all around the planet—that geology works.

Very often in science, after the resolution of a major mystery, the answers to many smaller puzzles fall into place. Geologists could finally understand how a small speck of rock in the middle of the Mediterranean was endowed with enough copper ore to lift the peoples of the Western world out of the Stone Age.

Many of the Roman tunnels and mines of that legendary island, where young geologist D. A. Gunther went prospecting at the turn of this century, lie in hillsides covered with large, swirling rock formations—pillow lavas. The dark stones bake in the Mediterranean sunlight; shepherds pasture their herds of goats and sheep among them, while farmers on the plains below tend vineyards and olive orchards. But once, the pillows lay a thousand leagues beneath the sea. Black smokers gushed among them, cornucopias of metals. Giant tubeworms just like those alive today swayed around the ancient smokers (scientists have recently found their fossils among the massive sulfides in the Cyprian hills). The tall sheets and pillars of basalt that geologists have found on the island of Cyprus, lying directly beneath its pillow lavas, are magma that hardened far beneath the black smokers while creeping upward toward the ocean floor.

The grinding and shuffling of plates have uplifted this mass of sea floor, complete with old, toppled chimneys, fossil tubeworms, and rich ores, and thrust it into the light of day. There the ancients mined it two millennia ago, and there D. A. Gunther rediscovered it for his boss, Seeley Mudd.

There are many other camouflaged bits of ancient sea floor exposed to sun and air and scattered around the world: one in Oman, on the southeastern coast of the Arabian peninsula; another in the Bay of Islands, on the western coast of Newfoundland; and others in Oregon and northern California. Halfway around the world, the Japanese have long mined a rich ore deposit they call the Kuroko—none other than gold, silver, copper, lead, zinc, and sulfur bound together.

Japan is a land of vulcanism, and its wealth of hot springs and mud pots led Japanese geologists to speculate as early as 1919 that the Kuroko deposits they were mining might somehow have been formed by the action of hot springs. It is one of the ironies of history that, because no papers on the subject were translated from the Japanese, Western geologists did not learn of the Kuroko deposits until the 1960s.

These days, Steve Scott of the University of Toronto, one of those who has explored black smokers in the great deeps, travels often to the Motoyama open-pit mines of Japan. He and Japanese colleagues work in the pit, studying the walls of what was once the interior of a hydrothermal vent more than 100 feet below the chimneys.

Now that they understand how black smokers form, exploration geologists are following telltale clues in search of other deposits. In the forests of northern Canada, a large, spooky-looking gathering of pillow lavas has helped point the way to a hidden cache of ore, the richest black smoker deposit yet found on land: the Kidd Creek Mine. Beneath a patch of land only 20 acres in extent lie an estimated $30 billion worth of ore reserves.

At the bottom of the sea, another Cyprus, Kuroko, or Kidd Creek probably is forming right now.

MINING THE SEA FLOOR

The great question with all the Earth's treasures is access. Cast up on dry land, the ruins of a single field of black smokers have now made fortunes for Phoenicians, Persians, Assyrians, Greeks, Romans, and the corporation of Seeley Mudd. But old black smokers at the bottom of the sea may never make a miner a penny, since it's too hard to get at them. What is a ton of silver worth if it is buried in the great deeps, or in the bowels of the Earth, or adrift in the asteroid belt, out in the dark frontiers of the solar system? Even if we could reach it and bring it home, the enterprise would cost far more than we would recover from the sale of the booty.

There are just a few places where mining the sea floor may soon be profitable. Among them are the brine pools of the Red Sea. Because the sea is narrow, its midocean ridge is near shore, and its ores are thus more accessible to mining. The brines are equidistant from Saudi Arabia, to the east, and Sudan, to the west; neither country can claim it from the other. However, no other country contests that either Sudan or Saudi Arabia is entitled to mine it. The two countries are lucky to be the only contenders. They have formed the joint Red Sea Commission to decide how best to exploit the sediments.

This commission has brought in a large West German mining firm, Preussag, which has developed a new technology designed to bring up the treasure in the pools. A long pipe is lowered from shipboard. At the end of the pipe is a great, vibrating sieve, and three high-pressure water jets. The combination of the vibrations and the jetting water loosens the sediment. Then a powerful vacuum pump sucks it through the sieve, up the pipe, and to the surface. Tests in shallow water have proved the scheme workable, and the two countries began vacuuming the Red Sea in the early 1980s. Market prices permitting, they hope to raise 150,000 tons of precious mud per year, from now till the year 2000. The sediments in the biggest of the brine pools, the Atlantis II Deep—named for the Woods Hole vessel that discovered it—hold a wealth of copper, zinc, silver, and gold. If it were on land and within easy reach, the top 10 meters of sediment might be worth billions of dollars. At the bottom of the Red Sea, its worth depends on the cost of the vacuum cleaning.

An even stranger sea-floor treasure hunt may begin soon. One century ago, HMS *Challenger*, on its historic 79,000-mile journey around the world's oceans, dredged up numerous russet cinders and charred black lumps, a few of which still are enshrined as curiosities in the British Museum. Nineteenth-century scientists mistook these cinders and lumps for meteorites. But in recent years, underwater cameras scanning the sea bottom have found that lumps literally pave great stretches of the floor. There are dark plains of ooze 20,000 feet beneath the sea that look like cobbled plazas.

These cobbles are rich in manganese, so they are called *manganese nodules;* but they also contain small percentages of other, rarer metals, including nickel, copper, and cobalt. The world already has plenty of manganese (which is an important ingredient in making steel) on land. It is the presence of nickel, copper, and cobalt that makes the nodules worth scrabbling for.

Manganese nodules are strewn like cobblestones across great stretches of the sea floor.

Manganese nodules are common in quiet deeps, far from the action of volcanic ridges and spreading centers. Like pearls, the nodules tend to grow around a nucleus: a grain of sand, a piece of broken shell, a bit of shark's tooth. Most of these nodules grow with agonizing slowness, adding concentric layer upon layer at a rate of only one millimeter per million years—which is about 10 million times slower, for instance, than the Atlantic Ocean or the Red Sea is spreading! Given their slow rate of growth, it is curious that most nodules are not buried by sediments and ooze. Something seems to keep them at the surface—which is fortunate, because it makes them at least a little convenient for mining.

Today there are three competing schemes for collecting the nodules, which are, at their densest, about 20 pounds per square yard of ooze. The first scheme is a replay of the *Challenger's* approach: Lower a bucket, or a chain of buckets. The second is the approach being used at the Red Sea: Suck them up with a gargantuan vacuum cleaner. The third is the fanciest, a NASA-style approach: Build a crew of robots (known variously as "water beetles" or "pearl divers") with head lamps and television camera eyes to swoop down to the bottom, scoop up a load of nodules, and return to the ship.

Assuming any of these schemes can be made to work at a profit—which some old hands doubt—would mining disrupt the ecology of the sea floor? Who owns the middle of the ocean—the country that gets there first, the countries that border it, or all countries in consortium? These questions currently are much in debate, and a long-sought global treaty, the Law of the Sea, recently faltered because of competing national interests. It may take longer for the world to agree on the

Salt harvesting in the San Francisco Bay Area in the 1920s.

answers to these questions than it takes metal pearls to grow at the bottom of the sea.

SCARCITY AND SUPPLY

Our high-powered age follows naturally from the ages of Copper, Iron, and Bronze—and even digs down into some of the same holes. But the pace of our progress sets us apart from the peoples who came before us, as the geologists Mead L. Jensen and Alan M. Bateman note in their recent book *Economic Mineral Deposits:*

> It is startling to realize that the rise of the industrial age has so accelerated the demand for minerals that the world has dug up and consumed more of its mineral resources in the period shortly before and after World War II than in all preceding ages. This insatiable demand for minerals to feed industry has made some sources of supply that we used to think were adequate now look rather small, and sources capable of meeting large demands are being depleted rapidly.
>
> Prior to and less than a century and a half ago, the rate of increase in the consumption of copper and iron was directly proportional to the increase in population. If the population doubled, the consumption of these metals doubled. In contrast, during the first hundred years of the Industrial Revolution, roughly from 1812 to 1912, the population increased threefold whereas the consumption of copper increased 80 times and iron 100 times!

In the year 968, notes minerals expert Richard P.

Sheldon, the average American used, each year, "a few pounds of flint and obsidian for tools, arrowheads, and ax heads, a few pounds of sandstone for mortars, a little salt and mineral dye." (A Stone Age Indian needed very little stone.) One thousand years later, in 1968, the average American used *20 tons of minerals a year*! Each citizen consumed this portion of the Earth's crust in the form of new paving stone, concrete, glass, oil, coal, asbestos, and metal. No wonder the naturalist Loren Eiseley called mankind "the world-eaters."

The great question of our age is: How long can we keep up this rate of consumption? Some would say forever. But in the 20th century, the global rate at which we mine minerals has doubled every 10 years. At this rate, resource geologist Brian Skinner calculates, by the year 2213, our descendants would have to produce 250 million billion metric tons of minerals a year. "This is absurd indeed," Skinner says; "that mass is equal to all of the land standing above sea level."

Clearly, the sweeping curve of exponential growth will have to level off long before that. We already know we are running out of oil in this country: National oil production peaked in 1970 and has been declining slowly since. Globally, some analysts think a number of metals are now becoming scarce, including silver, mercury, lead, and zinc. In the United States, the most threatening loss is copper, necessary for the wires and cables that, because they are good conductors of electricity, are the nervous system of the Industrial Age.

Scarcity and supply are hard to forecast, however. A banker can count the ingots in a vault, but a miner can't count all the ore in the ground. How much there is depends not only on geology but also on economics—it depends on how badly the world wants the metal. The gifts of the Earth's crust can be divided into two categories, *reserves* and *potential resources*. If we know the whereabouts and dimensions of a copper deposit and how to mine it, and if we are sure we can mine and sell it at a profit, then it is considered a reserve. It is on tap, so to speak. On the other hand, if we think we're on the track of a big copper deposit but haven't got the backing and equipment to prove it; or if we've found it but can't get at it; or if we can mine the ore only at a greater cost than the copper is worth on the market, then the deposit is classed as a potential resource. Reserves can be counted on; potential resources are speculative. If the market price rises high enough, a potential resource may become a reserve. If it doesn't, the potential resource will stay in the ground.

Experts in this subject can be divided into two sorts, too: optimists and pessimists (those in each camp call themselves realists).

Economist Julian Simons of the University of Illinois at Champaign-Urbana argues for optimism in his recent book *The Ultimate Resource*. It is reassuring, he says, to see how "shortages" have been worrying analysts for centuries. In 1864, an eminent British social scientist, W. Stanley Jevons, declared England's industry doomed for lack of coal. "We cannot long continue our present rate of progress," Jevons wrote. "[This] check for our growing prosperity . . . must render our population excessive." Jevons's prediction was very wrong. Because England needed coal, Simons says, "prospectors searched out new deposits, inventors discovered better ways to get coal from the earth, and transportation men developed cheaper ways to move the coal. Other countries did the same." Today in England and in the United States, coal is more plentiful and relatively cheaper than it was 100 years ago.

Reserves, Simons argues, are like groceries in the cupboard. We keep only as much on the shelf at one time as we think we need. When we need more, we go to the store. In the same way, when the world really needs more copper, Simons says, we will buy it. Mining companies will hire exploration geologists to find it, or, if that is prohibitively expensive, inventors will find a substitute. Doomsayers, says Simons, are counting the cans of soup in the cabinet and screaming, "We're about to starve!"

"Optimism and imagination are happy human traits," counters the geologist Preston Cloud of the University of California at Santa Barbara. But an exponential rate of growth, he says, cannot be sustained on an Earth that is not growing. The crust is not a cornucopia. When we burn a barrel of oil, that oil is gone. It will take Nature millions of years to make more. Given the Earth's limits and the population explosion, Cloud says, the only sane thing to do is to slow down our consumption of such irreplaceable resources. Instead, like lunatics, we are running through them faster and faster—urged on by the cheerful advisers whom Cloud terms "cornucopians."

Cloud calls for a careful census of the Earth's crustal materials. It is time, he says, to take stock of the globe. He says the modern notion that we can keep the economy healthy through overconsumption and waste "will prove, in the long term, to be a cruel and preposterous illusion."

Who is right? "On the answer to that question," says resources analyst Richard J. Barnet, in his book *The Lean Years*, "hangs the future of politics. A world of scarcity is a world of inevitable struggle. . . . War has been a favorite way for great nations to meet their resource needs, and if there is another world war the conflict will most likely be over what the industrial states have come to regard as the elements of survival—

oil, of course, and also iron, copper, uranium, cobalt, wheat, and water."

Both optimists and pessimists agree that we must find new reserves. Among the newest tools in the arsenal of modern exploration are keen robot eyes and giant robot brains—satellites and computers. Through the reconnaissance techniques of *remote sensing*, we can scan Earth from miles above.

    The first aerial snapshot was taken in 1858 by a friend of Jules Verne, the Parisian photographer Gaspard-Félix Tournachon, whose professional name was Nadar. Nadar climbed into the basket of a balloon, lifted off, and shot a village from 250 feet up—a high-tech adventure, since both ballooning and photography were still new enough to be glamorous.

    One century later, in 1963, the astronaut L. Gordon Cooper passed over Tibet in a Mercury space capsule, flying 160 kilometers above the Himalayas at a speed of 28,000 kilometers an hour. Scientists at NASA had assumed the atmosphere would blur an astronaut's view of Earth, just as it interferes with an astronomer's view of space. But Cooper, whose eyesight was 20/11 (even better for distance than 20/20), could on a clear day over Asia make out lamaseries, chimney smoke, and even movement on the roads. "I could first see the dust blowing off the road, then could see the road clearly, and when the light was right, an object that was probably a vehicle." He took two dozen excellent color photos with a hand-held camera, detailed views of glaciers, folds, and faults in Tibet and Southwest Asia.

EARTH AS UNEXPLORED

An aerial photograph of the Silver Bell District, northwest of Tucson, Arizona, a region rich in copper ore.

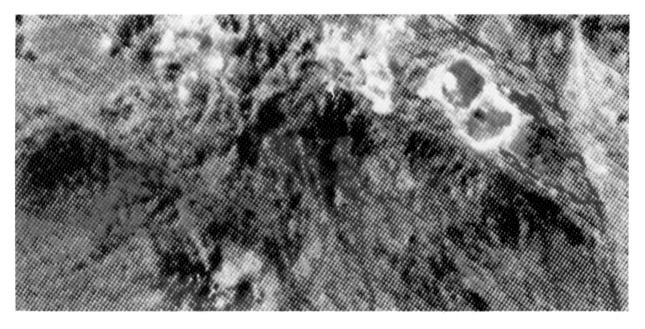

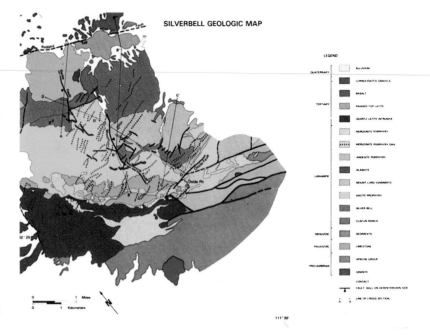

SILVERBELL GEOLOGIC MAP

The Silver Bell District,
mapped from space, in a test
of Landsat's *capabilities.*

Astronauts kept coming home with remarkable photographs, and geologists and other scientists began campaigning for a satellite program to exploit the lofty new view of the Earth. On July 23, 1972, the first of a series of robot earthwatchers—which have come to be called *Landsats*—was launched from the Western Test Range in California.

Jules Verne's comrade Nadar had photographed perhaps a few square acres of Earth. An airplane can record a few square miles. Landsat captures in each image 13,000 square miles of Earth, and the satellite can cover the whole planet in 18 days. It does not scan the Earth as a human eye would. Its sensors are designed to detect a wider range of the spectrum than the human eye can see, recording not only visible light but also infrared. The images from Landsat *multispectral scanners* (and the new *thematic mappers*, which record an even broader range of the spectrum) are radioed to Earth and assembled by computer, which tints them in brilliant, artificial colors to make various details stand out. More than 1 million Landsat images of Earth are now stored in a U.S. Geological Survey computer in Sioux Falls, South Dakota. The pictures are not only useful but also eerily beautiful. "It's like looking at the Earth with alien eyes," says a scientist at the Jet Propulsion Laboratory.

Lowman, inspecting early Landsat images of California, discovered fractures no one had seen before in the San Andreas Fault system. Agronomists found they could use Landsat's pictures to keep track of changes in the United States' and the world's crops, forests, and reservoirs. Analyzing the pictures, they could tell wheat from barley, freshly planted corn from ripe corn, and a healthy orchard from one diseased. Different kinds of vegetation, soil, and rocks were found to have their own special spectral signatures—fingerprints of light. Mapmakers used the pictures to correct the positions of rivers, lakes, and peaks in remote regions, including the Himalayas. One speck of land was named for the robot that put it on the map: Landsat Island.

The Landsat files in the supercomputer at Sioux Falls are the Space Age equivalent of treasure maps. For anyone canny enough to decipher them, they conceal clues to billions of dollars' worth of buried ore. This fact has not escaped the attention of the big oil companies.

In the early 1970s, Chevron assigned John Mill, then one of its senior exploration geologists, to help find out whether there might be any land worth drilling in the southern half of Sudan. Before the Space Age, this would have been a heartbreaking assignment. Sudan is the biggest country in Africa, and its southern half is a wilderness of deserts and papyrus swamps, with few people and fewer roads. No maker of maps, whether geographical or geological, had troubled to show the terrain with any great precision. There were hardly any outcrops of rock by which to judge what was below, and there wasn't an oil man on Earth from whom to get the lay of the land, because no one had ever drilled for oil in the whole region.

Miller put together a mosaic of Landsat photographs. Southern Sudan is so large that he had to patch together more than 100 Landsat images, each showing 13,000 square miles. He prospected across this mosaic in the comfort of his office. In a vast swamp called the Sudd, beside the White Nile River, Miller recognized the presence of a huge *sedimentary basin*.

Such a basin forms when sediments settle in one place for many eons—for instance, at the bottom of a lake, or a small sea, or in the delta of a river, where sluggish waters drop their brown loads in great spreading fans of silt, sand, and mud. Over time, as layers of sediment are piled one on top of the next, the lower layers are compressed and compacted by the pressure of the sands and clays above them. The lower portion of the basin turns slowly to sedimentary rock: siltstone, sandstone, shale.

The waters that lay down these sediments are often blue-green with algae and other microscopic plants, along with a miscellany of pollen, spores, and bits of wood. As generations of these plants live and die, trillions of their bodies rain down among the silts and clays.

Usually bacteria go to work on such organic debris and consume it, so that there is nothing left at last but pure carbon dioxide and water. Some of this gas and water is taken

When sedimentary layers are compressed and folded, they make good traps for oil.

in by new generations of living creatures. The rest is dispersed into air and sea.

Occasionally, however, a layer rich in organic debris, lying at the bottom of a lake, a delta, or a continental shelf, is buried suddenly by a layer of sediment. A torrential rainstorm, for instance, loads streams and rivers with sand and mud, which then settle quickly. In this way the ooze at the bottom is sometimes sealed off from the world by a thin blanket of earth and protected from being totally consumed by bacteria. The oozy layer sinks slowly into the depths, sandwiched between mud and sand.

Oil is rare because its formation requires a series of geological accidents. This is the first: Over a bed of rich ooze must be thrown a blanket of mud.

The heat and pressure deep in the Earth transform this dark mass by some chemical alchemy that is still poorly understood. If it is cooked just right (probably at the temperature of a medium oven, about 250 degrees Fahrenheit) for the right amount of time (usually tens of thousands or hundreds of thousands of years), the ooze turns to a thick, dark fluid, which we call *crude oil*. Further cooking makes the oil lighter in body and color and more valuable, and it turns some of it to a flammable gas, *natural gas*. More heat ruins it.

This is the second accident in the genesis of oil. A recipe so delicate and intricate that it has never been duplicated in a laboratory must be carried out to perfection, by pure chance, in the depths of the Earth.

The oil is under pressure and oozes upward. If nothing

A Landsat *view of the Mississippi Delta.* Landsats *are unmanned, downlooking robots, orbiting the Earth at altitudes of hundreds of miles. Each* Landsat's *sensors measure the amount of energy reflected or emitted from the Earth's surface in visible light, and in the infrared. The radiation is recorded electronically, and then converted into false-color images. Very deep, clear water is black; shallow water, or water carrying sediment, is lighter and bluer. Green, growing vegetation appears red.*

"Colonel" Edwin L. Drake built the first oil drill, in 1859, on the banks of Oil Creek, in Titusville, Pennsylvania. Here the colonel (left) poses with an investor.

blocks its way, it can rise buoyantly all the way to the surface of the Earth and seep out. Ancient tribes knew about such oil seeps; they used oil to light their sacred fires. According to the Book of Genesis, Noah used pitch—a thick, tarry petroleum— to caulk the ribs of his Ark. American Indians skimmed the oil slick from the surfaces of holy ponds and streams and rubbed it on their skin as medicine. But not everyone saw value in seeps of oil and gas. George Washington complained of a troublesome spring on his plantation, Mount Vernon. The spring was "of so inflammable a nature as to burn freely as spirits."

In the early 1800s, the world got most of its oil not from oil seeps (from which one could eke, at best, only a few gallons of fluid a day) but in the depths of the sea. Captain Ahab, brooding at midnight aboard the ill-starred ship *Pequod*, read his nautical charts by the light of butchered whales. The whaling captains of Nantucket rode as high as the oil magnates of Dallas do today. But by the mid-1800s, whales were getting scarce. Oil for lamps became expensive. In 1859, an unemployed conductor on the New York, New Haven, and Hartford railroad, "Colonel" Edwin L. Drake, was hired by a few entrepreneurs to drill on the banks of Oil Creek, in Titusville, Pennsylvania. An oil seep, Drake's employers reasoned, must be a sign of oil in the depths. Using an old steam engine, Drake built the first oil drill, and on August 26, 1859, after 69½ feet of slow, hard work (during which his backers gave up and his neighbors began talking of "Drake's Folly"), a dark, viscous liquid oozed nearly to the top of the hole. The colonel danced. This was the first modern oil well—and it is still producing today.

Oil prospectors soon learned that the biggest deposits were not always found near seeps; for if oil can reach the surface, it can also ooze away. A seep is nothing but a leak; the best wells are in vast underground oil reservoirs with no leaks. These are big pockets of oil that have been trapped on their rise to the surface. The most common trap is a place where the Earth's crust has been squeezed until it folds like a rumpled rug. Oil can be trapped in the tops of the folds. Such folds are called *anticlines,* and they hold three quarters of the world's oil. Another sort of trap forms when the crust cracks and shifts. The shift may block the oil's passage to the surface. Folds and faults that can collect oil in this way are called *structural traps.*

This is the third and final accident in the genesis of oil. First, it must be buried quickly; second, cooked gently; and third, trapped neatly. A series of three coincidences is much less likely than a single one. The three accidents that go into the making of an oil reservoir have coincided only rarely on this planet, and as a result only a small fraction of the world's total volume of organic debris—about 2 percent—ever became oil and pooled in a reservoir. Hence oil's rarity, and hence the astonishing speed with which the world has been using it up. Less than a century and a half has passed between Colonel Drake's first strike in Titusville and the high-stakes, high-tech, high-risk prospecting we must do today to find the last hidden deposits.

Chevron's John Miller, having compiled a full-color Landsat mosaic of the Sudanese wilderness, inspected it from corner to corner. He could see only the surface of the land, not the layers of Earth buried below. But he noticed an important fact about the Sudd swamp's rivers and streams. Most of them were wriggly with bends and meanders, because the land was fairly flat. (Where there is no great difference between uphill and down, rivers' courses tend to be indecisive.) But looking down from the satellite's God's-eye view, Miller could see long stretches where the riverbeds were so straight that they might have been inscribed with a ruler. These straight beds were signs that the water was following cracks in the Earth's crust, called *lineaments.* Lineaments gratify an oil man's desires. If the crust has cracked, strata may have shifted. If strata have shifted, they may have trapped oil.

The signs were auspicious. Agents of Chevron negotiated with the government of Sudan for rights to explore 200,000 square miles around the Sudd swamp—an area larger than the state of California. Armed with versions of the Landsat mosaic, geophysicists journeyed to Sudan and there, from airplanes and helicopters, they began *doodlebugging* the swamp.

Early prospectors often traveled with a forked twig, a

dowsing rod. When the rod, held loosely in the hand, dipped downward, that meant the prospector was standing over oil. Or water. Or gold—whatever the prospector was hunting for. Dowsers couldn't begin to say how the thing worked, or prove it did, but some old hands claimed to have struck it rich. One professional dowser even advertised that he could find major reservoirs of oil or water by dowsing a map of the world. Perhaps the rod allowed a prospector to express his intuitions about the lay of the land. Oil men call unscientific gadgets like the dowsing rod *doodlebugs*. They call the fancy equipment a modern geophysicist carts into the field doodlebugs, too. But while modern doodlebuggers are not infallible, there is at least one difference between them and dowsers: Geophysicists can explain what they're doing.

Chevron's doodlebuggers used a magnetometer to map the varying intensities of the Earth's magnetic field from one end of the swamp to the other. Sedimentary rocks often have weaker magnetic fields than other types, so the magnetometer helped scientists map more accurately the outlines of the basin. This is the same device that oceanographers in the early 1960s used to map "zebra stripes" of magnetic fields on the ocean bottom—work that helped prove the sea floor is spreading. At sea the instrument is towed by the ship in a sort of torpedo called a "fish." In the air, it is towed behind the plane in a small glider, a "bird."

Next, geophysicists on the ground surveyed the basin with *gravimeters*. A gravimeter measures slight—in daily life, imperceptible—variations in the tug of gravity from one place on Earth to another. It is really nothing but an exquisitely sensitive bathroom scale. Where there are large masses of dense rock beneath the ground, things weigh slightly more; where there are quantities of light and porous rock, things weigh slightly less. These studies, too, helped the geophysicists map the basin.

Field crews soon found out why no cartographer had lingered in the southern Sudan. Its deserts are some of the hottest in the world; and in the swamps, a jeep can't go six feet before its axles are hopelessly jammed in stalks of papyrus. What to do? Back to the satellite! In the Chevron home office, geologists further analyzed Landsat's photos of the Sudan, and from the images they made a detailed terrain map so the doodlebuggers could avoid the accursed papyrus. The satellite kept them out of the mire.

Now they brought in the vibrators. Scientists have long known that vibrations in rock—sound waves—can be used to map rock layers beneath the Earth's surface. The pioneering Yugoslavian geologist Andriya Mohorovičić mapped

This truck's wheels are not touching the ground. It has been jacked up on a central pedestal and set vibrating; the vibrations are traveling through the pedestal and the ground beneath it like the waves of a small earthquake. When the waves are recorded and analyzed, they show the rough lay-out of the rock and sediment far beneath the surface—a great help in the search for oil. Oman, Turkey 1981.

the bottom boundary of the Earth's crust using vibrations from earthquakes, as recorded by seismometers. Today, doodlebuggers make their own earthquakes. Sometimes they use dynamite. If that is unsuitable (as, for instance, in suburban Los Angeles), they use "vibrator trucks," which are perhaps the most bizarre doodlebugs in the whole arsenal. "These mechanical beasts," says one bemused observer from *Fortune* Magazine, "drop pads to the ground from their bellies; each truck then raises itself several inches from the pad on a hydraulic lift and shivers violently for up to 30 seconds."

To listen to the vibrations, field crews set up long lines of acoustic receivers called *geophones*. Geophones pick up sound waves as they reflect back from layers of rock thousands of feet below. The data are fed into a computer and translated there into a wiggly picture of the Earth's depths seen in cross section. Supercomputers can now generate such data in three dimensions—that is, the computer draws a picture of a great cube or block of crust, rather as it would look if it were quarried with a chisel a mile wide and 10 miles long and lifted out of the depths of the Earth. Sometimes this block of crust is displayed as a hologram: When seen in the light of a laser, a ghostly brick from the depths of the planet seems to float in space. In studying this cube from different angles, a trained eye can spot likely oil traps.

None of this work proved there was a drop of oil in the Sudd—not Landsat, the magnetometer, the gravimeter, or the vibrator, for no doodlebug actually smells buried oil. The gadgets can only point to places where the three key geological accidents *may* have made oil. "When you come right down to it," says one doodlebugger, "the only way to get an answer is to drill a hole." This Chevron did, again and again, in the late 1970s in the southern Sudan, at a cost of many millions of dollars . . . and came up empty.

At last, in 1979, a crew struck oil at Abu Gabra, some 400 kilometers southwest of Khartoum. Almost immediately, more drills struck in rapid succession at Unity, Melut, and Heglig. Probably the find will not prove to be a bonanza, a supergiant. But it is good enough. The drilling in the Sudd, reports Chevron's Floyd Sabins, a world expert on remote sensing, "has defined sufficient reserves to justify a 900-mile pipeline to the Red Sea."

Landsat and the doodlebuggers scored.

PROSPECTING WITH PLATE TECTONICS

In a way, the theory of plate tectonics could prove the biggest doodlebug of all. Plate tectonics experts have become well-paid consultants to major oil companies. With their special expertise, they can point to spots that may have been just right for the creation of oil and minerals hundreds of millions of years ago, though they seem unlikely and inappropriate today.

When the supercontinent Pangaea shattered and began to move apart, for instance, the Atlantic was just a narrow

A rock layer buried deep beneath the surface of the Sudan. This layer has been mapped by Chevron doodlebuggers, using vibrating trucks. Here the map is displayed on a computer screen. Using interactive graphics, an expert rotates the image, as if holding the great cube of earth in his hands, to look at it from all sides. The technique (which still is new and experimental) gives geophysicists the next-best thing to X-ray vision. Each edge of this cube is about seven miles long.

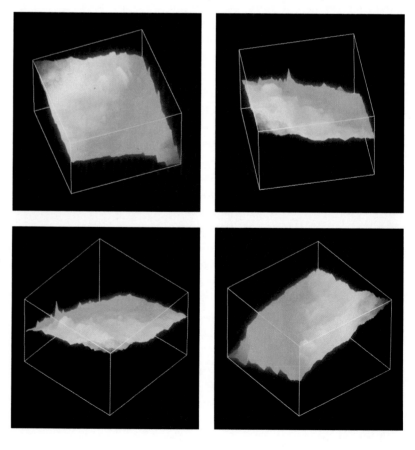

strip of seawater. Like the Red Sea today, it was an infant ocean. Being so narrow, the waters of the Atlantic Sea circulated sluggishly; the bottom was stagnant, and its organic debris—the muck and ooze of the sea floor—decayed only slowly. Under the strong tropical Sun, the water in this narrow sea grew highly salty, through evaporation. Salts rained to the bottom and helped to provide a coverlet for the organic ooze.

Thus the first condition for oil was met in the Atlantic Sea: Richly organic sediments were laid down and preserved.

As these sediments were compacted, sinking deeper beneath the weight of fresh sand, silt, and clay, they were heated from below. The subterranean fires that drive sea-floor spreading helped to cook the hydrocarbons. Where the cooking times and temperatures were right, the Atlantic Sea met the second geological condition, and oil was made beneath its floor.

Oceanographers with echo sounders have detected the presence of *salt domes* buried beneath the bottom of the Atlantic, up and down the eastern and western coasts. These domes—really pillars of salt beneath the floor of the sea—make good oil traps. If theory is correct, then, they are likely spots to look for oil. They may even prove to be major reserves. "It is reasonable to expect," geophysicist Peter Rona has predicted, "that petroleum accumulations will extend seaward under the continental shelf, the continental slope, and the continental rise to water depths of about 18,000 feet along large portions of both the eastern and western margins of the North Atlantic and South Atlantic."

Thanks in part to such predictions, more and more offshore drilling is now taking place on both sides of the Atlantic. But it is an expensive and dangerous business. A large oil platform, *a semisubmersible rig*, is a floating village, with crews of over 100 people. It is built to hold miles of anchor chain and drilling pipe, tons of drinking water and ballast, a sewage plant, and sometimes a small gymnasium. Each rig costs billions of dollars to build and a quarter of a million dollars a day to operate. When the oil is shipped to shore, accidents can cause big oil spills. And though precautions are taken, workers in the middle of the ocean are not as safe as they are on land. In the past decade, more than 300 oil men have been killed at sea. In 1980, a floating dormitory sank in the North Sea off the coast of Norway, and 123 people died. In 1982, off Newfoundland, an offshore drilling rig capsized in a storm and sank. Eighty-four people were drowned.

As we push north into Arctic waters, seeking oil in more and more obscure corners of the world, the hazards grow still greater. During violent storms, ice can frost a ship until it grows topheavy and capsizes. Off the coasts of Labrador and

Newfoundland, icebergs can loom out of a dense fog and snap drill pipes, or punch holes in ships' sides, even in June and July.

The International Ice Patrol helps ships and offshore oilmen avoid disaster. Icebergs are watched from satellites, planes, ships, and shores. The whereabouts of vagrant ice is broadcast daily. The International Ice Patrol was formed in 1914, after the *Titanic* hit an iceberg and more than 1,500 people died. Since then, the patrol has prevented countless disasters. Sometimes, if a huge drilling rig cannot move in time, members of the International Ice Patrol actually lasso a wayward iceberg and, with a tugboat, tow it out of harm's way.

The most amazing aspect of this drama is that, as yet, it still makes economic sense. Nothing shows more clearly modern civilization's hunger for the gifts of the Earth. To get a barrel of oil, we are willing to go to the far corners of the planet.

FROM SWAMPS TO COAL

Some 300 million years ago life on Earth basked in a warm spell, a luxurious planetary summer. Most lands were united in Pangaea, and the climate was generally so moist and mild that much of the supercontinent was green. We live today in the chilly margins of the last Ice Age. It is hard for us to imagine the endless forests of giant ferns 100 feet high, rising amid mists of vapor and swamp gas; the fetid marshes through which browsed some of the first amphibious creatures to make it out of the sea and onto the land; the inescapable, sickly-sweet smell of decay that rose from layer upon layer of leaves and stems, the foliage of centuries.

Those warm days at last ended and the supercontinent disintegrated, but much of the miasmic compost heap on Pangaea was preserved. Buried beneath layers of sediment, compacted, compressed, and heated, the compost eventually formed the black mineral we call coal. Partly because it is solid (indeed, a sort of rock made out of life), coal is much longer-lived than oil; it is believed that most of the coal ever formed on this planet still exists, in one place or another—except for the quantities we human beings have mined and burned.

There are several ranks of coal, depending on how much it has been compressed and heated. The first rank is *peat,* which is not much more than hard-packed humus. There are large peat bogs in parts of North America—including Quebec, Maine, the Pine Barrens of New Jersey, and the Dismal Swamp of Virginia. The peat may turn to coal in a few hundred thousand years, but meanwhile it is soft and crumbly turf, and does not burn as well as wood.

When peat is compressed it eventually forms *lignite,* or "brown coal." Lignite is a better fuel than peat, but it, too, is less than satisfactory (one mining engineer has been quoted as saying, "I'm not sure whether the stuff is low-quality coal or just high-quality dirt.") When lignite is compressed it forms the next rank, *bituminous* coal, which is the most abundant and the most commonly used. It is harder than lignite and burns well, though smokily. The top of the line is *anthracite*, which is hard, brittle, glassy, and almost pure carbon.

Ralph Waldo Emerson called coal "black diamonds," and indeed a diamond is merely carbon in another atomic arrangement, one that makes it harder than a chunk of anthracite, and transparent. Emerson might also have called coal "black sunshine," since coal is that, too. The ferns and mosses soaked up the Pangaean sunlight and, in effect, stored its energy in their greenery. As layers of Earth compacted the ferns, they concentrated this solar energy. When a coal miner digs up a shovelful of coal, and a suburbanite burns it in a patio grill, they release energy hoarded by the Earth for hundreds of millions of years.

Since its chief relic is carbon, the geological age that produced most of our coal is called the Carboniferous. And since coal and oil are, in a manner of speaking, fossilized energy, we call them *fossil fuels*. In fact, actual fossils are often found embedded within chunks of coal—the ghostly leaves and stems of the long-extinct giant ferns.

We have a lot of coal on this planet. There are reserves to last us 200 years, and a significant fraction lies in the United States. The United States is about as well endowed in coal as Saudi Arabia is in oil. Owners of coal companies wonder (sometimes vociferously) why anyone talks about an energy crisis when there is so much energy lying in the ground for the taking.

But coal is not an ideal source of energy. For one thing, the work of digging it is grueling and risky. Tens of thousands of coal miners in the United States in this century have been killed by explosions, floods, suffocating gases, and collapsing tunnels. Other miners died from "black lung" due to the coal dust they inhaled. The only alternative to tunnels is open-air strip-mining. Strip-mining is possible only when the coal deposit is near the surface, and it leaves huge craters in what were once pastoral landscapes.

Bituminous coal yields as much smoke as heat, and cities that once relied on coal for heat and power, such as old London and old Pittsburgh, were notoriously grimy places in which to live and breathe. The pollution problem probably was even worse than people realized at the time. Most bituminous coal contains sulfur. Released into the upper atmosphere, sulfur combines with water to form sulfuric acid. There is reason to fear that abnormally acid rains and snows are damaging mil-

We think of solar power as a new idea, and high-tech. But most of our energy sources, old and new, derive from the Sun. Even a windmill turns through solar power. The Sun drives the winds that turn the windmill's vanes.

lions of acres of woods, lakes, and streams downwind of giant factory smokestacks. Acid rain also corrodes limestone steps, marble monuments, and human lungs. It is difficult and expensive to "scrub" the sulfur from the smoke, and it is also costly to use only low-sulfur coal, anthracite.

Burning coal, like wood or oil, releases carbon dioxide into the atmosphere. Carbon dioxide the ancient ferns took out of the air is restored to the air when we burn the coal. A revival of the Coal Age would continue to exacerbate the greenhouse effect. Burn enough coal fast enough, and we could conceivably return the temperate zones to an age as damp and swampy as the Carboniferous.

As oil becomes more and more expensive, we probably will turn again to coal; but it is not a happy alternative. The mineral seems cheap, but the human price we pay for it is not.

If we rely on coal to maintain civilization's feverish pitch, we will burn through it all in the span of a few human lifetimes. Sooner or later, then, we need to find energy alternatives.

The most sophisticated alternative available today is nuclear power. If coal was once king, then uranium was crown prince. The slow and controlled splitting, or *fission*, of uranium atoms to release energy seemed in the 1950s and 1960s to promise the world a virtually limitless source of power. Pound for pound, enriched uranium contains nearly 3 million times more energy than coal.

Despite initial enthusiasm and enormous government subsidies, however, uranium's crown is now tarnished and the future of the industry uncertain. Nuclear plants are expensive to build and to run. The waste products are radioactive, and no one knows how to dispose of them safely. (It has been suggested that barrels of wastes be dumped into deep ocean trenches. The wastes would ride down, with the rest of the ocean floor, into what geologist Harry Hess once called "the jaw-crusher," and descend into the bowels of the Earth. Plate tectonics as garbage disposal. But no one can guarantee that the containers would not sometimes burst, releasing their poisons into the ocean. Then the currents in the abyss would distribute the stuff all over the world.) In 1979, the accident at Three Mile Island, near Harrisburg, Pennsylvania, confirmed public fears that fission reactors are hard to manage safely—and the Three Mile Island reactor still is not cleaned up. Finally, the most efficient kind of nuclear power plant, the breeder reactor, converts uranium to plutonium, and if a few pounds of plutonium ever fall into the wrong hands, we could have terrorists threatening to blow up not a bank but an entire city (though they would need to be sophisticated terrorists). All told, in the popular mind, nuclear power seems a close cousin to nuclear war. Orders for new nuclear plants in the United States peaked in 1973 at more than 40 and then plummeted in just a few years to zero.

There are a number of simpler alternatives. One is solar power. In regions with strong sunlight and clear skies, sunlight can be used to warm homes directly; or it can be converted into electric current. This latter feat is performed by a piece of electronic hardware called a *photovoltaic cell*. Such cells powered *Skylab* and other satellites in the brilliant sunlight of outer space. The cells are clean and long-lasting, and solar energy is, of course, renewed every day at dawn. But solar cells still are much, much too expensive to power whole nations.

Wind power—using sophisticated, aerodynamically designed versions of the ancient windmill—derives from solar power, since the Sun drives the winds that turn the vanes of windmills. Like photovoltaic cells, windmill power generators have not yet been made cheap and efficient enough to supply a large part of a nation's power.

Big dams convert river power into electricity, but dams form reservoirs that change the landscape, sometimes in unfortunate ways. The dams are expensive to build, and their river reservoirs eventually fill with silt, giving each dam a useful lifetime of only 50 years.

Ocean tides have been harnessed to produce electric power in the Bay of Fundy; but the technology works profitably only in harbors with unusually strong tides. There are inventors who dream of harnessing waves; other inventors have designed grand-scale floating power plants at sea, whose turbines would be driven by the difference in temperature between the cold bottom waters and the warm surface.

There is always wood—but we've tried that. With better forestry and husbandry, and clever furnaces, wood can be made to go farther than it has in the past; and it is still a major fuel in Third World countries. However, it will never sustain an industrial nation like our own in the style to which we are accustomed.

As we run out of oil in the next few decades, each of these alternatives is likely to get more attention. There is another alternative to oil and coal that is fairly far along in technological development and might supply a somewhat larger fraction of the world's energy budget soon. That is the warmth of Planet Earth itself.

Norsemen thought the fires of Iceland came from Hell. Today their descendants use those very fires to generate their electricity, run their factories, and heat their homes.

The core of the Earth is hot, 4 thousand degrees centigrade. So the planet's surface is warmed from below as well as from above. Donald E. White of the U.S. Geological Survey estimates that the energy in the crust's outer 10 kilometers is 2,000 times what we would get by burning all the coal in the world.

In part, the Earth is hot inside because it is still cooling off from the fiery days of its creation 4.6 billion years ago, and also because the decay of radioactive elements in the crust, uranium and thorium, releases heat. Since the hot core is well insulated from outer space by the bulk of the planet, and since the crust has plenty of uranium and thorium, the planet should stay warm for billions of years.

Living at the surface, we aren't normally aware of Earth's body heat. But miners in tunnels know all about it. The deeper they go, the hotter it gets. On average, the temperature increases one degree centigrade per 100 feet of depth. The walls of the deepest South African diamond mines are at 140 degrees Fahrenheit and the tunnels have to be air-conditioned to keep miners from cooking to death.

Most of this *geothermal energy* is too diffuse to be useful to us, unfortunately. Like other resources, the Earth's heat is worth gathering only in places where Nature has already concentrated it. These are, by and large, the geological trouble spots, which are cursed with volcanoes and earthquakes, but also, as if in compensation, blessed with gifts of oil, rich soil, and rare minerals.

For instance, the crust along the Ring of Fire that marks the edges of the Pacific plate is much hotter than the global average. A tunnel one thousand feet deep in California is warmer than the same tunnel in Connecticut. Heat tends to flow out fastest at plates' active and restless borders. This is not a coincidence: The plates are stirring and drifting precisely because heat is trapped within the planet and attempting to escape. The whole grand spectacle of plate tectonics can be described as Earth's way of trying to cool itself off.

In some places, the heat of the Earth literally boils out. It jets to the surface in the red lava of volcanoes, the towering steam of geysers, and the bubbling water of hot springs. Iceland, split down the middle by the Mid-Atlantic Ridge, is one of the hottest spots in the world for volcanoes and geysers (we get our word *geyser* from the Icelandic *geysir,* "gusher"). The first Vikings to row into the harbor that is now the capital city saw steam rising there, and that is how the place got its name (Reykjavik means "smoking bay"). Since ancient times, Icelanders have washed clothes in hot springs, bathed in them, and baked bread by burying loaves a foot in the ground, summer or winter. And in this century the descendants of the Vikings are profiting much more from life "under the volcano."

Reykjavik was once as grimy with coal smoke as old London. Since the 1930s, however, more than 30 holes have been drilled through the bedrock (a thick layer of hardened lava) to the hot water below. This buried reservoir was apparently left over from the melting glaciers of the last Ice Age and was trapped by the lava from volcanic eruptions. The water is 140 degrees Fahrenheit, hot enough to be pumped directly into radiators and hot-water tanks. It heats 99 percent of the buildings and homes in Reykjavik, the first city in the world to rely almost entirely on geothermal power. Home heating bills are surprisingly cheap in the capital of Iceland.

There are geothermal villages scattered across the island. Water heated by the Earth is piped up to heat homes and swimming pools, and it keeps hothouse orchids abloom in greenhouses through the long, dark Icelandic winters. At the fringes of some hot springs, where the heat of the Earth holds at bay the ice and snow, people sometimes take advantage of the rich volcanic soil to plant early in the spring and harvest late in the fall. The gardeners reap a double profit from their volcano country—once for the soil and once for the heat.

Geothermal energy is also tapped in Hawaii; in Klamath Falls, Oregon; in Mexico, Hungary, the Soviet Union, and Japan; in Melun, near Paris; and in Lardarello, Italy, where steam has been producing electricity since 1904. In Sonoma County, about 90 miles north of San Francisco, a certain remote canyon lies at a kind of geological crossroads, where two sets of faults intersect. "The Geysers," hundreds of great towers of vapor, roar in this canyon like the collective voices of the damned in Dante's Inferno. The Pacific Gas and Electric Company, working with Union Oil, uses the dry steam at The Geysers to turn the blades of turbines, producing electric power. Their geothermal power plants, hidden in the resounding canyon, now supply one half of San Francisco's electricity and may soon, as more plants are built, supply the other half, too (unless earthquakes kill The Geysers first, since any shift in the ground could easily shut them off; developers, like most Californians, keep their fingers crossed).

On the other side of the Pacific, North Island, one of the two main islands of New Zealand, has a strip of territory some 160 miles long and 13 miles wide, along which, every 10 miles or so, there is a volcano, a steam hole, a boiling spring, or a *fumarole* (dry steam hole). Maori tribes settled here in the 14th century, and they have been using the heat of the Earth ever since. They prepare vegetable dyes by dropping bark into boiling geothermal pools and letting the bark stew overnight. Children dunk sweet corn into a hot pool, where it cooks in moments. Maori ritual feasts, called Hangi, are structured around meats wrapped in a sort of foil of palm leaves lowered into steam holes in sturdy baskets.

Since the 1940s, this hot strip of Earth has been turned to high-tech applications. Buildings and homes in the area now are heated by wells drilled into the hot subterranean reservoirs. The Tasman Pulp and Paper Plant in Kawerau is the largest geothermal plant of its kind in the world. At Wairakei, near Lake Taupo, a large electric power station was completed in 1963. "Since that time," says Keith Wilson, the Wairakei power station director, "we have been running continuously—virtually continuously—over a period of 25 years. The advantages of geothermal energy have been that it is on tap practically 24 hours a day, 52 weeks a year. It is unaffected by the weather, or external problems in the world," such as coal strikes or oil embargos.

Tapping geothermal power has its disadvantages, too. Hot water from the depths often is saturated with minerals, like water in black smokers (and for the same reasons). Pump up the water and it clogs the pipes. The pipes get arteriosclerosis. (On the other hand, some plants are now mining the brines in their own pipes.)

Pumping up too much water can deplete the underground reservoir. Eventually the whole geothermal field may begin to fade and its geysers and hot springs disappear. This has already happened on North Island, to the sorrow of the Maori. Heavy industry has stolen away many of their ritual pools. In theory, this damage can be repaired by pumping water back down underground to replace what has been pumped up. But this is easier said than done. In New Zealand, when the power plants tried it, the ground began to shake. The engineers stopped the pumps.

The Maori believe the hot springs were the answer to the prayers of their ancestors. The high priest of the first Maori canoe to arrive there, had never seen snow before he disembarked on North Island, and he prayed for warmth. According to a Maori elder of Rotorua, named Bubbles, "Our people regard this as part of our heritage. My older grandaunts and granduncles and grandparents, when they talked about the legend, would always say, 'These are what have been bestowed upon us. These were gifts from the gods. And so, as they were gifts, gifts are to be used, but not to be abused.'

"Scientists might have a different theory, but ours has lasted 600 years, and as the descendants of the passengers of that canoe, and especially of the high priest, we still feel that ours is probably better than the scientists' theory, anyway."

A Maori tribeswoman prepares flax for making a Piu Piu (skirt), in Rotorua, New Zealand. The Maori have relied upon New Zealand's steam holes and boiling springs for centuries; they count them as gifts of the gods.

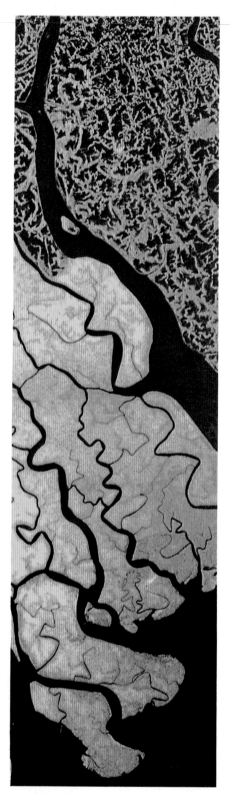

The Earth's first gift to us—the firm and solid base in space—is safe. No one has ever figured out how to blow up something as big as a planet (which, as one scientist has observed, is probably just as well).

But we can take none of the planet's other gifts for granted. Thanks to our success in mining, Earth's rich crust may be in some danger. We are unearthing treasures that took millions of years to fashion. We are consuming these treasures far faster than Earth can make more. Sooner or later we will have to admit that human hunger is infinite but the stores of Earth are finite. As resources expert M. King Hubbert once observed, "It is hard to know which is more remarkable, that it took 600 million years for the Earth to make its oil, or that it took 300 years to use it up."

Even the crust's common and bountiful gifts, its fresh water and rich soil, which we rarely think of as treasures—seldom think of at all—exist in limited quantities. Scientists are beginning to realize that we can exhaust these two fundamental elements of life, water and soil. Unlike wind and sunlight, they are not renewable. If we are greedy, we will drain the wells. If we farm carelessly, we will waste the good earth.

The human body is, by weight, 70 percent water, and each of us consumes about five pounds of water daily, in one form or another. A healthy adult can survive for weeks without food but only for a few days without water. Water is a prop of each individual life, and it is the lifeblood of society. Without water there would be no farming, since plants need water as much as people do. There would be little industry, for without plentiful water there could be neither lumber nor metal—all forests and most ore refineries require a great deal of fresh water. Commerce would be painfully constricted, since a country's waterways are its first and often its best throughways.

There is plenty of water on the planet, but most of it is in the oceans, and neither we nor our crops and animals can survive on salt water. We need fresh water, which is only 3 percent of the global supply. Even 3 percent is a vast resource. A trillion tons of water evaporate each day in the heat of sunlight—mostly from the sea; those trillion tons fall as rain, sleet, and snow. Some of this water is soaked up in the leaves and roots of plants and stored there; some gathers in lakes and pools. Much of it spills into streams and rivers and eventually flows back down into the sea, for another ride into the sky and down onto the land. This is the *water cycle*. The part of the cycle during which water is fresh keeps us alive.

This 3 percent of the planet's water is not spread evenly. In the United States, the East often is flooded while the

West goes thirsty. In the Soviet Union, nearly half the irrigated farmland depends upon two rivers, the Amu-Dar'ya and Syr-Dar'ya, and during droughts the rivers run dangerously low. Drought in Africa has brought about some of the worst famines of the century. In India, the Ganges River runs through endless cycles of flooding and drought. During the torrential monsoon season, the river overflows its banks, and often vast numbers of people are drowned or driven from their homes. (The flood-plains, being fertile farmlands, are as thickly settled as the slopes of some tropical volcanoes.) Then, during droughts, the river dwindles and the land becomes almost a desert. These life-giving and death-dealing cycles of the Ganges helped shape the Hindu vision of the universe as a place of endless creation and destruction.

Wars have been waged over water. In recent decades, India and Pakistan fought over rivers they shared; also Israel and Syria, and Iraq and Syria. In 1964, notes resources expert Richard J. Barnet, in *The Lean Years*, a water dispute between two states of the United States led to a legal battle and "language reminiscent of the sort that France and Germany used to employ just before they went to war." ("The aggressive policies of the State of Iowa," read one Supreme Court brief, "have caused great consternation to the State of Nebraska and its citizens, and have threatened to result in armed conflict on the part of landowners and the State of Iowa and its representatives.")

Such problems of unequal distribution have been with us since ancient times. But the twin explosions of the 20th century, in human population and in resource consumption, have put more and more of the world on the edge of "water famines." It is frightening how much water the United States now uses each day: In 1900, it was 40 billion gallons; in 1980, 700 billion gallons. The water that supports the American way is a veritable flood. The average American draws nearly 90 gallons of water a day for personal use, and far more has been drawn to supply him with the goods he takes for granted. "It takes thousands of gallons to produce a pound of beef for the table," says Barnet, "and more than 100,000 gallons to make an automobile." Include that water—the hidden springs and rivers that supply the American way of life—and the average American consumes an estimated 2,000 gallons of water a day.

The vineyards of California's Imperial Valley, and the sprawling suburbs of Los Angeles, draw water from hundreds of miles around, including massive amounts from the Colorado River. California's neighbors, many of whom are low on water themselves, resent what they see as a kind of city-state imperialism. The Colorado is fast becoming, in the words of one analyst, "water-short." It is the first great river in history that

This is the floodplain of the river Ganges, in Bangladesh, as seen on October 11, 1984, from the Space Shuttle. The river's floodwaters bring life and death to Bangladesh. The mottled gray and black areas near the coast of the Bay of Bengal (bottom) are cultivated fields linked by extensive irrigation and drainage channels. The more uniform gray area (top) is a region that often floods during the monsoon season. The area shown in this image is roughly 15 by 50 miles.

can hardly reach the sea. So many American cities and states tap it that by the time the river arrives in Mexico it has been reduced to a trickle. Adding insult to injury, the trickle is salty, because minerals and salts are more and more concentrated in the shrunken stream as it evaporates under the southwestern Sun. After years of protests from the Mexican government, the United States recently built a desalination plant near the border.

The American West taps another source of water: groundwater in sands, gravels, and porous rocks beneath the surface. There is 30 times more water in such buried reservoirs, *aquifers*, than in all lakes and streams combined. Beneath the High Plains, stretching all the way from South Dakota to Texas, is the Ogallala Aquifer. Water pumped up from the Ogallala irrigates a large part of America's most productive farmland.

The Ogallala, like the Colorado, is being overdrawn, and the water table—the height of water beneath the ground—is falling. In places, the ground itself has even begun to subside. It costs farmers more each year to pump water from the aquifer, because their wells must be sunk deeper, the water must be pumped up farther, and meanwhile fuel costs are rising. Some farms are running dry not for lack of water but for lack of money to pump it. Meanwhile, the aquifer is replenished so slowly that it may share the same fate as the oil fields of East Texas: The people of the High Plains may mine themselves right out of water. Experts believe the region will face severe water shortages before the end of the century. If used at current rates, the Ogallala Aquifer will run dry by the year 2020.

Rising populations, rising demand, and the high tide of 20th-century ingenuity have combined to put many parts of the United States in an untenable position. California and the Sun Belt have enjoyed extraordinary growth in large part through grand schemes for draining, pumping, and diverting Colorado River water. "Nonetheless," says Barnet, "the reality remains that some of the richest agricultural land and some of the fastest-growing population centers in the United States are in a desert."

The world picture is even grimmer, because poorer countries lack the resources to mount vast projects to try to save farmlands and alter geography. "World demand for water is quickly outstripping the supply," says environmentalist Bruce Stokes. "By the year 2000, population growth alone will at least double the demand for water in half the countries of the world."

LOSING GROUND   Soil, like fresh water, is one small part of a grand cycle in the life of the Earth. Molten rock rises up from the depths of the Earth. It hardens, and is worn by the erosive forces of wind and

*Galunggung volcano erupts
in Java, Indonesia, August 1982.*

water. Eventually (often after many eons of adventures and metamorphoses) it is reduced to bits, and washed by rains, rivers, and streams into the sea. This is the *rock cycle*. What we call earth, or dirt, is rock in the broken and pulverized part of its cycle.

If soil were only powdered stone, however, little or nothing would grow in it. Real soil also contains a rich mix of organic matter from the decay of living things that have died and been interred within it. Without this by-product of death, soil would be worthless to the living. With it, soil is alive with bacteria, fungi, mites, ants, millipedes, earthworms, and an occasional mole. They turn the soil and keep it full of air pockets and tunnels through which oxygen circulates, furthering more growth. In a myriad of ways, they keep soil a place in which a seed can sprout.

Because it is only a small part of the rock cycle, there isn't as much soil on this rocky planet as one might expect. Dig a hole almost anywhere in the world and soon you hit bedrock. Soil is just a thin layer; in some places it has drifted many yards thick, like snow, but in others it is only the thickness of a dime. Even where soil is thick, the topmost layer, or *topsoil*, which is most vital for plants, is only inches thin.

Plants help to hold this soil in place with their fine meshworks of roots, and their umbrellas of leaves, which break the wind, the rain, and the harsh light of the Sun. Farming encourages erosion partly because the plow breaks the natural ground cover, and each harvest exposes the bare soil to the sky for at least part of the year. Before man began farming the planet, erosion probably was around 9 billion tons of topsoil a year, slow enough to be replaced by the rock cycle. In 1984, according to a recent report of the Worldwatch Institute, erosion was about 25 billion tons. We are losing the ground beneath our feet much faster than Nature is putting it back, and soon we will start to feel the loss. Under topsoil there usually is a layer of subsoil, which is not nearly as productive, having less water and organic nutrients to offer plants. "Once you lose the topsoil, you're in trouble," says Tennessee soil conservationist Jim Bilyeu.

"Soil erosion is not new," says Bilyeu. "It's been going on since the world was created. But when man comes along and disturbs the soil and plants a crop on it, he accelerates the erosion process. Anytime we're using the land, we're going to accelerate erosion. What we have to look for is ways to slow those processes down, because we've kind of got used to enjoying three square meals a day."

The rich soil in western Tennessee is *loess*, silts from the edges of ancient glaciers. The loess was borne there from the North by colossal dust storms at the end of the last Ice Age, and ever since that time the land has been lush and green. American settlers, led by frontier guides such as Daniel Boone, found the country covered in fine, mature hardwood forests. A flowing spring and a tall walnut were signs of good farmland, and that was how many settlers picked their spot in the woods. They cleared the trees, plowed the fields, and made their farms the "breadbasket of the South."

Today the land is still rich and productive, but it is in trouble. At the start of this decade, farmers in western Tennessee were losing 14 tons of topsoil per acre each year. Nature puts back about 5 tons a year. So the farmers were losing ground fast: At that rate, they would lose an inch of topsoil in a dozen years. One lost inch of topsoil can mean a 6 percent drop in crop yields.

Responding to a statewide conservation program, many farmers stopped plowing in the fall and left the stubble of their summer crops in place, which helped prevent runoff. They also began double-cropping, growing wheat on the fields half of the year and soybeans the other half. Nearly 12 months of each year, there was vegetation of one kind or another growing on the field. In 1985, soil losses in western Tennessee had been cut to 10 tons per acre.

Nationwide, however, farmers feel they are being forced into more and more reckless patterns of working the land, because rising costs and bad years at the market have put many thousands of farms in danger of foreclosure. To keep production high enough to meet mortgage payments, farmers plow land that shouldn't be plowed—hilly land, dry land, tired land—and in a few years it is washed away in the rain, or gone with the wind. Worldwide, the problem is worse, as poverty and the population explosion are forcing more and more farmers onto poorer and poorer land. "So much soil from the Asian mainland blows over the Pacific Ocean," says resources expert Lester Brown, president of the WorldWatch Institute, "that scientists taking air samples at the Mauna Loa observatory in Hawaii can now tell when spring plowing starts in North China."

It is perverse of us, Brown argues, to keep such a careful inventory of oil reserves while we treat our soil like dirt. The loss of soil may be worse in the long run than the loss of oil. Bilyeu agrees. "When you get right down to the bare facts and weigh all the odds, I myself would say that soil is more valuable than oil or gold, because you can't eat gold and you can't drink oil and survive. But you can grow food in good soil. So if it comes down to a matter of survival, are we going to have enough to eat? Or are we going to have all the oil we want? I'll take the best land every time."

Our lives depend on an ultra-thin layer of the Earth—its soil. But many farms are losing tons of soil per acre per year. Madison County, Tennessee.

When we think of life on Planet Earth, we often imagine the two realms, life and Earth, as separate—as if life were a bird perching on a stony peak, or moss clinging to a boulder. In fact, however, life and Earth have been together so long they are virtually inseparable. In oil, in coal, in chalk, and in other rocks and minerals, one cannot say where one realm ends and the other begins. Soil is the best instance of the intertwining of biology and geology. Soil is literally a collaboration between life and Earth. It represents the disintegration of rock mingled with the death of living things; and out of this dark mixture rise the tasseled shoots of wheat and wild grasses. When the grasses die they enrich the earth from which they sprang. Indeed, the life cycle bears a family resemblance to the water cycle and the rock cycle—and soil is their common ground.

We, too, are part of the planetary life cycle. We spring from the Earth, and each of us will return to it. But as a race, we are taking more than we are giving. We are interrupting the great cycles of life and of the Earth. We run the risk of breaking the wheels that have turned rock to soil to rock, life to death to life. Or perhaps the grand cycles of Nature are too big to break—perhaps if we are foolish, they will break us. To sustain a healthy society, we must somehow strike a balance between our hunger for the things of this world, and our hope for a human future on the planet.

How much do we need in order to live the good life? How much can we safely take from the planet? What do the haves of this world owe to the have-nots? What do the haves of the present owe to the unborn of the future—who may be have-nots because of our excesses? These are among the great political, scientific, and moral questions that face our generation and the next.

There still are places on Earth that are almost un-touched. Yellowstone is overrun with tourists but otherwise intact—a landscape preserved by law. Antarctica is the last unpopulated continent—as of 1985, protected by international treaty. The floor of the sea is as remote as any spot on the surface of the planet. Should we mine these last pristine land- and seascapes? There are proposals to do so in each of these places: the first for geothermal power, the second for oil, the third for metallic minerals.

Yellowstone is a classic contest between the hunger for power and the desire to preserve the Earth. There probably is a huge, hot magma chamber beneath it. The heat of this magma powers Yellowstone's geysers, boiling mud pools, hot springs, and fumaroles. It is one of the world's best places for geothermal power.

No one is seriously proposing that we build a turbine

on top of Old Faithful. But power companies have leased land just outside the perimeter of the national park and are prepared to drill if granted the go-ahead by the government. No one knows if subterranean plumbing links the hot pools and springs just outside Yellowstone to the sources of the geysers inside the park. According to Donald White of the USGS, we cannot hope to exploit the geothermal energy of an area and also preserve its geysers. It is a clear-cut choice: one or the other.

The country needs every drop of electricity it can get, the utility companies argue. The country needs every drop of wildness it can get, say the conservationists.

Yellowstone is America's first and favorite national park, and its tallest geyser is an American symbol, like the Statue of Liberty. Probably it will never be chopped down and carved into kilowatts. As Senator Malcolm Wallop of Wyoming said at a Senate subcommittee hearing, "How would you like to go down in history as the man who ruined Old Faithful? I wouldn't want it on my record." But what about a thousand wild spots that do not have celebrity to protect them? How fast do we overrun the Earth before we admit we are going too far? How far do we exceed Earth's equilibrium before we realize we have to strike a balance?

"The issue," says Lester Brown, "is not whether equilibrium will eventually be reestablished. It will. If the deterioration is not arrested by humankind, then Nature will ultimately intervene with its own checks. The issue is whether . . . a new reverence for land will be forced upon us by wisdom or regret."

Fate of the Earth

In my beginning is my end. . . .
In my end is my beginning.

T. S. ELIOT *Four Quartets*

Overleaf: Monteverde Cloud
Forest Reserve, Costa Rica.

7 / Fate of the Earth

Aztec Indians thought the fate of the Earth depended completely on them. Long before they were born, their priests and wizards said, the Sun had died four times, and four times it had been reborn. The Aztecs lived in the age of Quetzalcoatl, the Fifth Sun, whose emblem was a human face. If this Sun died—amid earthquakes—it would be for the last time. With stone knives, the priests carved out the hearts of human sacrifices, hoping to keep the Sun alive and save the world.

In the Hindu vision of the fate of the Earth, there is nothing anyone can do to delay the end. On the other hand, the end is not truly final—death always is followed by rebirth. The eternal Brahma creates and destroys the universe as casually as a mortal might open his eyes and shut them again.

Old Icelanders, who endured a land of rock, ice, and fire, had a dark view of fate. The Norse gods lived in Asgard, a celestial city they built themselves, high above the clouds. Safe in a palace in Asgard, the gods played, sang, and feasted—except for their king, Odin. The lord of the gods neither smiled nor ate; he gave his share of food to two wolves that crouched at his feet, and two ravens that perched on his shoulders. He brooded because he could see the end of the world coming, the Twilight of the Gods.

As a young god, Odin had descended to the Well of Wisdom and begged its keeper, Mimir, for a single draught. Mimir told him he could take a drink only if he gave an eye for it. Odin paid an eye for wisdom. After he drank, Odin had a vision of the end.

He saw a dragon gnawing at the roots of the great tree whose lofty boughs sheltered Asgard. Someday the very trunk of this world tree would shake and totter. Then there would be "an ax age, a sword age, a wind age, a wolf age." The fallen god Loki, with a horde of giants, would gallop up on a rainbow and storm the heights of Asgard. In the battle, Earth would burn, and all the nine worlds. Odin himself would fall to the wolf Fenrir on the vast plain called Vigrid. Nothing good would be left alive.

Today scientists also entertain more than one scenario of the fate of the Earth. Of these, there is only one that is as sure, somber, and irrevocable as Odin's vision.

Astronomers believe an average star lives 10 billion years. The nearest star to Earth, our Sun, is an average star, and it is now 5 billion years old. One half its store of energy is gone—half of the hydrogen in its core has fused to the denser element helium. In another 5 billion years or so, most of its remaining hydrogen will have turned to helium. Then the Sun will collapse upon itself, and the energy released by this infalling will heat it rapidly to 100 million degrees centigrade. It will expand violently, becoming a red giant. As it grows, it will swallow first Mercury, then Venus, and then, perhaps—if it keeps expanding—it will engulf our Earth and Moon. Whether the conflagration actually reaches us or not, Earth will burn to a cinder. The Fang tribe of Gabon, West Africa, imagined something like this. They feared that the Sun would someday chase the stars, one by one, and then the Moon, and eat them.

There is no way to save the planet from this fate. But then, there is no urgency, either. Five billion years is a long time. (A student at an astronomer's lecture is supposed to have exclaimed, in relief, "Oh, five *billion* years. I thought you said five *million*.") It is one third the age of the universe since its creation in the Big Bang, and it is a little longer than the Earth has existed so far. That puts our planet in its prime, a young middle age, not the sort of vision to make us sit apart and brood at the banquet hall. The end has the cool inevitability of astrophysics; it must be the fate of many planets in many solar systems, those with life and those without.

However, there are other fateful scenarios, scenarios much closer to Odin's vision and much closer to our own lifetimes. Many scientists think we are moving—slowly or quickly—toward big changes on our planet. One of these scenarios eerily resembles the twilight of the gods. These nearer fates of the Earth are more difficult to accept—and fortunately, we may not have to. They are *not* inevitable, and this fact lends them a different color than Odin's vision, or the astrophysicists'. The immediate fate of the Earth is not determined solely by invisible powers, or inanimate forces of rock, fire, and ice. Rather, the near future is shaped by the fact that Earth is *alive*. Life has extraordinary influence on the Earth, far more than we ever realized. Life has the power to alter the world. The discovery of life's strength is among the most recent revolutions in the Earth sciences, and it may prove to be the most important, for at the moment, we are the dominant living things on the planet. To this extent, we control the fate of the Earth.

Earth scientists are not used to placing life in the foreground of their perspectives. Geology and biology (as an onlooker has observed) are two separate departments in the science building, with a long, echoing corridor between the two wings. Until recently, the two kinds of scientist could spend years without meeting—and then it was only by appointment, in the dusty mortuaries of the rock record, where they labored together to assign a date to the death of a fossil fish.

Today, however, more and more geologists and biologists share an extraordinary ambition: They hope to learn the ways that rock and life meet; to understand precisely how the presence of life, the sum of all the animals and plants, affects the planet.

The stretches of Earth that are mantled with life are called, collectively, the *biosphere*. The word connotes an attempt to think clearly about life in the round, life as a whole. Though the spheres of stone, water, and air—the lithosphere, hydrosphere, and atmosphere—are complex, the biosphere is more so. It is without question the richest, most varied, and most intricate of all the spheres of Earth. It includes perhaps five million separate species of animals and plants, only a small fraction of which have been named and studied. It includes ancient, single-celled organisms—bacteria—that are neither animal nor plant and that are invisible without the aid of a microscope, but that through sheer numbers carry enormous weight and influence in the world. The biosphere, of course, also includes us.

The sphere of life extends typically only about 10 to 20 feet into the soil, and it has no permanent home in the air. Seen from space, it is merely a thin veneer. Yet life does more than cling to the planet like lichen to a rock. It touches the lithosphere, Earth's stone foundations; the hydrosphere, our world's waters; and the atmosphere, our blue blanket of gas. It interlocks with these three inanimate spheres of Earth in ways only partly visible to us, like the massive gears in the "Imaginary Prisons" of the Italian master-etcher Piranesi. One well-known result of these interlockings is the series of chain reactions that we call, in shorthand, the greenhouse effect. Life, by altering the composition of certain gases in the atmosphere, notably carbon dioxide and methane, actually changes the composition of the air and hence the way the atmosphere handles the Sun's energy and therefore global climate. The biosphere is a kind of silent partner in many other grand transactions of the Earth, from the weathering of rock to the creation of it.

The term "biosphere" was introduced casually more than 100 years ago, in 1875, by a brilliant Austrian geologist,

An etching by the 18th-century Italian master Giovanni Battista Piranesi. Today, scientists' ideas of the architecture of the Earth are rather like the scene in this etching. Investigators can see the solid rock of the planet's foundations, overgrown with greenery, overrun with people, and canopied in cloudy sky. Over and above this, they sense the existence of a sort of vast, hidden superstructure, an invisible meeting of wheels within wheels, cycles within cycles. Somehow, rock, water, air, and life meet, fit and link together to make our world a living machine. The chemical elements of which life is built, including carbon, nitrogen, phosphorus, and sulfur, circle through this machine in mysterious ways. The details are still as sketchy as the airy architecture in Piranesi's etching.

Eduard Suess, toward the end of a book on the Alps. It was introduced again, more forcefully, 51 years later, in 1926, by a Russian mineralogist, Vladimir Ivanovitch Vernadsky, in lectures that were published in France a few years later under the title *La Biosphere*. But even at the dawn of the Space Age, during the International Geophysical Year, from 1957 to 1958, most experiments treated the Earth as an inanimate object. Measurements were made of Planet Earth's wobble, magnetic field, upper atmosphere, aurora; intensive inquiries were made into our world's volcanic eruptions, quakes, ocean eddies, and weather; but the life that mantles the planet was neglected.

Since the International Geophysical Year, as scientists have learned more of how the Earth works, they have learned greater respect for the power of the biosphere. They have realized that it is in some ways the fastest-working part of the living machine. It will get more and more attention in the next few years, not just because we ourselves are part of the biosphere, but also because its effects are dramatic during the spans of time we can all appreciate easily—our generation, our children's, our grandchildren's. According to a report sponsored by the National Research Council in 1983, "Improved understanding of the biosphere and its relation to the other great domains of the Earth has a special urgency." The study of the biosphere is urgent, the authors of the report say, because the changes that scientists are now predicting have profound significance for humankind and for every other species alive. It is urgent, too, "because of the rapidity with which changes are taking place."

THE FIRST CELL

It is hard for us to recognize the extent of life's influence upon the planet, because we are right in the middle of it. In fact, being the dominant form of life on the planet, each of us is at the biosphere's cutting edge.

If we look at the dim and distant past, however, the power of life stands out more plainly. Life's ability to change the Earth is one of the great lessons of the past.

As it is usually told, the story of the origin of life on Earth is a little misleading; it sounds like an immigrant success saga. Life, it is thought, probably started out on Earth as a single, humble cell somewhere in an ancient tidal pool. It was an assortment of molecules held together in a flimsy bag. It had five cents in its pocket, spoke no English, and hadn't the faintest idea of where to sleep. From this humble beginning, after years of hard work and almost unbelievable luck, that single cell multiplied and diversified. It became, from nothing, the soil king, the sea king, the air king. Its descendants colonized the highest peaks and the deepest seas. They found their way into the Sahara, and even to the dry, frozen valleys of Antarctica, where they set up shop inside rocks. The cell is an immigrant no more but a paterfamilias, with a nephew in every going thing on the planet.

Since we are the first part of the biosphere to learn to talk, it is perhaps natural that we like to brag a little. But this yarn about our shabby early years misses some of the real wonder of the story. Life was really not so much an immigrant on the planet as a founding father. The planet was here first, of course; but life got in literally on the ground floor.

It is easy to understand how the immigrant story got started. Biologists *used* to think that the world's first creatures were recent arrivals. The oldest fossils they could find had made their first appearance in rock at the start of the geologic period called the Cambrian. We can now date those rocks fairly accurately, by measuring their state of radioactive decay. They are 570 million years old. Rocks of that age contain trilobites (hard-shelled marine creatures like the larvae of horsehoe crabs) and a few other marine animals, along with algae. To generations of biologists and paleontologists, those seemed to be life's first notes. The rock record of the Earth goes back far beyond the Precambrian, but for most of those years, scientists thought, Earth had been as dead as the Moon.

No one really believed the first living thing was a trilobite, however. Trilobites are complicated creations containing billions of cells; in evolutionary terms, they are not much more primitive than antelopes and blue whales, daffodils and sequoias. Life had to have started more humbly, as a single cell, and worked its way up. Even a single cell is an enormously

Beginning some 570 million years ago, trilobites crawled along the bottom of Paleozoic seas. For a long time, they were thought to be the oldest fossils on Earth.

intricate affair and must have required a long time to come together. Compounds had to fumble together into a single cell, and then the first cells themselves had to gather together into many-celled creatures. Each of these steps in evolution must have required an enormous number of inventions and innovations. The fumbling could have gone on a long time and left no trace in the fossil record.

So life was unquestionably older than the Cambrian. Nevertheless, it seemed reasonable to suppose that the planet had lain barren for many hundreds of millions of years—perhaps billions—while the first chemical compounds somehow evolved into that first cell.

In 1953, Stanley Tyler, a geologist from the University of Wisconsin, was poking around old iron ore prospect pits on the northern shore of Lake Superior, just east of Thunder Bay. There he came upon a mass of rock 2 billion years old. The rock was chert, a form of quartz, and it was part of the Gunflint iron formation (so called because early settlers used to browse there for flints to spark the gunpowder in their muskets and blunderbusses).

Tyler knew that the walls of the abandoned quarry might hold treasures infinitely more precious than iron ore or flints. For a few years he had been talking with a brilliant young biologist at Harvard, Elso Barghoorn, about a new approach to fossil-hunting. This rock was just what they needed for their experiment, being exquisitely well preserved. With a diamond saw, Tyler cut samples of the chert into transparently thin slices and sent them to Barghoorn.

To the naked eye, the quartz held no fossils. But Barghoorn put one of Tyler's ultrathin slices under a microscope. The very first slice he looked at was filled to bursting with the fossilized remnants of single cells and with chains of single cells linked together. Some of them looked remarkably like cells still living today; others were unfamiliar. One star-shaped creature had never been seen before and apparently did not make it into the modern world. Barghoorn named it *Eoastrion*—the "dawn star." It was three times older than the oldest trilobite.

With a single glance through a microscope, Barghoorn had extended the history of life far back into the Earth's dim past. Biologists and geologists with microscopes immediately began slicing and scanning older outcrops of rock; they found microfossils that pushed the date of life's birthday even farther back. In September 1977, Stanley Awramik, a biogeologist from the University of California at Santa Barbara, discovered what are probably the oldest fossils yet. Awramik was working in a hot corner of Western Australia, a place so remote that 19th-century prospectors named it North Pole. The spot is famous

Eoastrion, the dawn star. This microscopic fossil was found preserved in the chert of the Gunflint formation, in 1953. It is nearly two billion years old.

among geologists for a hoary set of rocks called the Warrawoona Group.

Warrawoona rocks are about 3.5 billion years old, as measured by the state of decay of their radioactive elements. That places them among the most ancient rocks surviving on Earth. Yet they have been spared most of the Earth's revolutions and upheavals. Much of the Warrawoona Group has rarely been compressed or folded—barely even tilted. Awramik found microfossils in one of its older layers. If the fossils are indeed as old as the rock in which they were embedded and did not somehow sift down into it at a later date (a slight possibility that has not yet been ruled out), then life is at least 3.5 billion years old.

It is as eerie to see these ancient cells afloat in quartz as it is to look at ancient Romans lying sprawled, still in their togas, on the mosaic floors of Pompeii. The bodies of those men, women, and children (and even one Roman dog) are miraculously well preserved. Apparently they were killed by the hot, poisonous gases of Vesuvius and then covered over and entombed in an instant by the fine black ash of the terrible eruption. Some of them seem to have been running when they were struck down. The ancient cells, like the Romans, must have been entombed quite suddenly. The water around them, through some chemical process still poorly understood, literally turned to stone. Many cells were caught in the act of dividing in two; one can still see, preserved in stone, one of these primordial cells cinching in at the waist. To look closely at such an apparition can make a biologist's hair prickle, for it is not a cast or an imprint, as most fossils are. *It is the cell itself.*

"It is like a fly in amber, or a rattlesnake head in clear plastic, which you can go out and buy in the souvenir shops in the desert," Awramik explains.

Carefully, with drops of hydrofluoric acid, investigators have etched some primordial cells out of Gunflint silica. The body of the cell is still intact; the wall retains its shape. The chemicals the cell was made of have degraded over the years, of course, but they still are the same organic compounds of which all life is built—carbon combined with hydrogen, oxygen, and perhaps a little sulfur. We have been permitted to witness the birth and death of some of the first lives on Earth.

LIFE OUT OF HELL   One cannot fully appreciate those Adams and Eves of cell life unless one remembers what the planet was like in its early years, just before the first cells formed.

In the beginning, the Earth was so little like our world today that it might almost have been another planet. It was a desert without seas or shores, without soil or green leaves—a shimmering orb of red-hot rock from horizon to horizon. This first age of Earth began some 4.6 billion years ago, with the birth of the planet, and lasted nearly 1 billion years. It is called the *Hadean Aeon*, after Hades, the hell of the ancient Greeks.

For the Greeks, Hades was a realm of shades bounded by the rivers Fire, Woe, Wailing, and Oblivion. No mortal could descend there and come back up into the sunshine, unless by the special intervention of the gods. For modern scientists, the Hadean Aeon really is a kind of underworld, a lost land, because nothing of it has survived for our examination. The surface must have been pummeled continually by collisions with the millions of shards of rubble that littered outer space, remnants of the birth of the solar system. Any thin crust that formed, filming over a wound from one of these meteorites, probably was broken and melted down again in the churning planet, which was then still largely molten.

Every glimpse we have of Hadean days is hellish. Some astrophysicists believe the Moon was horribly close—perhaps only 11,000 miles off (now it is 250,000 miles away). So the present stately waltz of Earth and Moon was then a crazy jitterbug. The Moon revolved around the Earth not in a month's time but in about six hours. Its pocked face filled a large part of the sky and would have swept close enough to make you duck your head. The planet and its satellite were forever blocking each other's light, and total eclipses were common. Being so near, the Moon also raised massive tides—not of water but of molten rock.

The Earth spun much faster in the beginning; days and nights were only about five hours long. While daylight lasted, the Sun's deadly ultraviolet rays seared the surface. Each night, pools of swirling lava glistened in the red light of the molten Moon.

There was no air, or at least not what we call air today. The planet was surrounded at first by hydrogen and helium, the most common gases in the universe, and they formed Earth's first atmosphere. Very early, however, the infant Sun blew these light gases away as it flared to full strength. Thereafter, the only atmosphere the Earth had was what it made for itself—the gases that seeped up through cracks and fissures and volcanic craters. These gases probably were methane, carbon dioxide, ammonia, and water vapor. Shooting stars flamed through this primitive atmosphere day and night, as meteorites fell to Earth from space. They were like tons of coal tumbling down a chute from space, into a molten bin. They were a gift from space of millions of tons of organic carbon, and they shook the Earth as they splashed down.

Comets fell, too. If we are right in believing that comets are rocks encased in many tons of ice, then each comet must have brought in huge quantities of water. But the planet was still much too hot for water to exist anywhere except in the form of steam. If a single drop of rain chanced to fall, it vaporized instantly. Between the water vapor that poured up from cracks in the Earth, and the ice that fell with the comets, Earth acquired a vast water supply, but none of it stayed on the ground.

In short, there were no signs of a bright future, only the sorts of omens that were believed, in the Renaissance, to foretell the deaths of princes: eruptions, eclipses, earthquakes, and falling stars. There was virtually none of the gas we call oxygen. There was no life—none could have arisen in such a violent and chaotic world. If there were any lulls in the belching of volcanoes and the hissing of lava, those rare moments were silent as the grave.

Hundreds of millions of years passed. At last the Great Bombardment slowed and some of the terrible heat created by the Earth's formation radiated away and was lost to space. The planet's primitive atmosphere cooled to a temperature below the boiling point of water. Then, from the clouds of water vapor, rain began to fall. Gray skies showered black plains. Rain fell on the rivers of lava and steamed back up in thunderclouds. Rainwater pooled within the steep rims of craters that still pocked the Earth, left by the impact of the latest meteorites; and water flooded the vast calderas of extinct volcanoes. It flowed across the face of the planet in huge floods when the crust, heaving, shuffled the water from place to place. The primordial landscape became, as one writer has put it, a study in black and blue: the black of basalt, the blue of shallow seas.

Among innumerable pools, streams, and rivulets, each of them swirled by the great tidal pull of the nearby Moon, the Hadean passed at last into the *Archean Aeon*. Masses of rock dating back to the Archean have been found exposed to the air in Canada, Greenland, Africa, and Australia. There are smaller outcrops in South America, Scandinavia, southern India, and elsewhere in Asia, and there is a fringe of Archean crust along the northern shore of Antarctica. The Archean is the beginning of the historical record of Planet Earth; the Warrawoona Group is fairly early Archean.

Given this history, it is an astonishing fact, one whose significance we are only just beginning to take in, that some of the earliest rocks preserved on the planet contain cells entombed within them. There cannot have been much time, then, between the end of the Great Bombardment and the day Earth came alive. The conclusion seems inescapable: Life arose almost as soon as the planet ascended from hell.

Gustav Courbet's Marine. *From the primordial sea arose the first life on Earth—and perhaps the only life in this solar system.*

THE ORIGIN OF LIFE

How, then, did life arise? We do not know the answer yet, but what we do know suggests something about the nature of life on Earth and perhaps about the power of the modern biosphere as well; for, while the precise details of the creation remain one of the most baffling—and captivating—problems in modern science, many investigators feel that the results of recent laboratory experiments do help to illuminate the story in the fossil record. The genesis of life on Earth, these investigators say, could have been much quicker and simpler than biochemists once supposed. Earth may have slipped naturally, readily, and gracefully into life, given the first opportunity.

Most test-tube investigations of the origin of life are lineal descendants of what must be the most famous student science project in history. In 1953, while Stanley Tyler was slicing up quartz near Thunder Bay, Stanley Miller, a graduate student at the University of Chicago, asked a glassblower to make a simple apparatus. It was really little more than a circle of glass tubing, but it was designed to represent conditions on the early Earth. At the bottom, a big flask of boiling water was the primordial sea. Steam rising from the boiling water traveled up the tube to a second flask, where it mingled with methane, ammonia, hydrogen, and water vapor, gases of the early atmosphere. As the steam sank back down to the lower flask, it cooled and condensed back into water droplets—primordial rain. At the very end of the circuit, there was a bend in the tube. Any large particles that had formed in the liquid during its brief ride from "sea" to "sky" and back again would collect in this bend.

These are the flasks that Stanley Miller used in his famous experiment, while still a graduate student. The lower flask represents the sea; the upper flask, the sky.

It was a closed system; water circulated from the sea flask to the sky flask and back to sea, over and over, as it had on the Earth itself.

Miller, then 23, was a student of the Nobel Prize-winning physical chemist Harold Urey. Miller had asked Urey to suggest a good dissertation topic, and Urey had persuaded his student to tackle a problem that seemed as deep at the time as the riddle of the chicken and the egg. Biochemists knew that all life is made of complex molecules called *amino acids* and an assortment of other chemical building blocks. But scientists could find no amino acids in nature that had not been made by living things. Which came first, the chicken or the egg? Which came first, amino acids or living things? If only life can make these molecules, but no life can exist without them, how could life ever get started? Urey was convinced that conditions on the primitive Earth must somehow have spontaneously created the first amino acids.

At first Miller wanted to bathe his apparatus in strong ultraviolet light to simulate the primordial Sun. That proved impractical. Instead, he used a Tesla coil to send blue sparks, with the strength of 60,000 volts, crackling through the tubing just beneath the "atmosphere" flask to simulate lightning. He ran the apparatus for a week, and for hours he sat in the same room with it, with an open book in his lap, trying to study but too excited to focus on the page in front of him. The flask must sometimes have looked, in his imagination, like the Hadean sea itself. The crackling must have sounded like primordial lightning bolts. Inside the apparatus, the water slowly turned pink, and then red. When Miller analyzed the chemicals in the water, using standard techniques of paper chromatography, he found it full of amino acids. They were the very same building blocks out of which all plants and animals build their proteins!

News of this result electrified the scientific world. "It was the experiment that broke the logjam," says biochemist William Day in his book *Genesis on Planet Earth*. The flasks' simplicity and their high yield, says Day, "were enough to show that the first step in the origin of life was not a chance event but one that had been inevitable."

This experiment was easy to reproduce, and it has since been run successfully with many variations in the recipe, almost always yielding quantities of compounds once thought to be made solely by living systems. No one has made life yet, only its building blocks; but this kind of experiment proves that life does not hold exclusive patents on its own ingredients. Long before life arose, Planet Earth was in the amino acid business. Indeed, the primordial Earth, given nothing but the most plausible circumstances and the simplest chemical ingre-

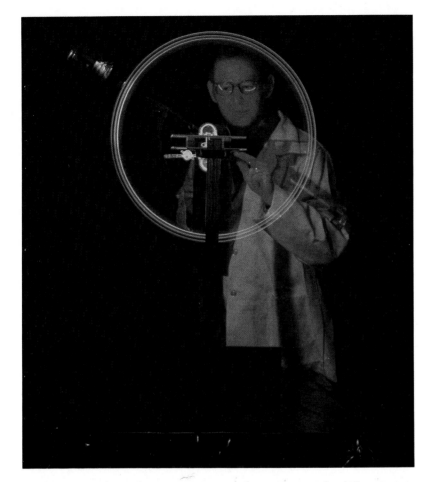

David Usher broods over his day-night machine, which simulates sunrise and sunset on our world some four billion years ago. In this machine, as in Miller's flasks, the simple precursors of life have come together readily.

dients, must have been stewing with amino acids. (The Great Bombardment contributed three of the most basic and necessary ingredients: water, carbon, and energy.) Through its constant agitation, the very hellishness of the young planet would have sped the birth of life by throwing these amino acids and organic molecules together in almost infinite combinations. The basic ingredients of life just fell together.

Miller's experiment is now being carried forward, with variations, all over the world. Currently Chris McKay, an earth scientist at NASA's Ames research facility near San Francisco, is experimenting with an apparatus that replaces Miller's relatively weak Tesla coil with something closer to the power of a thunderbolt. His apparatus generates sparks at upwards of 200 thousand volts. Lightning, McKay says, makes new compounds not because of its electric current but also because of the sudden wave it generates in passing through the air—the shock wave that we hear as thunder when it reaches our ears. McKay's "Michaelangelo Spark" is strong enough to make thunder. It yields simple organic molecules—in particular, hydrogen cyanide, ethane, and ethylene—which McKay believes represent some of Earth's first steps toward life.

In a gentler approach, David Usher of Cornell University uses a heat lamp. The lamp rotates slowly around a simple and ingenious arrangment of flasks. Usher's primordial soup is warmed gradually as the "sun lamp" rises; it bakes when the "Sun" is directly overhead, and finally it is chilled nearly to freezing in the darkness after the "Sun" sets. This "day-night machine" simulates neatly the conditions we think prevailed in the average ancient tidal pool. The machine can be left running for months, and the uppermost flask is subjected automatically and repeatedly to cycles of hot and cold, light and dark, wet and dry.

So far, Usher has used the day-night machine to examine only one small chemical step in the synthesis of ribonucleic acid (RNA). He is building upon work by the Salk Institute's Leslie Orgel, who proved that the building blocks of RNA and DNA can assemble easily under simulated Hadean conditions. At one crucial point in the assembly, there are two possible styles of construction, only one of which is actually found in living things. Both styles of construction occurred in Orgel's experiments. Usher hopes to demonstrate that if the experiment is allowed to run long enough, the only style that

When David Deamer mixes lipids (fatty compounds that compose the membranes of living cells) with water, the lipids form lovely and curious shapes, as seen in this photomicrograph. Deamer thinks such simple sacs, tubes, and bags formed readily in the tidepools of primeval Earth, and could have been the antecedents of cell membranes.

will survive in the flask is the one we find in the RNA of our own bodies.

David Deamer of the University of California at Davis re-creates day-night cycles on a glass microscope slide. He is interested in the way the cell membrane, the bag that holds all the cell's working parts, might have formed. Deamer coats a glass slide with lipids, the fatty compounds that make up the cell membrane, and then adds solitary strands of deoxyribonucleic acid (DNA), the ticker tape that holds all the cell's blueprints and plans. When he subjects this slide to cycles of warm and cold, wet and dry, the lipids automatically form tiny globs and spheres, like single cells; the globs neatly enclose and protect the strands of DNA. The resulting sphere of lipid and DNA is still a far cry from life, of course, but it is at least a quick sketch of a cell. Thus this step in the creation of life could have happened quite naturally and spontaneously in a tidal pool.

All these laboratory inquiries into the origin of life have a serious problem that no one has yet solved. In all animals and plants, strands of DNA are built up according to a universal and very beautiful arrangement of smaller molecules to form a double helix—a sort of spiral staircase made of molecules. This double helix is the code of life, perhaps the finest and most impressive piece of molecular architecture we know. It is ab-

In a variation of the experiment at left, David Deamer took lipid-like compounds found in meteorites and mixed them with water. As before, the substances on the glass slide formed microscopic structures that bear interesting resemblances to simple cells. Since meteorites rained down plentifully upon the early Earth, this is an experiment that Nature must have conducted many times.

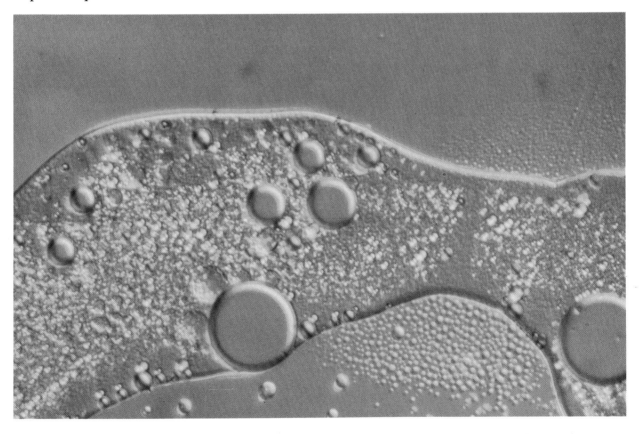

solutely essential to the functioning and reproduction of each living cell on the planet. Biochemists still can't imagine how it could have come together. Some scientists believe the DNA problem simply cannot be solved, that it is the ultimate logjam.

Lynn Margulis, a biologist at Boston University and an authority on the early evolution of life, is optimistic about the future of these experiments. "I'm not claiming life has been made in the laboratory," she says. "But I think it's a question of 15 years and it will be." Usher won't venture such a prediction. "It's always very hard to guess where science will be," he says. "The most exciting things are very often the most unexpected." Still, he hopes a grander version of his day-night machine, one with many more components and ingredients, will be constructed at some point, and allowed to run for a few years.

"It probably would produce something extremely interesting," Usher says. "Because after all, life *did start*. And maybe it didn't take as long to get going as people think."

If this line of thought is correct, then life is not a sort of waif, or immigrant, but a true native of the Earth. Life was born here almost as soon as the Earth itself had settled down into something approaching calm. Life was present here virtually on the third day of creation. Infant life and young Earth evolved side by side, and each changed the other. Very early, life molded the atmosphere of the Earth as powerfully as the hands of a potter shape the clay on a wheel. Life made the air breathable and the land livable.

These innovations came about through no conscious design, life being as yet nothing but a mindless sea of single cells. Indeed, life wrought these innovations while in the throes of two crises, the second of which was due to a blind and dangerous turn in its early evolution.

The two crises have a modern sound. They were global famine and toxic waste.

The very first cells on Earth probably had plenty to eat. They were in the same position a cell would enjoy if it arose by chance in one of Stanley Miller's flasks. They were floating in a virtual sea of chicken soup. They simply feasted upon the organic molecules in the water around them, molecules that had lacked the wit, grace, or luck to come to life. Fresh supplies of amino acids were constantly generated around them by ultraviolet rays, lightning bolts, and the bubbling cauldrons of submarine vents. Earth was for them an Eden, a Tahitian paradise.

Eventually, however, as cells prospered and multiplied, the supply of loose organic molecules thinned out through overgrazing. Life on Earth approached an early dead end. It is even conceivable that life failed, and then arose again, more than once, until a few pioneering cells finally invented a solution. They arrived at photosynthesis. Through this new process these early cells used the radiant energy of sunlight to build, within themselves, fresh supplies of organic molecules.

This was a creative answer to a fundamental problem, and it has never been rivaled or superseded. Life survived by courtesy of photosynthesis, and modern life could not endure without it.

Photosynthesis, however, did not immediately end the global famine. To grow, to make internal repairs, and to reproduce itself, each living cell has two fundamental requirements: energy and building materials. Sunlight could supply the energy. But it could not supply raw materials, the atoms and molecules that are the building blocks of organic molecules. Hydrogen is one of these essential elements. A cell that can't get enough hydrogen is doomed.

Now, when cells first learned to harness sunlight, they probably got their hydrogen from the same place they got all their food—loose organic matter. In effect, they used the great invention of photosynthesis merely to stretch the scraps of food they already had lying around. As the famine continued, however, such scraps got harder and harder to come by. Life was hanging by a thread.

It is our cosmic good fortune, as the lineal descendants of these primordial cells, that some of them at last hit upon a new source of hydrogen atoms. They got hydrogen by splitting up molecules of hydrogen sulfide, which spewed plentifully from the volcanoes and vents in the Earth's crust. Cells that could derive energy from sunlight, and also held this new patent for splitting sulfides, were truly independent of the bits of organic molecules in the primordial soup. With them, the global famine was finally past.

Life went along peaceably enough for perhaps 100 million years. Then a cell evolved a second innovation. It managed to split a molecule that was far more abundant than hydrogen sulfide—hydrogen dioxide, known as water. This molecule took 10 times as much energy to break apart, but the cell that could perform this trick had it made. Thereafter all the wealth it needed in the world was sunlight and seawater.

These new cells' brand of photosynthetic pigments tinted them bluish green, or cyan, and for this coloring they get their name, *cyanobacteria*. Beginning perhaps 2.6 billion years ago, cyanobacteria achieved unprecedented success. They swept across the seas like Attila's Huns. They multiplied so wildly, with their battle cry of "Sun and sea, sea and Sun," that

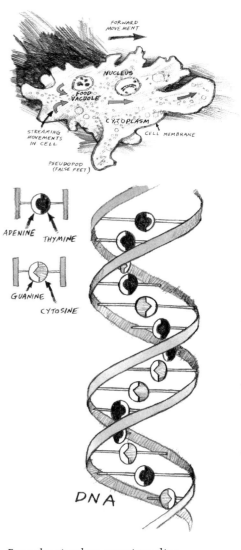

Even the simplest organism alive, a single cell, is an extraordinarily complex creation. Coiled within the nucleus of this amoeba is the miracle of DNA, the spiral staircase of molecules that contains all the information the cell needs to grow, to make repairs, and to reproduce itself. The four working parts of the DNA molecule—adenine, thymine, guanine, and cytosine—are fairly simple. However, no one knows how these parts came together to make DNA, or how the first cell leapt to life. Cells like the amoeba in this sketch were preceded by more primitive cells, whose DNA was not collected in a nucleus, but was scattered loosely throughout the cytoplasm.

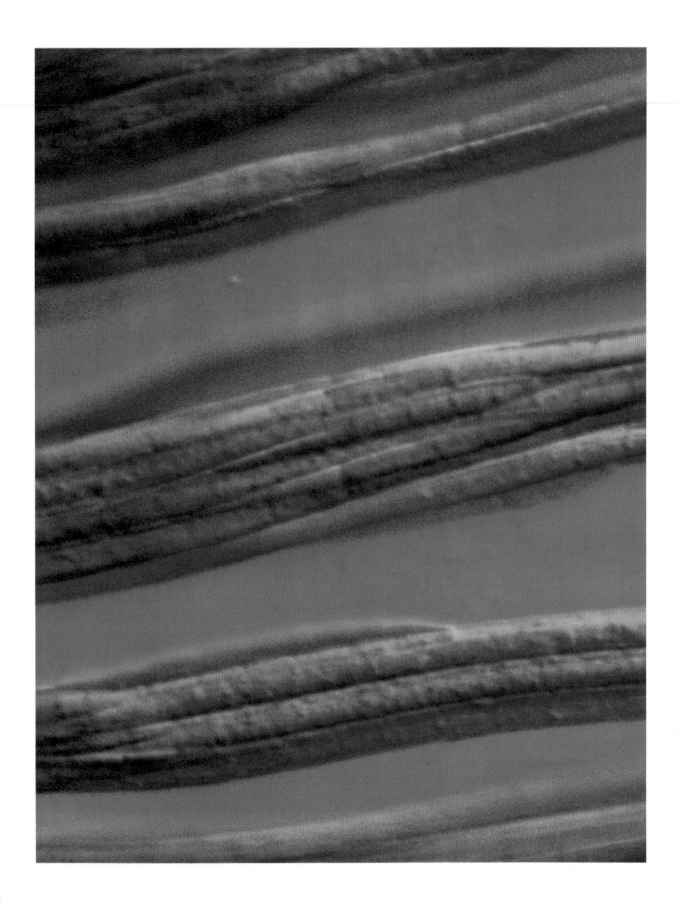

their numbers must have dyed deeply the face of the world ocean. The cells in the Warrawoona formation may have been of this type. By the end of the Archean Aeon, cyanobacteria ruled the Earth. But they brought about life's second crisis.

Each time one of these cells split a molecule of hydrogen dioxide (which is, of course, water), it seized the atoms of hydrogen and released the oxygen. Oxygen was garbage, a waste product, which the cells dumped into the water around them.

Now, oxygen—though not many people realize it—is a deadly poison. It is highly reactive and can burn living tissues almost as readily as it rusts iron ("burn" in a chemical sense; organic compounds, like iron, can combine with oxygen without the presence of a flame). There was virtually no oxygen loose in the Earth's early atmosphere. If there had been, the gas would have burned amino acids and dismantled organic molecules as fast as they formed. The journey of life would never have begun.

By exhaling oxygen, cyanobacteria were creating a toxic waste. At first they did no great harm, because in those days there were vast quantities of iron compounds—ferrous salts—suspended in the sea. There had been no free oxygen around to rust all this iron. The new oxygen combined with this iron; the compound ferric oxide was precipitated and rained to the floor of the sea. Layers of ferric oxide are still to be seen today in many parts of the world in what are called "banded iron formations"; among them is Gunflint, where Tyler and Barghoorn found the first microfossils. Banded iron formations supply North America with vast deposits of iron ore. They helped make Andrew Carnegie the "steel king." They are also indirect evidence that life and photosynthesis existed even earlier than Awramik's cells at Warrawoona. The oldest banded iron formation is 3.8 billion years old.

After 500 million years of oxygen pollution, cyanobacteria were spewing out more oxygen than ever. Ferric salts fell more steadily, forming massive iron deposits. Soon there were no more ferrous salts dissolved in the sea to buffer the environment from the cells' wastes. Poisonous gas diffused throughout the sea and air. There probably was still no life on land, for the violence of the Sun's ultraviolet rays made prolonged exposure in open places fatal. So the gas did no harm on the continents. But rising oxygen levels threatened everything alive in the seas—including the rulers of the Earth, the cyanobacteria themselves, which were adapted to low oxygen levels. They were manufacturing what might well have proved their own destruction. One atmospheric chemist calls this "the

POISON GAS

These are the inventors of photosynthesis—blue-green algae, also called cyanobacteria. They were also the first living things to make oxygen, and the first to learn to breathe it. This cyanobacterium is Microcoleus chthonoloplastes, *shown about 500 times larger than life. These cells live in large communities, called microbial mats, on arid shorelines around the world: places such as Solar Lake, in the Sinai; Abu Dhabi, in the Persian Gulf; and Baja, California, in Mexico, where these particular specimens are from.*

greatest pollution disaster ever to affect our planet."

Life had solved its energy crisis with photosynthesis. Now the dominant species' extravagant success was spoiling the planet. To survive, life had to make another leap.

A few fortunate cells developed special enzymes that could seize the dangerous compounds formed by oxygen and organic molecules and turn them into benign compounds. Cells with such fire-fighting enzymes were born survivors. As the gas gathered in sea and air, the cells had a greater and greater advantage over their neighbors, and they prospered.

Having learned to tolerate oxygen, some of these cells went further and found a way to turn it to advantage. They used oxygen to get energy, in the process known as *respiration*.

These cells were playing with fire, but they made it work. Among the creatures that succeeded with respiration were strains of cyanobacteria, which then spread even more wildly across the planet. Thus, after life had taken this decisive step, learning to tolerate oxygen and turn it to advantage, an old order faded and a new one emerged.

Cells that could survive the oxygen explosion multiplied in the seas. And because oxygen in the atmosphere made an ozone shield and cut drastically the amount of ultraviolet light reaching Earth, cells were soon able to diversify onto land as well. Life changed the face of the world, and life still is changing it—perhaps faster now than ever before.

GAIA: THE REBIRTH OF
MOTHER EARTH

The scientist who might be most impressed with the powers of the modern biosphere is the maverick British chemist and inventor James Lovelock. Lovelock developed, among other sophisticated devices, an "electron capture detector," which can measure minute quantities of trace chemicals in the atmosphere. The gadget revealed the presence of DDT and other pesticides in California condors and Antarctic penguins and in the breast milk of human mothers. These discoveries inspired Rachel Carson to write *Silent Spring*.

In the early 1960s, Lovelock flew often to consult with engineers at the Jet Propulsion Laboratory in Pasadena, California, where the two *Viking* space probes were being outfitted for their trip to Mars. Each robot probe was equipped with a mechanical arm to scoop up Martian soil. Lovelock helped design instruments to analyze the soil for amino acids and proteins, among other signs of life. These experiments, it was hoped, would prove whether the Red Planet—at least in those particular scoops of soil—was alive.

Shuttling between JPL and his home, a country farm in Wiltshire, England, Lovelock found himself worrying about

Inventor James Lovelock lives in seclusion on his country farm in Wiltshire, England. Here he poses with one of his creations, a gadget which allowed atmospheric scientists to detect fluorocarbons polluting the air in Antarctica.

the project's premises. It was designed to look for life as we know it. But what if Martian life was quite different in its chemistry?

What, after all, is life? Lovelock asked himself. He assumed the answer would be easy to find in any biology textbook. But biologists, he found, had sidestepped the question, or raised it and given up. A few 20th-century physicists had ventured a definition. It is a basic tenet of physics that things in our universe tend to run downhill, from order to disorder and at last to chaos. The principle is known to physicists as the Second Law of Thermodynamics. It is known to laymen by the buzzword "entropy." It is also familiar in Murphy's Law, "Anything that can go wrong, will."

Life, according to the physicists' definition, is a huge and intricate molecular contraption that manages for a while to reverse the general trend. The molecules make themselves an island of order in the sea of chaos and even manage to make more of their own kind. A living system is a triumph of order.

It keeps itself working far longer than most of its parts would endure if hacked into separate pieces and scattered.

In short, concluded such physicists as Eugene Wigner, Erwin Schrödinger, and physical chemist Ilya Prigogine, in a universe that is running downhill, life is matter that goes against the flow. However, because each cell consumes a great deal of energy in keeping itself together, it does not actually defeat the inexorable and depressing Second Law of Thermodynamics. Each creature's little victories of self-preservation are achieved at such great expense of energy that the inanimate world deteriorates slightly faster in consequence of life's presence. Each life, in any case, must come to an end. Thus the universe declines just as steadily as ever, with or without life.

Now, this sort of talk, Lovelock realized, was too general to be of much help in designing a space probe. In such abstract terms, even a hurricane was alive, since it was more orderly than the random winds that united in the storm and since it preserved its shape for days at a time (we acknowledge this resemblance to life by giving hurricanes names like Bob and Alice). Still, Lovelock thought, if life was an improbable chemical arrangement, then its inhalations and exhalations were also likely to be improbable. One might be able to detect the presence of life on a distant planet simply by analyzing the bubble of gas around it.

Consider our own atmosphere. It is 21 percent oxygen. If our world were in equilibrium—in other words, dead—most chemical reactions would have run downhill long ago and spent themselves. There would be no free oxygen in the air; being highly reactive, every bit of the gas would have bound itself to other chemicals, forming compounds like ferric oxide.

Hence, to an astute alien astronomer, the presence of so much oxygen in our atmosphere would suggest that there is something mysterious and unstable about Planet Earth. It would be like finding a sand castle on a beach. Left to themselves, sand grains on a beach lie flat, or at most, they are rippled and curved by waves and winds. Any beachcomber, coming upon the neat crenellations and tall towers of a sand castle, would conclude that they were raised up on purpose, that they were a sign of life.

Earth's oxygen, Lovelock decided, is like a castle in the air—and the atmosphere has many castles. It contains only .03 percent carbon dioxide, for instance. On an equilibrium world, that figure would be thousands of times larger—somewhere around 99 percent. Somehow Planet Earth was removing carbon dioxide from the atmosphere as busily as it was adding more oxygen.

The *Viking* experiments, Lovelock concluded, were

unnecessary. There was no life on Mars—or on Venus, either. Their atmospheres were well known to be in dull, chemical equilibrium. They contained no free oxygen and extremely high percentages of carbon dioxide. They must be dead worlds—no castles in the air.

This was Lovelock's first controversial conclusion. However, most scientists today would agree that there probably is no life on Mars or on Venus.

Earth's atmosphere, Lovelock now feels, is more than a mere by-product of life—and this is where he goes beyond the position of most of his colleagues. The atmosphere, he says, is too nicely adapted to life's needs to be accidental. With no oxygen, for instance, there would be no respiration. With just a little *more* oxygen, on the other hand—even 25 percent instead of 21—the whole living world would burst spontaneously into flames. Earth's air holds just the optimum amount. Similarly, without carbon dioxide, photosynthesis would fail, plants would die, and life would vanish from the Earth. With *more* carbon dioxide, however, so much heat would be trapped in air and sea by the greenhouse effect that the planet would descend into hell.

By consuming and exhaling these gases, the animal, plant, and microscopic kingdoms help to keep them in equilibrium. The biosphere also produces many millions of tons a year of methane and nitrous oxide. These gases combine quickly with oxygen and thus keep its level from climbing. Thus even termite mounds, stagnant swamps, and ruminating cows may help to keep the planet alive.

Life shapes Earth, Lovelock says, and Earth, life. They are intimately bound and work in harmony. The atmosphere

The arm of a Viking space probe scoops up a sample of Martian soil, to test it for signs of life.

"is not merely a biological product, but more probably a biological construction: not living, but like a cat's fur, a bird's feathers, or the paper of a wasp's nest, an extension of a living system designed to maintain a chosen environment." Rock and water—the lithosphere and the hydrosphere—are also part of this harmonious system, he suggests. The three spheres of Earth work with the biosphere to form "a complex system that can be seen as a single organism and that has the capacity to keep our planet a fit place for life." This organism he named after the Greek goddess Gaia, Mother Earth. In 1979 he published a book on the subject, *Gaia: A New Look at Life on Earth*. Its thesis: Earth is alive. All Earth is biosphere. Lovelock took the idea of a "balance of nature" to its ultimate conclusion and said that Earth is taking care of itself.

Lovelock did not declare Earth to be a thinking goddess. Rather, he said, the planet, acting like a single organism, unconsciously maintains the optimal conditions for life. Our own bodies, for instance, no matter whether we are in Iceland or Guyana, keep themselves neither too hot nor too cold, but always close to 98.6 degrees Fahrenheit. They do this by using a large array of automatic techniques beneath the level of consciousness—employing intricate checks and balances, of which sweating in the heat (which cools the skin by evaporation) and shivering in the cold (which warms the body by releasing heat from muscles) are only the most obvious examples. Such processes are part of our *homeostasis*—our bodies' ability to maintain themselves in equilibrium despite a variety of rude shocks from outside.

Earth, too, is homeostatic, Lovelock says, and must be capable of equally effective checks and balances, for our Sun, if it is like other stars, has not been a steady heat lamp. After the first convulsions of its birth, the Sun probably settled down to a level about one third as strong as it is today. Then it increased slowly to its present strength. Yet in all that time the planet has not overheated. Somehow it has remained at the optimum temperature for life.

We know at least one powerful way that life could help keep the planet at a steady temperature: by regulating the amounts of greenhouse gases in the atmosphere. Slightly more of these gases warm the planet, slightly less of them cool it. Another way life could help, Lovelock suggests, might be to darken or lighten the Earth's surface. Dark forests absorb much more light than white, sandy deserts. By absorbing more light, life would help the planet warm up; by reflecting more light, life would cool it.

Most of the planet's mechanisms of homeostasis are likely to be at least as complicated and subtle as the human

body's, and Lovelock admits that he cannot point them out and tell how they all work. But he is convinced they do exist, for, of all the Earth's four spheres, the biosphere is the most complicated and reacts to change in the most sensitive and varied ways. If these multitudinous reactions did not help to keep the planet livable, life would have disappeared long ago. Too much has gone right for us for too long to call it luck. Too much should have gone wrong and didn't. For more than three eons, as it spun dizzily through space, the Earth has stayed hospitable to life. "For this to have happened by chance," Lovelock says, "is as unlikely as to survive unscathed a drive blindfolded through rush-hour traffic."

From such reasoning, Lovelock decided that Gaia probably can handle human beings. "It is now generally accepted," he says, "that man's industrial activities are fouling the nest and pose a threat to the total life of the planet that grows more ominous every year. Here, however, I part company with conventional thought." Pollution is nothing Gaia hasn't handled in the past, he says calmly. Witness the pollution crisis brought on billions of years ago by the cyanobacteria when they first started producing oxygen. Gaia is a survivor.

A living world, seen from a dead one. What has kept our planet alive, without a break, for almost four billion years? Does the presence of life itself somehow keep Earth healthy? An Apollo astronaut snapped this picture from the Moon.

That kind of talk makes most of Lovelock's colleagues frown. To assume Earth can take care of itself is dangerous. How do we know when too much pressure from the human species—a species more powerful than any that has yet appeared on the planet—may not spoil the balance of nature? We work much too fast for Gaia's feedback mechanisms to clean up after us. Climatologist Stephen Schneider of NCAR argues, "Homeostasis on the Gaian scale is a billion years. Human pollution is on the scale of decades to centuries. So we can get severely hurt."

Scientists are always wary of the sin of anthropomorphism—of reading human emotions into rocks, streams, winds, and trees. Critics of the Gaia hypothesis say Lovelock is returning to the notions of the ancient Greeks—to the style of the poet Hesiod, for instance, who was the first Greek who tried to explain the birth of Gaia:

> Earth, the beautiful, rose up,
> Broad-bosomed, she that is the steadfast base
> Of all things. And fair Earth first bore
> The starry Heaven, equal to herself,
> To cover her on all sides and to be
> A home forever to the blessed gods.

It was all very well for Hesiod to speak of Earth giving birth to Heaven "to cover her." But a modern scientist never speaks of Nature as acting with such deliberation, except as a figure of speech. Earth did not intend the sky. Gases erupted from vents in the lithosphere, and gravity kept most of them from drifting out to space. Nature is not a planner. Nature is just what happens.

Quite true, Lovelock replies. But Gaia need not plan ahead in order for the end result of evolution to be harmonious. Harmony is on the average a product of natural selection and survival of the fittest. In the long run, over many generations, only those species that work well together and with their environment survive. Dangerous species, like the early cyanobacteria, eventually bring about a crisis for themselves and those around them. Then they either adapt to the new conditions or go extinct. There is no planning, and there are no police enforcing order. Yet the result is global harmony. Most of the time, most of the species on the planet are working more or less in concert.

Imagine, Lovelock says, a simple world in which there were only three kinds of life: white daisies, black daisies, and gray cows. Black daisies absorb more sunlight and so overheat faster than white daisies. Thus black daisies grow better in a cooler climate and white daisies in a warmer climate.

Suppose the daisy world is initially quite cold. Black daisies grow faster, and the planet's surface darkens. The darker surface absorbs more sunlight, and the planet begins to warm. The cows graze on the black daisies. Meanwhile, the rising temperature allows the white daisies to grow faster. Soon there are more white daisies than black. The planet's surface lightens again and it begins to cool. The cows turn their attention to the white daisies.

Whatever the starting conditions—warm or cool— the result is always the same: The daisy world settles down to a temperature comfortably in between. Thus such a simple system, with only three species, is stable (and it might even make do without the cows). The little ecosystem is capable of keeping its balance. It behaves like Lovelock's idea of Gaia.

Planet Earth, being a real world, is far more turbulent and full of change than the daisy world. On the other hand, there are far more species on our planet than the two or three on this imaginary world. With an estimated 5 million species on the Earth, there is room for far more diverse and intricate systems of feedback. The Earth is not really stable, though it seems so. It is constantly shifting and changing, like the rolling deck of a ship at sea. It puts constant demands on the balance of nature. If Lovelock is right, then—in the long run, at least— the adjustments of life's myriad species help to keep it livable. They maintain the Earth as what Hesiod called "the steadfast base of all things."

THE TROPICAL TURNING POINT

If Lovelock is right, then Gaia's vital parts must be in the tropics, where endless summer has led to the wildest profusion of species on the planet. Tropical rain forests are one of the richest and oldest realms of life on Earth. They grow in a green belt along the equator. The largest surviving forests are on three continents in just three countries: in South America, Brazil; in Africa, Zaire; and in Southeast Asia, Indonesia. These regions receive an average rainfall of as much as 400 inches a year, and their average temperature is 80 degrees Fahrenheit. The humid, hothouse climate supports biological extravaganzas of giant trees, tangled lianas, rare orchids, and monkeys, insects, snakes, and lizards.

The average acre of forest in North America holds only three or four species of trees per acre, and a Cub Scout can quickly learn to recognize them all. In a rain forest, however, an acre often carries 80 species of trees. The diversity of species is extraordinary. Charles Darwin and Alfred Russel Wallace might never have perceived the principles of evolution and natural selection if they had not seen tropical rain forests. Rain forests are known for teak, durian, greenheart, many kinds of baobob, and the strangler fig. Between their branches flit an explosive variety of birds—from the world's largest parrots and macaws to some of the world's smallest hummingbirds—and an even more bewildering variety of insects, including the black witch moth and the electric-blue morpho butterfly, which a naturalist once described as "the bluest thing in the world." There are leopards, moustached monkeys, epauleted fruit bats, and giant vampire bats; gliding squirrels, gliding geckoes, gliding lizards, and a gliding snake.

An average swath of tropical rain forest supports about 180 tons of life per acre, in dry weight, which is more *biomass* than in any other kind of forest. Whole ecosystems flourish at various heights in the forest—the life zone up in the canopy of the highest leaves, and the life zone down on the ground, attract such different sets of specialized inhabitants that the two levels might almost be separate forests. Of the perhaps 5 million different species of living things on Earth, nearly half live in tropical rain forests. The fossil record shows that many of these forests have stood for 70 million years, and some of them perhaps even 100 million years. Though individual species within them have come and gone, the rain forests still look much as they did when dinosaurs roamed among them, in the days when the supercontinent Pangaea was breaking up. They are the planet's oldest surviving ecosystems.

Until about 100 years ago, tropical rain forests, worldwide, covered an area twice the size of Europe. Now their territory has been halved. They are disappearing at a rate of 30 acres or more a minute, 24 hours a day, according to a recent United Nations report. The globe's expanding human population is fast pressing back the margins of the forests. Third World countries with tropical rain forests are also the countries with the most people living in absolute poverty and with the highest birth rates. An area the size of England and Scotland is cleared each year. "At the present rate of forest destruction," the report says, "all accessible tropical forests will have disappeared by the end of this century."

Though poor people do most of the cutting, few of them profit from the destruction of the forests. In Southeast Asia, foreign-owned corporations are "mining" cheap timber. In Latin America, many of the rain forests fall because North Americans like hamburgers. The forests are cleared to make pastureland for cattle. These ranches are owned by a small number of rich and powerful farmers, who export two thirds of the beef, most of it to the United States. Since the meat is a few cents cheaper than beef raised in this country, much of it is bought by fast-food chains. In a world full of unlikely links

A typical forest clearing near Jaru, Rondônia, in the Amazon Basin. This photo was taken in October 1984, 45 days after the forest was burned.

of cause and effect, this is one of the strangest—the hamburger connection.

In one sense, the razing of the tropics is nothing new. Vast forests in Europe and North America were cleared for the plow. Indeed, peasants in the tropics are doing no more than Theodore Roosevelt once recommended. Sailing along the Amazon on one of his big-game hunting trips, Roosevelt assumed that the profuse greenery he saw around him meant good farming. "Surely," he wrote, "such a rich and fertile land cannot be permitted to remain idle, to lie as a tenantless wilderness, while there are such teeming swarms of human beings in the overcrowded, overpeopled countries of the Old World."

But land beneath rain forests is often *not* fertile. The soil is old; eons of rains long ago leached away most of its chemicals and nutrients. The trees now get most of their chemicals from the sky. Their leaves and bark tend to be thin and specially adapted to soak up nutrients from rainwater. Their roots are typically shallow, concentrated in the top few inches of the soil, where they soak up rain as soon as it falls. Some roots even grow *up* the trees, closer to the sky. If it were not sheltered from the wind by the trees around it and propped up by branches and lianas, a tropical tree would soon topple.

Nor does death enrich the soil. With nutrients so scarce, every bit of dead vegetation that falls to the ground is quickly recycled by specialized plants, insects, and bacteria on the forest floor. As a result, the forest is usually much cleaner and freer of debris than those to the north. So the soil is not replenished by detritus the way it is in forests to the north.

Such land bears crops only as long as it is fertilized by the ashes of the jungle trees and plants that grew there. So farmers practice what is called "slash and burn" agriculture. They cut down a swath of forest, burn it, and stir the ashes into the soil. This buys them a year or two of decent crops. After that, the fertilizers are used up. Under the harsh sunlight and the rain, the soil is packed so hard that a plow can't cut it. Without sophisticated attention, expensive fertilizers, and good irrigation, the land is worthless. Farmers abandon it and press on into the forest.

In the North, when a field is abandoned, forests return. New England woods are crisscrossed with the half-tumbled stone walls of colonial farmers. But at the equator, rain forest heals only very slowly. Most of its plants and animals are specialists; they are adapted to the misty, shadowy, tangled world of the forest itself. They cannot tolerate the strong sunlight and the rain in clearings. The trees depend upon soil fungi called mycorrhizae to help their roots ingest minerals. This symbiotic relationship is vital to both the tree and the fungus. Indeed, many species of fungi can live only the roots of particular species of trees. Mycorrhizae often are killed by the heat of burning forest. The survivors may be killed by chemical fertilizers. It is then difficult for either tree or fungus to return to the burned place.

Cutting down rain forests usually does not make good farms. It may make deserts, instead, for the wholesale clearing of land probably will change even the precipitation patterns from which the forest takes its life and its name. It is a terrible waste of the biosphere's resources.

Rain forests already have given us coffee, quinine, rubber, and the wild ancestor of rice. Forest plants contain chemical compounds that help them survive in a jungle of close-living neighbors. These compounds have enriched the world's pharmacopoeia and support much of modern medicine. We owe the birth control pill to a wild yam in Guatemala, and we can now cure 99 out of a 100 cases of lymphocytic leukemia (a form of cancer most common among children) thanks to the rosy periwinkle of Madagascar. "When we pick up a medication or a pharmaceutical at our neighborhood drugstore," says conservationist Norman Myers, "there is roughly one chance in four that the product owes its existence, either directly or indirectly, to raw materials from tropical forests. The product may be an analgesic, an antibiotic, a diuretic, a laxative, a tranquilizer, or a cough pastille, among hundreds of other items. Over-the-counter sales of these items amount, worldwide; to $20 billion per year."

This, then, is the real value of the tropical forest: its

Loggers are fast making inroads in this rain forest, in Central Rondônia. Twenty-five years ago, according to ecologist Thomas Lovejoy, the population of this state was only about 10,000 (mostly Amerindians and rubber and tin prospectors). Now, it is about 500,000, and forests are being razed faster and faster. The view in this Landsat *image is about 185 by 185 kilometers. Some trees here grow as tall as 120 feet.*

extraordinary genetic diversity. Since so much of its life is unknown, the value of the lost forest is literally incalculable. Many tropical species live only on one island, or valley, or grow only on a single mountain slope. They can be destroyed forever in the clearing of a single farm. A lowly herb that could help us find the cure for cancer may fall tomorrow. Tropical biologists sometimes feel as if they are working in the legendary library of Alexandria. That city was built two millennia ago in Egypt by Alexander the Great. The library was a magnificent edifice, with all the learning of the ancient world collected on its shelves, perhaps half a million scrolls of papyrus. Among its many treasures, it held the complete works—in the original manuscripts—of the Greek tragedians Aeschylus, Sophocles, and Euripides. It also contained some of the earliest Greek scientific treatises, including the work of one Aristarchus of Samos, who held that Earth went around the Sun. Alas for posterity, the city of Alexandria eventually lost the love of learning and allowed the half million manuscripts to molder on the shelves. One day the building was sacked by a mob and burned to the ground. In the fire, some of the loftiest achievements of the human spirit were reduced to ashes, gone forever. It has been said that the loss of that single library delayed the Renaissance by a thousand years.

The rain forests, too, are a kind of library, in which scrolls have been stored with infinite pains. These scrolls are not papyrus but the tightly coiled loops of DNA concealed in every living cell. Some of them may hold secrets of infinite value. They may be codes we cannot yet read or put to use but that scientists in another decade or two, when they have learned the arts of genetic engineering, might bless us for preserving, for they may hold clues to ailments that had cursed mankind for a thousand years. The forest may also hold volumes that, while of no direct use to humankind, are of supreme value to the future evolution of Gaia. Who knows what priceless treasures are disappearing from this library every day, without our ever knowing they were there? Each vanished scroll of DNA may be as great a loss in its way as the missing plays of the Greek dramatists and the tattered wisdom of Heraclitus. We are witnessing another burning of the books. The loss is the more painful because these are masterpieces no human being has ever seen, and there have never been more than a few scholars in the beleaguered library.

"Against this background," says botanist Peter Raven, "the tiny effort that is being undertaken to learn more about tropical plants and animals and the natural communities in which they live is embarrassing. . . . Probably no more than 1,500 scientists in the world are able to catalog and describe tropical organisms or are even competent to make professional identifications of them. The number of unknown tropical organisms—five out of six have never been seen by any professional student—amounts to a staggering total of some 2.5 million species, or about twice as many as all species described during the past 245 million years."

Tropical biologist Thomas Lovejoy, a vice president of the World Wildlife Fund, is now working with officials of the government of Brazil on a vast experiment. As the forest is carved up, some 30 patches of various sizes are being left intact in northern Brazil. The smallest patches are only 2.5 acres, the size of a large suburban yard; the biggest are 39 square miles.

For 20 years or more, Lovejoy and many coworkers will monitor changes in the inhabitants of these islands and oases. They hope to learn how big a nature preserve must be if the species within it are to last. Lovejoy has found that the smallest lots deteriorate very fast. Even in bigger ones, the edges, exposed to sunlight and wind, wear badly, and only the core remains healthy. Even the very largest probably will fail in a few thousand years.

"The small reserves will give us a quick and simple picture of what we might expect," Lovejoy says, "whereas the larger ones should provide more sophisticated insights over a longer period. We expect the 10,000-hectare unit to be representative of unbroken forest for the duration of the study, except perhaps for some very wide-ranging species, such as the harpy eagle and the jaguar."

It is an experiment that may have been carried out once before in the Amazon, more gradually, by Nature herself. The theory is controversial, but many scientists believe that during the ice ages of the Pleistocene, between 1.8 million and about 11,000 years ago, the borders of the rain forest may have been reduced repeatedly to a few hot, moist spots, ice age refuges. Here, in their hothouse isolation, new species evolved and flourished in a cold, dry world. When the ice age lifted, the forests slowly expanded again, but many of the new species stayed where they were. The ancient refuges are still detectable in the forest because they contain unusual numbers of rare species. They are islands of ancient genes. It makes sense, says Lovejoy, to include these spots, which may hold many precious and still undiscovered forms of life, in the current experiment. Thus, wherever possible, the sanctuaries of the ice age and the modern age will be made to overlap.

We are razing the forests much faster than the ice ages ever did, however—too rapidly and completely to give the forest much chance of coming back. We are burning one of the wonders of the world, the greatest library of life on Planet Earth.

A NEW AGE OF MASS EXTINCTIONS

In the year 1984, there were 4.6 billion human beings on Earth—one of us, that is, for each time our planet had gone around the Sun. That is an unbelievable number. It is as hard to take it in as it is to apprehend the great age of the Earth.

Ten thousand years ago, there were only about 5 million people on this planet. In 1850, there were 1 billion. In 1950, there were 2.5 billion. By 2020, there will be at least 8 billion human beings alive on Planet Earth.

Our species achieved this success—if such a dangerous population explosion can still be called success—by one great talent. We, alone among the animals, can look ahead. We can weigh what we know of the past and present, and plan for the future. Earth scientist Roger Revelle, of the Scripps Institution of Oceanography, calls man an entirely new form of matter. No other living thing, so far as we know, is aware of itself and questions its own existence. If Gaia is Earth come alive, we are Gaia come awake.

Yet our own numbers are now a great threat to the rest of the biosphere. To make room for our own species, we are shouldering too many of the others aside.

Earth scientists and biologists met not long ago for a conference, "The Dynamics of Extinction." They came to a startling conclusion. In a very short while, a century or so, the deaths of species may rival or surpass the Great Dying at the end of the Cretaceous period 65 million years ago.

In that mass extinction, something—perhaps the black dust from a collision with an asteroid—not only killed off the dinosaurs but also destroyed about half the species then living. There are a number of such Great Dyings in the fossil record. The worst occurred in the late Permian period, 250 million years ago, when the continents jammed together to form Pangaea. During the colossal shifts of sea and land, more than 96 percent of all animal species died.

Few of us have considered, even in gloomier moments, that we might be living in such a time now. Yet we may in fact be on the verge of one. We are already losing perhaps one species per day. David Raup of the University of Chicago has estimated that the normal rate of natural extinctions is something like one every 13 months. So the extinction rate is already perhaps 400 times faster than normal. This pace is likely to accelerate as the human population continues to explode. In another few years, we may be killing species at a rate of one per hour.

Daniel Simberloff, an ecologist at Florida State University, estimates that sometime in the 21st century we will have so reduced the area of tropical rain forests that we will lose 66 percent of their plant species and 69 percent of their bird species. "All told," Simberloff says, "it is clear that the catastrophe we are facing is *not* the worst biological debacle since life began—the late Permian extinction must be that— but it certainly vies for second place." That is, we may be on the verge of the greatest dying in 250 million years.

Life did bounce back after the late Permian, of course. The survivors flourished in an emptier world. But this "bounce" took 20 million years, and even then there were only half as many species on the planet as there had been before the crash. Twenty million years is a long time to wait.

Neither are the survivors of a Great Dying likely to be the same sorts of species as those of the old regime. The ones that do best in an empty world are the opportunists, who can seize upon every vacant niche and cranny. They tend to be the ones with the fastest birth rates and the least scruples about what they eat. These are the kinds of species we call pests— flies, rats, and roaches, for instance. Specialists, especially the big ones, such as blue whales, elephants, and tigers, which are tied to one particular style of life and have slower rates of reproduction, tend to go first. In the wake of a Great Dying, our descendants would live in a world of weeds and pests, cockroaches and crabgrass. It would be a simpler place, but much less pretty and much less stable. Human beings would survive on shaky ground. As population biologist Paul Ehrlich stresses,

> You must understand that *all* human beings are embedded in ecosystems and are utterly dependent upon them for agricultural production and an array of other free "public services." These services include regulating climates and maintaining the gaseous composition of the atmosphere; delivering fresh water; disposing of wastes; recycling of nutrients (including those essential to agriculture and forestry); generating and preserving soils; controlling the vast majority of potential pests of crops and carriers of human disease; supplying food from the sea; and maintaining a vast genetic "library" from which humanity has already withdrawn the very basis of civilization—including all crop plants and domestic animals.

There is still time, Myers says. "The first great waves of extinctions are only beginning to wash over the Earth. We can still save species by the millions. Should we not consider ourselves fortunate that we alone among generations are being given the chance to support the right to life of a large share of our fellow species and to safeguard the creative capacities of evolution itself?"

NUCLEAR WINTER

"War is hell," said General William Tecumseh Sherman after blazing a trail through the South. For Planet Earth, with human numbers as vast as they are, even peace is hell. Our population's progress across the planet could lay waste to much of it within a century.

War, however, would compress this action into perhaps an hour and a half.

The secret power of nuclear weapons was discovered only four decades after the atomic bomb was dropped on Hiroshima. During all that time, presidents and military strategists considered nuclear warheads to be more or less conventional weapons, extra-strength. Physicists knew, more or less, the strength of nuclear warheads' actual blasts, and physicians and biologists pondered carefully the fate of human survivors. But no one thought enough about the fate of the Earth itself.

That this state of ignorance persisted from 1945 to 1982 is shocking. It stands as a remarkable oversight of 20th-century science. In the end, the discovery was made by chance and came as a surprise to the scientists who stumbled upon it.

Kayangel Atoll.

LIFE AND EARTH

The coral islands of Belau, in the Pacific, show how intimately the Earth's elements work together. These islands were originally created by volcanoes, which rose from the sea floor. Then the volcanoes' summits were worn down by ocean waves. Meanwhile, coral animals built upon the volcanoes' black summits. As the volcanoes slowly sank beneath the sea, the coral colonies grew steadily upward, and kept the islands nearly at sea-level. Life, that is, saved the islands from sinking. The coral reefs and atolls became a paradise for a bewildering variety of living things.

At Belau, life does not merely cling to the planet like a lichen to a rock. Life and Earth are in some sort of symbiosis; rock, sea, air, and life are collaborating. This archipelago would not exist without the volcanoes of the lithosphere, the waves of the hydrosphere, the warmth and winds of the atmosphere, and the creatures of the biosphere. Almost everywhere we look on this planet, the biosphere has altered the world so profoundly that it is hard to say where life leaves off and Earth begins.

This is not to say that life is always a creator. Like the volcano, life both creates and destroys. At Belau, certain species of small mollusks, called *chitons*, have metallic teeth that are hard enough to gnaw coral. These voracious creatures actually eat the islands: they undercut a coral island's banks until it topples like a tree felled by beavers. What the corals raise up, the chitons cast down.

The role of the human species, afloat on a small island in space, is still in question. So far, our kind has been both creator and destroyer, both coral and chiton. Our ultimate character may be decided by this generation and the next.

The story begins in 1971, when *Mariner 9* reached Mars. *Mariner* was the first satellite to orbit another planet, but it had the bad luck to arrive when Mars was in the middle of a global dust storm. The storm hid the planet. For months, scientists in the project had little to study but the dust itself.

The dust storm had begun while *Mariner* was en route to Mars, and through telescopes on Earth, astronomers had watched the storm grow. It started as a sandstorm in one of the Martian deserts. Winds kicked dust high into the atmosphere, and thickening clouds shaded the planet's surface from sunlight. The Sun warmed the dust and the upper atmosphere; the planet's surface, cast in shadow, cooled off, much as here on Earth we feel a sudden chill on a summer day when a thick cloud passes between us and the Sun. Massive, global storms are not uncommon on Mars. They last for weeks or months, until at last the dust particles slowly settle out from the sky. Then the surface warms up again.

Mariner was equipped with a device called an infrared interferometric spectrometer, which allowed scientists to measure temperatures from the very top of the dust cloud down to the surface of the planet. To analyze these data, Carl Sagan and two colleagues, O. Brian Toon and James B. Pollack (former students of Sagan's), developed a computer model that allowed

An icon of the modern age. The Pentagon dubbed this nuclear bomb "Priscilla," and dropped it from a balloon on June 24, 1957, in the Nevada desert. The bomb was as powerful as 37 kilotons of dynamite. This was the view from 6.5 miles south of Ground Zero.

them to throw clouds of small particles into a simulated Martian atmosphere. The model predicted fairly well the disturbances created by the Martian dust storm.

The scientists then applied their model to Planet Earth. Here, fortunately, a sandstorm in the Sahara never grows into a global disaster. Volcanoes, however, often send up huge quantities of aerosols and dust into the stratosphere, where the particles are caught up in the high winds, circle the Earth, and shade it. The stratosphere floats above clouds and weather and is very dry air. When particles find their way into it, they are not washed out by rain, and they often linger in the stratosphere for a year or more. Dust in the stratosphere typically cools the surface of the Earth, the same effect dust has on Mars. The effect was dramatic in April 1815, when Mount Tambora, in the Indonesian archipelago, exploded. It sent up about 100 times the fire and brimstone spewed out by Mount St. Helens in recent years. The dust made spectacular red sunsets all over the world for years—some historians think it colored the famous landscapes and seascapes of the British painter Joseph Turner. In New England, the four seasons that followed have been remembered ever since as "the year without a summer."

In 1980, Luis and Walter Alvarez made their now famous suggestion that the dinosaurs died in the dark, when a big asteroid or comet crashed into the Earth and heaved up masses of dust. Toon and Pollack had another application for their computer model. With Richard Turco, who was then at a Los Angeles think tank, R&D Associates, the scientists refined their computer model, tested the asteroid idea, and found the cloud would not last as long as the Alvarez group had thought. It would not persist for years, only for months. Nevertheless, such a cloud would indeed chill the planet. It would bring a sudden, dusky, bitter, worldwide, asteroid winter. The dinosaurs could have died in the cold and the dark.

Meanwhile, a Dutch chemist, Paul Crutzen, had become interested in the gases given off by tropical rain forests. Crutzen was a pioneer in the field of atmospheric chemistry. In the early 1970s, he had been one of the first to realize that life on Earth—in particular, soil microbes—affects the ozone layer. He had foreseen that certain kinds of human pollution (such as the flight of many supersonic aircraft) could damage or destroy the ozone shield. This had stirred one of the great environmental controversies of the 1970s.

In 1976 and 1977, Crutzen flew to Amazonia to find out which kinds of gases are being released as Brazilian farmers burn the jungle. His graduate student and assistant on the field trips was Pat Zimmerman, who later made a name for himself in studies of termites and methane. As Zimmerman recalls,

Crutzen sat in a jeep directing Pat to run through burning fields, between flaming trees and bushes, carrying a smoke collector—a sort of tin can on a pole. The two men took turns waving their scientific scepter in the burning jungle beneath the dark skies, singeing their hair and eyebrows. They found hundreds of compounds in their collector, but one of the chief products of the burning jungle, not surprisingly, was charcoal—the soot in smoke.

A few years later, the editor of a Swedish environmental journal, *Ambio*, persuaded Crutzen to write a paper on ozone: Would nuclear war damage the ozone shield? Crutzen hated this assignment. The subject depressed and repelled him, and in any case he assumed that during Armageddon the immediate damage on the ground would be bad enough without worrying about long-term effects in the atmosphere. Worse yet, after poring over the traditional forecasts and analyses of the aftermath of nuclear war, Crutzen and a colleague, John Birks, could find little evidence that a nuclear exchange would seriously damage the ozone layer. They did not want to cheer military strategists with news like that.

Crutzen still remembered the burning jungles and how the very sky had darkened in Brazil. He was by now an expert on fires; as one colleague puts it, he was "smoke-aware." Suddenly he and Birks realized that traditional analysts had been awed by visions of mushroom clouds, radiation, and firestorms. *They forgot about the smoke.* In a nuclear exchange, there might easily be a million square kilometers of forest around targets, Crutzen thought. Smoke from that kind of global forest fire—400 million tons of smoke—would be enough to darken the planet's skies. Never mind the ozone layer; the smoke layer was a terrible threat to life on land and in the sea. Smoke could be deadlier than fire and might even shut down photosynthesis.

Before the paper appeared in *Ambio*, Richard Turco saw a draft of it. From his earlier work with Toon and Pollack, Turco was dust-aware and dark-aware. He saw that the problem was even worse than Crutzen's calculations suggested. Many strategic targets of nuclear war are in cities, or just outside them. World War II showed us what can happen when a city burns. In July 1943, British bombers dropped more than 1,000 incendiary bombs on the German city of Hamburg. Like all cities, Hamburg was a maze of stockpiled oil, natural gas, gasoline, and other fuels. These spilled and exploded, and an enormous fire started; winds as powerful as hurricanes rushed into the city from all sides and rose skyward as if caught in the updraft of a gigantic chimney. Flames towered 15,000 feet; smoke, 40,000 feet. Temperatures in the heart of the holocaust reached

1,000 degrees centigrade. Glass windows and bottles and even aluminum melted. Human bodies, rubber tires, and even asphalt pavements melted, pooled, and burned. People went down on hands and knees in the cobblestone streets and crawled away from the flames; if they stood up, the wind blew them back toward the burning blocks. Forty thousand people died.

In February 1945, Allied bombers set another firestorm in Dresden, whose burning the novelist Kurt Vonnegut later described in *Slaughterhouse Five*. A month later, American bombers managed to set an even bigger firestorm in Tokyo, incinerating 16 square miles of city and 100,000 people. On August 6, 1945, at 8:16 A.M., a single bomber, the *Enola Gay*, dropped a single bomb, called "Little Boy," on Hiroshima. It was not the biggest firestorm of the war, but it was the simplest to ignite. All of central Hiroshima was gutted, and about 130,000 of the city's 350,000 people died. A pillar of black smoke rose miles above the burning city and darkened the sky. It was midsummer, but in the shadow of the smoke, survivors shivered. Black rains fell, each drop of water inky with soot.

Immediately, Turco teamed up with Toon, Pollack, and a third Ames scientist, Thomas Ackerman, and revived their computer model yet again. The results were frightening. Today's nuclear warheads are many times more powerful than the one that was dropped on Hiroshima 40 years ago. "Today," according to the British scientist and political adviser Sir Solly Zuckerman, "ten times—even a hundred times—the amount of explosive power that wiped out Hiroshima and Nagasaki can be packed in a single warhead weighing less than a tenth of those first two warheads." If even a small number of these exploded on the same day, the result would very likely be disastrous for the global climate. Most military strategists and analysts expect that if even a few missiles for nuclear bombs are ever fired, nuclear war will escalate within hours until hundreds of missiles are fired. If 5,000 megatons, half the world's arsenal of nuclear weapons, were detonated—a figure many analysts consider realistic—a thousand cities would burn at once. Smoke would shroud much of the northern hemisphere and some could cross over the equator to the southern. The study by Turco and his colleagues predicted that the average temperature in the northern hemisphere would plummet far below the freezing point within a week or two, and temperatures would stay below freezing for a few months. Turco called this "nuclear winter."

In the old Norse vision of the Twilight of the Gods, the gods battle against Loki and the powers of evil, and both sides lose.

The sun will go black
Earth sink in the sea
heaven be stripped of its bright stars;
smoke rage
and fire,
leaping the flame
lick heaven itself.

Then, according to the Norse tale, comes "Fimbul Winter." "Heavy snows are driven and fall from the world's four corners; the murder frost prevails. The Sun is darkened at noon; it sheds no gladness; devouring tempests bellow and never end. In vain do men await the coming of summer. Thrice winter follows winter over a world which is snow-smitten, frost-fettered, and chained in ice."

Earth scientists were reviving a Viking nightmare 1,000 years old.

DARKNESS AT NOON

Soon Turco, Toon, Ackerman, and Pollack were joined by Carl Sagan, who was struck by the resemblance of the nuclear winter scenario to the actual Martian dust storm he had observed, through the eyes of *Mariner*, a decade before. The five men's work became known by the somber acronym TTAPS, using the first initials of their last names. In April 1983, 100 scientists convened for four days in Cambridge, Massachusetts, to analyze and criticize the TTAPS report. Then, in late 1983, the TTAPS report was made public at a meeting in Washington. The date happened to be October 31, and Sagan noted the macabre relevance of the holiday. Halloween, he observed, began as a Celtic festival called Samhain. "It marked the beginning of winter. It was celebrated by the lighting of vast bonfires. And it was named after and consecrated to the Lord of the Dead."

According to the Halloween panel, even if a billion people were killed almost instantly during a nuclear war, the worst would be to come. "Biologists," says Paul Ehrlich, "can agree to that as easily as we all could agree that accidentally using cyanide instead of salt in the gravy could spoil a dinner party." With temperatures below freezing day and night, he said, rivers, streams, lakes, and reservoirs would ice over. The ground would grow hard and cold. It might even be difficult for survivors to melt enough water to drink. It might be impossible to bury the millions of dead bodies.

After a full-scale nuclear war, black clouds would hover above the lands of the superpowers, shutting out the Sun. Neutral neighbors would not be safe. Tendrils of smoke could reach out to touch any part of the globe.

Besides the sudden cold and darkness, there would be endless wildfires; toxic smog; radiation; and black, acid rains. Animals and plants find such assaults hard to survive when they are healthy; any one of these insults could be fatal to living things that were already sick and weak.

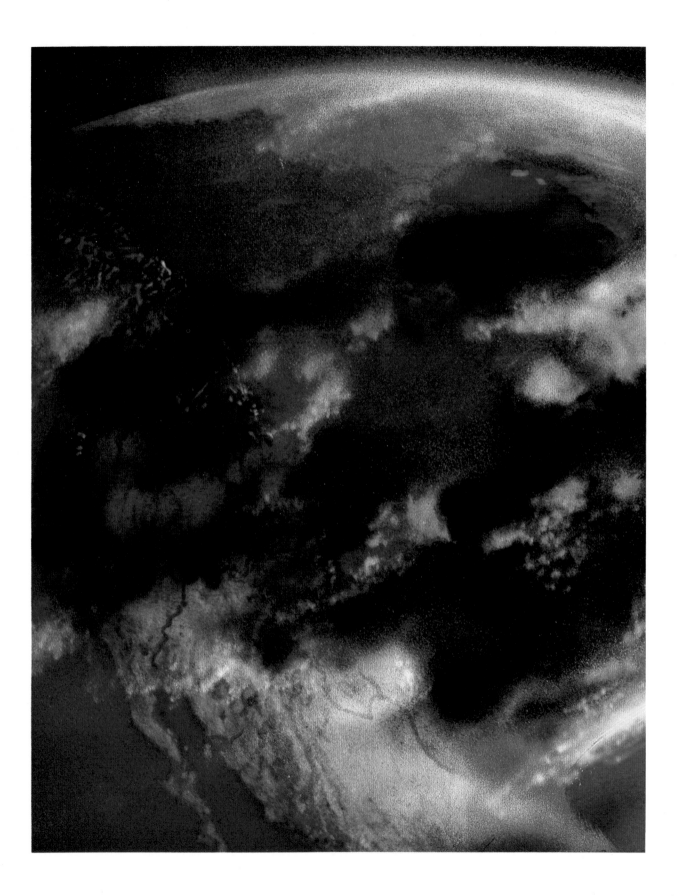

In a few weeks, black clouds would have circled the planet, and they could spread in long streamers and black fingers across the equator. Life in the tropics has no defense against cold, never having felt a winter. Many species of animals and plants of the rain forests might fail in a spasm of mass extinctions.

The sea would not freeze over, but life in it would be decimated anyway, because virtually all the food chains in the sea start with the phytoplankton near the surface, which live by photosynthesis. The phytoplankton would die off in days, or weeks, and after they were gone, fish, whales, and squid would starve. Only the creatures in the abyss would flourish, dining on the rain of death. Life in the vents in the Galapagos, and along the midsea ridges, probably would go on as before, with superheated water boiling up from chimneys, and giant worms and clams clustered around it. Indeed, fossil evidence shows that many of these creatures survived the Cretaceous extinction. In their bomb shelter of ocean, with the ceiling a few miles thick and with all their needs boiling up from within the Earth, they would survive this Armageddon, too.

Most plants' and animals' immune systems would be so weakened by all these assaults that they might succumb even to the least of the daily shocks. And if the planet can be said to have a kind of immune system also, this global ecosystem might be too shaken to recover its balance.

It is a tribute to the power of the evidence and to the importance of the issue that so many scientists accepted so quickly the importance of the TTAPS report. But the report was only a warning, a first statement of a global problem, rather than a definitive piece of research. As the TTAPS scientists themselves stressed in Cambridge and Washington, the subject was and still is full of tremendous controversy and uncertainty. The success of computer models of the atmosphere remains limited, and so does our knowledge of World War Three. Virtually all the targets would be in the northern hemisphere, of course, the homelands of the United States and the Soviet Union. But no one can know how many missiles would really be fired, how many firestorms ignited, how many cities destroyed, or just how much smoke would rise. No one knows what season of the year the war might come. Nuclear winter would be most devastating if it came in the spring or summer, before the year's crops had been grown and harvested. In the fall or winter, the onset of the cold and dark might be less murderous—at least at first—since the harvest would be in.

By 1985, after crash research projects by several climate modelers, the view was a little less grim. The scenario Ehrlich described was beginning to seem worst-case, or nearly so, although within the realm of possibility. A sophisticated climate model has been run on the supercomputers at the National Center for Atmospheric Research in Boulder. Stephen Schneider, who worked on the project with Starley Thompson and Curt Covey, says the supercomputer model "confirmed, denied, and extended TTAPS."

"We confirmed that there was cooling under dense smoke, especially severe in midcontinents," Schneider says. "We denied that it was as large on average as they said. The oceans cut down the averages by a factor of two or more; by a factor of ten near the coasts." The coasts might have some very chilly days.

The most important result of their study, says Schneider, was that large, thick, black smoke clouds could chill the Earth much faster than previously thought. Even a few days of darkness would lower temperatures nearly to freezing, or sometimes below. So a small and limited nuclear war could be far more dangerous than the TTAPS scientists had believed, because the cloud could cause a "quick freeze" over the region of each bombed city and far downwind of the war's "theaters." Random winds would blow this instant chill toward any point of the compass—"a sort of 'weather roulette.'"

"People think they needn't care about this because we're all going to be dead," says Starley Thompson. "The fact is, most people would still be alive the day after. You may kill several hundred million people, or even 1 billion. But the global population is more than 4.6 billion. Even in the combatant countries, many people would survive at first.

"But the ones who should be most concerned are those in neighboring, noncombatant countries—such as Brazil, Canada, Mexico, India, the countries of the Middle East and Southeast Asia. Nuclear winter knows no political boundaries. The day after, or the week after, you think you're doing fine—the superpowers have killed themselves off—and then a big smoke cloud comes overhead for three days and freezes you out. And suddenly you have become a casualty of a nuclear war."

Thompson thinks nuclear winter would be unlikely to last as long as a year—weeks, or at most, months. "Things change, though," he says. "Let's hope Ehrlich is not considered by future generations to have been overly optimistic."

Even after a year of the worst-case scenario of nuclear winter, Paul Ehrlich believes, there would be small groups of survivors in the northern hemisphere and many in the southern hemisphere. They would be living like the scavengers of prehistoric times. But hunters and gatherers in the past, Ehrlich notes, knew how to live off the land. Survivors of World War Three would be strangers in a strange land, stumbling about in an environment once home but now unrecognizable. The inevitable inbreeding of small groups marooned on islands would increase the rate of mutations and stillbirths. They would be living in isolation and ignorance, darkness and perpetual hunger. "The psychological state of the survivors," Ehrlich says, "is difficult to imagine."

In the long run, if there were a long run, these survivors would be hurled back down into the Stone Age. And they might never be able to climb back out of it. As Ehrlich notes, we have already used up most of the resources within easy reach. In the Old Stone Age, chunks of nearly pure iron and copper lay about on the surface; now we get these metals only by extracting them from tons of low-grade ores. Oil was once almost as easy to drill as water—essentially, as Ehrlich says, you could poke a pointed stick in the ground and get a gusher. Now we have to drill several thousand feet. After two centuries of full-tilt Industrial Revolution, it takes high technology just to dig out the fuels and minerals that make technology possible. There would be no blast furnaces or oil wells in the postwar Stone Age. The wreckage would rust away, and the world could not readily rebuild.

In any case, remembering what we had done to the world, our descendants might not wish to retrace our footsteps. The experience of a severe nuclear winter would impress itself deeply upon the psyche of the human race. The Black Cloud might replace the Great Flood in global mythology. Some survivors might become sun-worshipers, having been taught so bitterly Earth's thralldom to the day star.

What would primitive tribes, descendants of survivors, teach their children? How would the high-tech hell of nuclear war be remembered? Perhaps they would say that a man had stolen the secret of fire from the Sun, and to punish us, for one whole year the Sun withdrew its face and left us to suffer in the cold and the dark.

CODA   Since January 1983, a satellite has been circling the Earth and scanning the universe as part of a collaboration among the United States, Great Britain, and the Netherlands. The satellite monitors the infrared band of light's spectrum—the kind of energy emitted not by hot and brilliant stars but by cooler dust, smoke, and rock. The *Infrared Astronomy Satellite (IRAS)* has made, by chance, a discovery that alters our position in the universe.

IRAS has examined more than 100 stars. One out of five of them is surrounded by a disc of dark matter. The envelope of whirling matter is warmed by the star and so gives off infrared energy—as does our own Earth, for instance, and as does the dust in our atmosphere. The cloaks around these stars are more or less what our own solar system must have been like when it formed around the newborn Sun 4.6 billion years ago.

Among the dark-mantled stars detected so far by IRAS are Fomalhaut; HL Taurus; B Monoceros; and Beta Pictoris, which is 50 light-years away, in the constellation Pictor. The best known is the star Alpha Lyrae, often called Vega. Vega is one of the brightest stars in the night sky, and on summer evenings in the temperate zone of the northern hemisphere it is almost directly overhead. It is a very young star, between 100 million and 1 billion years old. It is also very near in cosmic terms—some 26 light-years away.

Vega's dark halo is about 15 billion miles in diameter. If theory is correct, it should subside eventually into something closer to the size of our own solar system, which is 6 billion miles across. Then planets will form in it, as they have in the neighborhood of our own star, the Sun. Vega's dark halo may already contain planets—the *IRAS* satellite cannot make out details that fine.

According to astronomer Bradford Smith of the University of Arizona, the *IRAS* evidence suggests that solar systems are quite common in the universe, that it is "perfectly normal in the formation of a star to have junk left over orbiting around it, which ultimately coalesces.

"We would like to find one that's 10 million years old, or 1 billion years old, or 2 or 3 billion years old," Smith says. "If we can find enough of them, we can get a picture of just how these systems evolved."

If Vega does have planets, they are still in their Hadean Aeon—too hot, turbulent, and collision-wracked for life to form. But there are about 100 billion other stars in our galaxy, and 100 billion galaxies in the universe. On how many worlds in the universe, however, is life at a stage like ours?

"I want to believe that we are not alone," Smith says, "that there are other systems very similar to our own; in fact, that the galaxy is full of them. I would really like to believe that intelligent civilization is not unique. I would hate to believe that we are just—this is the only one. Just seeing something out there that looks like we might have looked 4 billion years ago . . . !"

What are the two most powerful creations of our time? The nuclear bomb and the voyaging rocket. Both bid us, in imagination, to say farewell to our planet. We know the bomb could destroy our first home at any instant. The rocket could carry us off in a generation. We try not to think about the bomb, and we often forget the rocket. Yet they are there in the back of our minds, and they trouble our view of Earth. We were animals only a few moments ago in evolution, and though we dreamed of strength, we never really expected to achieve as much as we have. Ten thousand years ago, we were still in caves. Now we command some portion of the fire of the Sun, and we understand, in part, the forces that shake the Earth.

There are times when the Earth stands before us with a hallucinatory clarity. Despite all we know of its wind, rock, water, and fire, we do not know the sum of it; yet there it is before us, floating in space, in exquisite photographs. We never see a home so clearly as the day we first walk in, and the day we pause and look back across the threshold for the last time. That first day is so long ago for us that we have forgotten it. We can only guess at it, as we stare at a dawn star in a tiny bit of quartz.

But the farewell is now before us. We are living it. Our dreams are troubled by the bomb and by the rocket. We are the generation in the doorway. We are the first generation of the long good-bye. As we look around today, we see sky, hills, peaks, and waves with a peculiar attention. We stare, as if we were already looking back. This is the planet on which our species grew up. This is the planet from which, with luck, we will step toward the stars. If we survive, and make it up there, it will be because we have acquired a new measure of wisdom, and perhaps by then we will be worthy of the long and cosmic trip.

Thinking of that journey, this planet seems a small place. We stop for a moment in the doorway and stare back at the stone hearth before which we once loved to sit, dreaming of Odin, of Loki, of Gaia, of giants in the Earth.

Since the first sightings from the IRAS satellite, astronomers have been searching the skies to find more stars with solar systems. This is Beta Pictoris, a star 50 light years away, as seen from a mountaintop observatory in Chile. In this computer-enhanced image, we may be witnessing the birth of a new solar system.

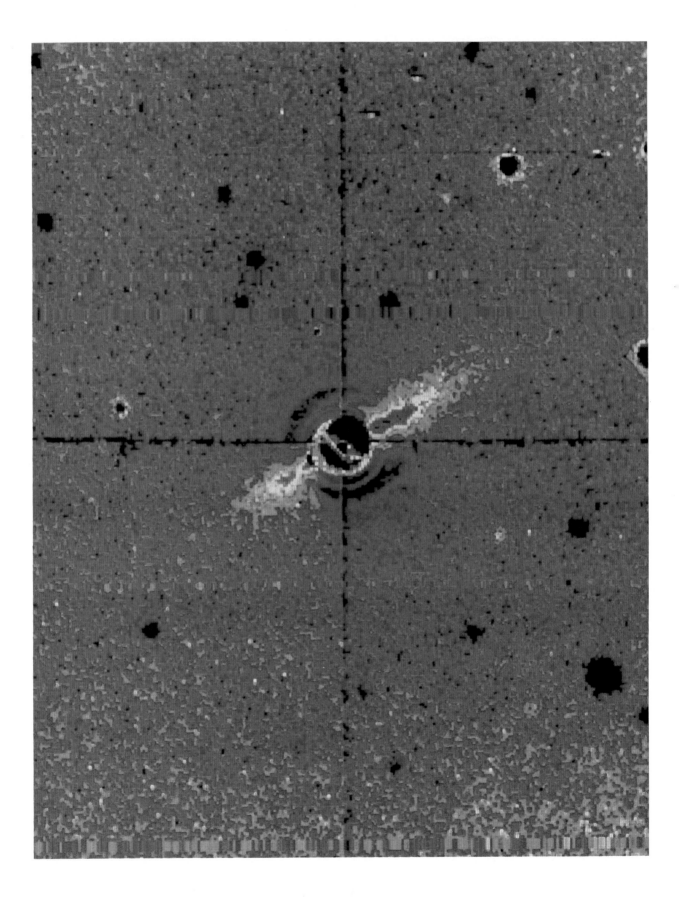

Bibliography

CHAPTER ONE: THE LIVING MACHINE

Alexander, Tom. "A Revolution Called Plate Tectonics Has Given Us a Whole New Earth." *Smithsonian*, January 1975, pp. 30–47.

Anderson, Don L. "Seismic Tomography." *Scientific American*, October 1984, pp. 60–68.

Bolt, Bruce. *Earthquakes: A Primer*. San Francisco: W.H. Freeman & Co., 1978.

Carr, Archie, and Coleman, Patrick J. "Seafloor Spreading Theory and the Odyssey of the Green Turtle." *Nature*, May 10, 1984 pp. 128–130.

Clark, Robert Dean. "J. Tuzo Wilson." *Geophysics: The Leading Edge of Exploration*, November 1982, pp. 17–23.

Dickinson, William R. "Plate Tectonics in Geologic History." *Science*, October 8, 1971, pp. 107–113.

Dott, Robert H., Jr., and Batten, Roger L. *Evolution of the Earth*. 3d ed. New York: McGraw-Hill Book Co., 1981.

Farmer, Penelope, ed. *Beginnings: Creation Myths of the World*. New York: Atheneum, 1979.

Geikie, Sir Archibald. *The Founders of Geology*. 1897. Reprint. New York: Dover Publications, 1962. A classic history of the field.

Glen, William. *The Road to Jaramillo: Critical Years of the Revolution in Earth Science*. Stanford, CA: Stanford University Press, 1982. Authoritative history of the plate-tectonics revolution.

Gould, Stephen Jay. "Uniformity and Catastrophe" and "The Validation of Continental Drift." In *Ever Since Darwin*. New York: W.W. Norton & Co., 1977, pp. 147–152 and 160–167.

Gribbin, John. *This Shaking Earth: Earthquakes, Volcanoes, and Their Impact on Our World*. New York: G.P. Putnam's Sons, 1978.

Hallam, A. *Great Geological Controversies*. Oxford: Oxford University Press, 1983.

Hammond, Allen L. "Plate Tectonics: The Geophysics of the Earth's Surface." *Science*, July 2, 1971, pp. 40–41.

Hammond, Allen L. "Plate Tectonics (II): Mountain Building and Continental Geology." *Science*, July 9, 1971, pp. 133–134.

Kerr, Richard A. "The Bits and Pieces of Plate Tectonics." *Science*, March 7, 1980, pp. 1059–1061.

Koestler, Arthur. *The Lotus and the Robot*. New York: Macmillan Co., 1961.

McIntyre, Donald B. "James Hutton and the Philosophy of Geology." In *The Fabric of Geology*. Reading, MA: Addison-Wesley Publishing Co., 1963.

McIntyre, D.B.; Craig, G.Y.; and Waterston, C.D. *The Hutton Lost Drawings*. San Francisco: Freeman, Cooper & Co., 1981.

McPhee, John. *Basin and Range*. New York: Farrar, Straus & Giroux, 1980. A literate and spirited introduction to modern geology.

Miller, Russell. *Continents in Collision*. Alexandria, VA: Time-Life Books, 1983.

Motz, Lloyd, ed. *Rediscovery of the Earth*. New York: Van Nostrand Reinhold Co., 1979.

"A Perfect Case of Serendipity." *Mosaic*, March/April 1972, pp. 2–12.

Playfair, John. *Illustrations of the Huttonian Theory of the Earth*. 1802. Reprint. Urbana: University of Illinois Press, 1956.

Press, Frank, and Siever, Raymond. *Earth*. 3d ed. San Francisco: W.H. Freeman & Co., 1982.

Scientific American. "The Dynamic Earth." September 1983. A special issue on scientists' new vision of our home planet.

Schmidt, Victor A. *Planet Earth and the New Geoscience*. Dubuque, IA: Kendall-Hunt, 1985. The classroom textbook based on the PBS series *Planet Earth*.

"The Seams of the Earth." *Mosaic*, November/December 1975, pp. 2–7.

Simmons, Henry. "Before Pangea." *Mosaic*, March/April 1981, pp. 27–37.

Sullivan, Walter. *Continents in Motion*. New York: McGraw-Hill, 1974.

Sullivan, Walter. "Sinking Slabs of Sea Floor May Cause Shifts in Earth's Crust." *The New York Times*, November 27, 1984, p. C2.

Vitaliano, Dorothy B. *Legends of the Earth: Their Geological Origins*. Bloomington: Indiana University Press, 1973.

Weaver, Muriel. *The Aztecs, Maya, and Their Predecessors*. New York: Academic Press, 1981.

Wegener, Alfred. *The Origin of Continents and Oceans*. John Biram, trans. 1929. Reprint. New York: Dover Publications, 1966.

Wesson, Robert L., and Wallace, Robert E. "Predicting the Next Great Earthquake in California." *Scientific American*, February 1985, pp. 35–43.

Wilson, J. Tuzo. "Evidence from Islands on the Spreading of Ocean Floors." *Nature*, February 9, 1963, pp. 536–538.

Wilson, J. Tuzo, ed. *Continents Adrift*. San Francisco: W.H. Freeman & Co., 1973. Readings from *Scientific American*.

CHAPTER TWO: THE BLUE PLANET

Barton, Robert. *The Oceans*. London: Aldus Books, 1980.

Bartusiak, Marcia. "Mapping the Sea Floor from Space." *Popular Science*, February 1984, pp. 80–85.

Bernardo, Stephanie. "The Seafloor: A Clear View from Space." *Science Digest*, June 1984.

Blakeslee, Sandra. "Satellites Giving Coast Fishermen Better Picture of Where the Catches Are." *The New York Times*, December 18, 1983, p. A40.

Canby, Thomas Y. "El Niño's Ill Wind." *National Geographic*, February 1984, pp. 144–183.

Carson, Rachel L. *The Sea Around Us*. Rev. ed. New York: Oxford University Press, 1961.

Clark, Jenifer Wartha. "Observations from the 1980 Newport to Bermuda Yacht Race." *Gulfstream*, November 1, 1980, pp. 3–7.

Cromie, William J. "The New Oceanography." *Mosaic*, July/August 1980, pp. 2–7.

Edmond, John. "Hot Springs on the Ocean Floor." *Scientific American*, April 1983, pp. 78–93.

Edmond, John. "Ocean Hot Springs on the Ocean Floor." *Oceanus*, Summer 1982, pp. 22–27.

Edson, Lee. "How It Might Have Been." *Mosaic*, May/June 1983, pp. 10–15.

Frye, John. "The Ring Story." *Sea Frontiers*, September/October 1982, pp. 958–967.

Gross, M. Grant. *Oceanography: A View of the Earth*. 3d ed. Englewood Cliffs, NJ: Prentice-Hall, 1982.

Hendrickson, Robert. *The Ocean Almanac*. Garden City, NY: Doubleday & Co., 1984.

Jones, Gwyn. *The History of the Vikings*. New York: Oxford University Press, 1968.

Laurs, R. Michael; Fiedler, Paul C.; and Montgomery, Donald R. "Albacore Tuna Catch Distributions Relative to Environmental Features Observed from Satellites." *Deep-Sea Research* 31, no. 9 (1984), pp. 1085–1099.

Ludwigson, John. "The Earth's Great Domesday Book." *Mosaic*, July/August 1980, pp. 29–36.

Martini, Frederic. *Exploring Tropical Isles and Seas.* Englewood Cliffs, NJ: Prentice-Hall, 1984.

Newby, Eric. *The World Atlas of Exploration.* London: Artists House, 1982.

Rasmussen, Eugene M. "El Niño: The Great Equatorial Warming." *Weatherwise*, August 1983, pp. 166–175.

Rasmussen, Eugene M. "El Niño: The Ocean/Atmosphere Connection." *Oceanus*, Summer 1984, pp. 5–12.

Schlee, Susan. *The Edge of an Unfamiliar World.* New York: E.P. Dutton & Co., 1973. A lively history of oceanography. I used it extensively in writing the historical sketches in my chapter.

Schlee, Susan. "Science and the Sea." *The Wilson Quarterly*, Summer 1984, pp. 48–69. The story of sea science in a nutshell.

Thayer, Victoria G., and Barber, Richard T. "At Sea with El Niño." *Natural History*, October 1984, pp. 4–12.

Thorndike, Joseph J., Jr., ed. *Mysteries of the Deep.* New York: American Heritage Publishing Co., 1980.

Van Andel, Tjeerd. *Science at Sea: Tales of an Old Ocean.* San Francisco: W.H. Freeman & Co., 1981. Literate, brief introduction by a sea scientist.

"Voyage to the Vents in the Sea." *Discover*, July 1982, pp. 13–14.

Waldrop, M. Mitchell. "Hot Springs and Marine Geochemistry." *Mosaic*, July/August 1980, pp. 8–14.

Whipple, A.B.C. *Restless Oceans.* Alexandria, VA: Time-Life Books, 1983.

Wiebe, Peter H. "Rings of the Gulf Stream." *Scientific American*, March 1982, pp. 60–70.

Wilford, John Noble. *The Mapmakers.* New York: Alfred A. Knopf, 1981.

CHAPTER THREE: THE CLIMATE PUZZLE

Bailey, Ronald H. *Glacier.* Alexandria, VA: Time-Life Books, 1982.

Brooks, C.E.P. *Climate Through the Ages.* Rev. ed. New York: McGraw-Hill Book Co., 1949.

Calder, Nigel. *The Weather Machine and the Threat of Ice.* London: British Broadcasting Corporation, 1974.

Chorlton, Windsor. *Ice Ages.* Alexandria, VA: Time-Life Books, 1983.

"Climate, Weather, Aridity." *Mosaic*, January/February 1977, pp. 15–19.

Dales, George F. "The Decline of the Harappans." *Scientific American*, May 1966, pp. 92–100.

Eckholm, Erik. "New Predictions See Rise in CO_2 Transforming Earth." *The New York Times*, August 7, 1984, p. C1.

"Faster Than a Speeding Glacier." *Discover*, April 1985, p. 7.

" 'Greenhouse Effect' and Methane Rise." *The New York Times*, October 18, 1984, p. C3.

Gribbin, John. *Weather Force: Climate and Its Impact on Our World.* New York: G.P. Putnam's Sons, 1979. An illustrated survey.

Hays, J.D.; Imbrie, John; and Shackleton, N.J. "Variations in the Earth's Orbit: Pacemaker of the Ice Ages." *Science*, December 10, 1976, pp. 1121–1132.

Herbert, W. "Long Hot Future: Warmer Earth Appears Inevitable." *Science News*, October 22, 1983, pp. 260–261.

Imbrie, John, and Imbrie, Katherine Palmer. *Ice Ages: Solving the Mystery.* Short Hills, NJ: Enslow Publishers, 1979. Readable and authoritative. My main source in recounting the history of ice-age research.

Imbrie, John, and Imbrie, John Z. "Modeling the Climatic Response to Orbital Variations." *Science*, February 29, 1980, pp. 943–953.

Jenkins, John A. "The Climes They Are A-Changin'." *TWA Ambassador*, May 1981, pp. 32–38.

Johnson, Diane. "Getting Behind (and Ahead of) the Weather." *Alumni Magazine Consortium*, November 1983, pp. 8–16.

Kellogg, W.W., and Schneider, S.H. "Climate Stabilization: For Better or for Worse?" *Science*, December 27, 1974, pp. 1163–1172.

Kerr, Richard. "The Race to Predict Next Week's Weather." *Science*, April 1, 1983, pp. 39–41.

Luoma, Jon. *Troubled Skies, Troubled Waters: The Story of Acid Rain*. New York: Viking Press, 1984.

Mason, B.J. "The Nature and Prediction of Climatic Changes." *Endeavor*, May 1976, pp. 51–58.

Matthews, Samuel W. "What's Happening to Our Climate?" *National Geographic*, November 1976, pp. 576–615.

McCarthy, John, and Serafin, Robert. "The Microburst: Hazard to Aircraft." *Weatherwise*, June 1984, pp. 120–127.

Mehta, Dilip. "Mystery on the Indus." *Geo*, August 1984, pp. 72–80.

"Modeling the Climate System." *Mosaic*, November/December 1979, pp. 2–8.

Olson, Steve. "Computing Climate." *Science 82*, May 1982, pp. 54–60.

Revelle, Roger. "Carbon Dioxide and World Climate." *Scientific American*, August 1982, pp. 35–43.

Roberts, Walter Orr. "It Is Time to Prepare for Global Climate Changes." *Conservation Foundation Letter*, April 1983, pp. 1–8.

Rotberg, Robert I., and Rabb, Theodore K., eds. *Climate and History*. Princeton: Princeton University Press, 1981.

Schneider, Stephen H., and Londer, Randi. *The Coevolution of Climate and Life*. San Francisco: Sierra Club Books, 1984. A long, thorough, and well-written review of climatology today.

"Tales the Tree Rings Tell." *Mosaic*, September/October 1977, pp. 2–9.

Wanning, Esther. "Interview: Roger Revelle." *Omni*, March 1984.

Washington, Warren. "Computer Simulation of the Earth's Atmosphere." *Science Journal*, November 1968, pp. 37–41.

Whipple, A.B.C. *Storm*. Alexandria, VA: Time-Life Books, 1982.

Witkin, Richard. "U.S. Is Pressing Efforts to Combat Wind Shear, Key Airliner Hazard." *The New York Times*, July 5, 1984.

Young, Louise B. *Earth's Aura*. New York: Alfred A. Knopf, 1977.

CHAPTER FOUR: TALES FROM OTHER WORLDS

"Back from the Moon." *Newsweek*, August 4, 1969, pp. 14–20.

Beatty, J. Kelly; O'Leary, Brian; and Chaiken, Andrew; eds. *The New Solar System*. Cambridge: Cambridge University Press, 1981.

Browne, Malcolm. "Antarctica: Earth's Early-Warning Station." *Discover*, February 1984, pp. 90–96.

Brownlee, Donald E. "Cosmic Dust." *Natural History*, April 1981, pp. 73–77.

Chapman, Clark R. *Planets of Rock and Ice*. New York: Charles Scribner's Sons, 1982. A readable guide to our corner of the universe, written by a planetologist.

Cooper, Henry S.F. *Imaging Saturn*. New York: Holt, Rinehart & Winston, 1981.

Cooper, Henry S.F. *Moon Rocks*. New York: Dial Press, 1970.

Davis, Marc; Hut, Piet; and Muller, Richard A. "Extinction of Species by Periodic Comet Showers." *Nature*, April 19, 1984, pp. 715–720.

Drake, Stillman. *Galileo At Work*. Chicago: University of Chicago Press, 1978.

Ferris, Timothy. *Galaxies*. San Francisco: Sierra Club Books, 1980. Extraordinary photographs of galaxies, nebulae, and exploding stars.

Fisher, Arthur. "The World's Great Dyings." *Mosaic*, March/April 1981, pp. 2–9.

Gore, Rick. "What Voyager Saw: Jupiter's Dazzling Realm." *National Geographic*, January 1980, pp. 2–29.

Gould, Stephen Jay. "The Cosmic Dance of Siva." *Natural History*, August 1984, pp. 14–19.

Gribbin, John. "Earth's Lucky Break." *Science Digest*, May 1983.

Hawkins, Gerald S. "The Stones Speak." *The Sciences*, July/August 1983, pp. 56–58.

Head, James W.; Wood, Charles A.; and Mutch, Thomas A. "Geologic Evolution of the Terrestrial Planets." *American Scientist*, January/February 1977, pp. 21–29.

Hiatt, Blanchard. "The Great Astronomical Ear." *Mosaic*, March/April 1980, pp. 30–37.

Hoffer, William. "Looking Up to Know Ourselves." *Mosaic*, September/October 1980, pp. 38–44.

Hoffman, Paul. "Asteroid on Trial." *Science Digest*, June 1982, pp. 58–63.

Ingersoll, Andrew P. "Saturn's Surprises." *Natural History*, September 1981, pp. 44–50.

Janos, Leo. "Timekeepers of the Solar System." *Science 80*, May/June 1980, pp. 44–55.

Kerr, Richard A. "Planetary Rings Explained and Unexplained." *Science*, October 8, 1982, pp. 141–143.

King, David A. "Faces of the Kaaba." *The Sciences*, May/June 1982, pp. 16–20.

Koestler, Arthur. *The Sleepwalkers*. New York: Grosset & Dunlap, 1963.

La Brecque, Mort. "The Terrestrial Planets." *Mosaic*, March/April 1981, pp. 11–19.

Lindbergh, Anne Morrow. *Earth Shine*. New York: Harcourt, Brace & World, 1969.

Lovelock, James. *Gaia: A New Look at Life on Earth*. Oxford: Oxford University Press, 1979.

Mailer, Norman. *Of a Fire on the Moon*. New York: New American Library, 1970.

Marvin, Ursula B. "The Search for Antarctic Meteorites." *Sky and Telescope*, November 1981, pp. 423–427.

Mason, Brian. "A Lode of Meteorites." *Natural History*, April 1981, pp. 62–66.

Miller, Ron, and Hartman, William. "Catastrophes That Shaped the Earth." *Science Digest*, April 1984.

Muller, Richard A. "An Adventure in Science." *The New York Times Magazine*, March 24, 1985, pp. 34–50.

Overbye, Dennis. "The Mystique of Mars." *Discover*, September 1984, pp. 24–25.

Pasachoff, Jay M. *Astronomy: From the Earth to the Universe*. Philadelphia: Saunders College Publishing, 1983.

Preston, Douglas J. "Wetherfield's Meteorites." *Natural History*, January 1984, pp. 86–89.

Raup, David M. "Death of Species." In *Extinctions*. Nitecki, Matthew H., ed. Chicago: University of Chicago Press, 1984, pp. 1–9.

Reeves, Sandra. "Brown's Space Men." *Brown Alumni Monthly*, December 1974, pp. 8–13.

Reeves, Sandra. "Exploration Lives!" *Brown Alumni Monthly*, November 1976, pp. 12–19.

Sagan, Carl. *Cosmos*. New York: Random House, 1980.

Sagan, Carl. "The Solar System." *Scientific American*, September 1975, pp. 23–31.

Sagan, Carl. "Volcanoes of Other Worlds." *Parade*, October 2, 1983, pp. 9–12.

Stuart, George E. "The Maya: Riddle of the Glyphs." *National Geographic*, December 1975, pp. 768–791.

Sullivan, Walter. *Landprints*. New York: The New York Times Book Co., 1984.

Waldrop, M. Mitchell. "First Sightings." *Science 85*, June 1985, pp. 26–33.

Wetherill, George W. "The Formation of the Earth from Planetesimals." *Scientific American*, June 1981, pp. 163–174.

Wood, John A. "Long-Playing Records." *Natural History*, April 1981, pp. 56–60.

CHAPTER FIVE: THE SOLAR SEA

Akasofu, Syun-Ichi. *Aurora Borealis. Alaska Geographic* 6, 2, (1979).

Akasofu, Syun-Ichi. "The Aurora: New Light on an Old Subject." *Sky and Telescope*, December 1982, pp. 534–537.

Brown, Bruce. "The Shining: The Mysterious Power of the Northern Lights." *The New York Times Magazine*, December 12, 1982, pp. 41–61.

Chen, Allan. "Tones of the Oscillating Sun." *Science News*, June 18, 1983, pp. 392–393.

Deitmar, Stephen. "The Observatories of Jai Singh." *Astronomy*, January 1985, pp. 18–22.

Eddy, John A. "Climate and the Changing Sun." In *1979: Yearbook of Science and the Future*. Chicago: Encyclopaedia Britannica, Inc., 1979.

Eddy, John A. "Climate and the Role of the Sun." In *Climate and History*, Rotberg, Robert I., and Rabb, Theodore K., eds. Princeton: Princeton University Press, 1981.

Eddy, John A. "A Historical Review of Solar Variability, Weather, and Climate." Keynote address, Second International Symposium on Solar-Terrestrial Influences on Weather and Climate, Boulder, Colorado, August 2–6, 1982.

Eddy, John A. *A New Sun: The Solar Results from Skylab*. Washington: U.S. Government Printing Office, NASA 5P–402, 1979. Well written and beautifully illustrated. Source of many of this chapter's photographs.

Finkbeiner, Ann. "What's Going On Inside the Sun?" *Science 85*, February 1985, p. 30.

Foukal, Peter. "Does the Sun's Luminosity Vary?" *Sky and Telescope*, February 1980, pp. 111–114.

Frazier, Kendrick. *Our Turbulent Sun*. Englewood Cliffs, NJ: Prentice-Hall, 1982.

Frazier, Kendrick. "The Sun's Back Pages." *Mosaic*, May/June 1981, pp. 2–8.

Friedman, Herbert. "Sun and Earth." In *Outlook for Science and Technology*. San Francisco: W.H. Freeman & Co., 1982, pp. 323–369.

Giovanelli, Ronald G. *Secrets of the Sun*. Cambridge: Cambridge University Press, 1984.

Harvey, J.; Pomerantz, M.; and Duvall, T. "Astronomy on Ice." *Sky and Telescope*, December 1982, pp. 520–523.

Kerr, Richard A. "Sun, Weather, and Climate: A Connection?" *Science*, September 3, 1982, pp. 917–919.

Lansford, Henry. "The Global Circuit." *Mosaic*, May/June 1983, pp. 16–21.

Maran, Stephen P. "The Inconstant Sun." *Natural History*, April 1982, pp. 62–65.

Maran, Stephen P. "Inside the Sun." *Natural History*, May 1983, pp. 82–85.

Mitton, Simon. *Daytime Star*. New York: Charles Scribner's Sons, 1981.

Mullan, Dermott J. "Tuning In to the Interior of a Star." *Astronomy*, December 1984, pp. 66–70.

"The Neutrino Shortage." *Scientific American*, October 1981, pp. 84–85.

Nicolson, Iain. *The Sun*. New York: Rand McNally & Co., 1982.

Noyes, Robert W. *The Sun, Our Star*. Cambridge: Harvard University Press, 1982. Clear, authoritative, and comprehensive.

The Smithsonian Institution. *Fire of Life*. New York: W.W. Norton & Co., 1981. A potpourri of articles and essays, beautifully illustrated.

Stafford, Edward Peary. *Sun, Earth and Man*. Washington: National Aeronautics and Space Administration, 1982.

Stahl, Philip A. "Sunspots." *Astronomy*, May 1980, pp. 66–71.

Sullivan, Walter. "Strange Subatomic Particles Herald a New Astronomy." *The New York Times*, February 26, 1985, pp. C1–C2.

"The Sun, the Whole Sun." *Mosaic*, January/February 1978, pp. 9–15.

Thomsen, Dietrick E. "Sunwatchers of the American Southwest." *Science News*, June 18, 1983, pp. 394–395.

Tierney, John. "On the Faint Trail of the Christmas Comet." *Science 85*, March 1985, pp. 16–20.

Tierney, John. "A Winter's Tail." *Science 84*, December 1984, pp. 38–41.

Washburn, Mark. *In the Light of the Sun*. New York: Harcourt Brace Jovanovich, 1981.

Willson, Richard C. "The Inconstant Solar Constant." *Sky and Telescope*, June 1984, pp. 501–503.

CHAPTER SIX: GIFTS FROM THE EARTH

Barnet, Richard J. "The World's Resources." *The New Yorker*, March 17, 1980. Analyzes the global politics of scarcity and supply.

Bateman, Alan M., and Jensen, Mead L. *Economic Mineral Deposits*. 3d ed. New York: John Wiley & Sons, 1979.

Bullard, Fred M. *Volcanoes of the Earth*. 2d rev. ed. Austin: University of Texas Press, 1984.

Canby, Thomas Y. "Water: Our Most Precious Resource." *National Geographic*, August 1980, pp. 144–179.

Carr, Donald E. *Energy and the Earth Machine*. New York: W.W. Norton & Co., 1976.

Decker, Barbara, and Decker, Robert. *Volcanoes*. San Francisco: W.H. Freeman & Co., 1981.

Duffield, Wendell A. "Developments in the Field of Geothermal Energy During the Past Half Century." In *Revolution in the Earth Sciences*, Shelby J. Boardman, ed. Dubuque, IA: Kendall-Hunt, 1983, pp. 355–367. Proceedings of a symposium held at Carleton College, Northfield, Minnesota, April 14–16, 1983.

Edelson, Edward. "Prospecting with Plate Tectonics." *Mosaic*, November/December 1981 pp. 9–13.

Facts About Oil. Washington: American Petroleum Institute, 1984.

Ferguson, Bruce K. "Whither Water?" *The Futurist*, April 1983, pp. 29–36.

"Fire in Iceland." *Science 81*, December 1981, pp. 63–67.

Gibbons, Boyd. "Do We Treat Our Soil Like Dirt?" *National Geographic*, September 1984, pp. 350–390.

Graff, Gordon. "Prospecting from the Skies." *High Technology*, March 1985, pp. 48–56.

Gregory, Cedric E. *A Concise History of Mining*. New York: Pergamon Press, 1980.

Gribbin, John. *Our Changing Planet*. New York: Thomas Y. Crowell Co., 1977.

Hamilton, Bruce. "Geothermal Energy: Trouble Brews for the National Parks." *Sierra*, July/August 1983, pp. 21–26.

Hopson, Janet L. "Miners Are Reaching for Metal Riches on the Ocean's Floor," *Smithsonian*, April 1981, pp. 51–58.

Joralemon, Ira B. *Copper*. Berkeley: Howell-North Books, 1973.

"Mapping the Continental Basement." *Mosaic*, November/December 1976, pp. 9–15.

Myers, Norman, ed. *Gaia: An Atlas of Planet Management*. Garden City, NY: Anchor Press, 1984.

National Geographic, February 1981. A special issue on energy: oil, synfuels, and conservation.

Nice, Joan. "Energy: Geothermal Lease Plans Threaten Yellowstone's Geysers." *Audubon*, May 1982, pp. 104–105.

Riva, Joseph P., Jr. *World Petroleum Resources and Reserves*. Boulder, CO: Westview Press, 1983.

Rona, Peter A. "Perpetual Seafloor Metal Factory." *Sea Frontiers*, May/June 1984, pp. 132–141.

Rona, Peter A. "Plate Tectonics and Mineral Resources." *Scientific American*, July 1973, pp. 86–95.

Ross, David A. "The Red Sea: An Ocean in the Making." *Natural History*, August/September 1976, pp. 75–77.

Sabins, Floyd. "Remote Sensing Assists Exploration in Sudan." *Chevron Oil Field Research Company News*, August 1983, pp. 4–5.

Sawkins, F.J. *Metal Deposits in Relation to Plate Tectonics*. Berlin: Springer-Verlag, 1984.

Skinner, Brian J. *Earth Resources*. Englewood Cliffs, NJ: Prentice-Hall, 1976. A short, solid introduction.

Simon, Julian. "The Scarcity of Raw Materials: A Challenge to the Conventional Wisdom." *The Atlantic*, June 1981, pp. 33–41.

Steinhart, Peter. "The Edge Gets Thinner." *Audubon*, November 1983, pp. 94–126.

Steinhart, Peter. "Soil: The Miracle We Take for Granted." *National Wildlife*, February/March 1985, pp. 15–23.

Stokes, Bruce. "Water Shortages: The Next 'Energy' Crisis." *The Futurist*, April 1983, pp. 37–47.

Stuart, Alexander. "Oil's Hired Ears Strike It Rich." *Fortune*, January 25, 1982, pp. 92-97.

Sullivan, Walter. *Continents in Motion*. New York: McGraw-Hill, 1974.

Tank, Ronald W. *Environmental Geology*. Oxford: Oxford University Press, 1983.

Watson, Janet. *Geology and Man*. London: George Allen & Unwin, 1983.

Weaver, Kenneth F. "Geothermal Energy: The Power of Letting Off Steam." *National Geographic*, October 1977, pp. 566–579.

Wilford, John Noble. *The Mapmakers*. New York: Alfred A. Knopf, 1981.

Young, Louise. *The Blue Planet*. Boston: Little, Brown and Company, 1983. A lovely set of linked essays on Planet Earth.

Zimmer, Heinrich. Joseph Campbell, ed. *Myths and Symbols in Indian Art and Civilization*. New York: Pantheon Books, 1946.

CHAPTER SEVEN: FATE OF THE EARTH

Bingham, Roger. "The Maverick and the Earth Goddess." *Science 81*, December 1981, pp. 77–82.

Brown, Lester R., and Wolf, Edward. *State of the World 1984*. New York: W.W. Norton & Co., 1984.

Brown, Lester R.; Chandler, William U.; Flavin, Christopher; Pollock, Cynthia; Postel, Sandra; and Wolf, Edward. *State of the World 1985*. New York: W.W. Norton & Co., 1985.

Caufield, Catherine. "The Rain Forests." *The New Yorker*, January 14, 1985, pp. 41–101.

Cloud, Preston. "The Biosphere." *Scientific American*, September 1983, pp. 176–189.

Day, William. *Genesis on Planet Earth*. New Haven: Yale University Press, 1984. The origins of life; an excellent and up-to-date introduction.

Doolittle, W. Ford. "Is Nature Really Motherly?" *The CoEvolution Quarterly*, Spring 1981, pp. 58–65.

Ehrlich, Paul R. "North America After the War." *Natural History*, March 1984, pp. 4–8.

Ehrlich, Paul R.; Kennedy, Donald; Roberts, Walter Orr; and Sagan, Carl. *The Cold and the Dark*. New York: W.W. Norton & Co., 1984. Speeches and papers on nuclear winter.

Farmer, Penelope, ed. *Beginnings: Creation Myths of the World*. New York: Atheneum, 1979.

Georgi, Dieter. "The Bombings of Dresden." *Harvard Magazine*, March/April 1985, pp. 56–64.

Groves, David I.; Dunlop, John S.R.; and Buick, Roger. "An Early Habitat of Life." *Scientific American*, October 1981, pp. 64–73.

Hutchinson, G. Evelyn. "The Biosphere." *Scientific American*, September 1980, pp. 44–53.

Lewin, Roger. "No Dinosaurs This Time." *Science*, September 16, 1983, pp. 1168–1169.

Lewin, Roger. "Parks: How Big Is Big Enough?" *Science*, August 10, 1984, pp. 611–612.

Lovejoy, Thomas E. "Hope for a Beleaguered Paradise." *Garden*, January/February 1982, pp. 32–36.

Lovelock, James. "Daisy World." *The CoEvolution Quarterly*, Summer 1983, pp. 66–72.

Lovelock, James. *Gaia: A New Look at Life on Earth*. Oxford: Oxford University Press, 1979.

Mackenzie, Donald A. *Teutonic Myth and Legend*. London: Gresham Publishing Co., 1912.

Margulis, Lynn. *Early Life*. Boston: Science Books International, 1982.

Myers, Norman. "The End of the Lines." *Natural History*, February 1985, pp. 2–12.

Myers, Norman. "A Fifth of All Species Headed for Extinction." *The Futurist*, October 1980, p. 13.

Myers, Norman, ed. *Gaia: An Atlas of Planet Management*. Garden City, NY: Anchor Press, 1984.

Myers, Norman. *The Primary Source*. New York: W.W. Norton & Co., 1984.

Overbye, Dennis. "Prophet of the Cold and the Dark." *Discover*, January 1985, pp. 24–32.

Patrusky, Ben. "Protolife's Clouded Beginnings." *Mosaic*, May/June 1984, pp. 10–17.

Ponnamperuma, Cyril. *The Origins of Life*. New York: E.P. Dutton, 1972.

Powers, Thomas. "Nuclear Winter and Nuclear Strategy." *The Atlantic*, November 1984, pp. 53–64.

Raven, Peter. "Global Futures: The Third World." Paper presented at conference, "Knockdown-Dragout on the Global Future," American Association for the Advancement of Science, New York, May 25, 1984.

Raven, Peter. "Tropical Rain Forests: A Global Responsibility." *Natural History*, February 1981, pp. 28–32.

Revkin, Andrew C. "Hard Facts About Nuclear Winter." *Science Digest*, March 1985.

Sagan, Carl. "Nuclear War and Climatic Catastrophe: Some Policy Implications." *Foreign Affairs*, Winter 1983/84, pp. 257–292.

Schneider, Stephen. "Nuclear Winter: The Storm Builds." *Science Digest*, January 1985.

Toward an International Geosphere-Biosphere Program: A Study of Global Change. Washington: National Academy Press, 1983.

Trachtman, Paul. "The Search for Life's Origins—And a First 'Synthetic Cell.' " *Smithsonian*, June 1984, pp. 43–51.

Waldrop, M. Mitchell. "A Solar System at Vega?" *Science*, August 26, 1983, p. 845.

Webster, Bayard. "Forest's Role in Weather Documented in Amazon." *The New York Times*, July 5, 1983.

Index

Credits